GROUP**W**ARE '92

GROUPWARE '92

Edited by David D. Coleman

Morgan Kaufmann Publishers
San Mateo, California

Sponsoring Editor   *Michael B. Morgan*
Production Manager   *Yonie Overton*
Production Editor   *Carol Leyba*
Cover Designer   *Studio Silicon*
Pasteup/Additional Composition   *Maryland Composition Company*
Printer   *Griffin Printing and Lithograph Co., Inc.*

Morgan Kaufmann Publishers, Inc.
Editorial Office:
2929 Campus Drive, Suite 260
San Mateo, CA 94403

95   94   93   92   4   3   2   1

Library of Congress Cataloging-in-Publication Data is available for this
volume.
ISBN 1-55860-261-5

TABLE OF CONTENTS

TRACK 2: TECHNOLOGY AND GROUPWARE DEVELOPMENT 207

ALTERNATES 531

Preface
Welcome to GroupWare '92

When this conference was originally conceived some 15 months ago, it was designed to meet the informational needs of the growing market for work group solutions and technologies. We have seen many changes in the commercial groupware environment since the inception of this project. My original research in May, 1991 showed that there were about 150 vendors offering commercial groupware products. Today we have identified over 400 groupware products and almost as many vendors.

Groupware has been predicted to be a $2 billion market by 1995 and to have an annual growth rate of over 30%. Groupware has also been called not a market at all, but a function, a solution, and "a cluster of tricks." Whatever groupware is, it does provide tangible productivity enhancements and a competitive advantage. In some cases, it even provides a cost savings to the user.

We are at the beginning of the growth curve for workgroup applications. With the LAN infrastructure rapidly moving into place, more and more commercial enterprises are looking to collaborative computing to increase productivity and give them the competitive edge they need in today's fierce global economy.

At the beginning of the development of any market, the most critical impediment to growth is information, or rather lack of it. GroupWare '92 was created to fill this informational void. The 600 plus pages in this proceedings is the first collection of information on commercial groupware products and the groupware market that I know of outside of the information available from market research firms. I feel that the quality of speakers and the topics covered at GroupWare '92 meets our initial goal of providing information and a forum for the groupware community.

But GroupWare '92 has a second and more important goal: that of aiding in the maturation of the entire groupware industry. By promoting the marketplace and providing a place for the exchange and discussion of critical ideas and issues, we hope that this conference will do for groupware in the commercial market what CSCW '86 did for groupware as an academic discipline.

Groupware is one of those technologies that is not easily defined. My (very liberal) definition is "computer-mediated collaboration that increases the productivity or functionality of a person-to-person(s) interactive process." This definition is broad enough to include electronic mail and FAX technologies. However, the focus of this conference is on LAN-based, workgroup solutions.

Because this is a new "market," many of the groupware vendors do not provide traditional plug-and-play solutions but instead offer tool kits that must be customized to provide a solution. One question that we hope will be begin to be clarified is "At what level will these tool kits reside?" The operating systems level, the applications level, at the user interface level, or all of the above?

Groupware is a broad field where computer technologies and social technologies intertwine in a dance of productivity that is being commercialized in its earliest form. We owe a debt of gratitude to Lotus Development Corporation for proving this to be a commercially viable market with their Notes product and for their support for this industry conference. Special thanks to Lotus for supplying the show network and electronic mail system. We would also like to thank our other sponsor, SRI, for their counsel and promotional support.

A great deal of thanks also go to <u>Network World Magazine</u> and their editorial, production and advertising staff. They were involved in both promoting the conference and also the collaborative computing market as a whole. They donated many hours of their time and also provided space in their magazine to help make this conference a success.

GroupWare '92 represents the largest collection of information, people, and vendors focused on commercial work group products, experience, and research to date. We envision this show as an annual event that will evolve in sophistication as the market grows. We will be using the same venue for next year's show (San Jose Convention Center, August 9-12, 1993) but hope to make some interesting additions in speakers, workshops and tutorials, panel sessions, and a groupware technology lab. This lab is conceived of as a multi-platform environment where groups of people can interact using groupware systems to see which one will solve their current collaborative challenges.

Our speakers this year include the management of the some of the top hardware and software companies in the computer industry, a wide variety of users, and well-known researchers from key academic institutions. Our original goal for the conference was to make it an international conference. Unfortunately, the infrastructure, technical and cultural support for groupware is less mature outside the U.S. than in the U.S. We are monitoring the progress in Europe and the Pacific Rim and hope to expand the show next year to include a more international flavor.

We also hope to use groupware more in the running of the show. This will allow attendees to register electronically, allow speakers to submit papers in electronic format, and enable E-mail discussions on various conference topics. Finally, the proceedings could be made available on CD-ROM to make them easily usable as a reference volume.

In your registration packet there is a request for presentations for next years show. We are asking that people who wish to submit abstracts to speak at next year's conference submit their abstracts earlier, so that we have more time for papers to be written and compiled into the conference proceedings.

Because this is a first-time event, we would greatly appreciate any feedback you have about GroupWare '92. Your input will help us evolve this conference to meet the need of the workgroup solutions marketplace.

We have provided free space for user groups to meet at GroupWare '92 in the hopes that this will also help move the market forward and allow GroupWare '92 to be used as the forum it was designed to be. This is an experiment, and we hope users and vendors will take advantage of it. If it proves successful, we will make this offer again next year.

The conference format is a cross between an executive conference (where all sessions are general sessions) and a user conference (where most sessions are split into tracks). We hope that this compromise format will provide attendees with a chance to optimize their time and maximize the information they receive.

We at The Conference Group, as producers of GroupWare '92 hope to provide a lively forum for the evolving commercial groupware market for years to come.

David Coleman
Conference Chairman
GroupWare '92

GENERAL SESSIONS

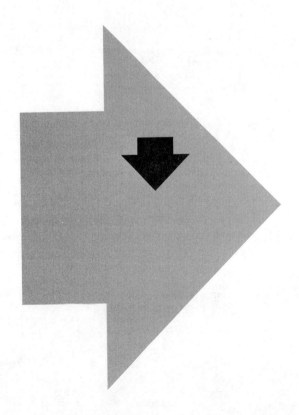

Working Together
By Jim Manzi
Lotus Development Corporation

In response to changing business, computing must embrace key technologies that support groups of individuals

The new reality is that it will take the collaborative efforts of people with different skills to create innovative solutions and innovative products... The classic perception that professional work begins with the individual decision-making unit and proceeds when management adds these units together to make larger and more complex decision-making units is tempting but ultimately wrong... The real basic structure of the workplace is in the relationship...

So says nationally-syndicated columnist and technology management consultant Michael Schrage in his most recent book Shared Minds: The Technology of Collaboration. And it is this reality that is driving fundamental changes in the way organizations operate. But these changes should be considered in conjunction with the computing technology that is inextricably linked with the way people work.

In the 1980s, personal computers brought increased efficiency by automating individual tasks. Spreadsheets, databases, word processing and graphics software made individuals more productive and, to some extent, more empowered. Yet the focus of personal computing was just that -- personal.

Today, people do less work in isolation. The flatter, decentralized global organization requires that people communicate, collaborate, share information and ideas more than ever. The new focus of computing is on automating processes, not just tasks; on processing knowledge; and on groups of people, not just individuals.

Organizational Revolution

Organizations are going through massive change. Layers of management are being peeled away, replaced by teams of people assembled on an ad-hoc, project or task basis. Teams are created according to the need at hand, then dismantled. Team members are selected based on expertise, not title.

Teams are not rooted in any particular location. They are more mobile, either physically or electronically. Voice, data and video communications networks unite far-flung team members.

The chief technologies driving this change are portable computing, user interfaces and networking -- the same technologies that are making possible the downsizing phenomenon in which organizations are using smaller, cheaper and more powerful processors to support their application requirements. They are also the source for such concepts as the "virtual office," or the workplace that is not bound by the four walls of a person's office. All provide greater mobility, flexibility and increased access to information.

Business has been built on the axiom that "information is power" and should therefore be doled out with extreme caution. To be competitive in the 1990s, organizations must adopt a new axiom, that "information sharing is power." For the simple truth is that the power of an organization is greater when everyone has access to the information they need to do their jobs.

Information technology is the largest and fastest-growing capital expenditure item for most companies. Yet it is money poorly spent if senior management does not consider information sharing as strategic. According to Peter G.W. Keen in his book, Shaping the Future: Business Design Through Information Technology, "To use it [information technology] competitively demands management discipline, time, commitment and skill."

Lotus' strategy is to enable people to work together by connecting disparate information systems and environments, connecting people to the information they need; connecting products with one another and connecting people with people.

Our goal is to provide our customers with the information technology tools they need to overcome the boundaries that exist between systems, organizations, companies and cultures -- to help bring about integration. Ultimately, customers will gain a competitive edge not through automation, or just a faster spreadsheet, but by achieving better information flow and increased flexibility in marshalling resources. And the integration of our products, across LANs and WANs, will contribute to organizations' abilities to reap the benefits of downsizing.

Portable Computing

While traditional personal computer sales are slowing, portable computer, or laptop, sales will triple over the next two years.

This growth stems from the amazing advances in technology over the past few years. The combination of increasingly powerful VLSI semiconductors enabling enormous amounts of computing power to sit on a single chip, and equally fast-paced advances in display technology -- particularly liquid crystal display -have made portable computing commonplace. Portable computers are one-third the size, twice the power and less than half the price they were just two years ago.

We have already taken the lead in hooking mobile users into the network. With products like Lotus Notes, a groupware communications package, and cc:Mail, our electronic mail product, a team developing a new word processing software package in Atlanta is able to communicate with the team building a new spreadsheet product in Boston on common technical issues, product linkage ideas and joint marketing concepts using electronic mail, group communications software and telconferencing. And similar scenarios are occurring between parties throughout the world.

Because laptop computers often require software that is specifically designed for their unique features, this is another very important technology for us. With the 95LX palmtop we developed with Hewlett-Packard, and our 1-2-3/Notebook application in Japan, we have taken a leading role in building "portable software" for this computing platform. We will continue to design applications specifically for the mobile user and the portable environment.

User Interfaces

User interface technology is aimed primarily at making computers easier to use. During the last five years, PC users have begun a transition from character-based user interfaces to graphical user interfaces (GUI). The latter feature icons, pictures, easy access to applications and menus, and a mouse. The GUI provides multiple concurrent on-screen views of information (text, data, graphics and images), so it is easier to manage increasing volumes of information.

We believe software products that bridge both character and graphical environments provide the greatest ease of training and use for today's customers. We built our leading position in applications software with a character-based command structure and interface that users found intuitive and easy to use. Today, we are supporting the industry-wide transition to GUI in way that is compatible with what users have already learned in our products. For example, in our new 1-2-3 for Windows and 1-2-3 for Macintosh, both of which take full advantage of the environment's graphical user interface, users familiar with 1-2-3 can call up the "1-2-3 Classic" menu simply by hitting the backslash key.

Our goal is to make computing easier across the board. To that end, we are focused on: User Interfaces, Common User Access (CUA), Visual Computing and Applications Integration.

In the first area, we have added graphical features to our DOS products so users have many graphical benefits normally attained in a more robust computing environment, such as WYSIWYG (What-You-See-Is-What-You-Get), without having to make the hardware upgrades necessary to support the Windows or OS/2 environments.

In the second area, our products for Windows and OS/2 go beyond the Common User Access conventions dictated by those platforms. CUA defines how user interfaces should appear -where functions appear on the menu, for example. But it does not provide for how applications look and act, or how a set of functions works across several applications.

A new concept from Lotus, Visual Computing, addresses the usability and aesthetics of computing by using objects based on graphics, illustration, color, typefaces, and annotation to perform a function. The goal of visual computing is to enable end users to develop sophisticated, fully integrated applications using point-and-click technique. We will provide an application development environment that gives users visual programming tools -- a palette of objects that they can point to and drag on-screen -- and a scripted language for the more complicated commands that can't be expressed visually.

Increasingly, we are finding that customers need to incorporate our products into their overall company-specific applications. With the visual programming environment under development, anybody who can write a 1-2-3 macro will be able to create an application that combines aspects of any products they already have -- like spreadsheet, word processing and graphics capabilities -- and any that they add in the future.

Another aspect of visual computing that we are working on is "active interfaces" -- as opposed to existing GUIs, which can be viewed as "passive graphical interfaces." In an existing GUI word processor, a user might copy and paste a piece of text by marking the text with the mouse, clicking on the "File" menu command, clicking on the "Copy" command of the pull-down menu, moving the cursor to where he or she wants the text to go, and clicking on the "Paste" command of the pull-down menu. While it is easy, the user still has to know which steps to take in order to accomplish the task.

An active interface will show a user, with animated symbols, what different menu items mean. For example, when a user clicks on the copy and paste menu items in an active interface, he or she might see a piece of text being copied to the clipboard and pasted to another part of a document, as well as animated instructions for what the user has to do to cut and paste the text.

While GUIs are a major step forward from the character-based user interface, we believe much more is needed to make computers truly easy to use.

Applications Software and Integration

The trend in applications software is toward suites -- or an "office" -- of applications that include a word processor, spreadsheet, graphics package, database and communications functions.

The goal of applications integration is to erase the vertical boundaries around existing software applications so users can move from one type of activity to another without having to close one application and open another.

At Lotus, integration involves three things -- appearance, behavior and compatibility.

Appearance means that all Lotus applications will look and feel alike to the user. Their screen layouts, menu bars and icon palettes (or SmartIcons), colors and fonts will have a common appearance.

Behavior means that all Lotus applications will have the same functions and controls. For example, a function such as spellchecker will require the same commands across products. Printing, opening files, getting help, and selecting colors or fonts are all invoked using the same controls across the suite of applications. In the near future, we will bring common user objects, or shared code, in all our applications. Already, drawing tools, table tools and text tools are the same in 1-2-3 and Ami Pro.

Compatibility means that all applications for all platforms are compatible with one another, so work on one platform is usable on another. This is more than 1-2-3 file and macro compatibility from DOS to Windows to OS/2, Unix and Macintosh, which already exists.

Compatibility across platforms means that if a user creates a document that includes spreadsheets, graphics and text, he or she can move from one machine to another and pull up each application and use it as if it resided on the desktop. This kind of sharing is important because it removes the boundaries that exist between individual applications and frees the user to focus on the actual work instead of file format and location.

Networking and Groupware

It is estimated that in 1992, 80 percent of all PCs will be connected to a local area network. According to other estimates, by 1994 there will be more PCs in business attached to local area networks than there were total PCs in 1989.

Networks tie computers together and enable people to share resources, such as printers. They give people access to company or departmental databases, and enable people to communicate via computer.

We believe that what software did for the personal computer in the 1980s, groupware will do for the network in the 1990s. We define groupware as applications software designed for networked PCs that enables people to work together. Essentially, it is software that brings groups together.

The product that best defines groupware is Lotus Notes. Notes moves beyond tying computing platforms together and swapping files to bringing people together and enabling them to share work. Notes is the natural complement to our electronic mail product, cc:Mail. While Notes connects individual groups to one another, cc:Mail connects individuals across an entire organization.

Groupware -- Enabled Applications

There are three tools required for people to work together: mail capabilities, annotation capabilities -- which allow users to perform controlled review of documents and to provide comments using text, voice and other media -- and a sharing capability. Users should be able to access documents by content, date, author, name, etc., with a method to control access and to ensure that data is updated across boundaries. This is possible today with Notes. And there should be a way to keep track of different versions of a document, as there is with Notes.

We are working on group-enabled spreadsheets, which will let users create, manage and share alternative scenarios for selected worksheet ranges. Users will be able to share spreadsheets, keep histories and audit trails of contributions by other users, and collaborate on the development of alternative scenarios.

Over time, other applications, such as text or presentation graphics, will benefit from group-enabling capabilities. The first step is to add mail capabilities to core applications, as we have done with our Windows applications, so users can mail documents directly from within their applications.

We can provide further support for groups by using applications such as a spreadsheet or word processor with Notes or cc:Mail in a complete system that allows users to share compound documents. For example, 1-2-3 worksheets and Ami Pro documents can be embedded in a Notes document, then sent to a Notes database and replicated to other users' databases around the world. A double click brings up the worksheet or Ami Pro document, and users can use the 1-2-3 file or Ami Pro document as if the software were on their computer. Laptop users can hook into Notes as well, so they can continue to be part of the group.

These types of capabilities, unique to Lotus, begin to address the changing nature of organizations by supporting workgroups, as well as individuals, across the boundaries of time, distance and functional organizations. And we are continuing to explore new ways to enable platforms, products and people to work together.

A FRAMEWORK FOR GROUPWARE

Esther Dyson, EDventure Holdings
375 Park Avenue
New York, NY 10152, USA

"Groupware" is about as useful a term as "singleware." Groupware applications and tools come in as broad a variety as single-user applications -- and more. Groupware can also be classified in a framework intrinsic to groupware -- and well beyond the well-known different-or-same time-and-place categories.

This paper provides a framework for classifying the tools and applications we'll be dicussing over the next few days. First of all, does a system manage the work (transactions or workflow) or does it manage the content of the work? (It could do both). Second, where is the center of control: with the users, centralized with the boss or with a group agent, or with the work itself? Technically, is it mail-based, database-based or object-based?

There are no right or wrong answers to these questions, but they're important in understanding the operation of any particular system and its suitability for a given set of tasks or corporate culture.

The case for groupware

Ideally, groupware will integrate the freedom, ad-hocness and personalness of a spreadsheet (or e-mail) with the integrity, globality and connectedness of a database. Users want local power along with global reach. Yet they want to deal with the global system through the local medium -- be it a spreadsheet or a mail-style interface or a document (cf. Microsoft or Interleaf's Active Documents, **Release 1.0**, 90-3).

Groupware can be powerful stuff, and the level of interest we're seeing from large vendors is exciting. But it will be important for vendors to remember that it's a concept that needs explaining -- albeit one embodied in products. Groupware's power and the difficulty it will encounter both within vendors and out in the marketplace stem from the same fact: It's orthogonal to most of what vendors are selling and customers have been buying. That is, it can link, integrate, coordinate and otherwise fit around existing applications, although that integration will not be a painless, automatic process. There won't be a lot of money in selling the concept or even the products, but there should be a lot of revenue for consulting and implementation services. More than a way of coding or building applications, groupware is a way to define, structure and link applications, data and the people who use them.

Groupware incorporates both the grand picture -- users and information and action (work) -- and a tool for implementing it. In a world where not just hardware but even applications, user interfaces and tools are becoming commodities, competitive advantage will consist of the ability to define and automate the *right* business processes. Currently, with widely available tools (and a little training) you can specify anything and (almost) automatically build a system to implement it; the remaining, unsolved challenge is to specify the right thing. (A handy marketing approach and a fundamental value-added offering will be preconfigured process templates for function- and industry-specific tasks, modifiable by customers.) Groupware will help both in defining, testing and implementing those specs, by helping customers understand and then automate their companies' missions.

But this design process is difficult. A groupware tool should be a thinker's aid: It should help the user to visualize and simulate a business process and try it out before committing, as well as implement and execute it later on. Current tools generally address only part of the whole problem; vendors show you what you *can* do, without elucidating how hard it can be to do it.

A tool for change

The challenge of the Nineties is change, and groupware is a tool for implementing change in organizations, rather than just in data structures and applications. It deals with business, rather than with computer processes. The danger is that groupware will be perceived as one more module, both within vendors and by the world at large: "And for Mr. Jones, we'd like to order one decision support system, one financial planner and a business process management tool." This is what has happened with such efforts at companies such as AT&T, NCR and Xerox, where Rhapsody and Cooperation got buried in a flood of product announcements and were never well articulated to the public. ("Yes, we have workflow management; see section 23A-b of brochure N2.")

Perhaps through fear of being grandiose or for lack of resources, vendors fail to comprehend the potential magnitude of the applicability of such a tool. It may be small in direct dollars, but it should be huge in impact (on account relationships as well as on business practices and system design). Larger vendors are uniquely positioned to market this kind of idea/product, which will require spreading the vision (as only a large, non-niche company can), providing support, and offering a truly useful tool to help make it work. Generally, large companies are too set in their ways to embrace such a vision (with an "installed base" of both systems and ideas), whereas smaller companies lack the resources and influence to do so. We'll be getting back to this problem later on.

What is information? Why, it's someone looking at and understanding data. Even a natural-language system or any other AI system doesn't really produce information until there's someone there to see it. The system may produce information and act on it, and then there's some value to the information. But beyond that, unless a person or a system acts in response, there's no value to the information. The action needn't be very physical; it could be a phone call, a command to a subordinate (cf. speech acts) that transfers an obligation, as well as a move to cut production, launch a new product, delay the price rise until after Christmas, solicit a certain customer. But until some action (or a decision to take no action) results, the information has had no value. Think about it....

A NEW FRAMEWORK FOR GROUPWARE: CENTER OF CONTROL

Overall, we classify groupware as information- or workflow-oriented, depending on whether the system managed information itself or simply the movement of information through a series of tasks where users manage the content. This is a useful and increasingly apparent distinction, but another framework classifies groupware by its "control center:" Does control lie with the individual user or does it reside with the work object itself? Or is the system process-centered, focused on a task that may involve a variety of users and work objects, and that has defined states from start to conclusion (just like a transaction)?

This distinction is orthogonal to whether groupware is information- or workflow-oriented (although there's necessarily a workflow aspect to a process-centered system). For example, the e-mail applications described below (page 11), with their user agents, are user-centered, and can manage both information or workflows depending on the rule sets built by their users. Interleaf's Active Document technology is best-suited for creating work-object groupware, with intelligence residing in the documents. So is Sidekick, for even though the information may be kept on servers, it is managed by individuals. Some workflow tools are halfway in-between; although they create complete tasks, they do so by moving a work object through a sequence of steps and branches without a conceptual model of task completeness.

The differences are subtle but deep. User-centered is managed locally, by, say, a mail client application or a tool such as Agenda; work-centered makes the work an active object, with its own rules attached; process-centered sees the work domain as a whole, and manages work from end to end as a single, complex transaction from a central vantage (virtual or physical). Work-centered is better for sending work outside the system and recapturing it, while process-centered is better suited for querying and monitoring. (Where are bottlenecks? Who has the Borkovsky report? How busy is Sharon?)

In any of these cases, a single "unit" may contain many others: A user's mail-handler may trigger a series of mail-handling processes or rules (every Monday morning, run these three processes); a work document may contain a number of subsidiary documents, each with its own behavior and rules (such as a folder of forms to be filled in by various people with the results to be reconciled at the end); a single broad task (approving a loan, say) may contain many subsidiary tasks (credit check, officer approval and so forth). And in the end, there's a sort of hierarchy, with a complete task perhaps incorporating or interacting with work objects and user agents.

Although you can take any of these approaches to building a system, the process of building it (and modifying it thereafter) will vary markedly, as will the flavor and the perspicuity of the resulting system. The underlying technology may vary, but results are generally best when the technical architecture corresponds to the user model (i.e. mail for user-centered, objects for work-centered, database transactions for process-centered).

User-centered

Let's start with user-centered. This is where the user builds his own agent -- something as simple as a macro or some calendar rules, or as complex as an expert system to execute rules he devises for interacting with other group members and data. The system he designs sees him as the center, and everything else as the outside world. He receives data and requests (commands) from the outside, and sends data, responses and requests back. He doesn't necessarily know much about what's out there; and even if he has a mental model of the group or workflow, it's probably not in his software. The tools he uses range from macro languages and "recorders" to higher-level packages such as Agenda or Beyond's and Agility's mail tools. He may also build views for himself in Lotus Notes (or he may use views built for him by a Notes administrator). He may be managing either workflow, delegating tasks, setting deadlines, moving work around -- or the content of the work, sorting information by topic or automatically updating a report.

Work-centered

Next is work- or object-centered. The archetype here is the document that knows how to mail itself, display itself, update itself from other sources. Here the user writes instructions that follow the work around: Go here, go there, get these approvals, come back. The work may even send itself out of the system and rely on someone to send it back. The problem is the closure: What happens if the document wanders around and gets lost? Who tracks it down? This approach doesn't offer a high-level representation of the cycle of work to be completed, but depends instead on a model in the user's or programmer's mind. Validation of work completion depends on the users rather than the system; it's as if you could make a withdrawal from the bank without the system requiring you to debit your account.

Process-centered

The process-centered approach makes sure that the work is completed, treating it as a complex, possibly nested transaction. Its model of the domain includes users, data (files) and applications, the cycle of work and the state of the transaction -- what's done, what's undone, who has what, what's next? (In work-centered, the object knows its own state, but not the state of the overall process; by querying broadly enough, you can get that information, but it's not integral to the system. It's like a flat file versus a relational database, if you like.) If user-centered has a user agent and work-centered has work "agents," then process-centered is closer to a group agent, working on behalf of and conscious of the entire group. Technically too, it's a more global system, typically managed by a database (perhaps physically distributed) that handles both information and work transactions.

The distinctions between work-centered and process-centered are subtle; one focuses on the work steps, and the other on the work cycle. In the end, the issue is the conceptual level of the task-building tool: Is it listing a series of steps and branches, or is it constructing a coherent task?

A subset or refinement of process-centered is the approach pioneered by Action Technologies (now licensed by Lotus and Da Vinci), which focuses on the relationships between requesters and doers of the work and "speech acts" such as delegation, commitment, counteroffers and so forth. The cycle (or transaction) is initiated by a customer or requester, and concluded when that customer is satisfied -- an excellent model for business overall.

MICROSOFT'S "INFORMATION AT YOUR FINGERTIPS" IN CONTEXT

There have been a variety of interpretations of the message promulgated by Microsoft and Co. -- delivered by Bill Gates in person, but very much a corporate message. As the press saw it, it's about viewing the world as a document rather than as files. Political analysts see it as an attempt to forestall HP NewWave, NeXT, Patriot Partners and GO and their followers. That's true too, in part. But it's also about object linking and embedding. A database lets you reuse data in (and maintain data integrity across) multiple database applications; object-oriented systems allow you to do the same with objects -- that is, reuse not just the data but also the applications (functions) and structure directly associated with the data. More importantly, objects can keep their character across applications; that is, a person is always a person (with name, address, discount level, salary grade or credit rating to be called as necessary), regardless of the specific application and rules applying to that person as a customer, employee, health-plan subscriber, or addressee of a letter.

Microsoft showed us the world-as-document (cf. Interleaf's Active Documents, **Release 1.0**, 90-3). But not everyone wants to use the document as interface to everything, and the concepts limned by Gates are much broader than the demos. Some people may organize their lives around time: Everything relates to a meeting or an appointment (see **Release 1.0**, 90-6). Architects or engineers may see the world as items organized by a hierarchy of diagrams; a doctor may see the world as patient charts (a specialized kind of document), while her medical assistant sees it as a schedule. One value of object linking and embedding is that you can get to any data from the medium of your favorite application/environment. (See **Release 1.0**, 90-3, 90-9.) The killer app is dead; the killer lib(rary) of objects is upon us.

The open get opener

Gates asserted that this won't be doable for another few years. Other vendors take exception, rightly pointing out that they can do this or that or the other right now. True, but can they do it with any other vendor's applications? They can do it only within their own proprietary, inward-looking environments, with imperfect connections to the outside world.

That's where Microsoft has an almost unassailable advantage: Do it our way, and you're open. Do it any other way, and you're closed (even with the interprocess communication tools from Userland for the Mac, also promised for System 7; **Release 1.0**, 89-4). The problem is that the Microsoft way is incremental and is less likely to foster fundamentally new applications than a revolutionary approach. But the revolution may never happen if people are kept content enough with the gradually evolving, gradually improving DOS. (In fact, DOS will almost disappear under the increasing functionality offered by Windows, and will become almost indistinguishable from OS/2.) The business fact of market dominance leads to the technical fact that Microsoft's approach will garner the most users and thus *become* practically, tangibly superior because of its interoperability with the rest of the world.

Until we have a standard way of loading just the functions that are needed (a transaction or two, say, or just the print routines) it won't be of much practical use. (Early efforts in that direction include Borland's VROOMM,

for Virtual Real-time Object-Oriented Memory Manager, **Release 1.0**, 89-6.)
Both Microsoft and NewWave are still wrestling with this object granularity
problem, as well as with issues of maintaining integrity across multiple
systems, what you do when an "object's" application happens not to be resident on the proper machine, or exists in a different version. Embedding
copies the object and makes a new standalone version; linking makes a link
to the original, which continues to be updated -- but you have to find it if
it has been moved. (DDE is simply a protocol for linking in data and some
display information, with no access to an application to manipulate it.)
Long-run, integrity maintenance will require an object-oriented database
(even if you call it an object-oriented environment) to keep track of all of
these. Did you want the data you put there, or the most current version?
What if the data in A depend on the data in B and so forth?

Every object a server; every server an object

Client/server devolves into object-oriented programming, where every object
is a little server, doing something in response to the messages it receives.
Long-run it's not practical (for memory and response-time reasons) to have
entire file/application objects, which is how NewWave and Microsoft's Vapor-
Wave (Object Linking and Embedding) do it currently. The trick is to call
code modules only as needed. An object is a virtual assemblage, with pointers to the appropriate functions and data; each bit is loaded only as
needed. And if you call two spreadsheet objects, you don't load the spreadsheet twice. A future system will let users and applications share small
modules and data instead of whole applications and monolithic servers.

One move in this direction is stored procedures such as Sybase's, which let
multiple applications share defined transaction sequences just as they share
data. At the user level, mail tools such as Beyond Mail and Wijit (page 11)
mediate among whole applications and let users define and reuse sets of
rules for handling various data items, which are encapsulated as mail messages. But they are an extra layer rather than a tool for modularizing existing applications and creating genuine objects. Take the new Sidekick 2.0
(page 16), which can create a quasi-object out of a name and address in its
address book (based on Paradox files) and paste it into a meeting in the
calendar. But it doesn't "remember" it as an object when we want that person's name and address later. Instead, we select the text and use it for a
database query; but if we know two Juan Tigars it doesn't know which one the
appointment referred to. In the same way, Agenda creates "object classes"
or categories by the simple act of creating columns and values, but those
aren't robust enough to carry across for use in other applications (at least
not without careful format handshaking).

Early examples of objects include not just the Windows graphical objects
everyone is promoting, but more powerful, behavior-rich application objects
such as HumanCAD's animated Mannequins, C++-based objects which come both
with variable parameters, display capabilities and behavior such as walking,
bending and reaching (more on this soon).

All these capabilities are headed in the right way, but as Gates says, if
you use a nonstandard approach you end up in trouble later on.... So where
else can we look for the standards?

MAIL IN MODULES

Whatever groupware looks like to the end-user, its technical underpinnings usually involve either a database or a file-transfer/mail system, which in turn hide the underlying network plumbing and remote procedure calls from the application developer (and save a lot of work). But the underlying technology also shows through, and e-mail is a natural for the user-centered approach to groupware. User-agent programming tools are ideal for building groupware, using the mail not as an application but as a utility or tool. Meanwhile, the very shape of mail is changing, from an integrated application that hides its architecture, to an open system comprised of clients and servers -- and open to attachment with foreign clients and servers.

Rather than disappearing into the network operating system at one end or the applications at the other, mail is resolving itself into a number of modules. Those modules will indeed turn up inside applications, but not because they're glued there by developers; rather, they will be facilities easily called from inside applications (cf. Microsoft's vision, pages 4-5).

Mail basically comes in four parts with a confusing variety of names that reflects the lack of visibility until now of these components. Traditionally, all four have been tightly coupled (quadrupled?) and hard to identify or distinguish and to communicate with from other systems. They are:

o   the so-called "user agent," the client application or user environment (including tools to program applications for mail-management and to link the mail system's functions with those of local user applications). The breadth of this facility is in part dependent on the quality of the local application's APIs.

o   the transport mechanism at the back end, which knows how to deal with network operating systems and protocols, and transfer files from one environment to another. It knows about the underlying hardware and plumbing so that applications and users don't have to.

o   the name or directory service, which maintains the physical locations of users who can thus be addressed by logical or virtual names. This can be a single file, a central database, a continuously updated distributed set of files or database (cf. cc:Mail's new automatic propagation service, for updating local directories).

o   the store-and-forward component. The store-and-forward or storage component could be either a file system or a database on the server, or it could be a set of local, distributed mailboxes (awkward if most machines aren't running most of the time).

In the past, you couldn't easily get at any component individually, and mail worked best when everyone was using the same system. The interoperability people touted worked through the addition of extra layers, translating back and forth, and so on. A number of vendors have written front-ends to PROFS, which convert its output into something intelligible and easier to use, but they can do little to increase its basic, limited functionality.

Now, however, we're seeing a sea-change in mail. Just as transfer of documents is about to disappear into a function that can be called from any application, limiting the appeal of traditional e-mail front-ends, a number of companies are starting to build separate programmable mailbox-management tools which go well beyond the display-and-dispose functions of existing e-mail. At the same time, a lot is going on at the store-and-forward end.

For transport, we're still at the stage of hide the plumbing, please, and talk to as many other systems as you can. Transport includes both connections to other hardware, connections to other mail systems (with proper transformations and addressing), and so forth. The transport properly also includes directory services, so that any message can get to any other person, location or service.

The directory server is also a component that can be offered separately, as Banyan is starting to do with its StreetTalk, one of the best directory services available and one of the closest to complying with the forthcoming X.500 standard. Separate from the directory service or name server is the database that holds the actual messages. In the first version, it may simply be a central file system, which holds them until called for, or in serverless mail systems, in and out boxes dedicated to the individual users. In the future (and in systems such as cc:Mail's) it's a database, so that messages can be stored, retrieved and manipulated by as many attributes (fields) as anyone cares to assign to them. Systems based on this model include OracleMail and cc:Mail and, soon, Wijit and Beyond Mail, below.

As mail modularizes, traditional vendors are threatened. Although they offer a complete solution, this is no longer a complete-solution world. Customers want interoperability, best-of-kind functions rather than a jack-of-all-trades complete solution. Third-party developers want something to hook into. Canny mail vendors see these modular third-party offerings as enhancements and support, whereas those reluctant to change see them merely as competition. Certainly, the old mail vendors will be squeezed on both sides, from (network) operating system vendors for transport and servers, and from application vendors for the user agent side. Certainly it requires clever strategy and good execution, but the model of Sybase -- which has opened itself up at both the client and server ends -- is a good one. Sure, people can compete with you at either end; but if you have the best solution what is there to fear? And if you don't, you can forget it anyway. The issue is to make your system if not a standard at least a widely used approach, and then to take a lead in the market you create by leading the way and (gently) controlling the evolution of the standard. (But don't be too successful, or some Open Hole Foundation will attempt to wrest it all away from you.)

MAIL-ENABLED APPLICATIONS

You can build groupware systems relatively easily from the ground up, with modules that talk to each other -- the model used by most group schedulers and other networked office-automation systems sold as groupware, such as WordPerfect Office and INTO, and Borland's Sidekick, below. Some of these include mail as one of their tools, with extensive features for fax, address lists, and the like. But these are mostly sealed systems; they deal intelligently only with their own data, and they load users' applications as foreign objects. Also, they rarely have any notion of workflow or tasks. The calendar is shared *information*, not obligations among users; the to-do list is a list, not a queue of tasks that the system knows about. Moreover, these systems have mostly wired-in functions are aren't really programmable; there's group data, but not a great deal of group intelligence.

For the moment, then, the most appealing approach is to start with user-centered groupware, and let the user supply the intelligence and applications -- or programmed user agents -- via an e-mail front-end. After all, what better application-independent way to communicate with other applications, whether locally, across a network or even across a country? (At least until we have the kind of global object-oriented, message-passing system described earlier.) Moreover, the e-mail system takes care of time delays, so that not everything need happen in real-time, and events can be programmed to happen at certain times or triggered by certain events.

Moreover, mail (inadvertently) provides some of the abstractions needed for groupware. You can use mail not just to send messages to people, but to send commands and data to applications and to chain these processes. The implementation requires a couple of capabilities: A tool for users that makes the messages easy to construct, and something that translates those messages into something the applications at the other end can interpret. But the translation-for-applications facility depends in large part on the applications in question, and in the existence or quality of their application programming interfaces (API) and macro languages.

The mailman cometh

Two different approaches are both offshoots of the MIT Information Lens project (see **Release 1.0**, 86-10). That project was LISP-based and ran on proprietary Xerox D-machines. It provided both information filters, user profiles and the ability to build and execute rules. A follow-on project, Object Lens, added some more object-oriented concepts, but both systems remain research projects without industrial-strength data management and other underpinnings. Information Lens is in the public domain; there are some patents applied for by MIT on certain aspects of the Object Lens system, but its licensing policies seem fairly unrestrictive.

Although the two products share many concepts and features, they are addressing different market segments with subtly different positions. One company, Beyond Inc., has acquired (nonexclusive) rights to the MIT patents, and is run by Chuck Digate, formerly senior vp of "analytic products" (spreadsheets) at Lotus; Soft·Switch's Michael Zisman (who wrote his thesis on groupware 13 years ago) sits on the board. The other, Agility Systems, was acquired last year by Dun & Bradstreet after it hired company founder John Landry (now at Lotus).

Both handle the world in terms of mail messages, which they can filter, sort and manage according to information in the header fields or a full-text search of the message body. Both also allow the creation of custom header fields and default values, or semi-structured messages, and can customize rules to handle them. You can also use either of them to delegate mail not just to other people but to other times -- a tickler file, in essence. Consider them another way to manage a to-do list or a project, with messages spitting out at appropriate times to all your correspondents.

Thus, both can create database applications acting as client to a server -- for example, processing an expense report or a subscription request. They can build rules to print out an invoice, send a welcoming (boilerplate) letter to the new subscriber, and finally post the transaction to the corporate database. Sure, you could build these another way, but the mail tools make it potentially within the capabilities of a single user (perhaps with help from a database expert and someone who knows how to work mail-merge in wp.)

Beyond is focused on the local user, allowing him to develop rules to deal with his mail -- call it inbox management -- and ultimately with applications and the outside world. The goal is both to reduce the information overload on each individual, says Digate, and to broaden the dissemination of information that people *do* want. The system is designed to work on pc-based local-area networks, although it can of course reach further through gateways. The target user is an individual within a group, dealing with messages from other users who have e-mail but may not have Beyond Mail.

While Beyond is focused on personal interactions, while Wijit is more information-intensive. Agility's target user is an individual dealing with external information, whether from outside databases or corporate or department applications. It starts off more outwardly-focused, allowing the user to go out and select what comes *into* his mail from external data sources.

Another differentiator is style: Beyond's tool, the aptly named Beyond Mail, will initially use character graphics, while Agility's Wijit is the ultimate in Windows glitz. Beyond has a simple, homespun feeling, addressing the largest possible audience at a low single-user price, while Agility is a more high-end product. Although Wijit offers a variety of templates for various information services, it's more likely that some kind of information center, help desk or MIS person will be involved with its installation (especially for a senior executive), whereas Beyond has more of that I-can-do-it-myself feel. Call Beyond a VW, with its capabilities clear, and Agility a BMW with an electronic dashboard -- all associations intentional.

Extending the group

While we would use Beyond Mail in the office, for interaction with other people, we would be more likely to take Wijit along on the road. It has a dial-up feel to it; it keeps you in touch with the outside world. Ultimately, with the developer's kit for either product and a willing customer base, you could use them for that holy grail, channel marketing. In other words, get your customers up on the system, so they can send orders directly into your system by e-mail. Just build them a form to fill in, and on your end, take the form and convert it into the order format required by your corporate mainframe -- probably not something either your MIS department or your customer really wants the customer to deal with directly. Of course, both systems could be used to build the same application; it's a question of the design center of each product -- which, if the two companies are smart, they will take care to differentiate themselves as much as possible.

A third approach is that of Reach Software, founded by Banyan founder Anand Jagannathan. Reach offers both a flexible e-mail package, MailMAN, and a tool for creating mail-based workflow scripts, WorkMAN.

Commercial issues

How to sell groupware? We spent an interesting lunch recently with a frustrated vendor of groupware. His product runs on pcs and networks and works
fine on that platform. The problem is that his customers don't have network
administrators; they know pcs are easy to use and don't need heavy-duty
administration. Accordingly, whenever something goes wrong with the network
(not with the groupware), the customers come back to his company for help.
But he can't find the necessary people to support those customer networks,
and he doesn't have the time or resources to train them. Neither, it seems,
do network vendors have time to support groupware. Evernet, the nationwide
company of local VARs specializing in servers and networks, is just getting
its affiliates up to speed with NetFrame and Oracle. Groupware tools and
applications are still off in the future.

The platform battle, in the end, may not be UNIX vs. OS/2, but UNIX vs.
LANs. UNIX may well pull ahead not so much because of product quality but
because it will sell to UNIX users who (1) understand that it needs support,
and (2) make such support and training are on site. This is good news for
vendors such as Hunter Systems (see **Release 1.0**, 88-11) who are helping
software vendors to make the transition to UNIX as painless as possible.

Likewise, groupware represents a big opportunity for the traditional vendors
who lost out to IBM in the mainframe business, to UNIX in the mid-range, and
to IBM and the clones in the pc business. Now their sales forces and support staffs can come into their own again, selling and supporting groupware
-- if they can rise to the challenge of articulating these concepts not just
to customers but to their own salesforces. Potential beneficiaries include
NCR (Cooperation), Xerox, AT&T (Rhapsody), HP (NewWave Office), Wang (with
its procedure automation tools) and even IBM (with an enhanced OfficeVision).

However, when we went to the AT&T booth at Comdex, the salesman there told
us Rhapsody was too innovative and difficult to understand to be
demonstrated at a trade show. Maybe he was right. At the NCR booth, the
company was demonstrating Cooperation, but the salesman couldn't really figure it out beyond showing us the icons. (The only other people who had
asked to see it, he told us, were from Seybold!)

Moreover, none of the groupware products has a compelling story yet. If
*all you want is personal productivity, a pc and some packaged software will
do the trick. If you want real office productivity for tasks and work and
business, you have to wait -- or have a specific problem to solve. Then you
can buy something like FileNet at the high end or some of the products described below for specific tasks, but it's early in the game.

CAN GROUPWARE ENHANCE PRODUCTIVITY

AND OFFER COMPETITIVE ADVANTAGE?

Susanna Opper

President, Susanna Opper & Associates
388 West Road
Alford, MA 01266

ABSTRACT

As groupware approaches maturity, it will have new responsibilities. One of
them is to focus on producing clear benefits for the enterprise. Only when
outcomes are clearly determined in advance and results are systematically
tracked can the groupware community even begin to prove groupware's benefits to
the organizations that invest in it. This article points to some beginning
steps all groupware implementers should take.

1   INTRODUCTION

Groupware's not a kid anymore. It's been 30 years since Doug Engelbart's early
experiments, nearly 20 years since the start of EIES (Electronic Information
Exchange System) at the New Jersey Institute of Technology, and more than a
decade since electronic conferencing was offered to the public on The Source.
Lotus Notes, the first mainstream groupware product, has been available for
two-and-a-half years.

The time has come to get serious about groupware's real benefits. Most of
us in the field assert that groupware is an enabling technology, that its
benefits can transform the way people work, and that it's the inevitable
flowering of a networked infrastructure. Many of the enterprises that
pioneered groupware did so without hard evidence of its advantages. But as
groupware becomes mainstream, warm feelings and heart-felt testimonials aren't
sufficient. It's time to ask the hard questions about groupware. Does it
really enhance productivity? How do we know? Will it really offer competitive
advantage? How can we tell? For a given set of users, how does groupware
really impact the way they work? If so, how?

2   MEASURING THE UNKNOWN

Groupware can't be justified in traditional ways. That's because, for the most
part, groupware's benefits are in areas that generally go unmeasured by
conventional techniques. How much time is wasted each year in American
businesses by telephone tag? No one knows. Nor is there a line item in
corporate budgets for miscommunications or time wasted having the same
discussion more than once. There's no accounting method for costing out the
inability to find the right piece of paper. So, it's difficult to point to a
column of numbers and say here is the evidence of groupware's value.

It's generally agreed that groupware substitutes for meetings, in one way
or another. That's why Bernie DeKovan invented the meeting meter. DeKovan, a
meeting facilitator based in Silicon Valley, wanted people to get a handle on
the true cost of wasting time in meetings. Almost as a joke, he invented a
device designed to keep track of the cost of meetings by multiplying the
salaries of the attendees by the number of minutes the meeting consumed. When
the meter was mentioned in The Wall Street Journal some years back, DeKovan
actually found there was a demand for the product.

A more chilling statistic is how people actually feel about the time they spend in meetings. During a US and European speaking tour earlier this year, I asked audiences to indicate by raising their hands how much time they spent in meetings. The average range was from 25% to 75%, with 50% being the median. Then I asked the same people to raise their hands if they believed they were more productive in meetings or working on their own. Of the hundreds surveyed, a scant four or five individuals voted for the productivity of meetings. For the rest, the majority of their time is spent in an activity that is minimally productive. This offers an enormous opportunity for groupware. So-called "roomware" or real-time meeting facilitation products such as Vision Quest, Ventana and Team Focus offer potential high return on investment. But so does all groupware since it potentially replaces some face-to-face meetings and can increase knowledge-worker productivity.

For the most part the savings from using groupware are made in increased flow of information and recovered time. Quantifying increased information access is nearly impossible in today's environment, but savings in time can translate into savings in dollars. Even here the savings are not typically directly quantifiable. The real bottom line about recovering time is that it lets companies be more responsive to their customers and helps individuals be more thorough in their work. It frees resources to be applied to projects that might not otherwise get done. These savings in time are key to what groupware will do for organizations. But how do we all of a sudden start accounting for these savings?

3   BASE-LINING WITH INTERVIEWS

Measuring the productivity of professionals, knowledge workers and creative people has never been simple. In the throes of a difficult implementation with many factors to coordinate, it's easy to overlook the fact that in the future, people will be interested in knowing what groupware actually produced.

In order to convincingly demonstrate the utility of groupware and to document its success or failure, you must know where you started and where you ended up. Base lining is a method of determining how a group or organization functions before the introduction of groupware so that changes can be isolated and measured later. The primary purpose of the base-line interviews is to get a fuller understanding of how the group currently works. Thus when the same questions are asked after the pilot is complete, the contribution of groupware can be measured.

The interview technique is recommended for gathering base-line information. Groupware is the merging of individual, group and organizational goals. The implementation process involves countless meetings, but the base-line interview offers an opportunity in the piloting process to pay attention to concerns of the individual. Additionally, in a group some participants may well be less candid than they would be in a private, confidential interview with a skilled data gatherer. Although data from these surveys is neither numerical nor highly scientific, such interviews can produce a wealth of information.

Base-line interview questions deal with fundamental work-process and group-effectiveness concerns for the organization. When people take time to talk about their work, they become sensitized to how they work as well as to what they do. Typically these issues are not given much attention in the normal workday. This is one reason why groupware is so challenging. It deals directly with concerns that have become habituated and unconscious for many knowledge workers. Thinking about these processes consciously and articulating opinions in the safe environment of an interview can be revealing. It should set the stage for the types of issues that will be of concern as the groupware implementation process progresses.

Base-line interviews should be conducted as the first groups are piloting groupware. Data from these interviews can be useful both for deciding who will use groupware and for building applications once groupware use has been inaugurated.

Combined with a thorough needs analysis, gathering base-line information provides the foundation for objective setting. The two together mean groupware implementers can establish success factors in advance of a groupware implementation. A few simple goals will usually serve better than many complex ones. In one client engagement, the initial goal was simply to reduce the length of a weekly status meeting that consumed up to three hours before groupware. Once the time was saved by putting status reports on-line, managers realized a second objective. There was time available to talk about more important issues--ones that could improve service and reduce inefficiencies.

3.1 Designing and Conducting Base-line Interviews

Base-line interviews should be designed and conducted by a skilled interviewer, if possible an objective outsider. It is important that the questions be responsive to business and systems concerns, so interviews should be designed with input from both of these areas.

Not everyone in the pilot group needs to participate in the interviews, but a good, representative sample is desirable. The list of questions shown below illustrates the kinds of questions asked in a base-line interview.

3.2 Sample Base-line Interview Questions

1. Describe some of the most frequent activities in your job currently. Roughly how long does each of these take to complete?
2. Who do you get information from? Give information to? What kind of information is this?
3. Estimate how much of the information you need comes from meetings, telephone conversations, E-mail, fax, regular mail. How important is each of these communication methods to you?
4. How many meetings do you typically attend in a month? How much meeting time is devoted to reporting? to decision-making? Could some of these meetings be eliminated if the information were available electronically? Could the necessary meetings be shortened, and if so how?
5. Do you have to repeat tasks or ask others to redo their work? If so, normally, what aspects must be redone?
6. Could the quality of your output and the projects you participate in be improved? What changes in the way you work would help facilitate improvement?

3.3 Presenting the Results

Compilation of the results of base-line interviews can take many forms, but it is most important that the data be organized and stored in such a way that it can be retrieved and used for comparison when the "after" set of interviews have been completed. In most cases the base-line interview data can be entered into the groupware system, providing an on-going measuring stick for progress and allowing for possible on-line follow-up during or after the pilot.

PAY NOW OR PAY LATER

After all these years of waiting, groupware is poised for success. But with the potential popularity comes a real risk that organizations will do the right thing for the wrong reasons. Simply jumping on the groupware bandwagon without clarity of purpose and clear business goals will spell certain disaster--sooner or later. In the sometimes mad rush to implement, eager systems managers ignore or discount the purpose of the installation and the outcomes management expects. Put simply, if your company's management doesn't know why the groupware system is being implemented, you are going to pay later.

Heed these words paraphrased with permission from an on-line comment by a veteran of organizational change:

> I will only get involved in redesign again if there's a clear understanding up front about both the hard and the soft criteria. All major stakeholders must participate in both the choice of the process and selection of desired outcomes. That way there's shared accountability for making results happen. I will make sure that measurement devices are set up in advance and tracked from day one.

Reference

Opper, S., Fersko-Weiss, H. 1992. **TECHNOLOGY FOR TEAMS: Enhancing Productivity in Networked Organizations,** New York, NY: Van Nostrand Reinhold.

COMPUTERS, NETWORKS AND THE CORPORATION*

Thomas W. Malone
Center for Coordination Science
Massachusetts Institute of Technology
50 Memorial Drive
Cambridge, MA 02139

John F. Rockart
Center for Information Systems Research
Massachusetts Institute of Technology
50 Memorial Drive
Cambridge, MA 02139

ABSTRACT

Computer networks are forging new kinds of markets and new ways to manage organizations. The result will be a major change in corporate structure and management style.

1 INTRODUCTION

About 150 years ago the economy in the U.S. and Europe began to undergo a period of change more profound than any experienced since the end of the Middle Ages. We call that change the Industrial Revolution. The industrial economies are now in the early stages of another transformation that may ultimately be at least as significant.

There is a critical difference this time, however. Changes in the economies of production and transportation drove the revolution of the last century. The revolution under way today will be driven not by changes in production but by changes in coordination. Whenever people work together, they must somehow communicate, make decision, allocate resources and get products and services to the right place at the right time.. Managers, clerks, salespeople, buyers, brokers, accountants--in fact, almost everyone who works--must perform coordination activities.

It is in these heavily information based activities that information technologies have some of their most important uses, and it is here that they will have their most profound effects. By dramatically reducing the costs of coordination and increasing its speed and quality, these new technologies will enable people to coordinate more effectively, to do much more coordination and to form new, coordination-intensive business structures.

The core of the new technologies is the networked computer. The very name "computer" suggests how one usually thinks of the device--as a machine for computing, that is, for taking in information, performing calculations and then presenting the results. But this image of computing does not capture the essence of how computers are used now and how they will be used even more in the future. Many of the most important uses of computers today are for coordination tasks, such as keeping track of orders, inventory and accounts. Furthermore, as computers become increasingly connected to one another, people will find many more ways to coordinate their work. In short, computers and computer networks may well be remembered not as technology used primarily to compute but as coordination technology.

---

* Reprinted with permission. Copyright (c) 1991 by Scientific American, Inc. All rights reserved. (*Scientific American*, September 1991, vol. 265, no. 3, pp. 92-99.)

2 AN ANALOGY: EFFECTS OF IMPROVED TRANSPORTATION TECHNOLOGY

To understand what is likely to happen as information technology improves and its costs decline, consider an analogy with a different technology: transportation. A first-order effect of transportation technology was simply the substitution of new transportation technologies for the old. People began to ride in trains and automobiles rather than on horses and in horse-drawn carriages.

As transportation technology continued to improve, people did not use it just to substitute for the transportation they had been using all along. Instead a second-order effect emerged: people began to travel more. They commuted farther to work each day. They were more likely to attend distant business meetings and to visit faraway friends and relatives.

Then, as people used more and more transportation, a third order effect eventually occurred: the emergence of new "transportation-intensive" social and economic structures. These structures, such as suburbs and shopping malls, would not have been possible without the wide availability of cheap and convenient transportation.

2.1 First order effect: Substitution

Improved coordination technology has analogous effect. A first-order effect of reducing coordination costs is the substitution of information technology for human coordination. For example, data-processing systems helped to eliminate thousands of clerks from the back offices on insurance companies and banks. Similarly, computer-based systems have replaced scores of factory 'expediters." Today computers track the priority of each job in the factory and indicate the most critical ones at each workstation. More generally, the long-standing prediction that computers will lead to the demise of middle management finally seems to be coming true. In the 1980s many companies flattened their managerial hierarchies by eliminating layers of middle managers.

2.2 Second order effect: Increased demand

A second-order effect of reducing coordination costs is an increase in the overall amount of coordination used. For instance, contemporary airline reservation systems enable travel agents to consider more flight possibilities for a given customer more easily. These systems have led to an explosion of special fares and price adjustments. American Airlines and United Air Lines, which provide the largest systems, have benefited significantly from the fees they charge for this service. For instance in 1988, American made about $134 million from its reservation system--almost 15 percent of its total income. In addition, access to up-to-the-minute information about ticket sales on all airlines enables American and United to adjust their fare schedules to maximize profits.

Otis Elevator Company also increased the amount of its coordination--primarily to improve maintenance service for its customers. With its Otisline system, highly trained multilingual operators receive trouble calls though a national toll-free number. The operators record the problems in a computer data base and then electronically dispatch local repair people.

The real-time availability of data has vastly improved the management of repair activities. For instance, if a particular type of part has failed during the past week on eight of 100 elevators, Otis can preemptively replace that part on the other 92 elevators. Although this kind of nationwide correlation of data was possible before, the degree of communication and coordination required was impractical. These capabilities have played a major role in reducing maintenance calls by nearly 20 percent.

In some instances the second-order effect of an increase in demand may overwhelm the first-order effect of substitution. For example, in one case we studied, a computer conferencing system helped to remove a layer of middle managers. Several years later, however, almost the same number of new positions (for different people at the same grade level) had been created.

According to people in the company, the new specialists took on projects not considered before. Evidently, managerial resources no longer needed for simple communication could now be focused on more complex coordination tasks.

2.3 Third order effect: New structures

A third-order effect of reducing coordination costs is a shift toward the use of more coordination-intensive structures. A prime example is Frito-Lay, Inc., studied by Lynda M. Applegate of Harvard Business School and others. At Frito-Lay, some 10,000 route salespeople record all sales of each of 200 grocery products on hand-held computers as they deliver goods to customers on their route. Each night, the stored information is transmitted to a central computer. In turn, the central computer sends information on changes in pricing and product promotions to the hand-held computers for use the next day. Each week, the main computer summarizes the centrally stored information and combines it with external data about the sales of competitive brands. Some 40 senior executives and others can then gain access to this information through an executive information system (EIS).

The availability of these data has enabled Frito-Lay to push key decisions down from corporate headquarters to four area heads and several dozen district managers. The managers can use the data not only to compare actual sales to sales targets but also to recommend changes in sales strategy to top management. This entire coordination-intensive structure has become possible only in the past few years because of the improved capability and reduced costs of hand-held computers, EIS software, computer cycles and telecommunications equipment.

Coordination-intensive structures do not just link different people in the same companies. Many of the most interesting new structures involve links among different companies. For example, the U.S. textile industry has begun implementing a series of electronic connections among companies as part of the Quick Response program. As described by Janice H. Hammond of Harvard Business School and others, these electronic connections link companies all along the production chain, from suppliers of fibers (such as wool and cotton) to the mills that weave these fibers into fabric, to the factories that sew garments and ultimately to the stores that sell the garments to consumers.

When such networks are fully implemented, they will help companies respond quickly to demand. For instance, when a sweater is sold in New York City, a scanner reading the bar-coded label may automatically trigger ordering, shipping and production activities all the way back to the wool warehouse in South Carolina. This new, multiorganizational structure will reduce inventory costs throughout the value chain. The textile-apparel retail industry spends about $25 billion in inventory costs every year; the Quick Response approach may save half that amount.

Wal-Mart has already established parts of a similar system that links the retailer to Procter & Gamble Company and several of its other major suppliers. In doing so, Wal-Mart has eliminated significant parts of its own purchasing groups and contracted with its suppliers to replace products as they are sold. In one such experiment, both unit sales and inventory turnover increased by about 30 percent.

Sometimes technology helps to create interorganizational networks--not just among buyers and suppliers but also among potential competitors. For example, Eric K. Clemons of the University of Pennsylvania has studied the Rosenbluth International Alliance, a consortium of travel agencies around the world that share customer records, services and software. The alliance also provides clients with toll-free English-language help lines in every major country. This consortium of independent agencies, led by Rosenbluth Travel in Philadelphia, can therefore manage all travel arrangements for international trips and for meetings of people for people from many parts of the globe.

The textile firms near Prato, Italy illustrate a related kind of interorganizational alliance. As described by Michael J. Piore and Charles F. Sabel of the Massachusetts Institute of Technology, the operation of a few large textile mills was broken into many small firms, coordinated in part by electronic connections among them. This network can flexibly adjust to changes in demand, sometimes shifting orders from an overloaded mill to one with spare capacity. The structure also takes advantage of the entrepreneurial motivation of the owners: in small mills, the owners' rewards are more closely linked to their own efforts than is the case in large ones.

3 MORE USE OF MARKETS

As these examples show, information technology is already facilitating the emergence of new, coordination-intensive structures. What do these changes mean for the organization of the near future?

A surprising result of our research is a prediction that information technology should lead to an overall shift from internal decisions within firms toward the use of markets to coordinate economic activity. To see why, consider that all organizations must choose between making the goods or services they need and buying them from outside suppliers. For instance, General Motors Corporation must decide whether to make tires internally or purchase them from a tire manufacturer.

Each of these two forms of coordination--internal and external--has advantages and disadvantages. As Oliver Williamson of the University of California at Berkeley and others have argued, buying things from an outside supplier often requires more coordination than making them internally. To buy tires, General Motors may need to compare many potential suppliers, negotiate contracts and do formal accounting for the money that changes hands. Coordinating the production of tires internally, on the other hand, can often be done less formally and at lower cost, with telephone calls and meetings.

Coordination mechanism	Production Costs	Coordination Costs
Markets	Low	High
Hierarchies	High	Low

Figure 1. Buying something from an external supplier, instead of making it yourself, allows you to exploit economies of scale and other production cost advantages, but it usually requires higher coordination costs to find the supplier, account for payments, and negotiate contracts.

But improved information technology should reduce the costs of both internal and external coordination, much as transportation technology lowered the expense of traveling. When trains and automobiles reduced the difficulty of traveling, more people chose to live in the suburbs rather than in the cities to reap such benefits as extra living space. Similarly, when information technology reduces the costs of a given amount of coordination, companies will choose to buy more and make less. The additional coordination required in buying will no longer be as expensive, and buying has certain advantages. For instance, when General Motors buys tires, it can take advantage of the supplier's economies of scale and pick the best tires currently available from any supplier whenever its needs change. Thus, we expect networks to lead to less vertical integration--more buying rather than making--and to the proliferation of smaller firms. More electronically mediated alliances (such as the Rosenbluth International Alliance) and an increased use of electronic markets to pick suppliers (such as the airline reservation system) will result.

3.1   Strategic implications of shift to markets

This argument implies that information technology will help make markets more efficient. Buyers will no longer have to exert great effort to compare products and prices from many different suppliers. Instead an electronic market can easily and inexpensively collect and distribute such information.

These more efficient markets threaten firms whose strategic advantages rest on market inefficiencies. For instance, as Clemons described, when the London International Stock Exchange installed an electronic trading system, the trading floor became virtually deserted within a few weeks. Trading moved to electronic terminals around the world. The system greatly reduced the costs of matching buyers and sellers. This change, in turn, dramatically reduced the profits of brokers and trading specialists who previously had had a monopoly on performing this function. The potential decline in profit may explain why many other exchanges still resist electronic trading.

Many other kinds of intermediaries, such as distributors and retailers, are becoming vulnerable as well. For example, consumers can now bypass retail stores entirely by using computer-based systems such as Comp-U-Card and Comp-u-store to buy household goods and services at substantial savings. Electronic traders can also make evaluating product quality easier. We expect that it is only a matter of time before networks contain extensive comments and evaluations from previous buyers, becoming a kind of instantaneous, on-line *Consumer Reports*.

Increasing market efficiency also implies that firms should focus more carefully on the few core competencies that give them strategic advantages in the marketplace. They should buy the additional, more peripheral products and services they need instead of making them. For instance, in the past few years Ford Motor Company and Chrysler Corporation have significantly increased their proportion of externally purchased components, such as tires and batteries.

Even though information technology can be strategically important, single innovations in information technology are seldom in themselves a source of continuing competitive advantage. For example, American Hospital Supply, now Baxter Healthcare Corporation, won high praise for its early system that let customers place orders electronically without requiring a salesperson. This system made ordering from American Hospital easier than doing so from competitors and reduced the time salespeople had to spend on the clerical aspects of taking an order. But contrary to original expectations, systems like these do not "lock in" customers in the long run. Instead customers eventually seem to prefer electronic systems that provide a choice among several vendors. Similarly, an automatic teller machine system that may once have been a competitive advantage for a bank is now largely a competitive necessity.

One way to maintain an upper hand is to keep innovating so rapidly that other firms always lag a step behind. Another way, as Clemons has noted, is to use information technology to leverage some other structural advantage. For instance, Barclay deZoete Wedd, a British brokerage firm, continues to benefit from an electronic stock-trading system because the company already controlled the trading of far more stocks than did any of their competitors.

4   ADHOCRACIES

In addition to markets, another coordination-intensive organizational structure likely to become much more common is what some management theorists call a networked organization or, more picturesquely, an "adhocracy," a term Alvin Toffler popularized in his book *Future Shock*. This form is already common in organizations such as law firms, consulting companies and research universities. Such organizations and institutions must continually readjust to a changing array of projects, each requiring a somewhat different combination of skills, and other resources. These organizations depend on many rapidly shifting project teams and much lateral communication among these relatively autonomous entrepreneurial groups.

The adhocracy contrasts with the conventional business organization of today: the hierarchy. Hierarchies are common partly because they provide a very economical way of coordinating large numbers of people. In principle, decision makers in a hierarchy can consider all the information known to anyone in the group with much less communication than would be needed if each person communicated with everyone else.

In practice, however, hierarchies have severe limitations. Central decision makers can become overloaded and therefore unable to cope effectively with rapidly changing environments or to consider enough information about complex issues. Furthermore, people at the bottom may feel left out of the decision making and as a result be less motivated to contribute their efforts.

As information technology reduces communication costs, the nonhierarchical structures (such as markets and adhocracies) may help overcome the limitations of hierarchies. For example, because of the large amount of unpredictable lateral communication, the adhocracy is extremely coordination intensive. New media, such as electronic mail, computer conferencing and electronic bulletin boards, can make the coordination easier and, therefore, enable the adhocracy to work much more effectively. Computer networks can help find and coordinate people with diverse knowledge and skills from many parts of an organization.

Moreover, computer-based technologies can transfer information not only faster and more cheaply but also more selectively. These capabilities help to mitigate information overload. Systems now exist to help people find, filter and sort their electronic mail based on topic, sender and other characteristics. Together these new coordination technologies can speed up the "information metabolism" of organizations--the rate at which firms can take in, move, digest and respond to data.

5 CENTRALIZATION AND DECENTRALIZATION

Abundant information poses two potential difficulties for organizational power. Some people worry that managers may become "Big Brothers" who use the information to exert stronger centralized control over those who work for them. Others fear that if power is decentralized throughout the organization, workers might use their newfound power to serve their own narrow interests, leading to organizational chaos.

In fact, neither dark vision has been realized. Instead what appears to be happening is a paradoxical combination of centralization and decentralization. Because information can be distributed more easily, people lower in the organization can now become well enough informed to make more decisions more effectively. At the same time, upper-level decision makers can more easily review decisions made at lower levels. Thus, because lower-level decision makers know they are subject to spot-checking, senior managers can retain or even increase their central control over decisions.

The changes at Phillips Petroleum Company illustrate this process. Previously, senior managers decided what price to set for petroleum products. These critical decisions depended on the recommendations of staff analysts several levels down. When Phillips Petroleum developed an executive information system, senior managers began to make some of these decisions more directly based on the global information provided by the system. The senior executives soon realized, however, that they could pass on this global information directly to local terminal managers, who could take into account information such as competitors' prices. By decentralizing the pricing decision in this way, the company made sounder, more profitable pricing strategies in each area of the country.

Another way of understanding this paradoxical effect is to realize that new technology does not just redistribute power, it can provide a sense of more power for everyone. For example, the agents of several insurance companies currently carry laptop computers when they visit the homes of customers. The agents use the computers to fill out applications and project premiums and benefits. But typically, underwriters at the corporate headquarters require several weeks to review the applications and to issue new policies.

Soon the underwriting rules for certain routine policies will be included in the laptop computer itself. The agent will be able to issue these policies immediately in the customers' homes.

These systems will thus "empower" the agents, who will control the time and place of the policy-acceptance decisions and can make sales immediately. The authority of the central underwriters will increase as well because the rules they have created will be applied consistently. The underwriters will also be able to devote more time to analyzing interesting and potentially more profitable nonroutine cases.

Information technology not only changes power, it also changes time. On the one hand, time has expanded. Electronic mail, voice mail and facsimile transmissions can be sent or received at any time of day or night, almost anywhere around the globe. Similarly, customers of automatic teller machines and some stock markets can make transactions around the clock. The "work day" has much less meaning, and companies can compete by expanding the times their services are available.

On the other hand, time has contracted. Companies can also compete on speed. For instance, effective coordination can reduce the time needed to develop new products, deliver orders or react to customer requests. Management teams, such as the one at Phillips Petroleum, have information available throughout the management hierarchy, which enables them to react to market conditions much more quickly. Decisions that might have taken days in the past can now be made within hours or minutes.

6   EMERGING ORGANIZATIONAL STRUCTURES

The changes discussed so far require no great predictive leaps; they are already happening. What will happen as information technology improves even more? What other kinds of organizations might emerge in the globally interconnected world that the technologies make feasible?

6.1   Answer networks

One possibility is the increasing importance of "answer networks," networks of experts available to answer questions in different areas. One might go to these services with questions such as "How many bars of soap were sold in Guatemala last year?" or "What are the prospects of room-temperature superconductivity in consumer products by 1957?" The services would include massive data bases and layers of human experts in many different topic areas. Some questions will be easily answerable from information in a data base. Others will be referred to progressively more knowledgeable human experts. Depending on how much one is willing to spend and how quickly one wants the answer, the response might range from a newspaper clipping to a personal reply from a Nobel laureate scientist. Similar but limited services exist today--product hot lines and library reference desks are examples--but computer networks and data bases will make such services much less expensive, much more valuable and, therefore, much more widely used.

6.2   Overnight organizations

Electronically mediated markets can also assemble armies of "intellectual mercenaries" virtually overnight. For instance, there may be a large number of consultants who make their living doing short-term projects over the network. If a manager has a job to be done, such as evaluating a loan or designing a lawnmower, he or she could quickly assemble a team by advertising electronically or by consulting a data base of available people. The data base might contain not only the skills and billing rates of prospective workers but also unedited comments from others who had used their service before. Although consulting firms and advertising agencies sometimes work like this now, pervasive networks will allow teams to be assembled much more quickly, for shorter projects and from many different organizations.

6.3   Internal labor markets

This kind of market for services might be used inside an organization as well. Instead of always relying on supervisors to allocate the time of people who work for them, extensive internal markets for the services of people and groups may exist. Murray Turoff of the New Jersey Institute of Technology has suggested how such a system might work. Someone with a short programming project to be done, for instance, might advertise internally for a programmer. Bids and payments for this internal market could be in real dollars or some kind of point system. The bids from programmers would indicate their skill and availability. The payments that programmers receive would reflect how valuable they had been to other parts of the organization.

6.4   Computer-mediated decision networks

Improved technology can also help create decision-making structures that integrate qualitative input from many people. For instance, in making complex decisions, such as where to locate a new plant, the amassing of many facts and opinions is critical. Today companies often make such decisions after incomplete discussions with only a few of the people whose knowledge or point of view might be valuable. In the future, companies may use computer networks to organize and record the issues, alternatives, arguments and counterarguments in graphical form. Then many different people can review and critique the parts of the argument about which they know or care.

For instance, someone in a remote part of the firm might know about plans for a new highway that completely change the desirability of a proposed plant location. As such information accumulates, people can vote on the plausibility of different claims. Then, using all the information displayed in the system, a single person or group can ultimately make the decision.

7   CONCLUSIONS

What will happen as the globally-networked society leads to a world in which vast amounts of information are freely available, or easily purchased? Clearly, this world will require services, both automated and human, to filter the tremendous amount of information available. In general, as the amount of information increases, people who can creatively analyze, edit and act on information in ways that cannot be automated will become even more valuable.

But what else people will do will depend on the values that are important to them. When trains and automobiles reduced the constraints of travel time, other values became more significant in determining working and living patterns. As Kenneth T. Jackson of Columbia University has documented, for example, American values about the importance of owning one's home and the moral superiority of rural life played a large role in determining the nature of suburbs in the U.S.

Similarly, when the costs of information and coordination are not a barrier to fulfilling people's needs and wants, other values may emerge to shape the workplace and society. The new information technologies will almost certainly help gratify some obvious wants, such as the desire for money. Some of the emerging corporate structures may be especially good at satisfying nonmaterial needs, such as those for challenge and autonomy.

But perhaps these desires are themselves manifestations of some still deeper needs. Psychologist sometimes refer to a need for self-actualization. Others might call this a desire for spiritual fulfillment. To use the new technologies wisely, we will need to think more carefully about what we truly value and how the technology can help us reach our deeper goals.

Further Reading

Malone, T. W., Yates, J., and Benjamin, R.I.. 1987. Electronic markets and electronic hierarchies. *Communications of the ACM*. 30: 484-497.

Johnston, R. and Lawrence, P.R. 1988. Beyond vertical integration: The risk of the value-adding partnership. *Harvard Business Review*. 66: 94-104.

Clemons, E.K. 1991. Evaluation of strategic investments in information technology *Communications of the ACM*. 34: 22-36.

Bradley, S. , Nolan, R., and Hausman, J. *Global Competition and Telecommunications: Proceedings of a Symposium Held at Harvard Business School*. May 2-3, 1991. (in press).

Supplying The Right Stuff For Groupware

Ronald J. Whittier
Vice President,
Architecture and Software
Technology Group

Intel Corporation

Introduction

As the PC starts its second decade, the pace of business is picking up around the world. Modern businesses of all kinds — be they industrial, technical, financial, or service-oriented — are critically dependent on their information resources just to keep up. Getting the right information to the right people quickly is a competitive necessity. New technology must facilitate people working together in teams to solve problems faster and more accurately. The ability to sustain the competitive advantage will be achieved through the effective linking of the technology to the people within the organization.

The networking of PC's is approaching critical mass. All members of an organization are being connected. The result is a dramatic reduction in the time required to get things done. This increased efficiency will allow people working together to make better business decisions in less time. We call this capability "Just-In-Time Business." My talk outlines Intel's vision of how Just-In-Time Business can be achieved through Computer-Supported Collaboration and the key capabilities required to make it happen.

Just-In-Time Business is Critical for Competitiveness

Just-In-Time Business is a little bit like Just-In-Time Manufacturing. I define it as the fastest and most accurate completion of business decisions and business transactions. The concept goes beyond the idea of getting the job done "just in the nick of time." As with Just-In-Time Manufacturing, it focuses on the continuous improvement of the business process and information management to produce a higher level of customer satisfaction and to gain a competitive edge.

The business world is becoming a more dynamic environment every day — change has become a way of life. A major rethinking of how to re-engineer the corporation's business processes is underway. There is an accelerating need to gather vast amounts of current information from anywhere by the fastest possible means. This must be combined with the ability to send that data to the people who can act on it. The focus is now on how quickly and how well a company can transform ideas into better products to be more competitive in today's global markets. JIT-Business techniques and tools enable a business to respond to its customers' needs in sufficient time to create a competitive edge and guarantee customer satisfaction. Our concept of JIT-Business ensures that the corporate information infrastructure enables companies to gain a competitive edge by accelerating their ability to respond to changes in business conditions.

In fact, some would say that the single most compelling competitive edge for companies today is in the ability to reduce the time to develop an idea, make a decision and bring a product to market. You are either "quick or dead." It's probably true in your industry and certainly true in mine. At the same time, making quick accurate decisions is getting harder — teams are getting larger and more dispersed, problems seem to be tougher to solve and business information sources are now global.

We have entered the age of Just-In-Time Business, where <u>moving data quickly to the right people, is as important as getting access to it.</u> More recently, organizations have come to depend on teams connected electronically to meet the rising competitive challenges of modern business. Members of these teams need to work across geographic boundaries. These teams face new obstacles not typically encountered when all members are in the same facility. New tools for collaboration are needed to support their interactions. The goal is to create a work environment where the quality and effectiveness of interaction for geographically dispersed teams is equivalent to that of local teams. New approaches are needed to help teams of workers develop ideas, make decisions, and market products faster.

Computer-Supported Collaboration Enables Just-In-Time Business

More than 10 years ago, a handful of researchers realized that computers would have a fundamental impact on how people worked together. They wanted to study how computers could enhance the effectiveness and productivity of a group or team of people. Over the years many more people and companies have joined in this research, which is now commonly referred to as Computer-Supported Cooperative Work or CSCW[1].

The CSCW research findings have laid the ground work for the development of commercial groupware applications. Intel shares the vision of CSCW with the people and companies that are involved in this research. However, as you might expect, Intel's efforts are focused on the technology required to realize CSCW.

Intel defines <u>Computer-Supported Collaboration</u> as cooperative work done using computers and interactive electronic communications. What this means is PCs enabled with powerful processors, connectivity, mobility, and natural data support. Together these capabilities enable the collaborative services of Inter-Personal Communications, Information Sharing, Inter-Office Automation and Real-Time Conferencing. CSC is Intel's vision of today and the future for the computer enhanced capabilities and technologies that provide the infrastructure necessary to support groupware.

We use the term *groupware* to mean the class of <u>applications</u> that take advantage of CSC. Groupware is also one of the first application segments in the computer industry to leverage the newly installed base of networked computers. Groupware is real today and is beginning to deliver some of the fundamental capabilities that will enable JIT-Business.

Computers have Improved Individual Productivity

Before we get into the details of supplying the right stuff for groupware, lets first look at where we have come from. The evolution of office work started with simple manual tools that improved individual productivity. These desktop tools were the: typewriter, calculator, Rolodex, and the story board. The worker adapted the work environment and his "skill set" to use the power of these simple tools.

Individual   

Manually   Computer
Supported

The first decade of the PC changed all this. The PC changed individual work and brought higher productivity to the individual, a first step for JIT-Business. In its first decade, the PC replaced the old desktop tools. The four desktop tools were replaced by a PC with a word processor, spreadsheet, database and presentation graphics application software. It's not an exaggeration to say that the PC has changed forever how workers accomplish their work.

Communications Improves Group Productivity

Meanwhile, a lot of other "manual" work (or "footwork") continued, because we don't work alone at our desks. We spend most of our time in meetings, on the phone, traveling, solving group problems, and so on. In other words, performing our work increasingly requires that we collaborate with others. New kinds of products have been developed to aid collaboration through enhanced communications services. For example, products and services such as fax, express package pickup and delivery, cellular phone service, 24-hour cable news, and video-conferencing have arrived to support JIT-Business.

The acceptance of these new tools has been dramatic. For example, the number of cellular phone subscribers jumped by over 40% in 1991 (vs. 1990) to 7.56 million! Revenues from roamer fees are up 50% for the same period. However, where the degree of computerization is concerned, these tools are still <u>primitive</u> and the best is yet to come.

---

[1]Paul Cashman co-chaired with Irene Greif the first workshop on CSCW and helped coin the descriptive phrase "Computer-Supported Cooperative Work".

The second decade of the PC will be the decade of Computer-Supported Collaboration. The 1990's will make the collaborative tools that we use today as obsolete as the PC made the typewriter and adding machine in its first decade! Using the general rule that there is a significant breakthrough in productivity per decade associated with computerization of anything, collaborative work that benefits from the computer will see a substantial productivity enhancement during the 90's.

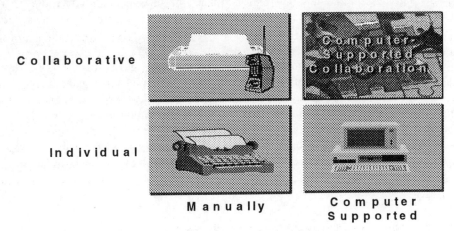

The PC's Second Decade

Computerized tools using CSC-enabled PCs will allow workers to perform tasks anywhere. In the office, these PCs will be as pervasive as telephones. One team member will use any available PC connected to the office network to contact another team member. At home, a team member will use his or her personal computer to "electronically transport" from the office to home. When traveling, a team member will use a portable PC on airplanes or in hotel rooms to electronically share information, participate in conferences, and exchange messages with other team members. Each team member can work at any task whenever he or she has available time or — and this is more likely — whenever the problem demands immediate action. Progress on team tasks can be made while other team members are working on other projects or are away from the office. You will be able to work efficiently as a member of a group wherever you have access to a computer.

Supplying the Right Stuff for Group Productivity

Teams of individuals require new services in order to collaborate effectively. Computers and communication improve team collaboration by enabling team members to exchange messages, share information, automate common office & business procedures and conduct real-time conferences.

Most CSC applications use several of these classes of service. For example, a claims processing application uses the information sharing capabilities of a database to store account information, inter-personal communications to route claim forms among multiple reviewers, real-time conferencing if two or more reviewers wish to jointly discuss some aspect of a claim form, and inter-office automation for assisting in the approval process of the claim. Now let's look at in more detail the underlying capabilities behind each of these four classes of service.

Inter-Personal Communications

Team members collaborate by sending and receiving mail containing information and requests for action. In the past, team members sent and received messages using the postal service. Today, team members send and receive fax, voice, and electronic mail messages, as well as postal mail. Unfortunately, fax messages contain only images and text, electronic mail messages contain only text, and voice messages contain only audio. A team member is often left wondering if and when his message was delivered. When team members are away from their offices, they have limited access to their messages.

Today electronic mail systems help team members exchange text messages and computer files. In the next 18 months, group members will send and receive messages using a variety of message data types — text, graphics, images, audio, video over various electronic communication channels. Users will be able to send and receive mail from within applications much as they can print from within an application today. PCs will be better integrated with one of the most important message delivery systems — the telephone system. Automatic acknowledgments will inform users when messages have been delivered. Filtering mechanisms will receive, categorize, and prioritize messages on behalf of users. Users will receive and act upon their messages at any time from any place using portable computers.

Information Sharing

Team members create information they want to share with other team members. Examples include documents, reports, memos, papers, spreadsheets, photos and pictures, and audio and video tapes. Information may be created with paper and pencil, typewriter, camera, tape recorder, video camera, or computerized applications such as word processors, spreadsheets, drawing tools, and "multimedia" applications.

Group members can share information by placing documents in filing cabinets or on bulletin boards that are accessible to all team members. Team members can search for, locate, and remove (check out) a document from a filing cabinet when they need to use it and return it (check it in) to the cabinet when they finish with the document. However, workers sometimes mis-file or remove documents without returning them, so other members of the team cannot access the documents. It is also difficult for team members to access a filing cabinet located at another physical site.

Computer applications, such as database management systems and document management systems, combine to overcome the problems with manual document management. In the future, team members will share information by capturing, storing, searching for, retrieving, displaying, editing, and printing electronic documents stored in an electronic filing cabinet. Powerful query utilities will be available to help users locate desired information. When a team member checks out a document from the electronic file cabinet, a copy always remains there for other team members to access. By using their PCs, group members will retrieve documents from remote electronic filing cabinets.

Inter-Office Automation

Inter-office automation allows computers to closely simulate the way people work in organizations. For example, inter-office automation can facilitate automation of workflow, tasks, forms and other objects and processes involved in moving a piece of work from one person to another.

In addition to helping users communicate and collaborate, the computer may also expand its traditional role to automating tasks that users find error-prone, tedious, boring, and repetitive. Many business procedures lend themselves to computer automation such as expense reports, claims processing, travel approvals, and status reports.

Real-Time Conferencing

Team members must collaborate by holding real-time conferences that often span physical locations. In the past, group members held meetings by traveling to an agreed-upon location at an agreed-upon time for a face-to-face meeting. Today, team members conduct conferences using the telephone and, in selected situations, video conferencing. While these systems enable team members to exchange information via audio and video, they fail to provide convenient, shared access to documents and tools needed during the conference.

What is needed is for team members to be able to interact via real-time conferencing, during which users at different sites can share a common electronic desktop and update electronic documents. Multiple users will be able to share applications designed for single users by taking turns interacting with the applications. In addition, new applications will be specially designed for real-time shared use by multiple users.

Additional real-time video conferencing capabilities will enable team members to see the physical gestures and reactions of other team members. This will bring Computer-Supported Collaboration one step closer to simulating real face to face interaction, driving yet another level of improvement to the quality of interaction supported by computers.

What Intel is Doing About CSC

Intel is focusing its efforts in four key areas: Processor Power, Connectivity, Mobility and Natural Data. These four key business thrusts are supported by leveraging our corporate competencies in: Silicon Technology and Manufacturing, Architecture and Platform, Design Technology, Information / Services / Support, and Brand Recognition.

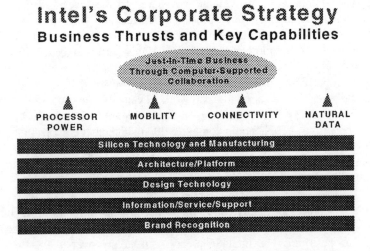

As mentioned earlier, Intel's objective is to deliver on the capabilities required for Computer-Supported Collaboration and groupware. I will now talk in detail about we are doing to make the vision a reality.

Processor Power

The first thing CSC requires is high-performance processors; there is always a need for more performance. This occurs because next-generation software is developed to run on the current high-volume CPU. The software runs slowly, however, because developers put on every bell and whistle and load down the CPU. It then takes the next generation of CPU to run the software well. We call this phenomenon; "The Power Spiral".

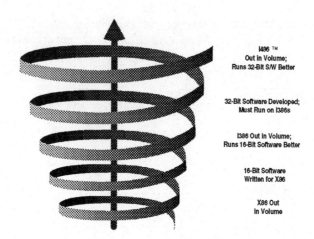

I486 ™
Out in Volume;
Runs 32-Bit S/W Better

32-Bit Software Developed;
Must Run on I386s

I386 Out in Volume;
Runs 16-Bit Software Better

16-Bit Software
Written for X86

X86 Out
In Volume

THE POWER SPIRAL

To illustrate this spiral: the 8086 and the 286 volume was driven by the success of the IBM PC. It used 16-bit software based on DOS, then the Intel386 microprocessor arrived and ran 16-bit software better and faster. Gradually 32-bit software was developed for the Intel386 CPU, but it really took the power of the Intel486 chip to run the software well. The Power Spiral motivates us to bring higher performance CPUs to the desktop.

If we break the desktop microprocessor market into three segments we see that at the high end are the computers used for critical business tasks and organizational group work. Typically, these computers cost over $5000. In the mid-range ($1000-$5000) we see broad business usage at work or home. And in the low end we have computer users who are very price-conscious. Their home computer often supplements work that they do at the office, so software compatibility is important. These computers are sold by mass merchandisers, and typically cost below $1000. Let's apply this model as a framework to review how we're feeding the insatiable appetite created by The Power Spiral.

Every three years or so, a new processor family comes out to occupy the high end in the marketplace. In 1985, it was the Intel386 processor, in 1989 it was the Intel486 CPU, and in 1992 the cycle will begin again. The new P5 chip will take the high-end position. The Intel486 processor is taking over in the mid-range market, and the Intel386 CPU is filling in the bottom of the market. These developments keep The Power Spiral rising.

Our current high-end microprocessor is the 50-Mhz Intel486 CPU, introduced in 1991. This processor runs at over 40 million instructions per second, outperforming most RISC processors that are typically used in engineering applications today. When we introduce the P5 later this year it will be more than twice as fast as the highest-performance Intel486 processor, and will bring new capabilities previously found only in mainframe-type applications. This processor will also be 100 percent compatible with all the previous software written for the Intel X86 architecture.

In the mid-range, the business world is rapidly making the Intel486 architecture the processor of choice on the desktop, partly due to the appearance of large numbers of Intel486 CPU-based computers below the $2000 price point. We recently introduced the Intel486 DX2 microprocessor, which permits the processor to run internally at twice its normal speed, without requiring the rest of the computer to speed up. It is easy for our original equipment manufacturer customers to adopt this technology and bring this higher performance to the marketplace because they can re-use their existing designs.

In the lower end of this three-tiered market model, the Intel386 CPU has now become the standard architecture for personal computers in the sub-$1000 market, meaning that many first-time users are starting out on 32-bit Intel-based machines.

Mobility

Mobility is the second key requirement of CSC. In the past, mobile computers required users to compromise between performance and true mobility. The 32-bit Intel386 SL microprocessor family extends battery life and provides "no-compromise" mobile computing. At Fall COMDEX last year, 46 manufacturers introduced 54 new systems using the Intel386 SL CPU, and since then, all of the top seven notebook manufacturers have begun shipping Intel386 SL microprocessor-based notebook computers in production volumes. This chip contains an exclusive power-saving technology called System Management Mode, which extends battery life in portable computers by selectively shutting down parts of the computer that are not being used.

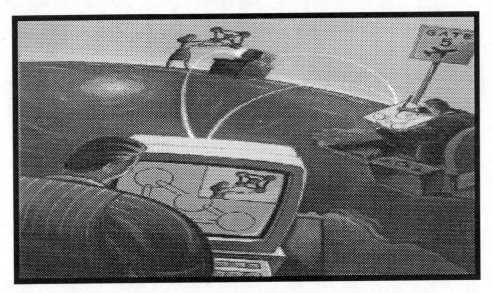

Connectivity

For any communication device to be useful, the technology has to reach all members of the relevant user community. Therefore, the third requirement for CSC and JIT-Business is to connect everyone together. Networking products is a new focus area for us. Our aim is to simplify building, using and managing PC networks. It shouldn't really be any harder to plug a PC into a network than it is to plug a telephone into a wall socket. Our goal is to make networks simple by providing truly "Plug-N-Play" solutions.

Natural Data

The fourth requirement of CSC is to communicate in the user's language. The networked computer world must operate using graphics, audio and video as well as keyboards. Data such as audio and video are difficult to incorporate into computing because they require enormous bit storage and network capacity. Our strategy is to use the power of silicon technology and software to squeeze down these images to a much smaller number of bits.

In 1989 we introduced a development system using Intel's DVI multimedia technology that required seven boards to implement the system. Today, our ActionMedia II board product, capable of displaying, recording and playing back full-motion video and audio, needs only a single slot in a PC, and performs 100 million operations per second, double the earlier version. We are now working on a third generation video processor: a single chip that can be added to a PC's motherboard with performance at over one billion operations per second.

In addition, we are working with Microsoft and IBM to define a common, standardized software interface for DVI products that is compatible with both the Windows and OS/2 operating systems. At last Fall's COMDEX, the ActionMedia II board received the "Best of Show Award." This product was developed by Intel and IBM, working as partners.

All of these pieces — powerful processors, mobile processors, connectivity and the use of natural data — are coming together to make it possible to use computers in new ways.

CSC — Supplying the Right Stuff for Groupware

The revolution of groupware and CSC has arrived. Intel's vision for CSC will supply the right stuff for groupware. In this decade, PC's will function transparently, allowing users to work together quickly, seamlessly, and naturally. The result: all of us will be delighted with the speed and ease of doing business. Just-In-Time Business requires computer-supported collaboration to exchange messages, share information and participate in real-time conferencing. To provide these services, PC's will need to continue to have increased processing power, be more portable, be better connected to other computers, and support a wider range of data types.

Intel is leading the way to Just-In-Time Business by enabling PC's with the capabilities of Computer-Supported Collaboration. These new capabilities are already finding their way into commercial products. Businesses who want to remain competitive will need to prepare themselves to take advantage of these new powerful capabilities and technologies.

[Contact: Marc Chardon, Digital Equipment Corporation, 110 Spit Brook Road, ZKO1-3/B10, Nashua, NH 03062, tel. (603) 881-1190]

GROUPWARE IN THE GLOBAL ENTERPRISE

David Stone
Vice President
Software Products Group
Digital Equipment Corporation

ABSTRACT

Groupware offers a compelling vision of more productive teams in a rapidly changing information-intensive world. Technology alone cannot produce collaboration, and working in community runs counter to our business tradition. Some advances in groupworking are technological; examples are given. Most critical will be a new spirit of cooperation among software designers, businesspersons, and social scientists in defining and supporting group work as well as groupware programs.

1 PRELIMINARIES

Based on our shared attendance at a GROUPWARE conference, my starting assumption is that we have some similar beliefs about the needs for group work and the technologies to support it.

Such beliefs probably arise from assumptions that the world is changing in fundamental ways. Growth is slowing, competition is increasing, business is becoming more global, organizations are flattening. We see computer-supported group work as a critical component in meeting the challenges of being flexible, effective, and efficient in the face of such changes.

This seems so compelling that many of us probably share similar future visions-- such as Apple's "Information Navigator" or something you might have seen recently on a PC screen at DECworld or HP's "1995" or something from "Star Trek."

It seems that we have the future well under control. It's the present that needs our attention!

2 THE THESIS AND SOME HISTORY

As an industry, I think we're only barely beginning to understand groupware and what effects it could have on the way we work. "Group" is a positive word these days. It connotes sharing, selflessness, openness. Who could object to that? And "ware" evokes wares--technology supporting the group. What could be more natural?

If it is so unobjectionable and natural, why doesn't it work?

I contend that the real barrier to effective groupware is as much the lack of *effective groups* as the lack of effective wares! Effective group work *can* use effective groupware support but *must* involve group change: process changes, normative changes, organizational changes. Only through a balanced approach to group process and technology can we be successful.

First, let's look at a little of the history that has put us where we are today:

We were eased into groupware in the late sixties through electronic mail, almost an afterthought in the development of ARPANET. ARPANET was really developed to move data around, but mail became one of its most attractive features. It moved ideas around and coordinated activities, despite the administrators who complained that this was not a good use of computer time.

By the late 1980s, groupware had come to mean technology designed to support small, dynamic, collaborative groups. This created a tension with the traditional organization and catalyzed organizational evolution. Peter Drucker, in an influential 1988 *Harvard Business Review* article, declared that "traditional departments will serve as guardians of standards, as centers for training, and the assignment of specialists; they won't be where the work gets done. That will happen largely in task-focused teams."

The future seemed secure. Technology and business theory would come together to suggest a kind of new frontier for computing, or let's call it a green pasture, where the wolf shall dwell with the lamb, and the leopard lie down with the kid.

Why haven't we made progress on this vision?

First, we simply haven't made it attractive enough for the individual user, let alone the group. We must examine the varieties of group work and of individual work--there can't be just one kind of each--and produce benefit for the user so we have a chance to benefit the group. When we talk about groupware we presumably don't have in mind a kind of intellectual hot tub; we still believe that at times individual human beings will have to sit by themselves to see, hear, feel, imagine, write, operate a train, or operate on a brain. Our current offerings don't respect the natural oscillation, the back and forth, between individual and group work.

To compound user dissatisfaction, people no longer know how to use what we have made--I don't mean what keys or buttons to press but how to change the way work is done, to capitalize on the technology so that what we call groupware is working with people, not apart from them or against them.

Second, we haven't made it attractive enough for the manager. Our business tradition pushes us in the opposite direction. The history of work in the latter part of the nineteenth century is the history of the migration of knowledge from labor to management. The rational approach to management practiced by people like Frederick Taylor focused on understanding the process of a piece of work so that it could be expropriated to management, which could then reorganize it to suit management's needs. Knowledge was hoarded by the privileged, by those in authority.

Now we come along and suggest that multiple, overlapping, task-oriented teams are where the most effective, efficient, and flexible work will be done in future. A person can both be attending to a machine-tool installation problem on a factory floor in Frankfurt and serving as a member of a quality circle back at home. Many analysts are suggesting that these teams should be to some degree--perhaps to a large degree--self-forming and self-managing. In a phrase, management's role and perquisites are threatened.

So, not only has groupware confused users, it has threatened their managers! It certainly should be clear that technology alone cannot produce collaboration, that we cannot bring a functional group into being simply by delivering a software package.

3 THINKING THE ISSUE OUT

How can we move out of this impasse? We need to start by reevaluating the mindset we must have if we are to provide groupware in a context that will encourage people to adopt it and use it productively.

First of all, I'd like us technologists to feel a suitable sense of humility. We'll probably never understand perfectly how our technology works. In fact, technologists often find out later than the users what disasters they have wrought.

An example: the early history of the application of iron to bridge construction. The expansion of railroads in the 1800s made it inevitable that iron would be used as a replacement for wooden trestles. Iron was strong, impervious, new. It was also quite unpredictable, and iron bridges during that period collapsed in extraordinary numbers, generally while trains were passing over them. The consternation of the designers, not to mention the passengers, is now rather amusing, though at the time of course it was not. Queen Victoria established a commission to try to determine causes and create standards, and in America, when a bridge in Pennsylvania broke under a train, the New York and Erie Railroad reversed itself and ordered that wooden bridges replace the new metal ones.

Well, we engineers finally understood metal fatigue and got the thing straightened out.

Second, let's admit that the most important effects of new technologies are often not the first-order ones--the effects the technology was designed to produce--but second, third, and even later orders of change. The typewriter was initially intended for authors and clergymen: think, among other things, about the effect it had for many years on the position of women in business. As another example of a second-order effect of dubious value, I have just read that software graphics packages on PCs have induced senior marketing staff in one Fortune 50 consumer-products company to spend more than a day a week, every week, preparing charts and graphs for presentations.

Finally, we need to realize that groupware is not about technology; it is about information and information processes--many kinds of information, highly structured and semistructured, facts but also people's judgments and feelings, symbols but also images and sounds, information within the building but also from and to anywhere on the globe. By this definition, Digital has been using groupware for years; people know us for our ubiquitous networking and the global communications and information access that it can provide.

Digital knows a lot about information; shareable intellectual property is the heart of our business. We have learned that information has some surprising characteristics. Information processes are not passive. They consume information but also produce information. They do things, but they also report what they have done. They take instructions but can also send back new ones. They grow, and when we try to manage that growth, they can grow still more.

Sometimes new information streams and processes become larger, more important, and more valuable than their sources. Not so long ago, the president of American Airlines declared that if he had to divest the airline or its SABRE reservation system, he would keep SABRE. When *TV Guide* was sold in 1987, the price was more than the then market value of ABC, CBS, or NBC.

4 WHAT WE CAN DO--USER STRATEGIES

Users and groupware providers are in the position of trying to figure out which comes first, the groupware-supply chicken or the groupware-demand egg? The only way out of this quandary is mutual action and cooperation--in short, group work.

Here are some strategies users can apply in this partnership:

Use quick-and-dirty automation of the current process. I used to suggest to customers that they redesign their business process before automating it. That still seems to be the right theoretical solution, but in practice it doesn't work. The majority of users seem to need to start automating the current process before they come to realize what requires changing in the process. So, automate using quick-and-dirty techniques, and *then* redesign the process.

Support knowledge authority, not positional authority. If group work and groupware are about better use of knowledge, then user organizations need to reward the development, sharing, and widespread use of knowledge, not the employment of knowledge to promote positional authority or individual interests.

Develop metrics that support team goals. An environment that reflects group values, rewarding team goals and driving individual recognition and benefit as a function of contribution to team achievement, will foster group work. Traditional peer-to-peer competition will stifle it.

Hook users on the individual benefits of groupware first. The PC revolution has shown us that users will accept technology only if they can relatively easily and quickly get benefit from it. So, successful groupware has to hook the user by providing prompt personal benefit, in order to gain the opportunity to deliver group benefits. Individual benefits could include interoperability, data access, easy mail addressing, etc.

Part of the answer, then, has to do with developing strategies such as these for responding to people's perceptions and needs as they move into teams, still seeking to distinguish themselves as individual contributors but increasingly willing to define their personal work in light of a common goal.

5 USER WANTS AND NEEDS FROM GROUPWARE TECHNOLOGIES

As the user community is moving towards productive group work, we on the technical side must support the partnership by responding to users' wants and needs on their terms, not technology's.

Here are some of the things that we and the industry are working on, in language that users might choose to describe what they want.

Among the things I want is a common computational workspace--not a computer desktop of the ordinary kind: that's too neat. I want a place where multiple, overlapping teams can share information, put drawings, clip pieces of charts and graphs, write on them with a stylus, attach voice notes and video snippets, build thought diagrams from flow-chart-type elements, display maps or ongoing sensor outputs--a kind of common dining-room tabletop for each task. And let this workspace be large; the usual monitor makes me feel as if my head is bumping against the ceiling. So it would be life-size computing.

People say electronic mail is a mature tool for groupworking, but they're wrong. Specific mail interfaces/functions are still pretty simple and traditional. The most important development--other than all popular mail systems' speaking together-- would be for incoming mail to coalesce automatically into task-oriented or person-oriented constellations (this would be an application for filters and agents) so that topic or team threads could be noticed, shared, and maintained to resolution. I call this facility "Nail" or "Motes" (cf. VAX Notes ^{TM}, the grandsire of Lotus' Notes^{TM}). Among other things, the interface should allow direct placement of yellow stickups on any team member's screen.

I want to be able to use the network to identify potential team members by screening for education, experience, special skills, recent business assignments, even notable failures (voluntarily registered). Mind you, the local area network won't do for this purpose. The reach has to be global, because I'm searching for "knowledgeable strangers."

I want to do true coauthoring and coediting of documents in the widest sense--not just memos or reports, I mean, but compilations of fact and judgment that are complete statements. The document-generation process would begin with the recognition of the "irritant" or "seed"--like the grain of sand in the oyster. It would include the generation of the team, and continue with the creation of a dossier of relevant existing information and a selection of methods of work (possibly changing in mid course). Examples: visioning, building off a paragraph from the dossier, creating an initial outline, sharing new writing tasks, reoutlining, editing through baton-passing, commenting in sidebars, making interlinear changes, etc., until a "final" version is produced.

Meetings are frequently an organizational wasteland, infamous for producing consensus by exhaustion, by misunderstanding, or by boredom. Most people who attend several hundred meetings a year in reality spend most of their time attending 5-7 meetings that adjourn and resume. I want to start each session more nearly at the point at which the previous one ended. We have the technology to provide a multimedia briefing package, automatically, prior to each physical (or electronic) meeting, displaying the most pertinent documents and other objects relating to the planned agenda. Agenda preparation could be shared, using "meeting templates"--frameworks for the meeting process. The "technographer" (a technologically qualified stenographer) could create a compressed video record of the meeting, revealing gaps and contradictions, and creating a sound starting point for further progress.

We must create highly visual interfaces, using design effects of the kind provided by video paintboxes, creating "visible" ways of seeing large aggregates of information. We would be able to observe information as a geography. That is what it is in a conventional library, after all, floors on which there are stacks in which there are shelves, but in my virtual library computation would allow us to cruise instantaneously--to rise above the library ("see more") or dive down into it ("see less but at much finer granularity"). We call this the "information glider," and it should have as many seats as there are members of the team with whom I am working at any point, and as many steering controls.

Much of the technology to do these things exists in labs or in diverse products. What is missing is the user-orientation and the ability to function in the context of a comprehensive framework.

6 CONCLUSION

In fact, there is an increasing need for the acceleration of action that workgroup computing can provide.

Groupware should offer a way of responding to these conditions, not just as a set of software products but as as set of new ways in which we can relate to one another in work. It should support processes by which a conventional organization can move in the direction of more sustained, more productive, more rewarding collaboration--including a process by which this new direction is defined.

Users and potential users of groupware technology need to start by taking some simple, concrete steps that will begin and foster changes in people, processes, and group dynamics: automate a process; reward information-sharing; measure team achievement; use analytical skills from researchers; hook the user on the personal benefit first.

Developers of groupware technology have to apply themselves, in partnership with users, to bring a broad range of effective new groupware into existence--technologies, of course, but technologies that are uncompromisingly related to observation of user behavior and choices, and include as-yet uncommon levels of education, mentoring, and feedback. In short, developers must be as focused about listening to and supporting each customer as they are when writing code.

The bottom line is that this partnership of users and developers must start now. Together, we can shape a future in which the group work of self-forming teams will help us act, react, and experiment more flexibly, effectively, and efficiently. . .and even have a little fun while we're doing it.

///HW

GROUPWARE MEETINGS THAT WORK

May 14, 1992

SUBMITTED BY: Carl Di Pietro, Vice President,
                 Human Resources
                 Marriott Corporation
                 International Headquarters
                 Washington D.C. 20058
                 Phone: (301) 380 7182
                 FAX : (301) 380 1043

ABSTRACT

This paper describes an organizational innovation, developed in a "skunkworks" environment, which favorably impacted the effectiveness of meetings and the quality of ideas/solutions at a large service corporation. A traditional meeting room called the Marriott Group Decision Center was equipped with linked computers which allowed meeting participants to enter their ideas/problem solutions anonymously into a personal computer. Then, individually, prioritize ideas and solutions developed by the group. The computer provided the vehicle needed for data collection, organization and analysis with the speed and efficiency not likely to be duplicated in a traditional meeting format. Research data were collected to evaluate the effectiveness of the "electronic meeting room". It was concluded that when compared to traditional meetings, a far larger number of high quality ideas/solutions could be collected and arranged in workable formats for analysis. Groups demonstrated a higher degree of team spirit and commitment to group consensus results. The productivity gains and other benefits of this type meeting room suggest significant efficiency improvements for large or small organizations that may chose to use the groupware approach to meetings and the decision process.

I. INTRODUCTION

As a business partner, human resource management at Marriott is responsible for assisting the corporation in meeting its goals and profit objectives.   The project described in this report was pursued because it represented a "rare" opportunity

   * to meet and surpass Corporate business goals and profit objectives

   * to recognize the profound impact employees have on the attainment of these goals and objectives

* to "shake up" the traditional boss/subordinate relationship and move it, through results, not rhetoric, to a partnership of progress

* to test and document the value of such TQM concepts as total involvement, empowerment, paradigms, continuous improvement, creativity and participative management

* improve the speed, quality and timeliness of business decisions

II. NECESSARY CONDITIONS

This project was based on the beliefs that:

1. "Teams flourish when
   - objectives are clear
   - opinions are valued
   - and communications are honest and timely"

2. Those closest to a problem, regardless or rank, sex, color, etc., are likely to be closest to the solution; particularly if they are expected to implement the solution.

3. Organizations, especially larger ones, have fallen short in tapping the creative, problem solving, power of its human resource. There are many reasons for this phenomenon but here are a few that are neutralized by the MGDC:

   a. Truth - the best business decisions are based on collecting accurate information and respecting diverse perspectives and the range of human emotion. Consensus without truth is a paradox. Offering candid opinions may place one at risk or may be seen as rude. Therefore, in traditional meetings, for these and other reasons, the best decisions are not always made. Participants, consciously or unconsciously, spend time and energy "feeling out" the boss and others. Groups often "agree" with solutions that are diluted or not supported by all participants (Abilene Paradox, etc.). Even the simplest of interpersonal communications; "How do you like my hat?", "Which movie would you like to see tonight?" makes an understanding of the truth tedious or impossible. Business meeting scenarios, considering the risks and rewards, greatly magnify this kind of dynamic. The MGDC moves groups more closely to the "truth" than traditional communication techniques.

   b. Shared Values - many times groups actively or passively focus on the differences among participants rather than similarities. This is even more evident when there is diversity within a group, which is almost always the case. Differences in rank, status, sex, color, etc., may have participant(s) question motives of others in the group. After ideas are prioritized in the MGDC, groups quickly realize that their shared values are far greater than their differences.

c. <u>Frustration</u> - according to studies completed by 3M corporation and others, 30% - 70% of work time is spent in meetings. Often, meetings are inadequately planned, stray from objectives, take longer than necessary, leave participants unfulfilled, provide inadequate/untimely documentation and feedback and otherwise fall short of participant/meeting leader expectations. The MGDC routinely lessons or eliminates these frustrations.

III. <u>PROJECT DESCRIPTION</u>

The MGDC is a traditional meeting room in every respect except that it is equipped with linked computer workstations. When appropriate, the meeting leader will have participants anonymously enter into the computer their responses/ideas/solutions to a question or problem. Use of computers provides:

- more truthful responses
- a simultaneous "dump" of ideas from participants
- immediate feedback to participants
- participant creativity through synergism
- participants with immediate written documentation of individual and group responses.

After collection, participants then "prioritize" the ideas in order of importance, profitability or any other appropriate standard(s) selected by the leader/group. The software currently used in the MGDC is VisionQuest by Collaborative Technology Corporation. The MGDC Project Team has developed a unique "process" that adapts the vendor's software to accomplish what other users of this or similar software rarely accomplished - unusual user friendliness and leaderless meetings.

In a "skunkworks" environment, for under $10,000, and in just 6 weeks the MGDC Project team:

* evaluated software alternatives (IBM Team Focus, Ventana, VisionQuest)

* installed the experimental MGDC

* developed a customized meeting process

* developed statistical measurements to evaluate the effectiveness of the concept; including engagement of academicians (see acknowledgements)

* marketed a concept/process which "clashed" with   traditional meeting values/culture but nevertheless flourished.

After opening the MGDC, October 1, 1991, and after 3 months of operation, the following results were reported:

* Over 1000 employees of Marriott and other companies (Federal Express, MCI, Westinghouse, GE, Bell Atlantic, C&P Telephone, Department of Navy, et. al.) used the MGDC with startling results

* Over 100 business meetings were held in the MGDC with the Center being occupied over 90% of the time for business meetings

* Users generated over 10,000 ideas/solutions with over 90% of ideas judged to be valuable and useful

* Users estimate that it would take 9-12 times longer to accomplish the same results in a traditional meeting. (e.g., a one hour meeting in the MGDC would take 9 or more hours in a traditional meeting format or require several additional meetings with its incumbent expense, confusion and scheduling difficulties)

* Annualized savings of over $1,000,000 and 35,000 manhours with only 10 computer terminals in operation

Fortune Magazine (March 23, 1992), the Wall Street Journal (January 28, 1992), and other publications learned about the Center, and published anecdotal comments about it in their publications.

IV. MGDC USES

Any issue that can be formatted as a question is likely to be an issue appropriate for the MGDC. How to increase profits, sales, ROA, etc.? How to reduce expenses, defects, turnover,etc.? What is our mission, goals, strategies etc.? These are just a few examples. Here are some actual issues that have been processed in the MGDC to date:

Total Quality Management; conflict resolution; development of vision, mission and strategy statements; document review; information systems design; financial reviews and resource allocations; team building; managing diversity; FOCUS group evaluations -

employee/marketing/client etc.; role clarification; ADA job descriptions; comparative analysis; training needs analysis; self-directed work groups; leaderless meetings; process engineering; and organizational design.

V. <u>MGDC vs. TRADITIONAL MEETINGS</u>

The MGDC concept works well when compared to traditional meetings because:

* <u>All</u> meeting participants provide input/ideas/solutions to issues. Traditional meetings are often dominated by a few (e.g. 20% of participants may do 80% of the input/talk - Pareto's Principle).

* Ideas are valued and not personalities. Ideas are viewed without regard to rank, race, color, creed, sex, etc. There is little if any chance that bias/prejudice will influence the decision process. The MGDC is also seen as a way of enlightening/training employees on the value diversity adds to the decision process. Groups are finding that they have far more in common than perceived differences (shared values). Also, participants are "routinely" surprised when they learn some of the best ideas came from participants not traditionally seen as "productive". Regularly, groups find it difficult, if not impossible, to "guess" who submitted which idea. In the MGDC, ideas instinctively become the property of the group as individuals quietly "release" ownership of the ideas they submitted and support the consensus.

* Anonymity provides participants with an environment that encourages directness and candor. For this reason groups develop higher quality decisions which they are more likely to support during the meeting and through the implementation phase. Politics/hidden agendas are not a factor.

* Participants are afforded time and space to "think" of ideas/solutions without pressure and criticism from others. Also, they are able to intensely examine an issue in a quiet, stressless environment. They have time, at their own pace, to examine an issue from different perspectives...wearing "different hats" to provide rich input. In addition, they are able to react and respond to the ideas of others without threat of reprisal or embarrassment to themselves or others.

* The "games people play" dealing with each other are virtually eliminated. The complex "interpersonal" skills needed to rebut, critique or otherwise to communicate with other are not required. Groups quickly move from fact finding to consensus with disarming ease. Participants report a strong sense of personal satisfaction, productivity, and self worth in MGDC meetings. Meetings have focus, produce

substantive results, and provide hard copy documentation of the participant/group efforts.

* The anonymous, quick and simple prioritization methods allow for group consensus that is quantifiable. Participants are at ease supporting the ideas/solutions of the group and "letting go" of their personal views which they might have defended exhaustively in the traditional meeting.

* Simultaneous input of ideas by participants results in an average of over 100 ideas/solutions being presented every 20 minutes. In traditional meetings only one idea at a time can be processed by the group. Furthermore, there is often more than one conversation ongoing at a time, interruptions occur, and discussions wander from the meeting objectives of the meeting.

* Without exception, decisions made by the group are documented. Each participant is provided with a hard copy of meeting results <u>before</u> leaving the meeting. Since the meeting results are on the hard drive/disk, the group can resume a future meeting exactly where the group adjourned.

* The group may be divided into smaller groups within the same meeting room. Therefore, multiple meetings may occur in the same room, at the same time, greatly increasing productivity and still in a quiet, stressless environment.

VI. <u>CREATIVE APPLICATIONS</u>

Marriott created unique processes and variations to the vendor's software formats. These variations were critical to the success of the MGDC. Examples of creative applications include:

1. Center may be operated, and meetings held, with little or no training of participants or meeting leader (15 minutes).

2. Meetings may be unchauffeured if desired. A facilitator is optional. Meeting procedures, learning aids, user friendly additions/instructions have made this possible. Currently, about fifty percent of meetings are unchauffeured.

3. Development of standard agenda templates that do not require pre-work or pre-planning. Meetings may be held impromptu. Ease of operation and "user friendliness" allows for spontaneous meetings with little or no advance preparation required of the meeting leader, participants or the Center.

VII.FUTURE CHALLENGES

Some challenges faced by the collaborative concept include:

1. Culture/Skill Shock - communicating using computers and keyboards represents a "culture change" that some find difficult to overcome. It is a perceived problem that some see since it may be seen as an "unnatural" way of communicating (to include inexperience using a standard keyboard). In contrast, to date, over 90% of users have found the computer/keyboard "easy" to use. Over 50% of users were skeptical of the value of the concept before using the MGDC but left feeling much differently. By design, senior managers (above Vice President level) have not been recruited to use the MGDC. This management level is voluntarily coming to the Center in increasing numbers as the "word" of success spreads (to date about 20% of users are VP level and above). Participants lacking keyboard typing skills have teamed with another participant who submits their ideas into the computer or have brought a typist to the meeting. Participants have consistently left the MGDC feeling that objectives have been met, the process was much easier than expected, and anticipated a return visit to the MGDC.

2. Fear - for some, particularly those who have not used the Center, the MGDC represents a fear that power and control will be lost. Concerns range from the group moving the decision process in a direction unacceptable to the leader, that sensitive/controversial issues may be raised, or that agendas and results may be manipulated.

In fact, most all leaders have found their power and control greatly enhanced. Fear of the unknown and of the MGDC is decreasing as reports of success spread.

VIII. MGDC FUTURE

The MGDC represents a profound breakthrough in human resource and business management. A positive impact will be realized in communications process, decision making, consensus management, and team building, to mention a few. When compared with the productivity of traditional communications/meetings, the economic savings to be realized are unarguable and are further enhanced with the installation of "anytime-anyplace" meetings. That is, meetings may be held without participants assembling in the "sameplace". Participants are able to join a meeting using their personal computer, 24 hours a day, from anywhere in the world. The benefits of total staff involvement in the decision process, continuous improvement (TQM processes), and the value of "anytime-anyplace" meetings is staggering.

ACKNOWLEDGEMENT

This project was made possible through the creative and prolific efforts of Marriott associates: Christine Bubser, who focused on the technical aspects of software/hardware coordination; David Kennedy who developed methods and process innovations; and Barbara O'Neil who reviewed documents and coordinated MGDC meetings, events and promotions. Also, technical support from Marriott associates Mark Cross, Mike Wakefield, Brad Crooks, Tony Neal and Lisa Olshan is acknowledged and appreciated. Researchers Maryam Alavi, University of Maryland, and Irene Liou, University of Baltimore, assisted in the design and collection of empirical and anecdotal data used to evaluate the effectiveness of the MGDC. Their objectivity and challenging views were critical to the success of the project. (Reference Table 1)

Table1: Descriptive Statistics from the Post-Meeting Questionnaires

Questionnaire Items	Mean	Std Dev	Percent agreed
Task Effectiveness			
Compared to a "traditional" meeting it took LESS TIME to GENERATE ideas today.	4.76	0.27	96.4
Compared to a "traditional" meeting, MORE IDEAS were generated today.	4.69	0.27	95.8
Compared to a "traditional" meeting, it took LESS TIME to PRIORITIZE ideas today.	4.65	0.38	95
Compared to a "traditional" meeting, the QUALITY of the ideas was better today.	4.06	0.41	75.4
User Satisfaction			
Using the computer was easy.	4.55	0.38	89.2
Compared to a "traditional" meeting, I was MORE COMFORTABLE in offering my ideas today.	4.35	0.38	82.6
Compared to a "traditional" meeting, today's meeting was LESS STRESSFUL.	4.34	0.38	80.8
Group Cohesiveness			
The group members worked well together.	4.24	0.34	77.8
In today's meeting, I felt I was a part of the group.	4.20	0.40	78.2
Use Again			
I would like to use the MGDC again.	4.87	0.12	98.2

Groupware Market Roundtable

Moderator: Ronni Marshak
Vice President
The Patricia Seybold Group
Editor-In-Chief,
The Office Computing Report: Guide to Workgroup Computing
148 State Street, Suite 700
Boston, Massachusetts 02109
617-742-5200

Panel Members: Marcello Hofmann, SRI
Paul Saffo, Institute for the Future
Bill Higgs, Infocorp

Focus of the Roundtable

The groupware market is just now being defined, and there are a lot of questions. To raise just a few:

- Where will the groupware market be in 1995? In the year 2000?

- Can groupware be sold through traditional distribution channels?

- How can we educate the market on groupware?

- Does groupware truly raise productivity? Are the promises being met?

- Who, exactly, will buy the groupware applications? And who will support it?

Groupware is not like personal productivity software—the applications that sell the best through retail channels. Groupware is more than just networked versions of the old-time favorites. It is an entirely new generation of applications that specifically addresses the needs of people working together on projects... people sharing information... people depending on each other, and on the software to facilitate the collaborative process. This new generation of application brings into question organizational and cultural issues that simply aren't relevant for the lone user. When you buy a groupware application, you aren't buying something just for yourself; you have to get buy-in from your colleagues. And, in order to get buy-in, you have to guarantee results.

This roundtable discussion with leading market analysts should prove to be a forum for lively debate on these and other groupware marketing issues. Rather than have each panelist give a 10-minute presentation, we plan a more interactive format, a la *Wall Street Week*, where everyone, audience included, gets his or her two-cents worth!

1. Definition of Groupware

At this conference, you will probably hear dozens of definitions of the term *groupware*. Here is yet another, but is one that I feel clearly differentiates groupware from other types of software aimed at workgroup use.

- Groupware is designed to be used by a group of people. It isn't just a networked version of a personal productivity tool.

- Groupware applications have less value standalone system or when used by only one person. I maintain that, although useful for the individual, the real value comes when the tool is used by a number of people working on a common problem or to achieve a common goal. Consider electronic mail--perhaps the most popular groupware application. When a group of people use via email, it increases communication and productivity. When one person emails to himself, it becomes narcissistic.

- Groupware enhances the productivity of the group without sacrificing the productivity of the individual group members. For example, if a user has to double enter all his lead information into both a personal information manager and a group database, the sacrifice is too great. Okay...I admit that the group system could be considered groupware, but it is bad groupware!

- Groupware is available to all appropriate members of the group. Consider, for example, an electronic mail environment where only the PC users can receive mail and the Macintosh users are out of the loop. Well designed groupware must take into account heterogeneous environments and offer some solution for allowing all group members to play, even if their involvement is at different levels--for example, a Mac user may not be able to create workflow application, but could be part of the workflow process via email connections.

- All applications used by a workgroup are not necessarily groupware; all groupware is, by necessity, used by a workgroup. This statement requires a definition of *workgroup*: a workgroup is a group of people working together on a common goal. A workgroup can be formal or ad hoc, permanent or temporary, in a single location or in multiple locations, intra-organizations or inter-organizations.

2. Implementing Groupware in the Organization

There seems to be some reluctance on the part of users to buy into groupware. I believe that the problem stems from the cultural issues of adopting group solutions in the organization. Group applications require a lot of preplanning before implementing, extensive training, and a willingness on the part of the individual group members to stick with it through the pilot period and on through the often steep learning curve. The most successful groupware applications, such as Lotus Notes and various electronic mail products offer immediate satisfaction to the user. Sending a message and getting a response may represent only a fraction of the functionality of the group mail system, but a user can feel good about using the product in a few short moments. Then he or she will be more willing to play with the product to seek out the added "group" functionality. Let me give another example, in our company, we have been building a "knowledgebase" which provides all users with access to our corporate database of customers. The knowledgebase has been sitting on my PC for several months, and I was encouraged to "play with it." Sorry, I'm a busy woman, I don't have time to play. But one day, after hours, I needed the telephone number of one of our consulting clients. Our consulting director had gone home. So I looked it up in the knowledgebase. And a few moments later, I had the number I needed! I have been using the knowledgebase for this type of lookup ever since, and have started to explore the other functionality built into the system.

Providing immediate value for the user will help get groupware used. Proving productivity gains for the group will get it sold. And that's hard to prove. Groupware is in its infancy and needs more of a track record before it becomes mainstream. In addition, groupware implies new models of software licensing and training. These issues also need to be addressed. However, I predict that, before the year 2000, the mystique of "groupware" will go away, and group applications will become *de rigeur*. The groupware market will cease to be a separate entity.

Groupware and Cultural Issues:
A New Challenge for Information Technology Development and Marketing

by Marcelo Hoffmann
SRI International

If individual preferences, expectations, and anxieties give computer system vendors cause for frustration, the world of groupware marketing is likely to be a major source of nightmares. Never before have vendors had to deal with the social and cultural complexities that are part and parcel of trying electronically to coordinate, facilitate, support, and mediate group interactions and behaviors.

Important questions abound. Under what circumstances are group coordination and collaboration appropriate? When is it effective to apply information technology to group tasks and when is information technology best left on the sidelines? How much capability needs to be built into a system and how much should be left to the end users to implement based on their specialized needs? Can products effectively cross organizational and geographic boundaries?

Even some of the simplest implementations of groupware can be sabotaged by "antigroup" behavior, for example, a group meeting scheduler that executives refuse to update because doing updates is "the secretary's job." Workers have also been known to deliberately fill up their electronic calendars to avoid meetings they do not want to attend (but may be expected to).

A classic example of a groupware product that failed is *The Coordinator* from Action Technologies. It stumbled for a number of reasons, but one of the most important was that it did not take into account the value of ambiguity in human interaction, and so it imposed excessive structure into messages.

Perhaps most intriguing are the prospects for developing and selling cross-cultural implementations of groupware. For instance, will collaboration technology that helps United States companies be effective also for Japanese companies? The contexts are, in many respects, strikingly different:

- Penetration of desktop computers in Japan is limited, and Japanese professionals tend to share computers or computer terminals; professionals in the United States, and to a limited extent executives, tend to have individual personal computers or workstations available to them and are relatively proficient at keyboarding skills.

- The architecture common in Japanese offices includes large, open rooms with professionals in close proximity to each other and a supervisor at one end; in contrast United States professionals tend to have individual offices, or have partitions separating.workers: Colleagues can rarely see each other while at their desks.

- Japanese behavioral tendencies lean toward reverence for experience and a business hierarchy based on tradition; face saving is crucial in Japanese group relationships. Open discussions and even potential disagreements in group forums are perceived as a way to reduce conflicts in United States organizations.

- The Japanese favor patience for trust building in negotiations and intolerance for aggressive interpersonal tactics; in the United States the precedent is for action, task orientation, and near term results rather than development of long-term relationships.

- Japanese individuals often subordinate their personal goals to their group goals and favor group success and harmony; United States organizations tend to favor individualism, a pioneering spirit, and individual rather than group competition.

- Japanese organizations use large meetings to give out information and ratify agreements; organizations in the United States may use large forums to air out differences and make management decisions on the spot.

- Japanese executives often use metaphors and symbolism for messages that may need refinement: subordinates are expected to pick out the core content of the message from its overall context and further refine it; executives in the United States tend to make statements explicit, without offering room for compromise or face saving by subordinates or colleagues.

- The formal style of Japanese language in use in business communications varies depending upon the relative positions within a hierarchy, and "translating" from one style to another slows the use of electronic text and makes it more cumbersome; communications in business English, whether spoken or written, do not have the same range.

These cultural, organizational, and behavioral characteristics will influence the development and use of groupware tools. Electronic-mail packages, for example, tend to reflect a bias toward United States communication values. How will such software need to be adapted to deal with Japan's informal face-to-face nemawashi and formal paper-based ringi processes for narrowing down options and making consensus decisions? Electronic forums currently make it almost impossible to include the contextual clues that allow differences to be smoothed over and consensus reached without losing face.

Although the differences between corporate Japan and corporate United States are obvious, subtle cultural differences may also create problems for vendors. For example, will Italian organizations, often characterized by loose associations among cooperating companies, seek the same features as their more highly structured German counterparts? If not, how much customization will be necessary?

The cross-cultural aspects of groupware are just now surfacing: global companies are starting to use collaboration technology across borders, and vendors outside the United States are seeking to develop products which match various environments. Global success will require an understanding of the cognitive, social and organizational elements that support collaboration in various markets. This requirement presents a significant challenge but also an opportunity for cross-cultural collaboration in the development of culturally-attuned groupware.

Marcelo Hoffmann
Senior Industry Analyst
Collaborative Technology Environments Program
SRI International
333 Ravenswood
Menlo Park, CA 94025
hoffmann@sri.com
(415) 859-3680

Making The Most of Information

By David L. Connor
Vice President, Lotus Consulting Services Group
Lotus Development Corporation

The Corporate Information Services group (CIS) of a large semiconductor company was caught in a downward spiral. The group, responsible for planning, developing and implementing business systems throughout the highly decentralized corporation, wascharged with finding faster and cheaper solutions to information sharing. To comply with the corporation's commitment to decision-making by consensus, the group first scheduled meetings with members of the organization's numerous business units. But while this helped accomplished the decision-making goals,the group fell further and further behind on implementation -- because they spent so much time in meetings.

CIS turned to an outside consulting group to help them implement a group communications system on a wide area network. The consultants worked with CIS to define various workgroups and their information sharing needs. They then devised a plan to develop and implement the new distributed system.

Once the infrastructure was in place, the business units were able to manage projects in new ways. People now spend less time in meetings because they are able to share ideas and resolve many issues using computer-based discussion databases. As new specifications, procedures, and programming techniques are developed, they are documented in shared databases and all relevant personnel contribute to and use them. New applications, users' requests for new software, and support requests are now distributed and tracked electronically.

CIS has been able to minimize the number of people required to fulfill the company's aggressive and expanding systems backlog, while increasing responsiveness. Also, the system acts as a vehicle for knowledge transfer between all employees, which has significantly improved the rate at which new employees become productive.

Until very recently, the above scenario would not have been possible. In the last decade, the focus of computing was on finding new and better ways to get information to people -- faster. Information is power, the thinking went, and the more information the better.

Today, anyone who has access to a computer probably has access to as much information as he or she can handle. In fact, many people are finding that they have more than they can handle. A new school of thought is beginning to question whether having this his much information so easily accessible really is such a good thing after all.

The recent flood of information has contributed to increased misuse of data. People feel they should use more data because it's so available; but they don't always use it in ways that make sense. Gary Loveman, an economics professor at Harvard Business School, cites as an example people who overload even simple memos with unnecessary facts obtained through costly information searches.

A vocal champion of this line of thinking has been Rear Admiral Grace Hopper, USN, Ret., who has been cautioning for nearly 20 years that before going about gathering information, people must determine what kind of information is valuable for any given project or situation. She has claimed that people fail toconsider the criteria for determining the value of information. And she cautions that unless people learn to better manage information and its flow, they will have only chaos, or confusion. [from interview in BYTE magazine, May, 1991]

But having access to extensive information isn't necessarily bad. In fact, when people have the right tools to manage the information, and know how to use them, increased access to information can be a plus. Several technologies developed in the last couple of years enable people to better manage information and use it to their advantage. For example, electronic news and data feeds, properly filtered, can help support better real-time decision making. Similarly, the ability to bring diverse types of information together into a compound document, combining for example numerical data, text, and graphics, addsvalue by increasing people's ability to understand complexissues. In particular, the ability to include graphics allows people to communicate ideas more effectively, with fewer words. Innovations like group-enabled software make it easier for people to share information. And Graphical User Interfaces make it easier for people to do all this work.

Until the recent arrival of some desktop computing tools, available types of information processing were, at best, cumbersome. At worst, they were impossible. New software tools, like Lotus Notes, provide people with new ways of using and sharing information, adding value in the process. Notes is an integrated communications and database network application, designed to gather, organize and distribute information among work groups, regardless of individual members' physical locations.

Using a tool like Notes, a real estate investor or analyst could review all of the information needed to make an informed decision about whether to invest in a particular property. This new technology can store and report traditional structured data, like the property's financial information, address, and ownership. But unlike traditional tools, it allows people to view the structured data together with unstructured information, such as images of the property, plot plans, location maps, surrounding properties, etc. Flexible "views" also allow the user to look at the information in many different ways. For example, the investor could structure a data search including all properties in his portfolio, or target in on one specific property or a group of properties.

This kind of tool was extremely useful recently, helping one of the leading U.S. insurance companies stay on top of claims that resulted from the devastating fire that swept through Oakland, California in October.

Within a day of the fire, which caused roughly two billion dollars in property damage, the insurer began the process of contacting each of its 1,200 policyholders in the four-zip code area affected by the fire. Employees from all over the company called policyholders and presented them with a list of questions aimed at getting assistance to those who needed it as quickly as possible. Within a few days, the Claims department had 1,200 pieces of paper filled with information -- and no way to summarize it.

The Claims officers passed the information on to the company's Office Systems group. The group downloaded information on the 1,200 policies -- including policyholder names, home addresses, policy numbers, types of coverage and amount of coverage -- from its batch policy systems to a network server loaded with this new software tool, and created a database. They added the information provided by the Claims group, and created multiple views by which to examine the information. This enabled them to cross-reference external information, such as the local newspaper's report of homes destroyed in the fire, listed by street address.

The database grew daily. The company had set up a catastrophe center in a hotel near the disaster area. Office Systems moved three workstations and a server that contained the database to the hotel. As the 35 adjusters working out of the center gained new information on claims, they added it to the database, and it was replicated to the server in the home office every half hour.

The key advantage of the system, according to the vice president of the Office Systems group, was its ability to pull together data from several locations and put it into a single database where it could be used by people in many different areas of the company for a variety of reasons.

For example, the Claims department was able to keep a running tally of the number of claims that had been submitted and which ones had been assigned to adjusters, as well as running totals of those that had been paid out. The Finance department could keep track of the company's potential liability as the damage estimates became more accurate. Policyholders benefitted from the company's ability to respond so quickly to their needs following what was a very personal disaster to many of them.

In a different kind of application, another company is taking advantage of new client-server tools to facilitate communications among a group of 30 managers located in four states whose only real link is that they report to the same executive. Until recently, the group interacted only through weekly conference calls and a monthly meeting. They concluded that client-server technology might help improve communications, as a way to better integrate the group.

A consultant helped the group define opportunities for improved communication using WAN-based electronic mail services and a discussion database. Through the latter, all 30 managers can share information that was previously limited to the executive and individual managers. They created another database with which individuals can submit agenda items for the weekly phone meetings, which has added structure to the phone meetings and helps ensure that topics important to each individual are covered. It also gives participants the opportunity to prepare for the discussions.

Connectivity and Interoperability

As described above, new and emerging technologies based on client-server and networked systems can bring many new tools and capabilities to end users. However, these new systems can also add significantly more value to the enormous amount of information stored in mainframes and minicomputers by making it more easily accessible.

In most organizations today, there is a gap between traditional computing resources -- mainframes and minicomputers -- and the new technology -- increasingly powerful PCs and smaller, more affordable desktop workstations, with new easier to use software. However, there is a shortage of people who are skilled in the design and implementation of client-server solutions. And the technology is changing so rapidly that it is difficult for practitioners to keep up with new developments.

A significant opportunity for client-server computing to have a positive effect on organizations lies in its ability to integrate desktop computers with the entire information system in a true enterprise-wide computing system.

This kind of system, built using networking technology to link desktops with other computing resources, requires software tools, commonly called "middleware," that operate across multiple hardware platforms and operating systems.

From the personnel perspective, it requires knowledge of the information and tools available on each platform; an understanding of the organization's business and information needs; and the expertise to devise an appropriate technical solution. As importantly, successful enterprise-wide computing requires a significant organizational commitment. The benefit of this new approach is a truly more efficient and valuable information system.

The Development and Manufacturing Finance group of a multi-billion-dollar business machine manufacturer is a case in point. This group, which is responsible for the financialmanagement of the company's development and manufacturing arms worldwide, recently streamlined its budget planning process by installing a system that linked Sun workstations with corporate host systems and integrated spreadsheet data with informationstored in traditional structured database systems.

Until the middle of 1990, budget planning for the group's 100 analysts, located in 10 locations around the world, was a paper-intensive process that involved much informed guesswork. The new system, implemented with the help of outside consultants, provides the group's financial analysts with tools to prepare all budget forecasts on their workstations, using 1-2-3 for Sun and a standardized template created for this purpose.

When the forecasts are completed, the data are uploaded to an Oracle database residing on a VAX cluster. Each quarter, the original forecasts are downloaded to the workstations, along with monthly financial performance, which the analysts use to compare the actual costs to the forecasts and make adjustments as needed.

This new system has significantly increased the value of the base financial data, which the company had all along, by easily moving it from the VAX to the desktop workstations, where the right people can use it and perform analyses that were previously impossible. As a result, the group now creates budget forecasts that are more reliable than before -- in much less time.

In an example that spans organizations, a consortium of six Wall Street firms recently formed a joint venture to disseminate proprietary bond information through a common channel. Their goal was to improve the efficiency and productivity of interacting with clients by linking them directly with the trading desks, and to protect their client base of institutional investors by giving them the most sophisticated tools available for evaluating bond prices and making trading decisions.

The venture was initially viewed with skepticism. On the one hand, industry participants found it hard to believe that such fierce competitors could cooperate on trivial matters, let alone a strategic business project. On the other, it seemed a nearly impossible technological challenge.

To address the technological issues, the partnership enlisted the help of consultants, who built an open-architecture platform that gives the partners' institutional clients access to fixed-income market data services and analytics. The front-end is based on user-friendly applications using 1-2-3 for Sun running on SPARCstation workstations, which retrieve data from a variety of sources and perform calculations via custom add-ins. Other windowed applications perform queries on the data and compute complex analytics. Back-end services include several databases, such as Sybase, historical databases, and real-time market data feeds.

The distributed architecture allows clients to download the data -- which includes information on individual bonds that has been collected from the trading desks, along with bond calculations that have been coded with the partners' cooperation -- to their desktop computers. Once there, users can apply their own proprietary models. The system can also electronically transmit analytics, research reports, computer models, new securities offering and indices.

Groupware And The Emergence Of Business Technology
Terry Winograd, Stanford University

We live in an era in which the interconnectedness and velocity of business has increased dramatically. Within the span of a few decades, the combination of computer and telecommunications technology has led to the networked international marketplace. Here, competitiveness depends on quick response and differentiation of service, not just product cost and quality. With more choices available, customers can and do demand greater attention to their particular needs, circumstances and concerns.

Computer technology by itself is not a sufficient solution to meet the new global challenge that it has helped to produce. The computer industry faces increasing competition, unpredictable markets and more skeptical clientele. That skepticism is fed by too many promises and too many failed solutions. It is increasingly difficult to justify large-scale investments in computer technology unless they offer real assistance with effectiveness and competitive position. Slowing sales in many segments of the computing industry are ample evidence of this uncertainty and distrust.

Modern American business leaders recognize the importance of changing traditional business practices in order to improve competitiveness and customer service. They see improvements coming with the introduction of computers and telecommunications into networks that coordinate their interactions with customers, suppliers, and the various parts of businesses. But so far, they see these solutions in a patchwork and used in a piecemeal way. When equipment and software vendors sometimes claim that it is the technology itself that is bringing the benefits, the customers are more than suspicious: sales of equipment has stalled at the very moment in which the full dimension of global competition is revealing itself.

Organizations are beginning to recognize that more computers per se will not improve their capacity to compete and respond to their customers. They recognize the importance of "redesigning" the workflows in their organizations, rather than simply augmenting and automating them. The missing offering -- which might be called "business technology" in distinction to "information technology" -- does not yet have a presence in the marketplace. The closest approach has been the promotion of something called "groupware," but this name is not an adequate description. Saying that a system is used by a group is not saying much about it at all. It was true of most of the early mainframe applications, and is true of a population of unrelated people using a shared file server.

The key element in looking to new business technology is not something that can be defined by the kind of equipment, or the networking, or by the size of the workgroup, but rather by the point of view from which the software is designed. Groupware is structured around the way people get their work done. The focus is on designing for the structure of the group activity, rather than the structure of the underlying computer system. The goal in building a system is to design productive workflow, supported by the technology, rather than designing a technology in its own terms.

Once we turn our attention to the structure of group activity, we need to find an appropriate theoretical framework in which to characterize and analyze that activity. Research on workgroup computer systems has historically focused on the technology itself---on developing gadgets that facilitate or automate the activities we observe people engaged in. But there has also always been a concern with the question of just what people are doing when they work, and how else they might be doing it. The series of conferences on "Computer-Supported Cooperative Work" suggests this emphasis in its very title. The focus is not on computers but on a particular kind of work, in which computers play a role. The challenge is to make this into more than a slogan by developing a discipline in which we can ground our designs.

For the past ten years, in conjunction with colleagues at Stanford University, Action Technologies, and Business Design Associates, I have been engaged in developing computer software for organizational communication and action, based on a theory of work structure as language action. A number of publications (see reference list) describe the basic elements of the theory and its application to computer-supported cooperative work:

1) Language acts, classified according to a theory of communications known as "speech-act theory".

2) Conversations, (or "workflows") which are coherent sequences of language acts with a regular structure of expectations and completions.

3) Explicit time points associated with completions of conversations.

4) Explicit mutually-visible representations of acts, conversations, and times, represented in computer systems as a way of facilitating communication in an organization.

In this paradigm, organizations do not consist of a collection of physical objects, structures of authority, fiscal entities, or information flows. Instead, an organization is a network of interleaved "workflows." The atomic and molecular structures of organizations, in this new interpretation, are made up of observable events that occur when people take certain classes of linguistic actions which have the effects of defining and fulfilling conditions of satisfaction with the organization's internal and external customers. These events, in addition to being observable, make up the permanent structures that make individual organizations what they are, including three key structures:

1) The declarations, appointments and authorizations in which roles and features of organizations are defined and people are given the authority to take action on behalf of the organization,

2) The offers and acceptances in which agreements are made with customers and suppliers, and

3) The requests and promises in which projects are constituted and carried out.

Each workflow constitutes a basic unit of work. In each, a "performer" commits to produce "conditions of satisfaction" defined in the workflow by the performer and a "customer," on or by a specified time. Four essential distinctions operate in each workflow:

1) Requests and offers start all the crucial actions and frame what is to be produced in terms of "conditions of satisfaction" defined by a customer.

2) Agreements (or promises) tie together the actions of customer and supplier with commitments to future action.

3) Assertions allow the participants to speak to each other in terms of standards and evidence that can be witnessed. This allows recurrence and continuous improvement to be built into designs of business processes.

4) Assessments allow the participants to speak with each other about consequences, to speculate about the best paths for resolution, and to interpret what may be causing difficulties or affording new opportunities.

Computers show up in a different light from previous accounts of "information processing." They appear as tools for managing commitments and their fulfillments and as tools for producing and "listening to" the assertions and assessments that structure the organization. Computers can make explicit the basic structure of human interaction and fulfillment of an organization, providing new operational means for generating and monitoring workflows, being a more effective observer and intervener in what is going on, determining what is needed for whom, when, and what is to be done. The computer can be the principal vehicle for navigating in the business' structure, assessing its performance, and redesigning its processes. Computers provide value through the velocity and global reach they offer, while affording a new opportunity for an organization to review and re-think "how we have always done things."

This approach sees "groupware" not as a technological fix for immediate problems. In looking at the work first and the technology second, it brings a recognition of the fundamental logic of business processes, with possibilities for analyzing, working with people in organizations and providing tools for facilitation. These are critical to moving forward towards providing new kinds of added value in business technology, and will be the starting point for much more.

REFERENCES

Bullen, Chris, and John Bennett, Groupware in Practice: An Interpretation of Work Experiences, in C. Dunlop and R. Kling (eds.), Computerization and Controversy, Academic Press, 1991, pp. 257-287.

Dunham, Robert, Business Design Technology: Software Development For Customer Satisfaction, IEEE Press, Proceedings of the 24th Annual Hawaii International Conference on Systems Sciences, 1991, 792-798

Flores, Fernando, Michael Graves, Bradley Hartfield and Terry Winograd, Computer Systems And The Design Of Organizational Interaction, ACM Transactions on Office Information Systems 6:2 (April, 1988), pp. 153-172.

Flores, Fernando, Management and Communication in the Office of the Future, Dissertation, University of California, Berkeley, 1982.

Keen, Peter, Shaping the Future: Business Design through Information Technology, Boston: Harvard Business School Press, 1991.

Kensing, Finn, and Terry Winograd, The Language-Action Approach To Design Of Computer Support For Cooperative Work, Proceedings of the IFIP TC8 Conference on Collaborative Work, Social Communications and Information Systems, Helsinki, Finland, 27-29 August, 1991.

Medina-Mora, Raul, Terry Winograd, Rodrigo Flores, and Fernando Flores, Workflow Management Technology: Examples, Implementations And New Directions, to appear in the proceedings of the Conference on Computer Supported Cooperative Work, Toronto, 1992.

Winograd, Terry, A Language/Action Perspective On The Design Of Cooperative Work, Human-Computer Interaction 3:1 (1987-88), 330.

Winograd, Terry and Fernando Flores, Understanding Computers and Cognition: A New Foundation for Design, (220 pp.) Norwood, NJ: Ablex, 1986. Paperback issued by Addison-Wesley, 1987.

Winograd, Terry, Where the Action is, Byte, December, 1988, pp. 256-260.

Graphics and Groupware: Increasing Intimacy through Broadening Bandwidth

Dr. Joel N. Orr
Autodesk Fellow

The degree of coupling among people—as well as between people and systems—is a function of the bandwidth of the communication paths: How much data can be exchanged in a unit of time? Pictorial communications are approximately 50,000 times as dense as verbal exchanges, so—for that reason alone—must figure centrally in groupware support.

But there are additional reasons for using pictures. Metacommunication issues regarding the structure of the group, the projects, and their progress can be explored graphically, as well as be reported on in pictures. Meanwhile, the underlying technologies are finally reaching the point at which participants can transcend the media—not to hypermedia, but to *im*mediacy, both spatial and temporal.

Intimacy is the goal. Graphics will help us get there.

The Goals of Groupware

What is groupware and what is it supposed to accomplish? The coinage has a self-evident meaning (stuff—hardware, software, and the like—for groups) with an underlying assumption: the existence of groups that need and want to work together. Groupware's purpose, clearly, is to facilitate such work. I propose four goals for groupware.

Groupware's first goal is to provide a medium for communication. Electronic mail (e-mail) systems, address that goal. "Thanks to E-mail on our corporate network of Macintoshs, international engineering proposals can now be developed in hours, rather than weeks," reports a telecommunications engineer at Motorola's CODEX. "I post the first draft on the network in the evening, and my European counterpart has it back to me with his comments by the time I come in to work the next morning. And the immediacy gives the writing a lively quality that seems to be working well, in terms of closed sales."

Where most e-mail systems fall short is in the second groupware goal-layer: *Metacommunication*. Groupware must provide an environment for communicating *about* communications—for annotating and marking up communications—in different ways.

The third goal of groupware must be to provide an *audit trail*—an easy way to find out who did what to whom, and when. It is not enough to save successive drafts of a document; we must be able to backtrack through the authoring and editing process.

Groupware's fourth goal is to provide a *secure environment*. We want to share information, but only with those with whom we want to share it.

The Need for Intimacy

We must not overlook how people interact with one another. We are used to a certain breadth/depth of contact with others, while standard alphanumeric programs offer a very narrow/shallow bandwidth for human communications. We can't see the other people's faces, hear their voices, or smell them. And only a very narrow portion of the population feels comfortable with exclusively verbal communications. By adding graphics to the basic lexicon of communication shared by the person and the computer, a much larger segment of the user population can be reached.

Good groupware should allow graphical interaction, but not require it. That way, the largest possible subset of the user community can be accommodated.

Graphics to the Rescue

Graphics are a wideband form of communications. So by incorporating pictures into the communicators' toolbox, we empower them to achieve the goals of groupware. Our brains hunger for non-quantitative data—the stuff the right half of the brain deals in. We need this other, left-brain, less orderly kind of information for orientation, for expression of non-verbal concepts, and for escape from the horrors of columns upon columns of numbers, row after row of dense text with no let-up. That's one reason why high-level managers in all organizations love pictures in business communications—when they are used appropriately. But though we recognize that cartoons and pictograms, for example, are helpful, they are expensive and difficult to produce; so we leave them to *BUSINESS WEEK, FORTUNE, USA TODAY* and their ilk.

Thanks to today's graphically powerful personal computers, however, anyone can produce diagrams and simple illustrations with "paint" packages and collections of software "clip art"—libraries of images that can be "cut" and "pasted" to create professional-looking pictures that add visual interest to any report. But these newly accessible tools give us power without knowledge. It is easy for someone who is not a graphics professional to spend hours on a chart or diagram, only to have it look terrible. Like any strong medicine, graphics systems must be employed judiciously.

The built-in graphics of the Apple MACINTOSH facilitate graphical playfulness, which does not always lead to greater clarity of communication. "The 'MAC-MEMO,' with seventeen fonts and six pieces of clip art for a four-sentence message, is part of a learning process," says Computer Associates executive Alan Paller. "Putting the ability to mix text and graphics into the hands of PC users has created a snowstorm of output, most of it inscrutable and graphically terrible. But it is encouraging people to think graphically, and identify their needs more clearly," says Paller.

There are many interesting and useful differences between words and pictures. For one thing, words are linear, in the sense that their sequence is important. If you start at the end of a paragraph and read backwards, you will not get the same meaning as when you read from the beginning forward. We read and write with the help of the left half of our brain, wherein resides our ability to process information linearly, according to Russian neurophysiologist A. R. Luria.

In fact, "alphabetic literacy reinforces left-brain patterns of cognition because of the linear, sequential way in which information is transmitted, letter by letter," claims R. K. Logan, in *The Alphabet Effect*. So the more we read words and numbers, and the less we look at pictures, the more analytical and left-brained we become.

Pictures, on the other hand, have no implicit sequence; you can "start reading" anywhere. They encourage right-brain, holistic thinking. Studies of geniuses show that it is a combination of right-brain and left-brain activity that yields the unusual creativity of a Leonardo, an Edison, or an Einstein. Some of the uniqueness of Oriental thought has been attributed to the pictorial nature of those cultures' written languages.

Pictures also represent a powerful and sorely needed form of data compression. More words are now printed in a single day than were published in the five hundred years between Gutenberg's invention of the printing press to the end of World War II (1450-1945). But since we only take in words at rates of up to about 1200 per minute, how can we absorb all this information? Marvin Patterson, now Director of Corporate Engineering at Hewlett Packard, estimates we absorb pictorial data at rates equivalent to fifty million words per minute—a difference of more than four orders of magnitude. So to communicate more data, we should be using pictures. But, generally, we do not.

There are historical and technological reasons for the dearth of pictures in human communications—especially technical ones. Mechanical typography made inserting graphics more difficult than when manuscripts were simply written out by hand. But today's computer-based word-processors enable us, once again, to create and incorporate pictures in letters and reports—without a great deal of effort. And laser printers make it possible to print them attractively.

Pictures are making computers themselves more usable than they ever were before. Because we have picture-capable computers, we also have the increasingly popular graphical user interface, or GUI—a pictorial interface that helps the user communicate with the computer. By allowing the user to employ right-brain pattern recognition abilities, and by taking advantage of existing knowledge in the user's mind, GUI's reduce the amount of time and effort needed to learn to use a computer. (E.g., a trashcan is where you put things you no longer want—so the function of a trashcan icon on a display can be grasped intuitively.)

The issue of precision, however, will always keep text and numbers an important part of most communications that include pictures. This is because the precision of a picture is limited by factors such as scale and the medium on which the picture appears, while the precision of letters and numbers is unlimited. Or consider ambiguity: Words and numbers are generally unambiguous; the meaning of pictures is context-dependent, and hence often ambiguous. So pictures cannot completely replace text and numbers, but can complement them. For instance, pictures can convey the concept, while text and numbers convey the details.

And Not Only Graphics

Having moved beyond plain text, we can begin to appreciate the communication-enhancing qualities of motion and sound. For instance, researchers at Ohio State University's Department of Psychology have demonstrated that motion is a more meaningful cue for perceiving depth than stereopsis.

A recently-developed human resource technology called neurolinguistic programming (NLP) reveals that everyone has preferred modalities for communication and "processing." Some people are primarily auditory, as indicated by their choice of predicates; they say things like, "I hear what you're saying"; "That sounds good." Others are visual, and things "look good" to them; they ask if you "get the picture" Yet others are kinesthetic, and need to "get a feel" for the situation while "impressing upon you" their sense of urgency. Graphics and charts are probably most appealing to people whose modality preference is visual or kinesthetic. Stored voice messages will appeal to others. Tactile communications? Smell? Taste? Not yet.

The Downside

A business organization is a structure under stress. The stress is the tension exerted by those who want information on those who have information. Automation of communication processes reduces that tension. Being under tension, as a member of the organization, equates to power. The more tension, the more power. Nobody, as Signor Machiavelli noted centuries ago, is anxious to give up power.

In addition, any improvement in organizational communications must bring about a loss of precious "information float"—a loss that is not on everyone's list of desiderata. (Information float is the time between the arrival of information and its departure, during which it should be processed. You may recognize the financial origin of the metaphor.) An organization lives in its float. It's where everyone gets to breathe and scratch. Loss of float time is loss of human re-creation time. The float is where organization people regain perspective...sanity.

When it comes to loss of information float, most people resist a change they think will affect their status. Most such change is procedural. Automation of isolated activities is welcomed by everyone because it makes them look good. It gives individuals more documentation to pass along per unit of time, thus increasing their perceived power in the organization. But automation of entire activities, with the concomitant loss of information float, is hard to sell—especially since people have difficulty admitting that their personal goals are at odds with those of the organization.

Where Are We Going?

What we can look forward to is what MIT Media Lab founder Nicholas Negroponte calls intimacy—contact with computers that goes far beyond our present notion of interface. In The Media Lab (Viking, 1987), Stewart Brand quotes a 1977 paper of Negroponte: "I coined the term 'idiosyncratic system' to distinguish a personal computer from a personalized computer, one that knows its user intimately and can accordingly invoke all the necessary inferences to handle vagaries, inconsistencies, and ambiguities. I offer," he says, "the following hypothetical scenario as an example:

  "Okay, where did you hide it?"
  "Hide what?"
  "You know."
  "Where do you think?"
  "Oh."

TOWARD HIGH-PERFORMANCE ORGANIZATIONS: A STRATEGIC ROLE FOR GROUPWARE

Douglas C. Engelbart
Bootstrap Institute
6505 Kaiser Drive
Fremont, CA 94555
Document #: (AUGMENT,132810,)

ABSTRACT

Achieving tomorrow's high-performance organizations will involve massive changes throughout their capability infrastructures. The complexity of implementing these changes will be daunting, and deserves a strategic approach. Groupware will support important, special new knowledge capabilities in these infrastructures, and also can play a key role in an evolutionary strategy.

1 INTRODUCTION

1.1 Shared Visions and the "Groupware Community"

Groupware to me, personally, is a strategic means to an important end: creating truly high-performance human organizations. My pursuit began in the '50s, aiming to make our organizations and institutions better able to handle complexity and urgency. By 1962 I had evolved a basic conceptual framework for pursuing that goal (Ref-1 and Ref-2). I have essentially lived and worked within that framework ever since, steadily evolving and enriching it via many relevant experiences.

It is becoming relatively common of late, in the increasing flow of literature about organizational improvement, to highlight the need for the members of an organization to have a shared vision of where and how the organization is moving, in its marketplace and in its internal evolution. I assume that the same principle should be applicable to a looser organizational unit, in this case, to the community consisting of organizations and researchers interested in the overlapping domains of organizational improvement and "groupware," and including the information-system marketplace whose business is providing products and services to end-user organizations.

From my experience, the nature of this shared vision will be the single most important factor in how directly and how well the digital-technology marketplace will indeed support significantly higher organizational capability — which I assume is our basic objective in the evolution of groupware.

My own vision about pursuing high-performance organizations has matured over the years into a quite comprehensive, multi-faceted, strategic framework. It may seem a bit radical in nature, but my continuing hope is that it will be merged into such a shared community vision.

The full purpose of our Bootstrap Institute is to promote constructive dialog with critical stakeholders in the community about this "bootstrap strategy," to facilitate its trial adoption, and to further the strategy's own "continuous improvement."

In this paper I summarize the key elements of this strategic framework and highlight the role that would be played by the "groupware community." In Ref-3 is an explicit historical treatment that provides a good deal of background on framework development up to 1986. Also, Ref-4 gives a relatively balanced description of our associated groupware and application developments with an underlying framework treatment.

1.2 Capability Infrastructure and its Augmentation System

Any high-level capability needed by an organization rests atop a broad and deep *capability infrastructure*, comprised of many layers of composite capabilities, each depending upon the integration of lower-level capabilities. At the lower levels lie two categories of capabilities: Human-Based and Tool-Based. The functional capabilities of groupware fit into the latter category, along with a wide variety of facilities, artifacts, and other tools.

In pursuit of higher organizational performance, this infrastructure is the obvious focus of attention. Then it is a matter of establishing system and goal perspectives to determine how much of this infrastructure to include as serious candidates for change, and how radical a change to contemplate. I arrived at a singularly global perspective from the following considerations.

Figure 1 shows the result of a great deal of thought about how over the centuries our cultures have evolved rich systems of things that, when humans are conditioned and trained to employ them, will *augment* their basic, genetically endowed capabilities so that they, and their organizations, can exercise capabilities of much higher nature than would otherwise be possible. For lack of a ready-made term, I named this our *Augmentation System*, and found it valuable to partition it into the two parts as shown — a Human System and a Tool System. I have developed many things from this model that have proved useful and valid over the years — including essentially everything I've developed in the groupware arena (tools, concepts, strategies).

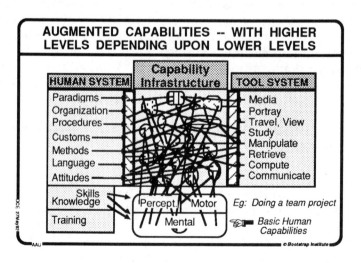

Figure 1

A bit of thinking about this model brought me the realization that we are far short of being able to do a one-pass re-design of any major portion of this capability infrastructure — if only because of their pervasive, underlying dependence upon human processes.

And as we pursue significant capability improvement, we need to appreciate that we will be trying to affect the evolution of a very large and complex system that has a life and evolutionary dynamic of its own. Concurrent evolution of many parts of the system will be going on anyway (as it has for centuries). We will have to go along with that situation, and pursue our improvement objectives via facilitation and guidance of these evolutionary processes. Therefore, we should become especially oriented to pursuing improvement as a multi-element, *co-evolution* process. In particular, we need to give explicit attention to the co-evolution of the Tool System and the Human System.

And, along with these foregoing perceptions, another factor popped into the scene to create a very significant effect on my emergent framework.

1.3 The Relevant Implications of Radical Scale Change

Some years earlier, I had studied the issues and prospects associated with extreme miniaturization of functional devices, towards assessing the likelihood of digital equipment becoming extremely small, fast and cheap. I was personally motivated because I would have to be relatively confident of very significant progress in that regard in order to commit a career towards facilitating widespread computer augmentation.

I learned enough to convince myself that, with the expected high industrial and military demand toward digital technology, the achievable limits on micro scalability were far beyond what would be enough to warrant my particular pursuits. And in the process, looking into references dealing with dimensional scale in living things, I became aware of a very important general principle: if the scale is changed for critical parameters within a complex system, the effects will at first appear as quantitative changes in general appearance, but after a certain point, further scale change in these parameters will yield ever-more striking *qualitative* changes in the system.

For example: The appropriate design for a five-foot creature is not that much different from that for a six-foot creature. But the design for either of these would be totally inappropriate for a one-inch creature, or for a thirty-foot creature. A mosquito as big as a human couldn't stand, fly or breathe. A human the size of a mosquito would be badly equipped for basic mobility, and for instance would not be able to drink from a puddle without struggling to break the surface tension, and then if his face were wetted, would very likely get pulled under and be unable to escape drowning.

The lesson: Expect surprising qualitative changes in structural assemblage and functional performance when a complex system adapts effectively to drastic changes in critical parameters.

I could only assume that the same is very likely to be true for the complex Augmentation System that supports an organization's capability infrastructure. Here, the radical change in the scale of Tool System capability — in speed, function, capacity, presentation quality, transmission, etc. of emergent digital technology — greatly transcends any other perturbation in system parameters that our organizations have ever needed to adapt to in so short a time as a few decades.

Much more could be said about the scaling issue that is relevant to the general theme of organizational change. Sufficient here to say that these thoughts drove me definitely to view as global and massive both the opportunity and the challenge that we humans were facing with respect to increasing the performance level of the organizations and institutions upon which mankind's continuing existence depends.

1.4 The Underlying Importance of Paradigms

In the ensuing thirty years since the model of Figure 1 first evolved, I have become ever more convinced that human organizations can be transformed into much higher levels of capability. These digital technologies, which we have barely learned to harness, represent a totally new type of nervous system around which there can evolve new, higher forms of social organisms.

In the face of mounting evidence that our organizations and institutions can not cope adequately with the increasing complexity and urgency of our society's problems, it seems highly motivating to explore every avenue that offers reasonable probability of improving their capability to cope.

Those were my thoughts thirty years ago; they seem even more germane today. The technologies have been demonstrated, and our organizations are aligning toward internal improvement. What seems still to be lacking is an appropriate general perception that:

    (a)   huge changes are likely, and really significant improvements are possible;

    (b)   surprising qualitative changes may be involved in acquiring higher performance; and

    (c)   there might actually be an effective, pragmatic strategy for pursuing those improvements.

In developing a basic, scalable strategy, the above issues of perception are important enough to warrant being explicitly factored into it. In other words, the strategy should provide for the need of significant shifts in our perception of our likely and possible futures.

Perceptions, shared visions, paradigms — their evolution is *critical*, yet they receive little or no direct developmental attention. The slow, un-shepherded paradigm drifting of the past isn't an adequate process for times when deeper global changes are occurring than ever-before accommodated by such massive social bodies. And the rates of such change are more likely to increase than to diminish.

I interject such thoughts here because I actually believe that what can be produced by the groupware community can make a very large difference (in a proper strategic framework) to our capability for coping with large, complex problems. The ability to acquire this new capability is heavily dependent upon evolving an appropriate paradigm, which result in itself represents the type of complex challenge that our institutions need to become more capable of handling.

This leads to an assumption that an important factor to hope for, in an early stage of the future paradigms possessed by key players in this transformation of our organizations, is the perception of importance and a can-do attitude about consciously cultivating appropriate evolutionary trends and change rates in our future paradigms. Shifting our paradigm about paradigms.

What role will *you* play?

2 IMPROVING THE IMPROVEMENT PROCESS

The next step in developing an explicit strategic framework was generated from the conceptual content of Figure 1 by asking what sort of investment principles would make sense. I hoped to solicit R&D money and wondered how we might get the best return on those funds in facing this very large, unstructured problem. I also was prepared to invest essentially the rest of my professional career: how should I invest that time to get best net progress? And what basic guidelines should be adopted for launching (bare handed, so to speak) such a program?

The only serious approach that I could imagine, towards really significant improvement, would be a long-term, pragmatically guided, whole-system evolution. I was addressing a very complex system, and the challenge would be further complicated by the fact that the subject organizations would have to keep functioning at better than survival level while undergoing large, systemic changes.

So the image depicted in Figure 2 emerged from realizing that the capability of an organization to improve itself would have to become much more prominent and effective. It then seemed natural to consider a strategy wherein the earliest improvement efforts might be concentrated upon improving this capability (i.e., to improve the organization's improvement capability).

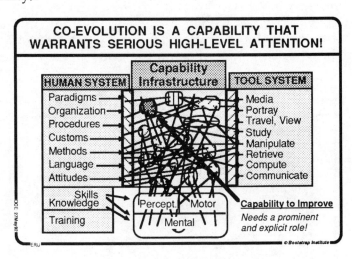

Figure 2

3 THE ABC MODEL OF ORGANIZATIONAL IMPROVEMENT

In doing some further thinking about improvement activities and the capabilities that support them, I found it useful to extract from Figure 2 a simpler abstraction dealing with organizational improvement, as in Figure 3. Here we separate the two types of activities, *A* and *B*, and show that the capability for each type of work is supported by its respective Augmentation System (comprised of Human and Tool systems).

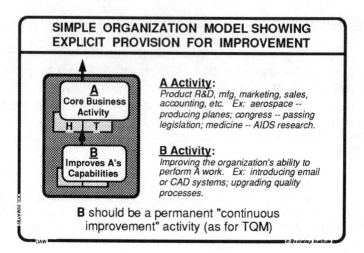

Figure 3

Given this model, we can now consider the prospects of improving the organization's improvement capability, as discussed earlier in Figure 2, as *improving the capability of the B Activity*. And for such a critical pursuit to be effective requires yet another explicit organizational activity, depicted in Figure 4 as the organization's C Activity. Executive efforts to assess and improve B-Activity funding, staffing, and high-level approach would qualify as a C Activity. C Activities would also include introducing new knowledge and skills into the B Activity, providing better means for participatory interaction with its A-Activity clients, or improving how pilot operations are managed.

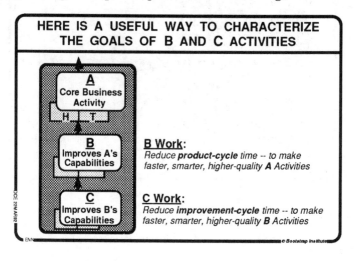

Figure 4

4 LOOKING FOR A MULTI-PAYOFF CAPABILITY CLUSTER

In considering the infrastructure elements that support this higher-level, self-improvement B Capability, I realized that many of its important subordinate capabilities are also actively employed by many of the higher-level A Capabilities that are important to the basic operations of the organization. For example, identifying needs and opportunities, designing and deploying solutions, and integrating lessons learned. This led to the following rhetorical question:

Is there a set of basic capabilities whose improvement would significantly enhance both the higher-level operational A Capabilities and this self-improvement B Capability?

The answer was a clear "Yes!" A core set of knowledge-related capabilities rapidly emerged as the prime candidate.

An investment that boosts the A Capability provides a one-shot boost. An investment that boosts the B Capability boosts the subsequent rate by which the A Capability increases. And an investment that boosts the C Capability boosts the rate at which the rate of improvement can increase. (To be slightly mathematical, investing in B and C boosts respectively the first and second derivative of the improvement curve — single and double compounding, if you wish.)

We are assuming here that selected products of the two capability-improvement activities (B and C) can be utilized not only to boost the capabilities of their client activities, but can also to a significant extent be harnessed within their own activities to boost their subsequent capability. This is depicted in Figure 5 by the "feedback" paths.

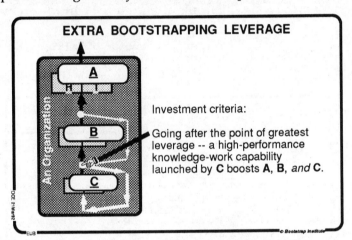

Figure 5

This was where the term *bootstrapping* became welded into my continuing professional framework. It turns out that there are many choices that we will face where balanced consideration of the bootstrapping possibilities can make a difference. I place much confidence in the potential payoff from thoughtful application of the principles that have evolved from such thinking.

5 THE CODIAK PROCESS CLUSTER: BEST STRATEGIC APPLICATION CANDIDATE

Over the years I have tried various ways to label and characterize the above-mentioned key knowledge capabilities. For lack of an established term, I have settled on an acronym that embraces the main concepts of this cluster of high-leverage capabilities — *CODIAK*:

> The <u>co</u>ncurrent <u>d</u>evelopment, <u>i</u>ntegration and <u>a</u>pplication of <u>k</u>nowledge.

As complexity and urgency increase, the need for highly effective CODIAK capabilities will become increasingly urgent. Increased pressure for reduced product cycle time, and for more and more work to be done concurrently, is forcing unprecedented coordination across project functions and organizational boundaries. Yet most organizations do not have a comprehensive picture of what knowledge work is, and of which aspects would be most profitable to improve.

The CODIAK capability is not only the basic machinery that propels our organizations, it also provides the key capabilities for their steering, navigating and self repair. And the body of applicable knowledge developed represents a critically valuable *asset*. The CODIAK capability is crucial in most A Activities across the organization, whether in strategic planning, marketing, R&D, production, customer support, or operations. It is also crucial in the B and C Activities, whether identifying needs and opportunities, designing and deploying solutions, or incorporating lessons learned — which of course is also used in key A-Activity work. As such, the CODIAK capability should be considered a core business competency in the organization's capability infrastructure, and is an ideal candidate for early improvement to achieve the extra bootstrapping leverage discussed above in Figure 5.

For best exposure to full CODIAK issues, it helps to consider heavy knowledge-intensive activities such as a large, complex project. Figure 6 represents the high-level core of such a CODIAK process. In the center is a basic organizational unit, representing the interactive knowledge domains of a single individual, or of individuals or groups within a project team, department, functional unit, division, task force, committee, whole organization, community, or association (any of which might be inter- or intra- organizational).

Each organizational unit is continuously analyzing, digesting, integrating, collaborating, developing, applying, and re-using its knowledge, much of which is ingested from its external environment (which could be outside of, or within, the same organization).

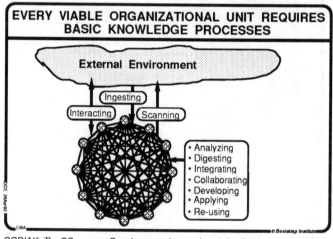

Figure 6   *CODIAK: The COncurrent Development, Integration, & Application of Knowledge*

A result of this continuous knowledge process is a dynamically evolving knowledge base as shown in Figure 7 below, consisting of three primary knowledge domains: intelligence, dialog records, and knowledge products (in this example, the design and support documents for a complex product).

Intelligence Collection: An alert project group, whether classified as an A, B, or C Activity, always keeps a watchful eye on its external environment, actively surveying, ingesting, and interacting with it. The resulting *intelligence* is integrated with other project knowledge on an ongoing basis to identify problems, needs, and opportunities which might require attention or action.

Dialog Records: Responding effectively to needs and opportunities involves a high degree of coordination and *dialog* within and across project groups. This dialog, along with resulting decisions, is integrated with other project knowledge on a continuing basis.

Knowledge Product: The resulting plans provide a comprehensive picture of the project at hand, including proposals, specifications, descriptions, work breakdown structures, milestones, time lines, staffing, facility requirements, budgets, and so on. These documents, which are iteratively and collaboratively developed, represent the *knowledge products* of the project team, and constitute both the current project status and a roadmap for implementation and deployment. The CODIAK process is rarely a one-shot effort. Lessons learned, as well as intelligence and dialog, must be constantly analyzed, digested, and integrated into the knowledge products throughout the life cycle of the project.

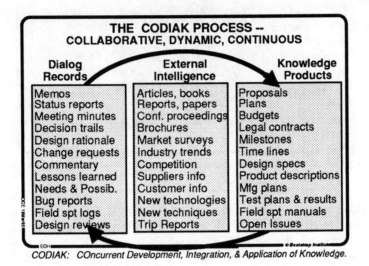

Figure 7   *CODIAK: COncurrent Development, Integration, & Application of Knowledge.*

With minor adjustments in the boxed lists in Figure 7, this basic generic CODIAK model seems to apply equally well to academic scholarship, heavy industry, government, medical research, social institutions, consumer product businesses, consulting firms, trade associations, small non-profits, and so on.

We need to note here that basic CODIAK processes have practically forever been a part of society's activity. Whether the knowledge components are carried in peoples' heads, marked on clay tablets, or held in computers, the basic CODIAK process has always been important.

What is new is a focus toward harnessing technology to achieve truly high-performance CODIAK capability. As we concurrently evolve our human-system elements and the emergent groupware technology, we will see the content and dynamics represented in Figure 7 undergo very significant changes.

More and more intelligence and dialog records will end up usefully recorded and integrated; participants will steadily develop skills and adopt practices that increase the utility they derive from the increased content, while at the same time making their contributions more complete and valuable.

Generally, I expect people to be surprised by how much value will be derived from the use of these future tools, by the ways the value is derived, and by how "natural and easy to use" the practices and tools will seem after they have become well established (even though they may initially be viewed as unnatural and hard to learn).

Inevitably, the groupware tools which support the CODIAK processes within and across our organizations will need to be fully integrated and fully interoperable. Consider the larger organization depicted in Figure 8 in which our representative complex project may be embedded (for example, in the Engineering Department of a manufacturing organization).

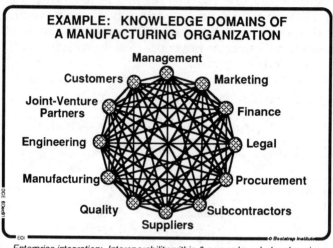

Figure 8

Enterprise integration: Interoperability within & across knowledge domains

Each of the enterprise's functional units studded around the circle represents an activity domain that houses at least one CODIAK process. Then, because of their mutual involvement with the operations of the whole enterprise, the CODIAK processes within each of these enterprise sub-domains would with strong likelihood benefit from being interoperable with those of the other sub-domains.

As operations between enterprises steadily become more closely knit, the interaction processes with customers, subcontractors and suppliers also want to become increasingly effective — and therefore the issue of knowledge-domain interoperability becomes ever more global.

As developed in the sections that follow, our framework assumes that all of the knowledge media and operations indicated in Figure 7 will one day be embedded within an Open Hyperdocument System (OHS). Every participant will work through the windows of his or her workstation into his or her group's "knowledge workshop."

With this in mind, consider the way in which the project group's CODIAK domain, with all of its internal concurrent activity, will be operating within the larger enterprise group depicted in Figure 8.

And consider that the whole enterprise, acting as a coherent organizational unit, must also have a workable CODIAK capability and possess its own evolving, applicable CODIAK knowledge base.

Here an important appreciation may be gained for the "concurrency" part of the CODIAK definition. CODIAK was introduced above with the sense that all of the development, integration and application activities within a given organizational unit were going on concurrently. *This establishes a very important requirement for the groupware support.*

In Figure 9 we get the sense of the multi-level "nesting" of concurrent CODIAK processes within the larger enterprise. Each of the multiply-nested organizational units needs its own coherent CODIAK process and knowledge base; and each unit is running its CODIAK processes concurrently, not only with all of its sibling and cousin units -- but also with larger units in which it is embedded, and with smaller units that are part of its own makeup.

Furthermore, there are many valuable organizational units that cut across the organizational structure — such as a corporate-wide task force — and each of these units also needs a coherent CODIAK process and knowledge base. And beyond that, significant working relationships will be going on with external organizational units, such as trade associations, professional societies, consultants, contractors, suppliers, special alliance partners, customers, regulatory agencies, and standards groups. Each such "external" unit needs to have a coherent CODIAK knowledge domain; all such domains will have some knowledge elements and evolutionary dynamics that are mutual with those of many other units in the enterprise's total CODIAK environment.

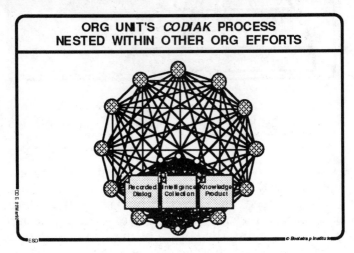

Figure 9

So, consider the much extended sense of concurrency and inter-dependency arising from the above picture: the CODIAK processes of all of the inter-dependent organizational units within the larger enterprise are going on concurrently; and further, among these concurrently active processes there is a great deal of mutual involvement with parts of the whole knowledge base.

It is easy to realize that significant parts of what the smaller group works with, as being in its "external environment" intelligence collection, will actually be shared-access knowledge from other domains within the enterprise — from other's dialog, from their external intelligence, or from their finished or evolving knowledge products.

Then the entire enterprise has a collective CODIAK domain, with knowledge elements that to some extent will be actually in a "whole-enterprise" domain, but where much of what lies in the collective enterprise domain is an active part of the CODIAK domains of subordinate organizational units within the enterprise.

And further, consider that as the availability of highly effective online CODIAK support becomes widespread, suppliers, contractors and customers will engage in a non-trivial degree of CODIAK-domain sharing with the enterprise. One needs only a brief glance at the supplier network of Figure 10 to realize the magnitude of critical, interoperable CODIAK processes and shared CODIAK knowledge domains that will prevail when (or if) suitable groupware becomes widely available.

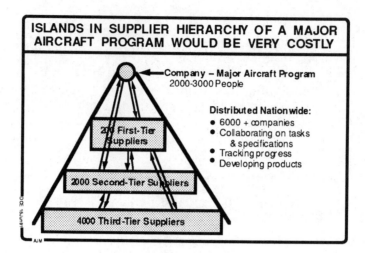

Figure 10

This is representative of the scale of global challenge that I think faces the groupware marketplace.

The foregoing dictates some very significant requirements for any groupware system that attempts to support the CODIAK processes of our future, high-performance organizations. Immediately apparent is the need for very flexible, wide-area sharing of pieces of the knowledge base. What has only recently begun to be generally apparent is the associated need for a new way of thinking about the nature of the knowledge packages we have called "documents." This above requirement for flexibly arranged sharing of essentially arbitrary knowledge chunks provides a very strong argument for documents becoming built from modular-concept nodes with arbitrary inter-node linking — *hypertext*.

So, how (and when) will the marketplace learn enough and be cooperative enough to develop truly effective OHS standards? The prospects for achieving truly high levels of performance in larger organizations and institutions pretty much await that day.

> This question is a significant part of what an effective bootstrapping strategy needs to address.

6 OPEN HYPERDOCUMENT SYSTEM (OHS): FOR GENERIC CODIAK SUPPORT

My early assumption, amply borne out by subsequent experience, is that the basic supporting technology for future high-performance knowledge work will be an integrated system based upon multi-media hyperdocuments.

Furthermore, there will be critical issues of interoperability within and between our organizations and their knowledge domains. The ever-greater value derived from online, interactive work within a hyperdocument environment will require a significantly higher degree of standardization in document architecture and usage conventions than heretofore contemplated.

It is inevitable that this service be provided by an "open system" of hyperdocuments and associated network and server architectures. The basic arguments for this Open Hyperdocument System (OHS) are presented in Ref-5; and the hyperdocument system features described below are assumed by me to be strong candidates for requirements for the eventual OHS whose evolution will be so critical to the productivity of industries and nations.

Following is a brief general description of the system design that has evolved from the conceptual orientation described in this paper, through the experience of many years and trial events. Please note that the term "system" is very important here.

Shared Files/Documents — the most fundamental requirement. Generalized file sharing is to be available across the entire global domain in which any online collaborative working relationship is established (e.g., world-wide).

Mixed-Object Documents — to provide for an arbitrary mix of text, diagrams, equations, tables, raster-scan images (single frames or live video), spread sheets, recorded sound, etc. — all bundled within a common "envelope" to be stored, transmitted, read (played) and printed as a coherent entity called a "document."

Explicitly Structured Documents — where the objects comprising a document are arranged in an explicit hierarchical structure, and compound-object substructures may be explicitly addressed for access or to manipulate the structural relationships.

Global, Human-Understandable, Object Addresses — in principle, every object that someone might validly want/need to cite should have an unambiguous address, capable of being portrayed in a manner as to be human readable and interpretable. (E.g., not acceptable to be unable to link to an object within a "frame" or "card.")

View Control of Objects' Form, Sequence and Content — where a structured, mixed-object document may be displayed in a window according to a flexible choice of viewing options — especially by selective level clipping (outline for viewing), but also by filtering on content, by truncation or some algorithmic view that provides a more useful portrayal of structure and/or object content (including new sequences or groupings of objects that actually reside in other documents). Editing on structure or object content directly from such special views would be allowed whenever appropriate.

The Basic "Hyper" Characteristics — where embedded objects called *links* can point to any arbitrary object within the document, or within another document in a specified domain of documents — and the link can be actuated by a user or an automatic process to "go see what is at the other end," or "bring the other-end object to this location," or "execute the process identified at the other end." (These executable processes may control peripheral devices such as CD ROM, video-disk players, etc.)

Hyperdocument "Back-Link" Capability — when reading a hyperdocument online, a worker can utilize information about links from other objects within this or other hyperdocuments that point to this hyperdocument — or to designated objects or passages of interest in this hyperdocument.

Link Addresses That Are Readable and Interpretable by Humans — one of the "viewing options" for displaying/printing a link object should provide a human-readable description of the "address path" leading to the cited object; AND, the human must be able to read the path description, interpret it, and follow it (find the destination "by hand" so to speak).

Personal Signature Encryption — where a user can affix his personal signature to a document, or a specified segment within the document, using a private signature key. Users can verify that the signature is authentic and that no bit of the signed document or document segment has been altered since it was signed. Signed document segments can be copied or moved in full without interfering with later signature verification.

Hard-Copy Print Options to Show Addresses of Objects and Address Specification of Links — so that, besides online workers being able to follow a link-citation path (manually, or via an automatic link jump), people working with associated hard copy can read and interpret the link-citation, and follow the indicated path to the cited object in the designated hard-copy document.

Also, suppose that a hard-copy worker wants to have a link to a given object established in the online file. By visual inspection of the hard copy, he should be able to determine a valid address path to that object and for instance hand-write an appropriate link specification for later online entry, or dictate it over a phone to a colleague.

Hyperdocument Mail — where an integrated, general-purpose mail service enables a hyperdocument of any size to be mailed. Any embedded links are also faithfully transmitted — and any recipient can then follow those links to their designated targets that may be in other mail items, in common-access files, or in "library" items.

The Hyperdocument "Journal System" — an integrated library-like system where a hyper-document message or document can be submitted using a submittal form (technically an email message form), and an automated "clerk" assigns a catalog number, stores the item, notifies recipients with a link for easy retrieval, notifies of supercessions, catalogs it for future searching, and manages document collections. Access is guaranteed when referenced by its catalog number, or "jumped to" with an appropriate link. Links within newly submitted hyperdocuments can cite any passages within any of the prior documents, and the back-link service lets the online reader of a document detect and "go examine" any passage of a subsequent document that has a link citing that passage.

Access Control — Hyperdocuments in personal, group, and library files can have access restrictions down to the object level.

External Document Control (XDoc) — (Not exactly a "hyperdocument" issue, but an important system issue here.) Documents not integrated into the above online and interactive environment (e.g. hard-copy documents and other records otherwise external to the OHS) can very effectively be managed by employing the same "catalog system" as for hyperdocument libraries — with back-link service to indicate citations to these "offline" records from hyperdocument (and other) data bases. OHS users can find out what is being said about these "XDoc" records in the hyperdocument world.

The overview portrayal in Figure 11 shows the working relationships between the major system elements described above. Note the shared catalog service that supports use of the Journal and External Document services.

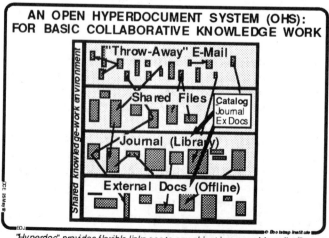

Figure 11

"Hyperdoc" provides flexible linkages to any object in any multi-media file;
"Open" provides vendor-independent access within and across work groups.

Details of features and designs for well-developed prototypes of some of the above may be found in Ref-6, Ref-7 and Ref-8.

7 FOUR GENERAL GROUPWARE ARCHITECTURAL REQUIREMENTS

Besides the aforementioned Hyperdocument Mail and Hyperdocument Library features that depend upon special larger-scale architectural features, there are at least four other important tool-system capabilities that are very important to wide-area groupware services such as being considered here:

Global and Individual Vocabulary Control — somewhat new in the history of computer services are issues regarding the evolution and use of a common "workshop vocabulary" among all the users of the forthcoming "global knowledge workshop." Common data dictionaries have been at issue, of course, but for a much more limited range of users, and for a more limited and stable vocabulary than we will face in the exploding groupware world.

Our own architectural approach (see Ref-6, Ref-9 and Ref-10) has been to introduce into every user-interface environment a common Command-Language Interpreter (CLI) module that derives the user's available operations (verbs) as applied to the available classes of objects (nouns) from a grammar file (individualized if desired with respect to the size and nature of the verbs and nouns utilized from the common vocabulary). The CLI interprets user actions, based upon the contents of the currently attached grammar file, and executes appropriate actions via remote procedure calls to a common application program interface of the "open system environment."

Each of us knowledge workers will become involved in an ever richer online environment, collaborating more and more closely within an ever more global "knowledge workshop," with multi-organizational users of widely divergent skills and application orientations who are using hardware and software from a wide mix of vendors.

Without some global architectural capability such as suggested above, I can't see a practical way to support and control the evolving global "workshop vocabulary" in a manner necessary for effectively integrating wide-area groupware services.

Multiplicity of Look-and-Feel Interface Choices — Based upon the same Command-Language Interpreter (CLI) architecture as above, a "look-and-feel interface" software module would be located between the CLI and the window system. Providing optional modules for selected look-and-feel interface characteristics would serve an important practical as well as evolutionary need.

There would be a basic constraint necessary here. When working interactively, no matter what particular look-and-feel style is being used, a user has a particular mental model in mind for the significance of every menu item, icon, typed command, or "hot, command-key combination" employed.

The necessary constraint needed here is that the resulting action, via the interface module that is being employed for this user, must be produced through the underlying execution of processes provided by the Command Language Interpreter module as derived from use of common-vocabulary terms. And the users should learn about their tools and materials, and do their discussing with others about their work, using the underlying common-vocabulary terms no matter what form of user interface they employ.

Besides relaxing the troublesome need to make people conform to a standard look and feel, this approach has a very positive potential outcome. So far, the evolution of popular graphical user interfaces has been heavily affected by the "easy to use" dictum. This has served well to facilitate wide acceptance, but it is quite unlikely that the road to truly high performance can effectively be traveled by people who are stuck with vehicular controls designed to be easy to use by a past generation.

As important classes of users develop larger and larger workshop vocabularies, and exercise greater process skill in employing them, they will undoubtedly begin to benefit from significant changes in look and feel. The above approach will provide open opportunity for that important aspect of our evolution toward truly high performance.

Shared-Window Teleconferencing — where remote distributed workers can each execute a related support service that provides the "viewing" workers with a complete dynamic image of the "showing" worker's window(s). Used in conjunction with a phone call (or conference call), the parties can work as if they are sitting side-by-side, to review, draft, or modify a document, provide coaching or consulting, support meetings, and so on. Control of the application program (residing in the "showing" worker's environment) can be passed around freely among the participants. Generic provision of this service is discussed in Ref-6.

Inter-Linkage Between Hyperdocuments and Other Data Systems — for instance, a CAD system's data base can have links from annotations/comments associated with a design object that point to relevant specifications, requirements, arguments, etc. of relevance in a hyperdocument data base — and the back-link service would show hyperdocument readers which passages were cited from the CAD data base (or specified parts thereof).

Similarly, links in the hyperdocuments may point to objects within the CAD bases. And, during later study of some object within the CAD model, the back-link service could inform the CAD worker as to which hyperdocument passages cited that object.

8 THE CODIAK PROCESS SUPPORTED BY AN OHS

With the above tool capabilities, together with well-developed methods and other human-system elements as discussed in section 1.2, the organization's capability infrastructure could support the following types of online CODIAK scenarios.

Note that the following online interactions are designed to work even if the users are in different organizational units, in different organizations, using different application packages on different workstations (assuming access to the data is not barred by the stringent privacy features, naturally). The real test of an OHS is when you can click on a link you received via email from someone in a different organization, jumping directly to the passages cited, and then comfortably maneuver through the "foreign" knowledge domain, possibly jumping up a level with an outline view to see the context of the given passage, following other links you find there, and so on, *without having to fumble through unfamiliar processes.*

Intelligence Collection: Now an alert project group, whether classified as an A, B, or C Activity, can keep a much enhanced watchful eye on its external environment, actively surveying, ingesting, and interacting with it mostly online. Much of the external intelligence is now available in hyperdocument, multimedia form, having been captured in an OHS Journal facility. When I send you an email to let you know about an upcoming conference, I can cite the sessions I think you'd be interested in, and you can click on the enclosed citation links to quickly access the cited passages (taking advantage of hypertext links and object addressability). When I do a search through the Journal catalogs to research a question for the proposal I am writing, I can see who has cited the material and what they had to say about it. If the material is offline (i.e. in XDoc), I can quickly discover where it is stored and how to obtain a copy, probably requesting it via email. If the material is online, I can access it instantly, usually starting with a top-level outline view of the document's titles (taking advantage of the OHS document structure and custom viewing features), possibly setting a simple filter to narrow the field, then quickly zooming in on the specific information I require. I can quickly build an annotated index to the intelligence documents, or objects within those documents, that I want to keep track of. I can share with you a macro I wrote to trap certain incoming intelligence items and reformat them in a certain way, and you could fire this up in your own environment to work off your pet keywords (taking advantage of the common-vocabulary architectural feature). All the intelligence collected is easily integrated with other project knowledge.

Dialog Records: Responding effectively to needs and opportunities involves a high degree of coordination and *dialog* within and across project groups. In an OHS environment, most of the dialog will be conducted online via the Journal. Email would be used mostly for "throw-away" communiqués, such as meeting reminders. All memos, status reports, meeting minutes, design change requests, field support logs, bug reports, and so on, would be submitted to the Journal for distribution. Asynchronous online conferencing would be supported by the Journal, with each entry tagged and cataloged for easy future reference. Document exchange would be a matter of submitting the document to the Journal with a comment such as "Here's the latest version — please note especially the changes in Section G, differences are listed in File Y" including links to that section and that file for easy access. The reviewers would click on the links, and proceed to review the document. To make a comment, the reviewer would click on the object in question, and enter the comment, such as "Replace with 'Xyz'," or "Watch out for inconsistencies with Para G4!" with a link to the passage in G4. The author then gets back the indexed comments, and has many options for quickly reviewing and integrating them into the document. Such dialog support will obviate the need for many same-time meetings.

Same-time meetings, when needed, would be greatly enhanced by an OHS. The dialog motivating the meeting would already be in the Journal. Agenda items would be solicited, and the agenda distributed via the Journal. At the meeting, the agenda and real-time group notes can be projected on a large screen, as well as displayed on each participant's monitor (using the "shared screen" feature), and any participant can point to the displayed material (e.g. using a mouse). Controls can be passed to any participant to scribble, type, or draw on this virtual chalkboard. Any presentation materials and supporting documents can be instantly retrieved from the knowledge base for presentation. All resulting meeting documents, along with references to supporting documents cited, would subsequently be submitted to the Journal for immediate access by all authorized users.

In addition, tools will soon become generally available for flexibly contributing, integrating, and interlinking digitized speech into the OHS knowledge base. Early tools would be available for speaker recognition, for special-word recognition, and even for basic transcription to text — and for installing and following links between modules as small as a word embedded in a long speech string. This will greatly enhance the development, integration, and application of dialog records. More elegant tools will follow, and as human conventions and methods evolve to make effective use of the technology, the quantity and completeness of recorded dialog will become much more significant.

Knowledge Product: Throughout the life cycle of the project, the online OHS knowledge product will provide a truly comprehensive picture of the project at hand. Intermediate project states, including supporting intelligence and dialog trails, can be bundled as document collections in the Journal for document version management. All knowledge products will be developed, integrated, and applied within an OHS, with concurrent contributions from many diverse and widely distributed users. These users can also work as if sitting side by side, reviewing a design, marking up a document, finalizing the changes, etc. (using the shared screen feature). Finding what you need among the thousands of project documents will be a simple matter of clicking on a link (provided by the Journal catalogs, or by your project's indices), and zooming in and out of the detail, or by having someone else "take you there" (using the shared screen feature). Accountability is absolute— Journal submittals are guaranteed to be authentic, and each object can be tagged by the system with the date and time of the last write, plus the user who made the change. Documents can be signed with verifiable signatures.

Everyone is but one quick "link hop" away from any piece of knowledge representation anywhere in the whole knowledge collection. Smart retrieval tools can rapidly comb part or all of the collection to provide lists of "hit links" with rated relevance probabilities.

Conventions for structuring, categorizing, labeling and linking within their common knowledge domain will be well established and supportive of a high degree of mobility and navigational flexibility to experienced participants — much as residents get to know their way effectively around their city if they get much practice at it.

As a group adapts its ways of working to take better advantage of a tool system such as projected here, the classes of knowledge objects will grow, as will the functions available to operate upon them—and that growth will be paralleled by the concurrent evolution of an ever richer repertoire of the humans' "workshop knowledge, vocabulary, methodology and skills."

There is tremendous potential here, and many methods, procedures, conventions, organizational roles to be developed in close association with the tools. And, if the OHS is to be *open*, there is much deep exploration to be done into different application domains, such as Computer-Supported Cooperative Work (CSCW), organizational learning, Total Quality Management (TQM), Enterprise Integration (EI), program management, Computer-Aided Software Engineering (CASE), Computer-Aided Engineering (CAE), Concurrent Engineering (CE), organizational memory, online document delivery and CALS, and so on. This will require many advanced pilots, as will be discussed further on.

9 RECAP: THE FRAMEWORK TO THIS POINT

To this point in the paper, we have outlined steps in the development of a strategy to provide a high-leverage approach toward creating truly high-performance organizations.

We considered the concept of the organization's *capability infrastructure* upon which any of the organization's effectiveness must depend.

Further, what enables humans to exercise this infrastructure of capabilities is an *Augmentation System*, which is what provides the humans with all capabilities beyond their genetically endowed basic mental, motor and perceptual capabilities. It was useful to divide the Augmentation System into two sub-systems, the Human System and the Tool System. "Organic style co-evolution" among the elements of our Augmentation System has been the process by which it evolved to its current state.

New technologies are introducing an unprecedented scale of improvement in the Tool System part of the Augmentation System. This promises that subsequent co-evolution of our Augmentation Systems will likely produce radical qualitative changes in the form and functional effectiveness of our capability infrastructures, and hence of our organizations.

Very large and challenging problems are envisioned in pursuing potential benefits of such changes, towards truly high-performance organizations. A strategy is sought to provide an effective approach.

It would be profitable to consider early focus on improving the organizational improvement process so that further improvements can be done more effectively.

To help with this analysis, the *ABC* categorization of improvement-process was established. And the thesis was developed that the *CODIAK* set of knowledge capabilities — the concurrent development, integration, and application of knowledge — is important to all three types of activities. Therefore, if CODIAK improvement was concentrated upon early, the result could improve the first and second derivatives of the return on future improvement investments.

An Open Hyperdocument System (*OHS*) would be a key "Tool System" development towards improving general and widespread CODIAK capabilities within and between organizations. And creating a truly effective OHS would in itself be an extremely challenging and global problem for our groupware marketplace.

So, high-performance organizations: great opportunities, interesting concepts, tough challenges. What next regarding strategy?

10 C COMMUNITY: HIGH-PAYOFF BOOTSTRAPPING OPPORTUNITY

Returning to the basic ABC Model in Figure 4, we can make a few useful observations toward a next step in strategy development. This model will be useful even if the Bootstrapping approach is not followed; it is valuable to become explicit about differentiating responsibilities, functions and budgets between the two levels of improvement activity (B and C).

If explicit C roles are designated and assumed, basic issues will soon arise for which the C-Activity leaders find it valuable to compare experiences and basic approaches with their counterparts in other organizations. For instance, what budgeting guidelines and targets make sense for these improvement activities? How much can it help the B Activity to document the way things are done now? What role should pilot applications play? How large an improvement increment, for how big a group, does it make sense to try for a pilot? How much "instrumentation" of a pilot group — before, during, and after transition — to measure the value of the effort? These are all relevant to making the B Activity more effective.

So let us consider formalizing and extending the above type of cooperation among improvement activities, especially the C Activities. In the mid-60s I began to think about the nature and value of communities of common interest formed among different improvement activities. This led me very early to build explicit planning into the bootstrap strategy for forming improvement communities.

In Ref-11 (1972), I presented the concept of a "community knowledge workshop" -- outlining the tools we had developed for supporting it (including many of the hyperdocument system capabilities outline above), and described the three basic CODIAK sub-domains: recorded dialog, intelligence collection, and what I then called the "handbook" (or knowledge products).

After the ABC Model emerged in the framework, this evolved into a special emphasis on an important launching phase, for forming one or more special bootstrapping C *Communities* as shown in Figure 12.

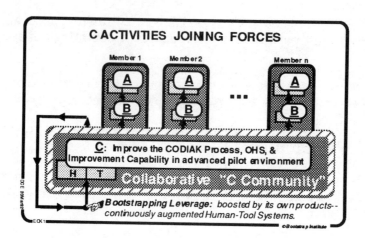

Figure 12

The value of such a cooperative activity can be very high — we'll unveil some of that later. First, there are some other questions that naturally arise which need to be addressed. An early and common pair of comments are: "I can't imagine sharing things with my competitors, there is so much about what we do that is proprietary;" and, "If they aren't in the same business, I don't see what useful things there would be that we could share."

About proprietary matters: The A Activity of each organization may be very competitive, with considerable proprietary content. The B Activity of each would tend to be less so — having quite a bit that is basic and generic. The C Activity of each would be much less involved in proprietary issues, and much more in basic, generic matters. So even competitors could consider cooperating, "out of their back doors" — "while competing like hell out of our front doors," as a trend that seems to be appearing among companies heavily into Total Quality Management and pursuit of the Malcolm Baldridge Award.

About being in very different business: Again, their B Activities will be much less different, and their C Activities surprisingly alike in important basic and generic issues.

Now, consider how a C Community could operate if it had the basic hyperdocument tools described above. For several decades, my colleagues and I have had such a system available, so all of our scenarios began there, using that system and calling it our "OHS, Model 1" — or "OHS-1."

And how would an ideal bootstrapping C Community operate? Its earliest focus would be on augmenting its own CODIAK capability. Using OHS-1 to do its work; making an important part of its work at first be to establish requirements, specifications and a procurement approach for getting a set of rapidly evolving prototype hyperdocument systems (e.g. OHS-2, -3, etc.), to provide ever better support for serious pilot applications among the C Community participants.

The Community's basic knowledge products could be viewed as dynamic electronic handbooks on "how to be better at your improvement tasks," with two customer groups: its B-Activity customers; and the C Community itself. Pooling resources from the member organizations enables a more advanced and rapidly evolving prototype CODIAK environment, which serves two very important purposes:

1. It provides for the Community getting better and better at its basic "C Activity;"

2. It provides advanced experience for its rotating staff of participants from the member organizations. They thus develop real understanding about the real issues

involved in boosting CODIAK capability — this understanding being absorbed by "living out there in a real, hard-working CODIAK frontier."

Note that it would be much more expensive for each member organization to provide equivalent experience by operating its own advanced pilot. Also the amount of substantive knowledge product developed this way would be very much more expensive if developed privately.

An important feature: once the Community stabilizes with effective groupware tools, methods and operating skills, the participants from the respective member organizations can do most of their work from their home-organization sites. This provides for maintaining the organizational bonding which is very important in effective C and B activities.

This home-site residency also facilitates the all-important "technology transfer" from the C Community into its customer B Activities. And, while considering the issue of "technology transfer," note that a strong feature of an augmented CODIAK process is the two-way transfer of knowledge. Developing dialog with the B clients via joint use of the hyperdocument system not only facilitates directly this two-way knowledge transfer, but provides critically important experience for the B people in the close witnessing of how advanced CODIAK processes work.

To characterize the value of facilitating this two-way transfer, consider Figure 13, which highlights the basic importance of improved CODIAK processes in the organization's improvement activity. The "1, 2, 3" points all are basic to the CODIAK process. As augmented CODIAK capabilities make their way up from C to B and into A, the over-all improvement process can't help but improve. And also, note that when the A Activity for this organization, as well as those for its customers, become based on interoperable CODIAK processes, the dynamics of the whole business will begin to sparkle.

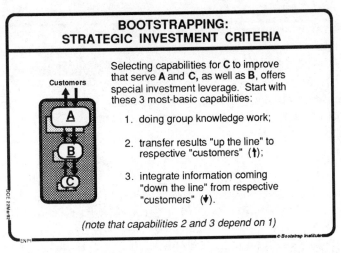

Figure 13

Now consider Figure 14, and note that the indicated types of knowledge flow are basic to the CODIAK processes, and that augmenting those processes for the C Community directly boosts one of its core capabilities. Conversely, Figure 15 emphasizes the previous basic point of the naturalness for enhanced CODIAK to improve this outflow, and highlights again the basic bootstrapping value that is obtained from early focus on these CODIAK processes.

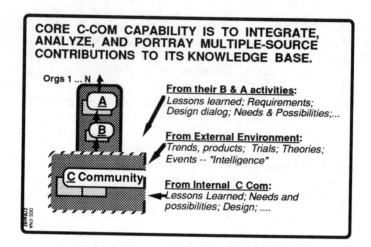

Figure 14

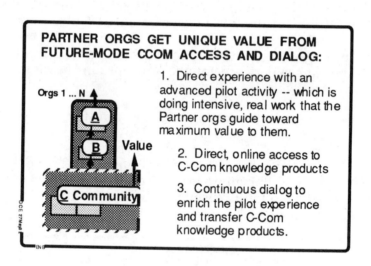

Figure 15

In the organizational improvement domain, there are several immediately apparent large and explicit issues for which a lone organization would need to consider a multi-party alliance. An immediate such issue, from the bootstrapping point of view, is to procure appropriate groupware systems that can support advanced pilot applications. Other large-sized issues have to do with "exploration and outpost settlements."

Relative to the options opening to our organizations for transforming into new states, there is a very large, unexplored, multi-dimensioned frontier out there. Both its dimensionality and its outer boundaries are expanding faster and faster. To really learn about that frontier, in order to decide where we would want to "settle our organizations," we must somehow do a great deal of basic exploration work. We also need to establish a significant number of outpost settlements in promising places so as to find out ahead of time what it would be like to really live and work there. (Translate "outposts" into "advanced pilot groups.")

Yet we are launching very few exploratory expeditions and developing very few significant outposts.

From the viewpoint that I have acquired, there is a great need for such explorations and trial settlements. Much of my motivation for advocating such as C Communities, bootstrapping, CODIAK and OHS pursuits, etc., is to find a strategy for exploring and settling that territory. It is almost like a military strategy: "first we get a firm settlement here in

CODIAK territory; then with that as a base, we encircle the OHS and C territories; when we get those under reasonable control, we will be in a most advantageous posture to pour through the rest of the B and C Improvement Territories to get the whole area under control and ..."

As the C Community and its working relationship with its "B customer" matures, there can be integrated into the substance of their joint efforts an ever larger sphere of involvement with the whole set of issues of organizational improvement.

Potential customers for augmented CODIAK capabilities can be seen everywhere in today's global society: e.g., all of the "Grand Challenges" earmarked in the U.S. for special support. Essentially every professional society will eventually operate this way; as will legislative bodies and government agencies, and university research programs.

In short, our solutions to every other challenging problem that is critical to our society will become significantly facilitated by high-performance CODIAK capabilities. Provides a stimulating challenge for the groupware community, doesn't it?

In closing, I would like to re-emphasize the comments in Section 1.4 about paradigms. I am convinced that cultivating the appropriate paradigm about how to view and approach the future will in the pursuit of high-performance organizations be the single most critical success factor of all.

[Note: The Bootstrap Institute has developed basic plans for several scales of C-Community launching — a medium-sized consortium approach on the one hand, and a more conservative, organic evolution approach on the other hand. Interested inquiries are invited.]

REFERENCES

Ref-1: Engelbart, D.C. 1962. *Augmenting Human Intellect: A Conceptual Framework*, Summary Report, Stanford Research Institute, on Contract AF 49(63-8)-1024, October, 134 pp.

Ref-2: Engelbart, D.C. 1963. A Conceptual Framework for the Augmentation of Man's Intellect. *Vistas in Information Handling*, Howerton and Weeks (eds), Washington, D.C.: Spartan Books, pp. 1-29. Republished in Greif, I. (ed) 1988. *Computer Supported Cooperative Work: A Book of Readings*, San Mateo, CA: Morgan Kaufmann Publishers, Inc., pp. 35-65.

Ref-3: Engelbart, D.C. 1988. The Augmented Knowledge Workshop. Goldberg, A. [ed], 1988. *A History of Personal Workstations*, New York: ACM Press, pp. 185-236.

Ref-4: Engelbart, D.C. and Lehtman, H.G. 1988. Working Together, *BYTE Magazine*, December, pp. 245-252.

Ref-5: Engelbart, D.C. 1990. Knowledge Domain Interoperability and an Open Hyperdocument System. *Proceedings of the Conference on Computer-Supported Cooperative Work*, Los Angeles, CA, October 7-10, pp. 143-156. (AUGMENT,132082,). Republished in Berk, E. and Devlin, J. [eds] 1991. *Hypertext / Hypermedia Handbook*, New York: Intertext Publications, McGraw-Hill, pp. 397-413.

Ref-6: Engelbart, D.C. 1982. Toward High Performance Knowledge Workers. *OAC'82 Digest*, Proceedings of the AFIPS Office Automation Conference, San Francisco, CA, April 5-7, pp. 279-290. (AUGMENT,81010,). Republished in Greif, I. (ed) 1988. *Computer Supported Cooperative Work: A Book of Readings*, San Mateo, CA: Morgan Kaufmann Publishers, Inc., pp. 67-78.

Ref-7: Engelbart, D.C. 1984. Collaboration Support Provisions in AUGMENT. *OAC '84 Digest*, Proceedings of the 1984 AFIPS Office Automation Conference, Los Angeles, CA, February 20-22, pp. 51-58. (OAD,2221,).

Ref-8: Engelbart, D.C. 1984. Authorship Provisions in AUGMENT. *COMPCON '84 Digest*, Proceedings of the COMPCON Conference, San Francisco, CA, February 27 - March 1, pp. 465-472. (OAD,2250,). Republished in Greif, I. (ed) 1988. *Computer Supported Cooperative Work: A Book of Readings*, San Mateo, CA: Morgan Kaufmann Publishers, Inc., pp. 107-126.

Ref-9: Irby, C.H. 1976. The Command Meta Language System. *AFIPS Conference Proceedings*, NCC Vol. 45, Montvale, NJ: AFIPS Press. (AUGMENT,27266,)

Ref-10: Watson, R.W. 1976. User Interface Design Issues for a Large Interactive System. *AFIPS Conference Proceedings*, Vol. 45, Montvale, NJ: AFIPS Press, pp. 357-364. (AUGMENT,27171,).

Ref-11: Engelbart, D.C. 1972. Coordinated Information Services for a Discipline- or Mission-Oriented Community. *Proceedings of the Second Annual Computer Communications Conference*, San Jose, CA, January 24,. Republished in Grimsdale, R.L. and Kuo, F.F. (eds) 1975. *Computer Communication Networks*, Leyden: Noordhoff. (AUGMENT,12445,).

Ref-12: Grenier, R., Metes, G. 1992. *Enterprise Networking: Working Together Apart*. Digital Press. (Very relevant general treatment; special emphasis given to "Capability-Based Environment" along the lines outlined in this paper.)

Ref-13: Parunak, H.V.D. 1991. Toward Industrial Strength Hypermedia, *Hypertext / Hypermedia Handbook*, Kerk, E. and Devlin, J. (eds), New York: McGraw Hill, pp. 381-395. (Provides very useful considerations relevant to requirements for the Open Hyperdocument System as discussed in this paper.)

Daniel Petre

General Manager
Workgroup Division

Microsoft Corporation

Groupware : Evolution not Revolution

Microsoft 1

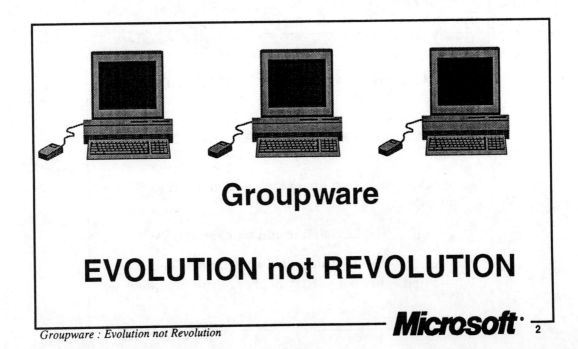

Groupware

EVOLUTION not REVOLUTION

Groupware : Evolution not Revolution

Microsoft 2

The Challenges of Groupware

◆ Definition of Groupware

◆ Where are We today

◆ What Needs to Happen to Facilitate
Enterprise Wide Groupware Utilization

◆ Planning Groupware Implementations

Groupware : Evolution not Revolution   ***Microsoft*** 3

What is Groupware?

"Workgroup computing promises to help groups and
organizations automate processes" - Summit Strategies
1992

"...groupware is the facility that allows a set of people
with common interests to use [network] resources and
processors in support of a common objective." --
Network Computing November 1991

"...it's a floor wax, it's a dessert topping..." -- Saturday
Night Live

Groupware : Evolution not Revolution   ***Microsoft*** 4

Categories of Groupware

◆ Products that help communications and sharing
information

◆ Products that help in creating and managing
information

◆ Products that help define and manage processes

◆ Products that are integrated environments or "shells"
that contain a variety of groupware functions

Groupware : Evolution not Revolution   ***Microsoft*** 5

Estimates of the Market for Groupware

PC networks

"20% of PCs connected in 1990 will grow to 50% by 1995" --Summit Strategies

"10 million PC networks installed by 1995" -- Intel

"more PCs connected in 1994 than PCs in existence in 1989" -- Lotus

Groupware

"from $11 million in 1991 to $600 million in 1995" - IDC

Groupware : Evolution not Revolution — **Microsoft·** 6

Groupware Today = Closed

Niche Group Memory Applications

- ◆ Serve a Purpose
- ◆ Limited use of Operating Systems Infrastructure
- ◆ Proprietary At Every Corner

Groupware : Evolution not Revolution — **Microsoft·** 7

Groupware Today = Limited

- ◆ **Not Pervasive**
- ◆ **Not Accessible by the Masses**

Groupware : Evolution not Revolution — **Microsoft·** 8

Groupware Direction = Open

- ◆ **Pervasive Facilities**

- ◆ **Accessible by all Users/Applications**

- ◆ **Supporting Facilities in the Operating System**

Groupware : Evolution not Revolution ——————— **Microsoft**· 9

Groupware Direction = Open

System Extensions
- ◆ Allow Client and Server Applications to Interchange Messages
- ◆ Access Replicated Data Structures
- ◆ Access Common Sharing Tools (Address Book, To Do List)

Development Toolkit
- ◆ Easily build Applications to be Messaging Centric
- ◆ Utilize "Standard" Development tools
- ◆ Be Open at all levels

Groupware : Evolution not Revolution ——————— **Microsoft**· 10

Taking Advantage of Groupware
Vendor Responsibility

Widely Propagated Facilities
- ◆ Enable all applications and Systems
- ◆ Available on all Systems (ie comes with the OS)

Incorporate Groupware in the Operating system
- ◆ User Interface
- ◆ **File Server**

Open
- ◆ Client Applications
- ◆ Server Applications

Groupware : Evolution not Revolution ——————— **Microsoft**· 11

User Implementation Where to Start?

Mainframe Database Strategies

- ◆ Historical choice of Application over Data Base architecture

- ◆ Long terms Data Management Issues

- ◆ Lesson learnt -

Defining Messaging/Groupware Strategy/Platform

- ◆ Integrated with Operating System Advancements

- ◆ Allows Selection of Best of Breed Applications

Groupware : Evolution not Revolution **Microsoft** 12

Roadmap - Implementing a Workgroup Solution

- ◆ Determine Company Wide Messaging Architecture

- ◆ Determine Company Wide Directory Service Architecture

- ◆ Integrate Current Disparate Messaging Systems

- ◆ Enhance Messaging Systems with Messaging Applications

- ◆ Develop next generation Business Application to be Groupware enabled

Groupware : Evolution not Revolution **Microsoft** 13

Roadmap - Implementing a Workgroup Solution

- ◆ Use any Development Tool to develop Groupware Applications

- ◆ Purchase only Apps that Utilize the Standard OS Shell

- ◆ Make sure Applications access OS Messaging APIs

- ◆ Each Application should be separate, best of breed

- ◆ Utilize non-standard Systems sparingly

- ◆ Watch for the Foxes in Sheep's Clothing

Groupware : Evolution not Revolution **Microsoft** 14

TRACK SESSIONS

TRACK 1:
Management and Cultural Issues

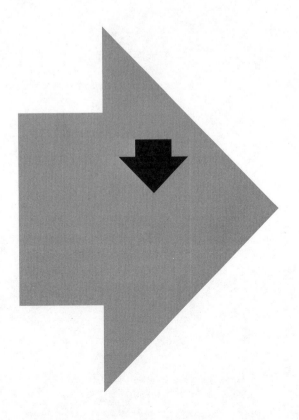

Groupware and Corporate Culture;
Panel Overview
By William J. Ryan
Susanna Opper & Associates

MODERATOR:
William J. Ryan, Partner, Susanna Opper & Associates Will has a diverse systems background. Over his 30 year career, he has been in technical, sales and sales management positions for major vendors, and a systems executive for two Fortune 500 companies. Will is currently a consultant specializing in groupware. Susanna Opper & Associates is a groupware consulting firm addressing the needs of groupware vendors, the distribution channel and the end user community.

PANEL PARTICIPANTS:
Donald Coleman, President, Ventana Corporation Donald has been president and chief operating officer of Ventana Corporation for three years. He brings more than 25 years of experience in management, systems design and computer product development gained as an officer, vicepresident and division general manager of NCR Corp.

Bob Johnson, Computer Associates. Bob has extensive experience in PC, Macintosh and mini computer platforms. He has managed the development and marketing of workgroup software, worked with numerous organizations on workgroup and network application issues, and received an award from the national computer graphics association for his contribution to the field of computer graphics.

Peter+Trudy Johnson-Lenz, Awakening Technology Peter & Trudy began working with computer-mediated communications in 1977 on EIES, the Electronic Information Exchange System. They coined the term "groupware" in 1978, describing it as the whole system of "intentionally chosen group processes and the software to support them." Their work on EIES covered the spectrum from software and groupware development to on-line group facilitation to sociological research and evaluation.

In 1986 Peter & Trudy founded Awakening Technology. They designed and developed their own tailorable groupware system and have provided a variety of on-line group seminars and workshops. These have been the laboratory for ongoing action research in the psychological, social, and cultural factors that contribute to high-trust, small-group, collaborative work and education via computer. Awakening Technology's current action research project focuses on computer-supported structure dialogues among people with diverse and potentially conflicting viewpoints on the challenging issues of our times.

Peter Olson, Vice President, MCI. Peter has organizational responsibilities that include planning for network systems, switch systems and business systems. He is also responsible for technical standards management and for the development of applications and the deployment of information technology to fully automate the business process. Prior to joining MCI in 1990, Peter spent 26 years in a variety of management and executive positions with IBM.

OBJECTIVES
This panel of users, researchers, consultants and developers will focus on the many impacts groupware has upon corporate cultures. The panelists will focus on adoption strategies and how to prepare a corporate culture to accept and nourish the seeds of team-oriented productivity tools. Other issues discussed include: how to measure the impact of groupware, implementation obstacles, and building internal momentum for groupware.

APPROACH
After the moderator's introductory remarks, a brief opening statement will be made by each panelist. Next, panelists will discuss and respond to a selection of questions from the list below. As time allows, the audience will be given an opportunity to ask questions.

QUESTIONS FOR THE PANEL

1. As we consider the impact and acceptability of groupware in our corporations, we wonder which comes first, a team-oriented organizational culture or the groupware itself?

2. What can be done to prepare an organization's culture so that groupware will be realistically implemented and its benefits achieved?

3. In what ways can we analyze an organization to determine how its existing culture will respond to the changes brought about by groupware?

4. If we start with the assumption that top management commitment is essential to the success of groupware, how do we take the pulse of the organization to measure the level of commitment?

5. How can we adopt an implementation approach that is compatible with the groupware to be used and the culture of the organization?

6. What changes, both positive and negative, will result from implementing groupware?

7. What suggestions do you have for dealing with the negative reactions to groupware?

TRANSFORMATION AND TECHNOLOGY

Peter Olson, Vice-President
MCI Systems Planning
2400 North Glenville Drive
Richardson, Texas   75082

1   TRANSFORMATION

Transformation leading to individual empowerment requires three simple components: culture change, organizational architecture and information technology.

2   CULTURE CHANGE

Positive attitude is the most important measure of an organization's culture. Positive attitudes create individual hardiness to economic uncertainty, competitive pressure, and difficult project demands. Positive attitudes do not just tolerate change but foster it at the pace required. Positive attitudes allow people to meet impossible challenges while maintaining balance in their lives. Positive attitudes are flat-out healthy.

Attitude is contagious. People are attracted to other people, projects, and organizations where there is a strong vision, where everyone is dedicated to working together, and where "good things happen". A source of positive attitude radiates energy outward in ever-widening circles and behaves like a magnet that draws others in.   The result is positive behavior change throughout an organization.

In preparing our corporate-selves for the 21st century the simplest objective is to create an environment that fosters, maintains and spreads positive attitudes.

P.S.

The 1991 morale index of the first organization at MCI to introduce groupware is 88% (compared to the historic range of 62% to 75%!!!) A tremendous reflection of positive attitude at work.

3   ORGANIZATIONAL ARCHITECTURE

Organizational architecture is based on the definition of clear roles and responsibilities (R&R), individual R&R ownership, and teamwork.

Roles and responsibilities are defined at the individual level and tied to both corporate goals and project objectives. This provides a clear sense of direction and a measure of progress.

Ownership reflects personal identity with the tasks. Individuals are encouraged to be innovative, to actively manage the task approach, and to remain open to change as a result of people interaction. Managers are asked to let go of control and influence paradigms and to view themselves as coaches of individual development and catalysts of organizational change.

Teamwork is the alignment of individual R&R to accomplish corporate goals and project objectives. Objectives are clear, resources are available for the necessary roles, and individual ownership is established and highly visible.

4   INFORMATION TECHNOLOGY

Information technology raises the visibility of positive attitude, roles and responsibilities, ownership, and teamwork, and becomes the high-speed circulatory system through which culture change and organizational architecture flow. The faster information flows and the more ubiquitous access becomes, then the faster culture change can occur.

Roles and responsibilities are communicated effectively when they are electronically accessible and tied to living organization charts and directory services. It becomes easier to identify a person responsible for a project role, to understand the project-specific extent of that responsibility, and to keep this person informed and involved.

Ownership is heightened when the results are highly-visible throughout the project team. Groupware provides simultaneous, information-rich, many-to-many communications that is not filtered through store and forward organizational hierarchies. People interact directly and have instantaneous access to shared information to accomplish project objectives.

Teamwork is raised to new levels because of the increased understanding of roles, the visibility of ownership and contribution, and the access to shared information.

INTEGRATING GROUPWARE INTO CORPORATE CULTURES

Presented By
Donald E. Coleman
President, Ventana Corporation
1430 E. Ft. Lowell Rd., Ste. 100
Tucson, AZ 85719

ABSTRACT

Ongoing studies covering the impact of groupware that supports collaboration in use at large companies have found that culture shifts occur. "Regardless of the culture, techniques can mold behavior," one study respondent said. "I have no doubt that if you designed software to successfully model the steps of basic problem-solving, you would gradually change the whole organizational structure," said another. The effects on meeting times and on project schedules are documented to be more than 60% with Computer Supported Collaboration groupware. The change in culture associated with such dramatic change in organizational behavior is a fact but not well documented.

1 INTRODUCTION

In order to understand how groupware effects corporate culture, one must consider the types of groupware available, the types of organizations being effected and the types of collaborative processing being utilized.

The desire to provide a more conducive environment for collaborative endeavors is not a new concern. Historically, group activities have taken place at meetings. Individuals gathering together to collaborate for a better outcome of a joint endeavor, seemingly, has always presented problems.

A quote from Benjamin Franklin during the Constitutional Convention, September 15, 1787, poses the same problem for today's collaborative efforts.

"When you assemble a number of people to have advantage of their joint wisdom, you inevitably assemble with those people all their prejudices, their errors of opinion, their local interests, and their selfish views. From such an assembly, can a perfect production be expected?"

Benjamin Franklin spoke of his impressions about cultural and organizational environments with regard to collaborative efforts. Groupware, especially interactive groupware that supports collaboration, can assist with the concerns addressed by Benjamin Franklin and experienced by today's managers. Until the creation of this type of groupware, project teams have used manual processes and tools in the meeting room. New groupware technologies will change the way we communicate and interact and will have a significant impact on organizational cultures.

2 CONDITIONS FOR INTERACTIVE GROUPWARE INTEGRATION

To understand the cultural integration of groupware one should become familiar with the type of groupware available and map the functions to organizational needs through three variables (see figure 1). The organizational impact may be determined by evaluating the type of groupware - data sharing/viewing or interactive, to be implemented into the type of organization - democratic or autocratic, and by determining where these collaborative activities will require individuals to meet - face-to-face or distributed environments.

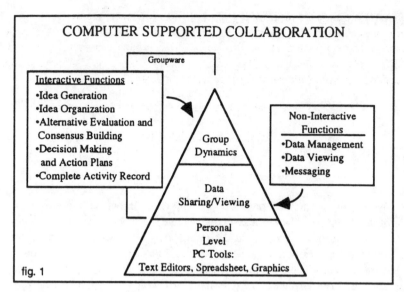

fig. 1

Types of Groupware

The evolution of electronic media in the workplace has a progressive history. Mainframes have been well imbedded into the major corporate cultures. Today, the PC has moved into these organizations with 60% or more of those PC's being networked. Today' networked PC's represent individual productivity enhanced by the ability to share data and send and receive communications between group members. The cultural impact of this type of groupware has been limited to change in individual work habits and behavior (see figure 2). Interactive groupware now offers collaboration support tools which extends the meeting process outside the meeting room - meetings at any time and in any place. This same interactive groupware dramatically modifies group behavior within the meeting room environment. The cultural effect of this type of software is more pronounced (see figure 2).

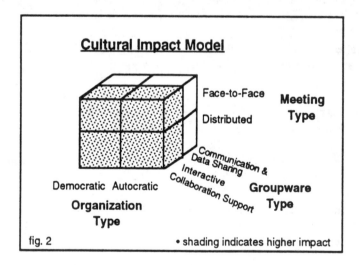

fig. 2   • shading indicates higher impact

For the autocratic and hierarchical organization that is accustomed to heavy filtering of information and centralized control of decisions, the major increase of useful information associated with groupware at all levels introduces pressure to de-centralize decisions and to increase group member participation on a much broader scale. On the other hand, for the more democratically oriented organization, this type of software provides more than information exchange between group members. The democratic organization embraces this technology as a desired "process enabler."

Types of Organizations

In an organization that is democratic, group relations are developed and information flows freely (see figure 3). This culture invites employee participation as a competitive advantage. The impact of groupware in this organization type is minimal as its major effect is to provide efficiency improvements. A challenging and unsuspected transition may await the <u>autocratic or top-down</u> organization, (see figure 3), implementing today's groupware. Empowering individuals at varying levels and managing communications and interactions in different-time/different places electronically creates process change an the organization. For these organizations a continual shift toward the democratic style is probable.

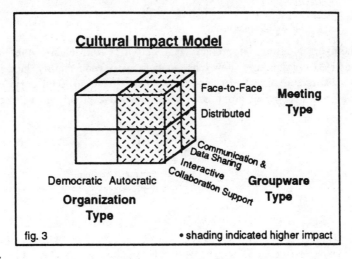

fig. 3 • shading indicated higher impact

Types of Meetings

People who come together over time for an activity are called a group. A group coming together at the same time is called a meeting. A group coming together over time is called a project, and projects coming together over time are an organization. In order for an organization to benefit and grow from its group activities, individuals, and groups, must communicate and interact. This interaction is enhanced by new groupware which allows the group to collaborate face-to-face or distributed, i.e.. different times/different places. Both democratic and autocratic organizations are familiar with face-to-face collaborative processes (meetings, (see figure 4)); neither have been familiar with distributed collaborative processes as a norm.

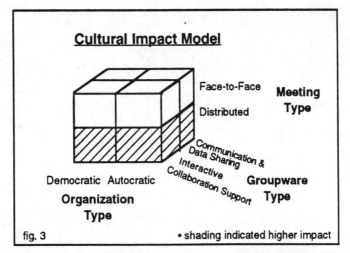

fig. 3 • shading indicated higher impact

Interactive groupware in the <u>face-to-face</u> setting produces increased information, increased participation, increased commitment to group actions, improved organizational memories, reduces the meeting count over a project's life, decreases project schedules and improves the quality of group decisions and actions. All of these effects tend to increase participation of the individual and dispersion of the decision making process. These are normally welcomed cultural changes, but they could be seductive "eye-openers" to the unsuspecting.

A new phenomenon occurs with interactive groupware. The asynchronous meeting, which is an outgrowth of the distributed environment (see figure 4), can now remove the barrier that "time" places on group work, and is an extension of the face-to-face meeting. Subgroup activities - information gathering, requirements definition, document preparation, evaluation of alternatives, and decision making can now be conducted at the individual's convenience within the allotted time frame for the project or task. This should lead to even more individual interaction and feedback, empowerment of the individual, and dispersed decision making. As a result, the cultural impact is potentially quite strong.

3 SUMMARY

Groupware technologies focusing on project team activities will change the organizational culture. Collaborative or interactive groupware, allow individuals to speak anonymously, increases participation to all group members, facilitates consensus and commitment, creates more powerful organizational memories, and improves the quality and quantity of group activities. Interactive groupware will have the most dramatic cultural effects.

Introducing Workgroup Technology
"How To Build Momentum And Success"

Bob Johnson
Computer Associates International
201 University Avenue
Westwood, MA 02090

INTRODUCTION

Introducing workgroup technology to an organization represents a significant challenge. Proponents need to consider group-related issues and new techniques to affect and assist the process of workgroup technology discovery. This paper discusses a number of issues that must be addressed in introducing workgroup technology to an organization, and suggests areas that corporate proponents and software vendors can focus on to enhance product penetration and use.

The basis for this paper is experience in introducing new technology, including workgroup products, to organizations. In addition, informal discussions and a survey of workgroup technology evaluators provided insight and ideas.

Summarized here are the findings. They suggest that if proponents consider "group-oriented" issues they can build positive awareness, alleviate concerns, focus interest and optimize group product evaluations. When proponents and software vendors reuse standard "standalone application" techniques in introducing workgroup technology to an organization, the evaluation process frequently remains undefined, the buy/no buy cycle lengthens, and trial use fails to focus on common tasks. In making observations and drawing conclusions it was apparent that many organizations suffer from this problem, and have the opportunity to replace "standalone" processes and procedures with new techniques when considering workgroup products. This situation has not been helped by software vendors who fail to provide marketing materials that address the "group" education challenge. Proponents need help, and outlined below are areas they can address on their own or with vendor assistance. Here, then are the key points of this paper.

KEY ISSUES AND CONCLUSIONS

1. One individual's support for the purchase of a workgroup product does not insure success. The group that will be affected by the technology cannot be ignored. The proponent responsible for introducing the new technology must effectively talk to the needs/concerns of the group, not just the individual. Vendors must also assist this effort with marketing materials that help focus on individual <u>and</u> group benefits.

2. Building awareness and acceptance among a group is an "internal education" process that helps potential users understand the impact and benefits of workgroup technology, and addresses their concerns. Education must be accomplished in an open, clear and understandable manner that addresses the "unknown" before it becomes an impediment to acceptance. When the proponent is convinced about the value and importance of the technology, the acceptance and education process has just begun. Current materials and techniques fail to carry forward the education process.

3. Each proponent faces various levels of perceived risk both individually and as part of a group. Vendor marketing efforts must address those risks to make a "champion" want to be a "hero." They must take the initial sense of "religion" held by the proponent and help that individual clarify product use, develop need understanding, focus on common tasks, build consensus, raise priority, and, manage the process of product discovery. Proponents generally have a good idea of why they are interested in workgroup technology but they need help to clearly transfer that understanding to others.

4. A product evaluation should be presented as a chance to "discover" a new way to work, not simply another evaluation. Materials should provide the process structure and move it along. They include organizing tips, lead evaluator responsibilities, defining evaluation scope, tasks and group size.

5. Qualitative benefits such as improved quality of work and decision making must be experienced to appreciated. They represent a "fuzzy" understanding trap that should not be overemphasized or relied on. Because workgroup technology affects a significant segment of an organization (a group), success at uncovering the bottom line of money saved and competitive advantage gained becomes more important. Proponents can use such information to counteract discomfort that accompanies the thought of doing certain tasks in a new way. Vendors should help focus attention on quantitative benefits by offering a flexible formula to calculate financial benefits.

6. Effective acceptance strategies need multiple prongs. Proponents should attempt to trickle down interest from upper management, bubble up enthusiasm from individual users, and, focus on a "middle exposure" program that identifies initial "niche" groups and applications. In addition, the electronic highway provided by the network should be used as much as possible to spread awareness, understanding and acceptance.

7. An overall challenge is to move the group's view of the technology from "neat" to "needed." Proponents can facilitate this by identifying those tasks that have are currently somewhat "painful" to accomplish, ones that rely on processes that are closer to being unacceptable rather than inconvenient.

8. Once initial acceptance and implementation takes place the proponent must work to maximize ongoing visibility and education to spread understanding, use, and implementation. Without this effort, individuals and groups will fall back into old habits and momentum will be lost.

9. Workgroup technology's momentum and success can increase if products offer "individually oriented" features and benefits that can stand on their own. This will help move group members to conclude that even if the group will not implement the technology they themselves would still gain enough benefit to justify a purchase. This workgroup "prospect beachhead" approach, can assist a product's long-term penetration.

It is possible to avoid the situation where a workgroup application does not get a fair chance during the initial process of awareness, evaluation and acceptance. It requires addressing group factors and putting some structure around the process. This mind set is significantly different from historically successful ways of bringing "standalone" technology to an organization. This paper will help you understand group issues and offer some techniques and strategies to boost the impact and acceptance of workgroup technology in networked organizations during the 1990's, the Group Decade.

INTRODUCING WORKGROUP TECHNOLOGY

LIMITATIONS OF CURRENT TECHNIQUES

Workgroup technology. For a category so young, it has prematurely grayed many proponents and software vendors. The reason for this is simple. Regardless of the product, workgroup technology requires new "group-oriented" programs and skills that can move a group of people through the process of technology discovery. Unfortunately, many proponents and vendors have difficulty understanding this fact, and believe that old "individual productivity application" or standalone techniques will succeed. Not true.

As group-oriented applications evolve, the days of simple software marketing and evaluation disappear, where you could influence one person to evaluate, purchase, and implement. The simple fact is that workgroup technology has difficulty coming in the back door to spread the old fashion "word of mouth" way, even if it has strong individual uses and benefits. Although individual features can provide a marketing beachhead, the technology affects other people, LANs, and WANs, changing the decision to innovate from a personal to group affair.

Marketing effectively to a group is significantly more complex than the "standalone" process. Think how dramatically different the complexity is of making a decision among five people versus making it yourself.   The proponents task is to keep the group focused on common tasks, objectives, capabilities and results. Without guidance and structure to the process, workgroup product evaluations slow down as they go in multiple directions, pulled by the dispositions and interests of individual group members.

Proponents should think about the following issues when introducing workgroup technology to their organization.

- -finding a critical application
- -building consensus
- -individual and group benefits
- -the evaluation as a process of discovery
- -maintaining the "criticality" or "priority" of the process
- -avoiding fears of the "unknown" becoming acceptance barriers
- -"pain level" of current procedures and processes
- -perception of risk
- -quantifying benefits

- The reality is that marketing workgroup technology is hard work

Bringing workgroup technology to an organization is a complex challenge, where proponents often find it difficult to focus on real, meaningful applications, and problems appear that delay the priority and consensus to embrace the new technology. At this point this paper will go through these challenges and offer suggestions that, when addressed, will enhance the likelihood of success.

AREAS NEEDING ATTENTION BY PROPONENTS AND VENDORS

Initial interest in workgroup products can often be termed "need awareness." This is the initial impression that there is some value or benefit in a particular technology. This impression is most often generated by advertising, articles or word of mouth. With workgroup technology the initial interest tends to be general rather than specific, such as a general feeling that reviewing documents among a group is somewhat difficult, and "there must be a better way." This means that the intended implementation and use is not that well thought out at the time of initial awareness.

Less frequently, there is a specific need shared by the proponent and the group exploring the technology. Initially having a specific need significantly increases group focus, otherwise, building an understanding, of what that need is, provides an important challenge.

- Take need awareness and turn it into need understanding

The "need understanding" challenge is to take a group from the state of mind that a particular technology is "neat" to the belief it is "needed." Important to individual and organizational success. The result of this cognitive metamorphosis moves the groups to a point of need understanding. That is, individuals now understands the technology as it relates to a "critical application" or use. They understand why it's important. That moment is when the proverbial light bulb goes off and they group members exclaim "we will use it for that," and "that" is important to the group as a whole.

- Help prospects find critical uses with three dimensional marketing materials

Introducing an organization to workgroup technology is a three dimensional challenge. The third dimension is the group. This additional dimension is difficult to address with two dimensional, product/individual thinking. Proponents must develop a process that allows people to clarify product use on both an individual and group basis.

One way that vendors can help this process is to provide materials that lay out a flexible framework for the individuals to self-select, with simple guidance, their own "hot buttons." A visual metaphor is a sphere. Visualize that an individual is at the center point of the sphere, free to move in the most appropriate direction. From the starting point the options are almost limitless and initial views are broad versus narrow. The sphere approach allows individuals to work their way outward moving first through individual tasks and benefits. Their journey then takes them into group tasks and benefits. A self selected path delivers them to the sphere's outer surface, at a point of need understanding.

Whereas this approach may seem to lack sufficient focus, the reality is that many individuals when first considering workgroup technology have only has a general idea of why they view it as interesting. Two dimension materials, such as a matrix are too rigid to optimize successful development of need understanding. The columns and rows lead down narrow alleys to very specific uses that lack a broader, organizational context, that often gives the use its "criticality." Other problems with two dimension marketing materials are inability to find the specific factor that spurred initial interest, or material organization and headings that are not defined or presented in a meaningful way. Individuals are left at a cognitive dead end because they are often not exactly sure of what was driving their interest, beyond the sense that it sounded like a "good idea." They are left no closer to understanding their need.

The reality is that people face a tremendous number of possible uses and tasks when a workgroup product's capabilities are laid out. By offering a flexible framework and some simple guidance or suggestions on how to mentally explore the technology you can lead them down a path to more quickly identify their critical application.

- Turn your champions into heros

Individuals vary in their need to avoid risk. When considering workgroup technology, an important factor that heightens the perception of risk is that it affects a group, not just an individual. This leads many people to shy away from the task of presenting the technology to others in the organization. Innovation is often a very personal thing. One person does it for himself, others see it, and, one by one embrace the idea. You can't often do that with workgroup technology. When group members explore workgroup technology, they quickly see that acceptance and implementation affects a group, all at once. This causes a negative reaction by some individuals, who want the risk to be personal, rather than subject to the possibility of negative reactions by others. The challenge for the proponent is to increase understanding to the point where the "risky" impression is replaced by the perception that there is an opportunity to be part of something positive where they can be a hero.

Proponents can change individuals perception to that of the hero by first giving them a strong sense of what is "in it for them," a clear, simple path to follow, and turning concerns into benefits.

– Work at multiple levels to build awareness and acceptance

To maximize the chances for workgroup technology acceptance, proponents should use a three-prong strategy. Each will, depending on the organization, bring out individuals who can be moved from being champions to heroes. The first, directed at upper management, the second at specific workgroups or task types, and the third aimed at end users. This combination of trickle down, middle thrust and bubble up will optimize a proponent's ability to identify the best ways to advance the workgroup technology discussion.

– Get upper management to delegate workgroup technology investigation

In dealing with some American corporations, one is struck by the frequent lack of strategic focus among employees. That responsibility is said to fall to upper executives. But reality reveals that often upper executives take too little time to think strategically, instead focusing on short term, revenue-driven objectives.

When you encounter less than optimal strategic focus, the upper prong of a triple-pronged strategy should get executives to delegate workgroup technology investigation. Only in certain cases will the problem be acute and visible enough for an executive to state that something must be fixed in a certain way. If a proponent brings a situation to the attention of executives, and is successful in getting the topic delegated for someone else to look into, positive things can result. Software vendors should treat the person to whom the executive delegates the task as a champion. As you turn them into a hero they have the added confidence of a certain level of upper management authorization to propose the technology to the rest of the organization.

– Identify shallow verticals and niche task workgroups

One possible view of the middle prong of a triple-prong strategy might be those individuals who act as network administrators. Unfortunately, their ability to lead application innovation is frequently reduced by their focus on keeping the network up, running, and expanding. A better middle prong is corporate workgroups or shallow verticals that have niche tasks assisted by the new technology.

Evaluate how certain tasks are currently accomplished to map out an approach to building awareness within shallow verticals. Initially, quick, informal analysis is required. Simply look for opportunities that would have maximum impact, before mapping out the entire discovery process.

- Understand individual benefits that can stand on their own

Product functionality can also lend a helping hand to a middle prong approach. If the product contains enough features that can be used for personal benefit, beachheads within shallow verticals can be obtained. An initial sale to a member of a shallow vertical, justified by individual benefits, will provide visibility and aid momentum towards group acceptance. That is why the sphere concept presents individual benefits first and foremost to the organization. If the individual product uses and benefits are strong enough, initial acceptance can be driven by that alone, while more general need understanding develops.

- Build up a groundswell of end user interest

The bubble up strategy attempts to leverage individual discomfort in completing various group-oriented tasks. Reaching end users with new technology can develop a groundswell of interest. The intent is to have requests to explore a new way of accomplishing tasks reach a certain "pitch." When this takes place, the risk factor on the part of those who respond to the buildup of requests, sometimes the network administrator, is reduced by their ability to fall back, in the event of any problems or negative feedback, on the adage of "you asked for it."

AFFECTING GROUP DECISIONS

Getting a group of individuals to the point of need understanding provides a good foundation for success, but many additional challenges face proponents from that point forward. The initial momentum and interest must be built and nurtured with a process that reduces the unknown, the perception of risk, builds consensus, clarifies priority, and quantifies the value to both the individual and the group.

- Help people understand what is in it for them

An individual group member is probably looking to satisfy some type of personal need when initial exposure to workgroup technology spurred their interest. The case is rare where a person participates for the sole reason of "benefiting the organization." The workflow or task completion pain level has most often reach a point acute enough for the person to seek relief. Success builds if that person perceives that their career and work will be enhanced by being part of the group pushing the new technology.

- Provide something for everyone else

Once the individual needs and benefits are addressed, proponents should focus on organizational benefits that are both important and tied to the individual. The key objective of organizational benefits is to bring a better understanding of the beneficial group changes offered by the new technology. That is, the affect on groups will be positive, not disruptive. Issues about the degree to which the way one works will be changed should be addressed head on rather than sugar-coated. Claims that the technology will enhance rather than change work process and habits fail to clearly address concerns and issues, leaving the "unknown" factor to cloud understanding, raise the sense of risk, and delay acceptance.

- Drive internal momentum towards consensus

Your heroes need help to build awareness, interest and consensus within an organization. The sphere approach has brought each to a point of need understanding. But unless the group or proponent is in position to dictate to the rest of the organization, the acceptance process has just begun. Those initial converts that have "religion" must be given a framework to successfully move forward.

Involving others in any decision is a two-edged sword. It complicates things as diverse opinions drive the process in different directions. But it is necessary to build consensus and avoid the perception among others that something is being pushed upon the organization without a chance for input. Granted, a proponent can simply throw consensus building to the wind and embrace the technology within ones own domain but that reduces the widespread "distributed" potential of workgroup technology. Therefore, a proponent should position the process of building consensus among groups as one of discovery. A discovery map should be conceived and offered to help move the organization from point A to point E beginning with smaller groups and gradually expanding in size and distribution.

- Present looking at workgroup technology as a process of discovery

Meeting new workgroup technology for the first time should be positioned as discovery. Individuals asked to take part of members of a team and the lead proponent represents the team leader or coach. Many organizations will require a thorough hands on evaluation of a new product. Materials should be put in place that help people who have not previously reviewed group-oriented products to insure that group specific issues are considered and addressed. Some suggestions that can be incorporated into the process provided below.

Laying The Groundwork: Workgroup technology enhances the way people work but also changes it to a degree. Suggest that key decision makers and individuals who will ultimately use the program are kept aware of the evaluation, and asked for input. Make sure they feel involved.

Task Types: Suggest that program performance be measured against a set of benchmark tasks, to make the review of features and capabilities meaningful. Make the tasks "real world" and choose ones that are common. Propose that, in order to stretch program flexibility, the number of tasks is not as important as the variety. The variety should have a unacceptable pain level caused by procedural bottlenecks, communication barriers, and work load conditions. Make sure the evaluation targets problem focal points that the technology may improve.

Follow The Leader: Suggest that one person be the lead evaluator. Lead responsibilities include knowing the timeline, current progress, defining individual responsibilities, and, communicating discovery status to others. This is a group effort. Successful discovery requires that the group be well informed and coordinated.

Group Size: Advise that the discovery be done by a group of manageable size. Physical proximity is important to allow face-to-face meetings. This should be balanced against testing an applications ability to support "distributed" tasks involving a group spread over multiple locations. A suggestion is to try to keep the group to seven or less.

Group Members: Teams take commitment, time and energy. Recommend that the lead evaluator select team members that represent a cross section of user types but make sure everyone shares an interest in exploring something new, and they all understand their specific, important roles.

Common Tasks: Discovery materials for group members should focus them on solving tasks that are repeated fairly frequently, common to a group or groups, and having a good degree of visibility. Current techniques for accomplishing the tasks should be viewed by the majority of group members as unacceptable rather than inconvenient, significant problems rather than irritations, and negative in terms of competitiveness and work quality.

The degree to which initial tasks considered for workgroup technology are common and problematic will have a major impact on acceptance, degree of implementation, and long-term value. Work habits will more easily be modified if the group has less vested in current techniques. Therefore, proponents should help the organization focus on common problems that are currently both painful and cumbersome to accomplish.

Evaluation Length & Steps: Suggest a set time period and steps. Deadlines are more critical with groups. Provide a framework to lay out evaluation steps, individual roles to avoid group fallout and insure availability. Have the lead evaluator communicate this, or the product evaluation can face bottlenecks that bog down the process.

Provide the evaluation team a framework to help organize the results and feedback. Depending on the product, the topics outlined below in five areas may be appropriate. In any case, provide a means for the results to be summarized.

Flexibility:

1. Adequate flexibility for various tasks.
2. Usable by users of various aptitude.
3. Ability to accomplish future tasks types.
4. Support for simultaneous work.
5. Allowance for task interruption and resumption.
6. Multiple ways of viewing the task in process.
7. Multiple roles for group members e.g. author/reviewer.

Communication/Coordination:

1. Task progress/status information on both individuals and group.
2. Automatic task notification of group members.
3. Task routing and completion notification.
4. Organization of task inputs and actions.
5. Communication between group members.

Audit Trail:

1. Organized audit trail.
2. Inclusion of names, dates and times.
3. Results summary.

Network:

1. Network bottleneck or performance impact.
2. Security support.

Overall Performance:

1. Level of task enhancement in accuracy, completeness and quality.
2. Reduction of task time requirements.
3. Technical support required.

- Use the product to build product awareness

Workgroup products are network-based. This fact provides proponents the opportunity to use the "electronic highway" to spread awareness, build product interest, and counteract the always present "new technology" barriers during the evaluation process. Whenever possible, the product should be a integral part of communicating evaluation progress and results. When group members use a product to communicate progress and results it becomes more familiar, comfortable, and are likely to develop positive impressions.

A good technique is to see if the product, upon installation, can make network users aware of its existence. This notification can be combined with an electronic reward offer for a certain number of individuals who take a few minutes to explore it. Vendors should assist proponents by providing this evaluation feature. However, this should not be done automatically by the program without some notification to the installer, that a notification option is available and can be selected. "Early explorers" represent additional "product-use beachheads" that the proponent can use to expand awareness and acceptance.

- Work to prevent the "whisper factor"

Workgroup technology is especially vulnerable to the fear that many people hold towards any type of new technology. Unless this factor is addressed by the proponent or lead evaluator, negative remarks can increase the number of misconceptions, that develop and spread to damage the likelihood of acceptance.

The negative effect the unknown factor can have on workgroup technology relates well to a line game we have all played in the past. That game worked by a line of people whispering a sentence from one person to the next until the last one in line said it out loud. The result, when spoken, was usually not even close to what was initially said. With groups the same effect can happen as people talk about how any new technology under evaluation will affect either communication or the way tasks are performed. The answer is to counteract the unknown factor with ongoing application "warm fuzzies."

- Build acceptance with "warm fuzzies" that address effects, advantages and control

Proponents should build visibility during the discovery process. This visibility must be more than a simple restatement that "we are looking at this." Instead, communication should help clarify workgroup affects, working techniques, group advantages, and how users maintains some level of control. This periodic, positive visibility will provide ongoing application "warm fuzzies" where individuals feel more and more comfortable with the idea of embracing the new technology. This objective can be assisted by vendors who provide supporting materials such as discovery guides, sample program documents, tasks or demonstrations. The result is to counteract new technology barriers and the whisper factor before they impede the acceptance process.

- Raise the priority level

The evaluation and purchase of workgroup technology needs constant attention to maintain an understanding of objectives and keep the process at a high priority in relation to other organizational projects. In most organizations, project difficultly and complexity is directly related to excuses and delays start and finish dates. Evaluating workgroup technology is somewhat complex and therefore, unless the priority is kept at a high level, this fact can lead to longer than expected evaluation cycles.

- Make sure initial exploration clarifies some quantitative value

Proponents can work raise the priority level of investigating workgroup technology by focusing on factors that are quantitative (time and money) or enhance competitiveness. General reminders of the pain level provided by alternative techniques for group tasks like workflow, communication, coordination, consolidation, approval and review can also be restated in various, systematic ways.

The restatement of priority-oriented "hot buttons" must be done periodically to maintain awareness and momentum. This is to prevent the situation where the group at some point scratches its collective head and asks "so why are we doing this?" For example, every week something that hits a priority type hot button might be delivered to at least some, if not all group members. It can include new ideas on product use as well as quantitative benefits.

Organizational success at building priority is directly tied to reaching additional group members beyond the hero. The concepts of using the product to sell the product, ongoing warm fuzzies, quantitative focus, and clear intent and visibility can help expand audience reach during the evaluation/implementation process.

CONCLUSIONS

Proponents who wish to build acceptance of workgroup technology within their organization must modify their techniques to build positive awareness, momentum, quantify benefits, organize the discovery process, maintain visibility, clarify objectives, and use the product build product acceptance. The evaluation, acceptance and implementation of workgroup technology is significantly more complex than that posed by standalone applications. If workgroup technology is to significantly expand its reach into organizations, this reality must be accepted and dealt with, rather than ignored.

The primary goals of leading the discovery of workgroup technology is to:

- Manage the process
- Build need understanding in terms of critical uses
- Focus on common tasks
- Provide a process of discovery and framework that helps the organization reach implementation consensus
- Keep the process visible, and, at a high priority level by measuring quantitative benefits

Software vendors have the opportunity to enhance success by offering flexible introduction/understanding tools, that organizational workgroup technology proponents can use to enhance acceptance and use. Few proponents have the time or inclination to design the internal marketing tools that address the third dimension of workgroup technology, the group. The key is for software vendors to understand this, and that the evaluation, acceptance and implementation process is significantly different than that found with standalone applications. Once this happens, they can develop and provide more meaningful information, programs and tools, to turn champions into heros and spread awareness and understanding with application "warm fuzzies." Without that focus and effort there are acceptance barriers that will appear due to the way individuals and groups react to, and accept new technology. This will unnecessarily delay the implementation and acceptance of workgroup technology.

Thinking about the needs and dynamics of both individuals and groups can have a dramatic impact to reduce the sense of risk, avoid the whisper factor, build momentum and consensus.   The results will accelerate the penetration of workgroup technology into networked organizations.

GROUPWARE IS COMPUTER-MEDIATED CULTURE:
SOME KEYS TO USING IT WISELY

Peter and Trudy Johnson-Lenz
Awakening Technology
695 Fifth Street
Lake Oswego, Oregon 97034

Groupware is computer-mediated culture. The more we use it, the more our organizational cultures will be shaped, reinforced, or broken by the cultural patterns groupware carries.

There are two keys to using it wisely: (1) a good fit with the organization's style and culture, and (2) a whole systems approach.

A GOOD FIT

Just like non-silicon culture, groupware comes in many varieties. Each system is an embodiment of the worldview of its designers, reflecting their beliefs about people and how we work together effectively.

No culture is inherently better than any other. Just as we need a rich diversity of non-silicon cultures, we need a diversity of groupware. What matters is whether particular groupware fits an organization's culture and whether it supports its growth in a healthy direction consonant with strategic goals.

The best groupware fits like a well-tailored suit. Not too loose, not too tight! Make sure the groupware design expresses a culture in which you want to live, work, and spend time. Murray Turoff said that within a computer communications system, it's as easy to program a dictatorship as a democracy (Turoff, 1982). In fact, democracy may be more challenging!

A WHOLE SYSTEMS APPROACH

Groupware is more than just software. Douglas Engelbart calls it a co-evolving human-tool system (Engelbart, 1988). In 1978 the authors first defined groupware as "intentional group processes plus software to support them" (Johnson-Lenz, 1981). Now they also include other cultural factors like purpose, myth, values, norms, and etiquette. The software can't hold all of that for us. People play an *essential*, irreplaceable role.

People bring meaning and purpose to the system. We choose our organizational purpose — what matters most to us, and we choose our means to that end. It is up to us to decide where to go and how to get there. The best groupware supports those purposes and the processes we use to realize them.

People shoulder vital responsibilities the software cannot carry. Teams work best in an atmosphere of trust where each person feels comfortable expressing himself openly *and* listens to others with respect. Team intelligence and creativity is greatest when each member brings all her knowledge to the meeting table (Senge, 1990), electronic or not. Human judgement and creativity will never be fully replaced by technology. Instead, the technology will free us to do what only we can do. Groupware can support or hinder shared purpose, an atmosphere of trust, and effective team work.

REMEMBER THE UNKNOWABLE

The part of groupware we can express in software is *explicit* culture. We can program anything we can completely describe, but much lies beyond our descriptive grasp, including much of ourselves and our interactions with each other. We are mysterious creatures.

Groupware is persistent. Once programmed, it shapes our actions whether we know it or not. When first learning to use it, we consciously acquire new skills which then become more automatic, almost unconscious habits. The spell of explicit cultural forms embodied in groupware can be so compelling that we often forget the vitally important implicit parts of the whole. Its persistence in digital memory often tempts us to forget that it has a dynamic, changing nature as well.

Groupware is not only the forms or processes we use to shape our interactions. It is the capacity to create, shape, and change forms as appropriate (Johnson-Lenz, 1991). The most effective groupware leaves room for the elusive, paradoxical, ambiguous, mysterious side of who we are and how we work together. And it helps us remember to keep choosing the most appropriate forms for our electronic organizational life.

Groupware is a living, co-evolving human-tool system.

LEARNING AS WE GO

Groupware is a frontier recently discovered. It will take us generations to explore and inhabit it fully and wisely. Looking back from the future, we will be as amused by today's state of the art as we are now by predictions in the 1950s of a worldwide market for computers saturated by six or maybe seven machines!

The first attempts to inhabit this electronic frontier reflect the industrial era patterns we already know well. The computer's power is perhaps the ultimate expression of the age of the machine. Looking back from the future, we will see these are natural starting points, but ones which leave out vitally important parts of the living whole.

The following examples from recent groupware history show we are already learning important lessons on our path to using it wisely.

THE COORDINATOR

Winograd and Flores' The Coordinator (Winograd, 1986) was inspired by a good idea which when implemented explicitly in groupware yielded surprisingly negative results. The idea still makes sense. Managers spend much time repairing breakdowns that occur when commitments are not fulfilled. Computers can manage and monitor requests for action, commitments, and their fulfillments very effectively.

With The Coordinator, two unanticipated consequences resulted from requiring all communications to fit within a framework of explicit commitments. First, many people resisted the system, refused to use it, and in some cases literally threw it out. Second, counter to the expectation that it would fit best in team-oriented cultures, The Coordinator worked best in traditional top-down, hierarchical organizations (Robinson, 1992).

By requiring all commitments to be explicit, any ambiguous, fuzzy, implicit, tentative commitments were excluded. By persistently reminding people of unfulfilled commitments, The Coordinator left no room for simply forgetting them or quietly letting them go. Clear and fulfilled commitments are vital to organizational success, but they become oppressive if taken to the extreme made possible by computer enforcement. Could the inevitable ambiguities and incompleteness in human relationships be just as important to vital team work as clarity and completeness?

Learning as we go, more recent versions of The Coordinator and its progeny are less rigid and more flexible. Each step takes us closer to a more mature, balanced way of designing and using groupware, broad enough to hold apparent opposites in creative relationship. On one hand, experiences with systems like The Coordinator teach about letting go of tight control. On the other hand, "open space" systems are teaching us not to let go too much.

OPEN SPACE SYSTEMS

"Open spaces" are inspired by the idea that people can self-organize into effective teams if given a chance. All that's needed is an open space in which to meet, raise topics, and organize into groups around subjects of mutual interest. Open space systems emerged as an alternative to fixed hierarchical organizational patterns. Open space computer conferencing is the most common form of different-time/different-place groupware. Examples include the burgeoning variety of Internet newsgroups, Lotus Notes topics, CompuServe forums and special interest groups, and most bulletin board systems.

Experience with such groupware is teaching us that open space by itself is rarely enough. Some guiding forms are needed. Harrison Owen's pioneering open space process for face-to-face meetings (Owen, 1987) has a clear beginning and end and follows a defined sequence of steps. Norms, etiquette, and communications skills we've used for generations to guide our face-to-face meetings are also necessary for effective computer-supported meetings. Otherwise, they tend to degenerate into "flaming" or sporadic, scattered activity without much purpose or focus.

Learning as we go, more recent groupware designs offer a dynamic balance between form and emptiness, holding and letting go. The authors have recently discovered groupware building blocks based on principles found in all living systems — rhythms, boundaries, containers, context, timing, and procedures. These tools are used to persuade rather than control group activity, to hold group life flexibly, with respect. Feeling for how alive and creative the flow of group energy is, they adjust the groupware forms to fit (Johnson-Lenz, 1990).

ROOMWARE

"Roomware," or same-time/same-place groupware, is now in the spotlight, helping groups be more effective and productive than ever before. Using IBM's TeamFocus groupware, The Boeing Company reports an astonishing 91% reduction in flowtime to decision and a 170% return on their investment (Post, 1992). Simultaneous parallel input and anonymity work together to encourage free expression of more ideas. Group intelligence increases as more knowledge is available to the group.

While yielding unprecedented gains, roomware also teaches us unexpected lessons about balance. While electronic meeting support tools are important, they can be ineffective and even dangerous without a skilled facilitator to guide the group. Research at the University of Arizona is discovering that anonymity is not always appreciated nor warranted. Groups are sometimes more satisfied with less "effective" approaches (Nunamaker, et al., 1991).

Anonymity encourages expression of minority viewpoints and is useful for issue formation. But it can be counterproductive during implementation when cooperation among potentially competing interests depends on mutual respect, trust, and authentic contact.

While speed is essential for many decisions, organizational governance often involves keeping some aspects of issues open, using opposing perspectives like stereoscopic vision to navigate more skillfully in three dimensions. Team, group, and organizational intelligence needs a diversity of viewpoints. The clarity with which those viewpoints are expressed and mutually understood is at least as important as the speed of decisions which are but stepping stones on the journey.

Paradoxially, for every groupware answer there seems to be an opposite answer which also contains some truth. The answer that fits varies from one situation to another. It all depends....

WISDOM CULTURE

Our worldview shapes our thinking and actions. It evolves as we learn from feedback. Since Newton and Descartes our actions have been shaped by a mechanistic worldview. Inspired by our success with machines, we saw the universe, the world, and ourselves as machines. Control over ourselves and nature was idealized. For every question we sought a single, right answer.

The scientific and industrial revolutions unleashed more human creativity than ever before, but with disastrous results for our environment, organizations, and even our very social fabric. Naturally, our first designs for groupware reflected this worldview. The Coordinator took the answer of explicit commitments to its logical, mechanized extreme, trying to *make* groups work. While that fits in some situations, it fails in others.

In an attempt to step outside the mechanistic worldview, other designs have taken a polar opposite approach. Open space systems aim to *allow* groups to work by letting them self-organize. While this also fits some of the time, it also fails in others.

A new worldview is emerging which is not the polar opposite of the mechanistic worldview, but rather includes it as an instance of something larger (Johnston, 1991). This new worldview embraces the power of both making things happen and letting things be, our need for explicit forms as well as the fuzzy, ambiguous, and creative unformed. It is based on values, rather than mechanism. Our survival as a species depends on groupware that reflects and embodies this new worldview.

Choose groupware that fits your culture. Remember the dynamic interplay of people and software. Leave room for mystery. Pay attention to feedback, and keep learning....

REFERENCES

Engelbart, D. 1988. Bootstrapping and the Handbook Cycle. Presented at CSCW '88, Conference on Computer-Supported Cooperative Work. Portland, Oregon.

Johnson-Lenz, P+T. 1981. Consider the Groupware: Design and Group Process Impacts on Communication in the Electronic Medium. *Studies of Computer-Mediated Communications Systems: A Synthesis of the Findings*, S.R. Hiltz and E. Kerr (eds). Research Report #16, Computerized Conferencing and Communications Center, New Jersey Institute of Technology.

Johnson-Lenz, P+T. 1990. *Rhythms, Boundaries, and Containers: The Creative Dynamics of Asynchronous Group Life.* Research Report #4, Awakening Technology, Lake Oswego, Oregon.

Johnson-Lenz, P+T. 1991. Post-Mechanistic Groupware Primitives: Rhythms, Boundaries, and Containers. *Computer-Supported Cooperative Work and Groupware*, S. Greenberg (ed.). London: Academic Press. pp. 271-294.

Johnston, C. 1991. *Necessary Wisdom: Meeting the Challenge of a New Cultural Maturity.* Seattle, WA: ICD Press.

Nunamaker, J.F., Dennis, A.R., Valacich, J.S., and Vogel, D.R. 1991. Information Technology for Negotiating Groups: Generating Options for Mutual Gain. *Management Science* 37:1325-1346.

Owen, H. 1987. *Spirit: Transformation & Development in Organizations.* Potomac, MD: Abbott Publishing.

Post, B.Q. 1992. Building the Business Case for Group Support Technology. *Proceedings of the Twenty-Fifth Hawaii International Conference on System Sciences.* Washington, DC: IEEE Computer Society, pp. 34-45.

Robinson, M. 1992. Computer Supported Co-operative Work: Cases and Concepts. *Proceedings of Groupware '91.* Utrecht: SERC.

Senge, P. 1990. *The Fifth Discipline: The Art & Practice of The Learning Organization.* New York: Doubleday.

Turoff, M. 1982. Management Issues in Human Communications via Computer. *The Management and Evolution of Electronic Office Systems*, R. Landau, J.H. Bair, and J.H. Siegman (eds.). Norwood, NJ: Ablex Publishing. p. 255.

Winograd, T. 1986. A Language/Action Perspective on the Design of Cooperative Work. *Proceedings of the 1986 Conference on Computer Supported Cooperative Work.* New York: ACM.

Capturing Organizational Memory

E. Jeffrey Conklin, PhD
Corporate Memory Systems, Inc.
8920 Business Park Drive
Austin, Texas 78759
512 795 9999

Abstract

Contemporary organizations have only a weak ability to remember and learn from the past, and are thus seeking to gain the capacity for "organizational memory." Networked computers might provide the basis for a "nervous system" that could be used to implement the capacity for organizational memory, but the technology (software and hardware) must provide for easy capture, easy recall, and learning. Moreover, for an organization to augment its memory it must shift from the currently pervasive document- and artifact-oriented paradigm (or culture) to one that embraces *process* as well. This process-oriented paradigm requires a new kind of computer system which integrates three technologies: **hypertext**, **groupware**, and a **rhetorical method**. Groupware allows the organizational record to be built in the course of everyday communication and coordination. Hypertext provides the ability to organize and display this rich informational web. And a rhetorical method, such as IBIS, structures the memory according to content, not chronology. In addition to the computer technology, a **shift in organizational culture** toward an appreciation of process is required to implement organizational memory.

1 What is organizational memory?

By "organizational memory" I mean the record of an organization that is embodied in a set of documents and artifacts. Note that collective memory (i.e. the pooled memory of individuals) is excluded from this definition. Organizational memory has become a hot topic recently due to the growing recognition that it appears to be so thoroughly lacking in contemporary organizations. (As M. Graham as pointed out in Graham 1991, organizations in the first half of this century were not so amnesic.) The problem is not a scarcity of documents and artifacts for the organizational memory, but rather the quality, content, and organization of this material. For example, an effective organizational memory would be able to answer such often asked questions as "Why did we do this?" and "How did such and such come to be the case?" Rarely is this possible now.

Organizational memory is perhaps most clearly missing in industries where large numbers of people engage in the design and construction of large, complex systems over long periods of time, such as defense, aerospace, utilities, pharmaceuticals, and telecommunications. Engineering organizations in these industries have serious limitations in transferring previous learning to current problems. The design rationale of large, complex systems is thoroughly and systematically lost. Such phrases as "reinventing the wheel", "going in circles", "having the same discussion over and over," often heard in large engineering organizations, point to a striking phenomenon: while organizations don't seem to learn or remember very well, this limitation was, until recently, regarded as normal and inevitable.

2 Why is organizational memory so poor?

It is thus highly desirable to increase the capacity of organizations to remember and to learn. According to our definition, this means capturing more of the "documents and artifacts" of the organization in a way that they can be effectively recalled and reinterpreted. The growth of networked computers for all phases of information work promises to provide the "nervous system" that would support this increased capture and reuse.

However, within the current "artifact-oriented" paradigm (see Figure 1), the only thing we have to capture is that in which we are already drowning: more "data", documents, and artifacts. These are not what is missing from organizational memory -- what is missing is the *context* (i.e. the sense or rationale) that lay behind these documents when they were created. In short, organizations fail to capture any record of the *process* behind the artifacts.

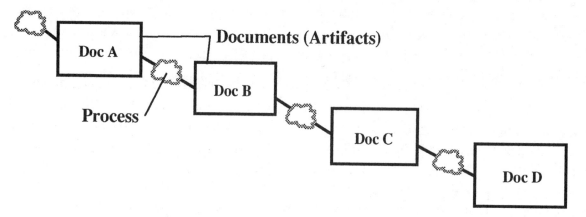

Figure 1: In the artifact-oriented view of work the artifacts (such as diagrams, documents, letters, reports, etc.) are the focus of management attention. Moreover, tools and methods are solely for the production and modification of these artifacts. The process by which this work is done is regarded as secondary.

This is because the current paradigm of work focuses almost solely on the artifacts (or products) of work. For example, in software engineering it is the documents (e.g. requirements, functional specifications, designs, code, etc.) that really count -- the process of creating and revising these artifacts is only recently receiving any attention.

This artifact-oriented paradigm is slowly giving way to a new "process-oriented" paradigm (see Figure 2). Organizations are finding the artifact-oriented way of capturing work to be too impoverished a model to support the complexity of work in the information age. They are turning to a richer, more complete view which embraces the messy (and sometimes chaotic) nature of *process*. No longer ignored are the assumptions, values, experiences, conversations, and decisions which lead to and constitute the context and background of the artifacts. Still, few tools exist for supporting and capturing these elusive but critical aspects of design and action.

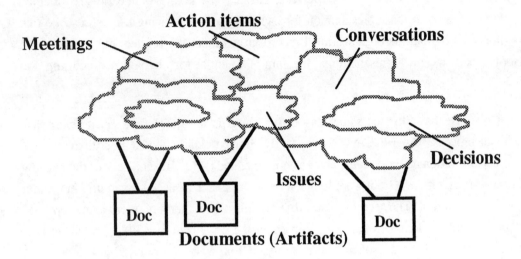

Figure 2: In the process-oriented paradigm there are still artifacts, but they are seen as being no more important than the interactions between *people*.

3 Tools for organizational memory

The most immediate barrier to capturing more of the process of work and making it part of organizational memory is that it seems to present an insurmountable and onerous documentation burden on the people doing the work. *The key to overcoming this perception is to shift the notion of capturing the process data from being an additional documentation burden to "tapping into" the flow of communication that is already happening in an organization. Not surprisingly, this shift is also a shift from an artifact-oriented to a process-oriented perspective.*

For example, one might argue that electronic mail (email) already provides a kind of organizational memory for organizations which use it, and that it does so at no additional documentation cost to the members. While email does indeed have an acceptably low capture cost, it does not provide an effective record because email messages are strictly personal and are stored that way, and because the email record, even for an individual, is so poorly organized and structured that it cannot effectively augment even an individual's memory. So, with email the cost of capture is low, but so is the value of that record for organizational memory.

During 6 years of research on gIBIS (in the MCC Software Technology Program) we learned much about the necessary characteristics of a technology that could provide acceptable capture *and* recall costs for organizational memory (Conklin & Yakemovic 1991). This technology embraces hypertext, groupware (or computer-supported cooperative work), and a rhetorical method. In addition, we learned that computer technology is not enough -- the organization itself must embrace the technology adoption process as part of a larger shift in the corporate culture.

The first element of the computer technology is **hypertext**, because the nature of the process-oriented approach is essentially non-linear, so the representation for capturing and organizing it must also be that rich. Moreover, as time goes by and the organizational record grows more convoluted and complex, the unlimited flexibility of hypertext as a representational medium is essential for ongoing restructuring and summarization.

The second element is **groupware** -- for the same reason that email is a natural first step toward easy capture of organizational process. An MCC/NCR field study showed clearly that it is critical that the technology of used to capture rationale be as transparent as possible, and that it must closely fit the existing practices and tools of the organization. Groupware by its very nature is not focused on capture, but rather on communication and coordination. The secret to capturing organizational memory, then, is to "tap into" the existing flow of process interactions between the members of the organization, and to crystallize this, ongoingly, into the key elements of the organizational memory. Groupware can provide the medium for organizational dialogues which, because they occur via the computer, create a computable record of semi-structured documents. The ability then exists to manipulate, distribute or share this information and intelligence throughout the organization or team, effectively and ongoingly creating a memory and learning tool.

The third element of the technology for capturing organizational memory is the use of a **rhetorical method**, or conversational model, for structuring the conversations occurring with the technology. The reason for this is twofold. A simple rhetorical method provides a structure for discussion of complex problems which can immediately improve the quality of the dialogue process. The IBIS (Issue-Based Information System) method (Kunz & Rittel 1970) provides this kind of process improvement. Secondly, such a model provides a basis for structuring the conversational record which is not simply chronological (as in an email or bulletin board type system). For example, conversations in the IBIS method are structured according to the *issues* being discussed. This provides a *content-based* indexing structure within which the cumulative record of the organizational process is preserved and organized.

The technology for organizational memory must, at a minimum, incorporate hypertext, groupware, and a rhetorical model. But this computer technology is not sufficient to create an effective organizational memory. While the technology must be very good and the user interface transparent, the *organization must also shift* to making capture and use of organizational memory an important and natural practice. This shift towards a process-oriented paradigm and culture requires organizational commitment, and it is the most challenging part of establishing a capacity for memory and learning in an organization.

However, this shift is consistent with the trend already under way in organizations toward quality, customer service, reducing time to market, and all of the other forms of process awareness and improvement. Thus, a new symbiosis is emerging between the human and technological aspects of work: tools for organizational memory and learning can support and maintain a beneficial culture shift, and the culture shift highlights the value of the new tools and promotes their use.

Corporate Memory Systems, Inc. is now offering CM/1, which combines software and consulting technologies based on our MCC gIBIS experience. CM/1 is a groupware system developed to support organizational learning, better decision making, and collaborative work group productivity.

References

Conklin, E. Jeffrey and KC Burgess Yakemovic. 1991. A Process-Oriented Approach to Design Rationale. *Human-Computer Interaction,* Vol. 6, pp. 357-391.

Graham, Margaret. 1991. Notes on Organizational Memory: Practice and Theory. Unpublished Xerox PARC working paper.

Kunz, W. & H. Rittel. 1970. Issues as elements of information systems. Working Paper No. 131, Institute of Urban and Regional Development, University of California at Berkeley, Berkeley, California, 1970.

Groupware '92 Telecommuting Panel
Panel Chairperson Position Paper
J. Robert Martinson
President and CEO, Futurus Corporation

Over the past several years, an increasing number of companies
have implemented telecommuting programs. Managers within
many of these companies have found that telecommuting is an
economical conduit for doing business. If you, the session
attendee, have questions regarding telecommuting and whether or
not you should implement this technology in your company, we
welcome you. In today's session, the other panel members and I
will provide you with background information on telecommuting
as well as some of the "do's and don'ts" we have learned in our
years of experience with this technology.

Basically, there are three types of telecommuters: The first, a
full-time telecommuter, has a desktop computer system at home
provided by the employer. This type of knowledge worker tends to
be in marketing and sales and he uses his computer primarily for
contact management, word processing and electronic
communications with fellow workers at the office.

Another kind of telecommuter travels with a notebook or laptop
computer and communicates with his corporate office workers
while "on the road." Traveling telecommuters have the same
application needs as the home-bound telecommuter but obviously
they require the portability of smaller computers without
sacrificing power. In essence, telecommuting provides these
workers with a "microcosm" of their offices by duplicating their
desktop tasks (word processing, contact management, electronic
mail, etc.) into a portable environment.

Finally, there is the part-time telecommuter who spends a portion
of his time working in his home (or at another location) and some
of his time in his office. This kind of telecommuter needs
frequent face-to-face interactions with his fellow workers but he
also needs a quiet work environment to complete tasks that
require a high degree of concentration. Examples of part-time
telecommuters include software development engineers who
create code, manuscript writers, and consultants.

Telecommuting has become so popular in recent years because employers are recognizing the benefits of telecommuting. When workers telecommute from home, companies are able to save significant amounts of money because office space is no longer needed for those workers. Telecommuters can be strategically located in the same geographical areas as their customers -- regardless of where the employer's corporate offices are. This is a major competitive advantage because when a company's sales and support staff are geographically close to its customers, then that company has the ability to respond much quicker to its customer needs.

A few years ago, I visited a bank outside of Portland, Oregon in a somewhat remote area. The bank was a large Novell customer and the bank's MIS Director needed immediate technical support for their NetWare network. After receiving a phone call from the MIS Director, Novell Corporate in Provo, Utah sent an electronic mail message by modem to one of its support engineers in Portland. Because the support engineer was a telecommuter and located very close to his customer, he was able to solve the problem much more efficiently than if Novell had sent personnel by plane from Provo to Portland.

When considering whether or not to implement telecommuting, employers should know that they will incur initial capital expenditures for hardware and software installations for their telecommuters. However, the benefits of increased productivity and quicker response time to customer needs far outweigh the initial installation costs.

In my experience as a manager, I have given some of my employees the opportunity to telecommute either full-time or part-time. What typically occurred as a result is that productivity increased significantly. When workers are offered alternative work environments that suit their needs without sacrificing output, then managers can expect to see greater employee work satisfaction and loyalty.

The most important aspect of a successful telecommuting program is that a corporate-wide electronic mail system is in place and that this communications link is really used by everyone in that company. Remember, the whole idea of telecommuting is to provide the remote worker with all the tools he needs to be "part of the team" even though he is geographically elsewhere.

Electronic mail has the addressing functionality required for text-based communications between workers. It is important to note that the telephone alone is not an appropriate vehicle for all communications because of the fast paced schedules workers have -- people are not always at their desks to receive calls. Also, text messages (as opposed to voice mail) are more apt to be accurately understood by the receiver. Therefore, electronic mail is the necessary transport mechanism for telecommuting in order for companies to recoup their initial hardware and software investments.

I also suggest that companies consider an electronic mail package that offers additional groupware functionality for their telecommuters. For example, some groupware packages have personal and group scheduling along with phone message centers. This type of software extends the telecommuter's connectivity with his office -- the telecommuter can function with the same ease outside of the office as he does inside the office.

One objection regarding telecommuting has frequently surfaced: Employers believe that they will have a difficult time managing their telecommuters because supervisors cannot actually see what their subordinates are doing. This can be easily overcome if the employer has installed a groupware package that allows the manager to monitor the telecommuter's personal schedule, to-do list accomplishments, and phone messages. As a result, the manager can see how productive the telecommuter is out of the office.

Another objection is that certain industries are not well suited to telecommuting. For example, an architect who travels cannot carry an expensive and heavy plotter with him to print blueprints. Therefore, the architect must rely on overnight delivery services which lengthens the time for him to complete his projects. However, the architect can still benefit from telecommuting by using his modem and portable computer to obtain his electronic mail, phone messages and appointments from his office when it is convenient for him, not only when his assistant is available for a voice call.

Telecommuting in the future will be very exciting, and the growth of this technology will parallel the growth of WANs (i.e., moving more data much faster). This growth will take the form of dramatic improvements in software. For example, using his palmtop computer equipped with a video input/output device, an analyst would take environmental measurements of an area and transmit the video results to his lab thousands of miles away.

Also, ISDN (Integrated Services Digital Network) will play a role in the future of telecommuting because it will increase the connectivity capability of telecommuting in an economical way. Telecommuters will undoubtedly benefit from ISDN's multiple channels which provide simultaneous voice and data transfers.

In conclusion, I would like to challenge smaller and mid-sized companies who think that telecommuting is only for the "Fortune 500" type of corporations. I encourage you to take a closer look at telecommuting and how it is a viable option for reducing your overhead -- especially when telecommuting is paired with an effective electronic mail and groupware solution.

"Meanwhile back at the Ranch"

A presentation on telecommuting

By Thomas C. Cross - Chairman

CROSS COMMUNICATIONS COMPANY

1881 9TH STREET - SUITE 302

BOULDER, COLORADO 80302

303-444-7799 FAX 444-4687 BBS 444-9003

Abstract

Telecommuting, or working at a site, neighborhood work center, and time-independent way with the aid of information technology, is on the increase. Time is what we have so little of. Telecommuting does not give us more time but more control over time. Its claimed advantages include reduced office overheads, increased productivity, and various psychological and environmental benefits. These claims are assessed here, together with several problems which face the implementers and participants of telecommuting. The main problem appears to be the isolation of the telecommuter. Rather than real isolation, the notion by employees that once you start telecommuting you can never, ever work in the office again. This area will require further study of the socio-communication needs of remote work. As you will see, telecommuting is not for everyone but everyone can do it.

Telecommuting - an Introduction

Today in 1990, with an estimated 25 million people currently working at home at least part-time (Atkinson), futurists forecast that 45 million people on all business levels will be telecommuting two or three days each week by 1995 (Hellman). Thus, telecommuting in its many forms is emerging as a significant social "quiet revolution" and economic trend; and the "electronic cottage," foreseen as the evolving home setting for office work, is becoming one of the more talked-about business office scenarios.

Prospect for the growth of telecommuting could be even rosier, however, given the current pace of technological developments in the computer and telecommunications industries, and the fact that 60 percent of American jobs currently involve information handling (Wiegner and Pairs). Electronic Services Unlimited (ESU) of New York estimated in late 1980s that some 7.2 million workers were potential telecommuters, although only about 100,000 people were engaged in formal and informal remote work programs for 450 companies (Gluckin).

What is telecommuting? - Not at home but anywhere, anytime

Telecommuting means performing job-related work at a site away from the office, then transferring the results to the office or to another location.

Telecommuting usually supplements other office activities, although many jobs can be handled entirely in this way. Among the popular terms that cover telecommuting, one hears: remote work, home office work, telework, location-independent tasks, and "home-distributed data processing" ("Viewpoint"). Control Data Corp., Minneapolis, calls its program "homework" (Slatta) and federal agencies refer to telecommuting as "industrial homework or *flex-place*."

hough telecommuting may assume that telecommunications or other technology is required, however, the role of technology is only to enhance or supplement the work activity not to create it or replace it. That is, to say that telecommuting has and can occurred without technology. The role of technology is like a dishwasher to give the home worker more time, more control, and other facilities to perform work more efficiently and more effectively.

Telecommuting or remote work is often performed on a personal computer or terminal that is connected by modem and telephone line to a mainframe computer for processing the work. Remote work is also often performed and processed on a stand-alone microcomputer (also known as a personal computer or PC). The completed task is transmitted over telephone lines (uploaded) to the company's computer facilities, or the disks on which the work is entered are carried or mailed to the office. The work is then entered into the company's main computer.

When remote terminals are connected to an organization's communications network, employees can use electronic mail or groupware conferencing software systems to call up electronic files or database information onto their screens. The results can be transmitted back to the office, to a supervisor, or deposited in the appropriate file. Any number of people can be working remotely for an organization at the same time. Electronic mail and groupware conferencing software systems are highly strategic telecommuting tools that are explained later.

Telecommuting can be handled in other ways as well. Reporters have telecommuted for years by sending their stories to newspaper "city rooms" via telephone, teletypewriter, or facsimile equipment. Sales representatives and customer service employees, when calling on clients, regularly connect their portable computers to the clients' telephones. This has enabled computer users to reach their company's computers and query them on inventory information, product availability, current prices and delivery schedules. Salespeople can then use the same linkage to place product orders and perform other related functions.

Telephone conference calls can be used to communicate information (work) and to coordinate activities, as well as to avoid costly face-to-face meetings. Facsimile or FAX machines can move documents anywhere in the world in seconds. Electronic mail and online conferencing systems also allow participants to send their work directly to other people or place it in electronic files which others can access. Today, telephone lines are not required for sending and receiving information. Mobile cellular telephone, paging systems, and new broadcast technologies make it possible for the employee to work from virtually any location.

Thus, for all practical purposes, remote work can be accomplished at the time and place one chooses, then moved via voice, data, FAX, image to the person or place needing. Depending on the nature of the material and the transmission it requires, the site could be a telephone booth, an online meeting, a client's office, in or out of town, around the country or world. This way of operating is often called operating asynchronously or being "time- and site-independent."

Telecommuting does not necessarily mean working only at home, nor using a computer or telecommunications technology to link the office and home. Offices located at any distance: from headquarters, at a neighborhood or satellite work center, hotel room, airplane, or telephone booth can be telecomuting sites. Surprisingly, the telephone booth is the second most frequently used place for work outside of the office. The following are some, but not all of the options:
- o Phone booth
- o Home
- o Restaurant
- o Customer premises
- o Car
- o Hotel/motel - "space shuttle"
- o Airplane/boat
- o Satellite-neighborhood work group centers

In addition, there are a number of ways to transfer the work product, including bicycle couriers, to accomplish the task.

It should be noted that not all office tasks lend themselves to telecommuting. Jobs are inappropriate which require employees to frequently interact face-to-face with associates or clients, to handle products, or to manage resources (microfiche or paper) not electronics based. The principle behind telecommuting is the old "cottage industry" concept where workers do piecework at home then turn it in to the employer, but the current telecommuting trend is influenced by many other factors. Primary among them is the decentralized work process of the automated office, and the management's need to process ever-increasing amounts of information. Currently, decentralization of office work has put most office tasks in the machine, and the machine-now located almost anywhere-enables employees to access databases, graphics, electronic mail, work processing and other software system applications. However, understand that even the most traditional face-to-face jobs such as bank tellers are being automated to the point where the worker could work remotely.

Overview of the telecommuting community

Who telecommutes? Because there are many ways to work remotely, the telecommuter can be an employee or consultant on the payroll of one or more companies, a freelancer who contracts for agency projects, or entrepreneurs who run businesses from home. Executives who carry their "electronic briefcases" home in the evenings and on weekends telecommute. Online participants who transfer the results of their work to central files or to other people telecommute. Table 1 shows actual and predicted preferences of employees for work locations in the USA, in terms of percentages of the total "white collar" workforce, over the period to the end of this century.

Table 1. Distribution of employees (%) among work locations

	1990	1995	2000
Go to office	40	40	30
Split time between office and home	30	25	20
Work "on the road" anywhere	10	15	20
Work at neighborhood work center	10	10	15
Work at home	10	10	15

Sources include *Wall Street Journal*, Honeywell Information Company, Cross Market + Management Company, Bureau of Labor Statistics

The changing roles of management and technology

The manager in today's rapidly changing office environment is faced with an increasing number of technological and personnel issues. New organizational and management styles will be required to handle these issues before telecommuting becomes widespread in today's homes, satellite or neighborhood work centers, or office building settings. This section focuses on the changes in business operations and management that support telecommuting in the new environment, and on the technologies that are required for effective remote-work programs.

Communications technology influences organization hierarchy

Technology is creating a number of major structural changes in traditionally organized "smokestack" organizations. One change is to reduce the number of management levels between corporate presidents and line workers in large organizations. Several factors influence this reduction, as follows.

(1) The computer permits businesses to respond faster and more effectively to clients' needs. Before the days of automated office technology, upper-level decision makers in large, authoritarian organizations tended to receive delayed, distorted, and inaccurate product/market information after it passed through many management levels. For example, FAX machines allow people to send information in seconds rather than overnight. This is increasing the "organizational velocity" of companies.

(2) The computer facilitates business information flow by allowing all managerial levels to access it easily and without its being handled or set aside by intervening layers of personnel. Electronic mail, voice mail, and cellular telephones is making more and more information both available to you and hundreds of other people in the organization simultaneously.

(3) The computer enables managers and telecommuters in different parts of a plant, or in company offices dispersed throughout an organization, to access information and communicate via electronic mail. Thus, the manager does not need to be at any particular location, inside or outside of corporate walls, to communicate or receive required information. As a result of the widespread access to necessary online information, management perspective has shifted one step farther from the traditional, centralized office. This notion of "shift work" will disappear altogether in a global 24-hour day trading environment.

In the future, companies will reorganize around technology, using technology as human, financial, and other company resources are developed. The term "virtual management" coined by Cross refers to the concept of a department of technology that creates, coordinates, and facilitates all forms of technology not just information technology.

Satellite or Work Group Centers emerge

Management's new time-place perspective has produced a number of business trends. The trend most relevant to telecommuting is the development of small, independent business operating units (IBUs). IBUs can comprise a single person or a large group and can be located at the corporate office or almost anywhere else. In fact, they need not be located in any physical proximity to one another. These operating units generally comprise professional or informations workers such as engineers, clerks, floor managers, lawyers, and other worker categories.

Electronic communications technology allows IBUs to work with any type of task force, ranging from an Equal Employment Opportunity Commission (EEOC), to committees concerned with toxic waste, benefits, new products, sales, or education. IBU personnel may work from home, from the office, "on the road," or at a resort.

The concept of the satellite work center is being rapidly developed in Japan. In fact, according to research at Cross Market + Management Company, has found that the Japanese are "far ahead" of the United States in telecommuting. Many Japanese companies such as NEC, Mitsubishi, and Espon have developed satellite work centers where small work groups perform work as though they were "down the hall" from their superiors, colleagues, and other associates. The work group center will, for many companies and individuals alike fill the role of the "real" office work environment.

Groupware communications become key

The subtle but important point is groups within the organization are able to exchange information and work with one another- and in effect, telecommute. As shown in Table 2, manager's spend an enormous amount of time, in fact almost all of it, telecommunicating. Telecommuting workers are considered by many to be "communications-intensive" in nearly every aspect of their work activity. For example F International's communication costs account for one third of the cost to the client.

Furthermore, as the numbers of decentralized information workers at distant locations grow (internationally and across many time zones), the need for effective, efficient technology and management leadership becomes imperative. Managers will spend more time guiding, coordinating, motivating, and educating their employees than managing in the traditional sense. It should be noted that professionals require more interaction with supervisors than do other employee levels.

Table 2. Present and predicted distributions of working time in typical "white collar" jobs

---

Present manager's distribution of time
o Communications/information transactions
  -meetings   30%
  -telephone   20%
  -travel   20%
o Seeking information transactions
  -desk work   30%

Future manager's distribution of time
o Communications/"communinections"/people interfaces   40%
  -meetings
  -presentations
  -audio conferencing
  -video conferencing
o Travel   10%
o Seeking information transactions/system interfaces   50%
  -dictation
  -telephone/voice mailbox
  -groupware conferencing
  -viewdata-data systems
  -decision support systems-assisted "thinking"
  -computer-assisted retrieval
  -document management

Present manager's distribution of time
o Gathering information/communications - "communinections"
  -researching, manipulating
  -data entry and proofreading
  -document management   20%
o Interpreting information
  -telephone, mail   35%
  -away from desk   30%
  -waiting for work   10%
  -absent   5%

Future non-manager's distribution of time
o Information analysis   10%
o Information transactions   50%
  -project research
  -meeting coordination
  -arranging travel
  -budget tracking
  -purchase order tracking
  -researching/conferencing
o Administration coordination/support for meetings
  -telephone, mail   35%
  -absent   5%

Source: Cross Market + Management Company
Note: Telecommuters generally spend the same proportions of time as do non-telecommuters in various activities; however, where they spend that time is different. In F International, over the whole organization, people work at home less than 40 percent of the time.

(c) 1992 - CROSS COMMUNICATIONS COMPANY

Technologies associated with telecommuting

Telecommuting equipment

There is a wide range of technologies available for telecommuting and for what is expected to be the supportive system behind telecommuting. Some of the most important technologies are:

"NO-TECH TOOLS"

However, before getting started by assuming that you will need a "clone" of your office in your home before you start telecommuting, take a look a what office tools you use today. Many of the tools that can be used to telecommute require NO technology. These "no-tech" tools include:

- o Meetings
- o Yellow pads
- o Calculators
- o Staplers/supplies - we forget we need these too
- o Micrographics
- o Dictation
- o Answering machines

When you begin to consider the role of technology and how it can help you, take a "step a a time" approach before moving ahead. That is, some technologies work for some and not for others, while other technologies can take more than a week or two to get used to. Allow people and the technology to get to know one another. **Remember, technology will be blamed for everything, e.g. getting fat or smoking too much.** Consider the following issues carefully:

The home working environment

- o Access - lost on your desk but which desk
- o Storage - keeping it from getting lost
- o Communication - courier, FAX, modem
- o Quiet - understand waiting time

Some of the of the other physical environment issues include:

Home support system
- o Comfort heating, cooling, lighting, humidity
- o Ergonomics-sitting, standing, moving about
- o Psychological-visual, convenience, flexibility

"HIGH-TECH TOOLS"

Some of the technologies most suited to telecommuting are:

Any technology can telecommute - "high tech" tools

- o Personal laptop computers
- o Facsimile
- o Electronic mail
- o Voice mail
- o Communications - cellular, pagers, phones

Remember technology will likely be used to increase time for other activities including aerobics and other "lifestyle" time activities. Consider the following "lifestyle" considerations:

    Personal lifestyle support system
    o Parking
    o Exercise
    o Daycare
    o Offices - "windows"
    o Power lunches
    o Social

If we consider the many facets of why people work, telecommuting because it increases significantly the amount of time and "freedom" workers have. And, the more there is, the more they will do it.

"Home smart home"

The telecommuter's immediate work environment is the workstation, its furnishings, and surroundings. The blending of these elements, and their ergonomic characteristics, have considerable effect on the remote worker's performance. A recent National Bureau of Standard's study cites the design of the workstation and its job features as being essential to VDT-based work. The study also points up the need to accommodate work areas to the physical differences and preferences of workers and indicates the following.

o The individual should have some say in the design and selection of furnishings and equipment, as well as an opportunity to personalize the workspace.

o Special, separate devices should allow the user to adjust the height of work surfaces, keyboard level, source documents and terminal screen.

o Chairs with high back rests and adjustable inclinations are recommended.

o Forearm/hand supports should be available for keyboard work, and keyboards should be movable.

Computer specialists from the Department of Computer Science, Concordia University, Montreal, Canada, are designing an "ideal" professional remote workstation for the home (Goyal and Desai). It is expected to provide a personal information system and a secure communications gateway for information, and to integrate all normal office functions for the telecommuter. This facility will simply appear to be another office workstation to together office personnel who interact with the remote worker.

All vital home management information will be readily accessible on the computer, and the device will be used to control appliances, energy, and resource consumption. In addition, the computer will enable the worker to access various information services such as consumer networks and banking.

Whether the telecommuter works at company headquarters, in a work center, or a home setting, office space design flexibility is especially important because manufacturers are currently producing equipment that increasingly reflects changing technology and upgrades the power and versatility of the worker. "Make is really flexible and easily changeable," advises a workspace design specialist, because "some very responsive clients do change the configuration of workstations as many as 10 times per year of the work demands it (Haas)."

In any organization, goals of office efficiency and cost figure highly in choosing technologies. Companies that consider telecommuting must balance their potential costs as they apply to both "hard" dollar and "soft" dollar savings.

While people remain the most important factor in any telecommuting environment, the significant aspects of using telecommuting equipment include:

(1)   easy installation and compatibility with the existing data processing equipment,

(2)   choice of appropriate type of personal computers from among the many available,

(3)   security and archival issues, i.e. protecting both the users and corporation from loss,

(4)   communications technologies involved,

(5)   networks to be used-the advanced "highways" where information travels-current telecommunication systems are hardly more then "dirt roads" when compared with the systems becoming available.

Telecommuting comprises a complex set of systems for which understanding of which tool to use, and when, is required. Furthermore, a company that telecommutes needs to plan for system expansion and increases in numbers of people using the program, as well as in the productivity of those who are already telecommuting.

The integration of management and technology creates a balance between human resources and the computer "power tools" that assist people in accomplishing their tasks. The following equipment provides some of the advanced systems with increased capabilities:

o computers,
o copiers/graphic scanners,
o telephone systems,
o networks,
o smart desks and chairs,
o electronic typewriters/word processors,
o mail systems,
o electronic file cabinets,
o buildings/cars/homes.

The telecommuter's ability to reach out and communicate through these devices in one force behind his/her ability to work. The business community expects that as international standards are applied in the computer and telecommunications industries, these systems will communicate using the same language.

The ability to communicate from many sites has spurred users to use their equipment in increasingly more mobile work conditions. Equipment mobility, in turn, affects the physical needs and design of the office environment-possibly more dramatically than it affects the telecommuter. When office designers can truly address the increasing speed and efficiency of office work, as will as the psychological work environment, productivity may increase yet further.

For more than 300 years, offices have been created by interior designers and architects rather than the people who understand office functions and procedures. This has resulted in work environments becoming poorly suited to today's office tasks, and has also fueled general interest in telecommuting from other settings. In other words, technology can now allow workers to relate to the office *electronically* rather than *physically*. As a result, people increasingly realize technology can bring the job to them. They have the option of not moving where the job is.

It must be noted that technology often places pressure on managers and staffs. In many instances it forces them to:

o improve productivity,
o reduce "information float"- "time-to-decision cycles,"
o increases their effectiveness, efficiency, and spread,
o decentralize business activities,
o integrate information systems.

Each of these areas can be significantly improved through appropriately integrating and applying telecommuting programs. In addition, remote work can offer the "pressures" office worker a way to perform effectively at home, instead of in hostile conditions. The technologies which may make the greatest impact will be those, like telecommuting, that *complement* rather then *replace* the office workplace.

Conclusion

There is no standard approach to integrating telecommuting technologies. Whereas many remote workers use nothing more than their kitchen table and telephone, others require elaborate video/computer/telephone automation systems with robots. As the reader has probably noted, this paper emphasizes communications. This is because, in business, people, whether upper-level managers or payroll clerks, spend much of their time communicating. For the telecommuter, isolation appears to be the most limiting factor. Thus, the type of communications system used for remote work may be the most important factor to consider when designing an effective telecommuting system.

In summary, bringing together management commitment, an ergonomically sound environmental setting, and appropriate technology, provides the most suitable business conditions for telecommuting.

REMEMBER TELECOMMUTING IS NOT FOR EVERYONE

BUT EVERYONE CAN DO IT!

We at Cross Communications would like to work with you in developing and expanding your telecommuting needs.

Cross Communications develops innovative inbound and outbound communications software specifically for the telecommuter.

"Telecommuting through an Electronic Information Marketplace"

Written & Submitted by:
Marc Stiegler
General Manager of AMIX, an Autodesk Information Business Systems Unit
(415)856-1234

We are all very aware of, and some of us have personally witnessed within the last several years, a major shift in corporate structure -- the downsizing or "flattening" of the organization. Economic decline is certainly a major impetus to corporate trimming, but the emergence of new technologies has also driven downsizing.

There's a large chicken or egg question here. Which came first, the technology or the downsizing? As a result of downsizing, new technologies have been forced to emerge that will help workgroups adapt faster to changing demands and coordinate activities. Conversely, as collaborative technologies succeed, they drive the downsizing of companies. Groupware allows work environments to function more smoothly without the need for middle management to direct and coordinate. Every member of the workgroup becomes involved and responsible for the coordination of the entire group.

One of these emerging technologies that will have a significant impact on the way future work environments evolve is an "electronic information marketplace." Through means of a PC and modem, people can work independently yet be linked to the workgroup. The term "telecommuting" normally evokes visions of an employee working out of her home and communicating to the main office through her computer. But now we are going to see a new breed of telecommuters -- the information providers who may act as consultants as much as they act as employees.

As companies undergo downsizing, there is an increasing need for outside consulting services and information sources. No more are there employees or the time to rummage through volumes of information sources just to find one answer. What's wrong with the existing communication mechanisms like the phone? Well, just think of the last time you got put on hold for five minutes or were transferred to three different people only to find out they cannot help you. Electronic information marketplaces can easily bring the consultant into the organization without the pains of finding the "needle in the haystack."

MIT's Thomas Malone talks about coordination technologies in the September issue of Scientific American (page 128, "Computers, Networks and the Corporation"). He talks about how networks and coordination technologies have begun to restructure the way businesses conduct transactions. Companies are faced with cost decisions to either make the products or services themselves or buy the goods from outside sources. Malone predicts that information technologies will create an overall shift from internal bureaucracies to using outside contractors.

The overhead is typically high when contracting outside sources. Even prior to entering into contract, a company has to find out who to call, explain the parameters of the job, check references, do some comparison shopping and negotiate contracts. Once they have hired someone for services, there is maintenance and coordination of the projects. While there is less coordination required if the jobs are done in-house, the company does not benefit from the efficiencies of competition that come with a free market.

With the development of information technologies, like an electronic information marketplace, there is less coordination required for both internal and external activities. The effect of an electronic information marketplace will be the lowering of the cost to coordinate work done by outside consultants. For instance, I could send out a specific consulting request with predefined parameters and budget to a particular individual or to the entire group within a market. I would then receive replies bidding for the job. In one location, I can read each consultants' resume, comments from previous buyers and descriptions of their products or services. I can quickly do comparison shopping and reach a decision.

How does this differ from just picking up the phone and calling a consultant? Well firstly, not all of us can reach the well-known experts. How many of us can actually pick up the phone and get through in one attempt to computer industry figures like Esther Dyson, Mitch Kapor or Patricia Seybold. And secondly, perhaps the Esthers and the Mitches don't always have the best answers. An electronic information marketplace opens the door for smaller consultants to directly compete against the more well known and established. Through new technologies like this, little time is wasted in searching because the consultants come to you when you post your information request.

Because electronic information marketplaces can reduce the cost of finding resources and information to complete tasks, companies will rely more on outside sources rather than internal production. What we will see is the dispersal of the organization -- people not having to be in one central location in order to conduct transactions. Using these information technologies, people will be telecommuting either as employees or contracted consultants.

Of course there is always the fear of any new technology "replacing" humans. Does telecommuting eliminate face-to-face interaction? Will technologies like electronic information marketplaces drive corporate downsizing until there is no one left? The answer is "no." Innovations in information technologies will actually bring people together and create meeting opportunities that otherwise would not have been possible. Electronic information marketplaces will never displace the individual because it's the individual that makes up the marketplace.

Workflow Software: A Primer

Authors: Ann M. Palermo and Scott C. McCready
IDC/Avante Technology, Inc.
5 Speen Street
Framingham, MA 01701

Workflows exist in many forms. The type of workflow that will be successful in a give application depends upon the degree of structure which is inherent to the process, the types of activities native to the process, the number of people involved in the process, and the areas within the organization of where these people are located.

Through the years, companies have built into their organization design more and more levels of management. They have also increased the number of products and services they must support. In many cases, what has been created is a bureaucracy which is choking itself. The time to get products out the door has expanded, and acceptable levels of customer service and support have declined.

Few would argue that technology, and more particularly, business automation, has made huge strides. Despite the avalanche of new technologies, there are still limits in the scope of business problems that computer technology can address.

The early 1980s were full of promise in terms of what office automation would deliver. The vision of the paperless office became a recurrent theme of futuristic discussions. But the 1990s have arrived and we appear further way from a paperless office than we were in 1980.

Certainly we have some very useful tools today that we did not have in the early 1980s, such as CASE and CIM, which address discrete problems. What we do not have is a general set of tools which are flexible enough to manage a wide range of business objects and processes -- sort of an "open computer integrated manufacturing environment." In our opinion, this is the challenge for workflow software to fulfill.

Workflow Definition

Workflow software is the tool which empowers individuals and groups of individuals in both structured and unstructured environments to automatically manage a series of recurrent or non-recurrent events in a way which achieves the business objectives of the company. Simultaneously, workflow software should allow feedback to management ensuring them the opportunity and ability to extend or modify those business processes as the business environment changes.

Certainly, this is a very high level definition, but we believe that workflow software is all inclusive. Workflow software is the largest fundamental shift in automation in the past five years. Its implications go far beyond image technology, transaction processing systems, document management, or office system technology. In fact, workflow software will become so pervasive that it will for many companies become the front-end to all their strategic business processing applications.

Origins of Workflow Software

FileNet Corporation has been a strong advocate of both the concept and product of workflow software since 1984. Workflow software has its initial historical roots firmly planted in the world of image technology. Image and workflow have become nearly synonymous for a simple reason: to at minimum mimic, and at best improve, formerly paper-based processes. Image system technology represents the first attempt at interfacing our existing computer systems with the paper flooding in from the outside world. The challenge that image system technology must meet is to provide an economical method of effectively processing information external to the organization and selectively interfacing with existing investments in office automation.

To place external information into a financial context for a moment, IDC/Avante estimates that US business will spend over $1 billion to design and print paper forms in 1991. Since paper forms are currently the only generally available method for most companies to control how their external information arrives at their doorstep, $1 billion may seem like a relatively small price to pay. IDC/Avante provisional estimates suggest that the cost of processing these forms , however, exceeds $60 billion. If you add up the cost of the entire document lifecycle, the total cost to US companies is likely to exceed $100 billion.

Simply digitizing a document and displaying that document on a workstation does not necessarily improve the equation. It does not change the flow that the document is required to complete in order to be efficiently processed. Having a digital copy as opposed to the original paper allows a company to introduce the concept of workflow software. What workflow software can achieve is to:

- reduce the number of individual steps to complete the processing cycle of the document,

- minimize the complexity of the tasks for the individual operators, reduce the amount of human intervention, and

- shorten the processing time.

The basic nature of image technology has allowed us to eliminate the gaps among people, machines and documents. The challenge for workflow software is to address the remaining issues:

* High-level workflow software is necessary since the cost of building workflow applications are quite high when using conventional development environments, which are commonly made up of low-level software tools and structures.

* Workflow software must be flexible enough to address the unstructured nature of many processes. This would include the ability to handle exceptions, interruptions, and improvisations. It must be easily reconfigurable to reflect a change in business conditions or new competitive environments.

* Workflow must address the need to link isolated areas of automation.

* Workflow software has to address the gap between businesspeople and technologists.

Types of Workflow Software

There is an old axiom in the computer world which suggests that you cannot automate an activity that resists definition, therefore those activities which cannot be reduced to a limited number of prescribed activities simply cannot be automated. In some cases, a set of tools are delivered to bring some degree of management to the "undefinable" process. On the other hand, many companies have erred on the side of establishing too many policies and procedures as a foundation for automating certain processes, forcing structure where it need not necessarily exist. The result is a stagnant environment for creative beings and no effort to solve business problems which by their very nature resist definition.

Since the policies and procedure strategy does not work in solving all our business problems, it is equally naive to believe that one form of workflow software is capable of doing the same thing. As a result, IDC/Avante believes that there are at least two discernible types of workflow software -- production or transaction-oriented workflow software, and ad-hoc workflow software.

Production Workflow Software

Production or transaction-oriented workflow software is used in business systems which are by there very nature definable and governed by a series of policies and procedures. This includes such areas of business as mortgage loan processing, insurance underwriting, or even new employee hiring. The basic premise is that the company has developed a prescribed set of policies and procedures for these activities to occur which results in an acceptable level of business risk and return. These activities are completed day-in and day-out with little or no variation in how the work is processed. Even within these structured processes, exception processing occurs and workflow software must not only streamline the definable everyday activities, it must also handle those exceptions which occur infrequently.

As a result the workflow software for this kind of environment must be robust. It should resemble conventional programming languages in terms of debugging tools and text editing. At the same time, it should also be relatively easy to change as business systems respond to competitive pressures and customer needs.

The users should have their work presented to them in such a way that they do not have to be concerned about the source of their work or who it is going to next. The tasks at hand should be the operator's sole concern, and even those tasks should be made more simple. The system should automatically establish host communication sessions for the operator if that is what is required for them to process a particular case or document. In addition, if an operator needs information from an outside database or is required to complete a response to a customer inquiry, all the tools necessary for this to occur should be part and parcel of the workflow script.

As a users, evaluating this type of workflow software package can be difficult. The following list of questions, although not exhaustive, are some of the questions a potential purchaser of transaction oriented workflow software should pose to a vendor:

Can the workflow procedures access objects which are external to the workflow routine?

Can applications outside the workflow procedure access objects within the workflow application?

What hooks are inherent to workflow that are available to the user?

Can the workflow leverage MS/Windows Dynamic Data Exchange (DDE) facilities? or similar functions such as Digital Live- Links?

Transaction processing automates well-defined complex business processes. Workflow software for this environment should offer a correspondingly sophisticated and feature rich set of development tools. To now, these tools have included a language specifically designed to automate workflows.

For example, the FileNet Workflo language includes a rich set of calls and intrinsics which can be called for such complex activities as automatically opening a host session, sublaunching another application, retrieving information from an external database, indexing an image from a host database, to the simplest functions such as image scanning, display, rotation, and printing. The result is a dramatic shortening of the application development time and a significant improvement in the time and effort required to update the application.

AD-HOC Workflow

There are activities within all large companies which defy definition and thereby limit the use of policies and procedures to govern their outcome. Developing a strategic plan, reviewing a new product design, or perhaps simply designing a new corporate brochure are some which come to mind. Certainly all these tasks involve an identifiable group of people and there may be some scheduled deadlines. But, individual responsibilities may change almost daily, deadlines can slip, the creative people may not work well on Monday and by Friday they're burned out.

Ad-hoc activities are very time intensive to manage and coordinate. Communication problems quickly arise when people are unsure of their responsibilities. Typically, ad-hoc environments are short-lived, unstructured, and vary greatly in complexity. As a result, the end users must be able to construct and modify the workflows of ad-hoc processes. In its most simple form, workflow layers an added level of co-ordination over and above the familiar automation tools such as document processing and spreadsheets.

Ad-hoc workflow software should be able to quickly define the people involved in the project, assign appropriate roles and work, determine the deadlines and appropriate methods of communication, and what dialogue facilities are needed for different portions of the project. The result is a coordinated effort with flexibility built in, as opposed to forcing a structure on a process which resists structure. For individuals, workflow software frees them from the mundane tasks of manually tracking who got what and when. .. and if they got it did they do their part and send it to the next person. Ad-hoc workflow software manages the co-ordination of tasks in the background.

The Elevator Definition

So, on your next skyscraper elevator ride, when the next person asks you what workflow software really is. you have a pat answer. Workflow simply provides a language and tools for design of work processes. Workflow provides links between islands of automation. Workflow allows a company to deal with exceptions. Workflow offers high level programming for reducing development costs and time. And, finally, workflow is the first method for coordinating functions and actions that are completed by people, machines and paper (or its electronic equivalent).

METHODS FOR SUCCESS
WITH NEW WORKFLOW SYSTEMS

James H. Bair[1]
Competition Technology Corporation
1797 Austin Avenue
Los Altos, CA 94024

ABSTRACT

New workflow systems require the same methods for effective use as does groupware. These methods must ensure user acceptance of the system and provide work-system design. User acceptance can be achieved by involving users in the work-system design -- the technology cannot be installed with user training alone. Users can be involved through "participatory design" which employs workshops, interviews and questionnaires. User needs are uncovered while simultaneously engaging users in identifying the necessary work changes and learning about the technology. Workflow systems, especially those with optical filing, necessitate the significant change from paper manipulation to computer assisted work.

1 THE COMPONENTS OF SUCCESSFUL WORKFLOW SYSTEMS

Workflow systems must bring together management, end-users, and customers into a process that ensures the effective utilization of workflow technology. There are three components to this process.

- Technology: computer and communications systems used by people working together in offices such as document & image management systems, electronic mail & shared filing systems, data-base applications, and groupware (e.g., Lotus NOTES).

- Utilization: the technology will be used in a way that gives the organization ROI (return-on-investment), competitive privilege, integrates end-users into the design and ongoing success of the system, and provides increased support of management's objectives.

- Methods: proven techniques for involving end-users and management in the design of the work-system based on Total Quality Management and communication science. The work-system includes how the technology is used, the activities and processes that have to be changed, and the ongoing support requirements.

---

[1] PHONE: 415.968.7592

2 METHODS FOR PARTICIPATORY WORKFLOW DESIGN

The methods include a set of workshops, interviews, questionnaires, and analysis tools that an organization uses to ensure that workflow systems are effectively utilized. The end-users, managers and customers of a new system participate in its design. This results in (1) acceptance by users and the rest of the organization and (2) valuable application design guidelines. For example, a workflow product from FileNet or Hewlett-Packard (called "AIM") provides hardware, software, and a high level language for specifying workflow. The methods would provide input to the workflow specification such as work roles, tasks, series of tasks, types of documents, and types of actions. The methods are constructed so that respondents feel involvement in the workflow system. Their issues, concerns and needs are captured in the process of defining the work-system.

New workflow systems are likely to change the way users work together, not merely replicate the current processes. Changing work processes and activities requires an understanding of the current work-system and then consciously "re-engineering" to take advantage of the technology. The methods gather the collective insight into work objectives, the inhibitors to achieving objectives, how the new technology can remove inhibitors, and the action plan, going far beyond traditional systems analysis. The methods analyze the key success behaviors including team membership, communication patterns, workflows, document life cycles, information sources, and customer relations.

The methods use a team approach in the following steps:

   1) Clarifying work objectives for teams

   2) Identifying the inhibitors to achieving objectives

   3) Determining how new workflow systems can remove the inhibitors

   4) Developing an implementation action plan

A work-systems design project can include the appropriate combination of the following methods. Which methods are used depends upon the level of effort a user organization is willing to invest. In general, the more methods used, the more likely the success of the workflow system.

   • *Key-product tracking* maps the flow of work units such as documents or forms as they are processed by one or more workgroups. It quantifies the labor required to produce the product.

   • *Communication network analysis* measures the amount of communication between individuals according to media -- meetings, phone, paper, e-mail, teleconferencing, etc. It also shows who needs to communicate with whom and how that can be done more efficiently.

   • *Interviews* provide a broad range of information from mission, goals, objectives, and requirements to specific design issues such as workflow bottlenecks. They are crucial to obtaining the involvement of management and users. They also are designed to help educate interviewees.

   • *Workshops* bring together the users of the workflow system and their management. Group process techniques such as Fishbone diagrams for cause-effect analysis, PARETO charts, and paired-weighting comparison lead to a consensus on inhibitors to faster, more efficient workflows. Current workgroup efforts are examined to see how the workflow technology could be used to better meet workgroup objectives.

- *Questionnaires* are employed to survey an organization for user needs, management issues, and predictors of work performance. A series of attitude questions can uncover important attitudes and values and correlate them with self assessments of performance.

- *Shadow function analysis* uncovers hidden, low-value uses of time which cause delays and increase labor costs. The most common kind of shadow function is not being able to reach the right person for needed information in a reasonable time. They are hard to predict, but they are prevalent and costly in white-collar work processes.

- *Media transformation analysis* identifies the conversions of one media to another which are a source of delay and inefficiency. A common example is conversion from paper to digital media.

3 NEED FOR THIS APPROACH

These methods are needed when computers are used for information work such as co-authoring a document, circulating a memo, preparing a briefing, sending mail, filing and retrieving documents, managing engineering drawings, etc. They are also needed for applications based on forms such as filing expense claims, personnel action requests, budget planning documents, travel requests, etc. The methods also can be used for more data-based work, such as insurance claims processing, loan applications, airline reservations, and purchase order processing, but these applications do not require as much user involvement. In data-based applications, most of the information flow and processing can be designed by the systems analyst. But, PCs and distributed computing are changing applications development requiring more user involvement in design and operation.

Research into why there has been such a "puny payoff from office computers"[2] has brought attention to the necessity of designing the flow of office work not just installing computers. Office work cannot be designed without the participation of office workers. Office work is less structured requiring worker discretion in the treatment of each work object, usually a document. Decisions are often made on the spot regarding the actions to be taken and when. This is the nature of professional, white-collar work: it requires decision making capability on the part of each worker. For example, consider the array of alternatives and tradeoffs in making business travel arrangements, or developing a marketing plan. In office work, the end-users are vital to identifying the inhibitors to meeting their objectives.

---

[2] Bowen, *The Puny Payoff from Computers*, **Fortune Magazine**, May 26, 1986.

Using a proven set of methods provides an approach to successfully involving end-users by:

- Systematically obtaining end-user input to the analysis and design of the work-system

- Involving management to ensure the execution of their responsibilities

- Involving all the success influencers including senior management, customers, related members of the management team, and other stakeholders

- Promoting a shared understanding of the technology

4 THE BENEFITS OF USING PARTICIPATORY METHODS

Participatory methods that we use ensure that computing applications reflect the work being done in organizations rather than an abstract representation. It will enable organizations to obtain payoff from the widespread use of networked PCs. New workflow systems applications will achieve ROI because of increased organization acceptance and design that meets user needs.

- Workflow systems will be accepted by the organization

- Technology will leverage the organization's mission critical processes

- Workflow systems will increase competitive position or services through enhanced capability

- Information will be a corporate resource through planned access

- Options for increased organizational effectiveness will emerge

  - Labor is reinvested in revenue activities, not in communication overhead
  - Alternative activities and processes are selected for increased efficiency
  - Workflow inefficiencies will be re-engineered

- Workflow systems will better meet user needs

  - The use of the technology will be planned, not left to chance
  - User needs will be fed back to workflow systems designers
  - Methods for the continued improvement of work processes will be part of the system

5 FOUNDATIONS OF THE METHODS

The methods are based on two disciplines, Total Quality Management (TQM)[3] and communication science. TQM provides techniques for workshops such as Fishbone diagrams of cause and effect, PARETO charts for visualizing priorities, voting and other techniques to reach consensus, and a focus on customers and objectives. TQM emphasizes user participation in the design of the <u>use</u> of the technology, not necessarily its selection. User needs can be obtained before workflow systems selection, using these methods. TQM also emphasizes measurement to quantify system performance, and scientific methods are available for use with the methods, for example, in the evaluation of a pilot installation.

Communication science is an interdisciplinary field with academic departments and industrial applications. The focus is on understanding and improving human communication media such as meetings, telephoning, and documents. Communication is viewed as the critical process in the functioning of organizations, for example, 75% of all activities in organizations are communications with an average of 35% in meetings alone.[4] Over the past fifteen years, an organizational model has been developed based on pioneering work at Stanford Research Institute.[5] This model shows how to improve the performance of teams and organizations based on experiments with workflow systems, and its validity has withstood the test of time and use. Most recently, workflow has been recognized as a communication process in which the behavior of participants must be a major consideration in the design of the technology implementation.

The author has developed and tested the methods referred to here in three major corporations, an international engineering company, a large bank, and a major satellite communications company. Several other companies have employed them to varying degrees. They provide powerful insights to improving the performance of organizations through workflow systems.

---

[3] Tenner, Arthur R. and Irving J. DeToro, **Total Quality Management: Three Steps to Continuous Improvement**, Addison-Wesley, Reading , MA, 1992.

[4] Bair, James H., and Laura Mancuso, **The Office Systems Cycle**, HP Press, Palo Alto, 1986.

[5] Bair, James. H., *A Layered Model of Organizations: Communication Process and Performance*, **Journal of Organization Computing**, (2)1, 187-203 (1991).

ActionWorkflow™ Technology and Applications for Groupware

Dr. Raul Medina-Mora
Senior Vice President
Chief Technical Officer
Action Technologies, Inc.
Alameda, CA 94501

Abstract

This talk outlines Action Technologies' ActionWorkflow technology. It reviews the ideas behind the technology, complete with a review of its overall architecture and various components. The functionality that is added to groupware environments is presented; and the technology's integration with existing environments, including database and messaging environments, is discussed. The talk concludes with examples of business applications that have been successfully implemented.

1 INTRODUCTION TO ACTIONWORKFLOW TECHNOLOGY

ActionWorkflow technology enables computer-supported work; specifically, it is designed to reorganize, automate, and manage the flow of work within an organization. It results from the convergence of two key insights: 1) The idea that every organization and the work in it exists as a network of commitments between people and 2) that today's markets are increasingly knowledge-based and global, and that this new reality requires that all companies commit themselves to the following business goals,

. Satisfy customers,
. Constantly reduce cycle times,
. Constantly increase the quality of offers,
. Create a structure that matches the new global reality.

It follows that a business process should be viewed as a network of commitments. Indeed, the application of the technology is guided by an associated business design methodology whereby work is restructured into a series of customer-performer commitments in which the actions, roles, and completions that comprise the flow of work are explicitly represented. The commitments are contained within structures referred to as "workflows," which can be depicted as ellipses divided into four phases of interaction: *Preparation*, *Agreement*, *Performance*, and *Acceptance*. Distributed throughout the four phases are 12 acts that define all possible work interactions. Thus within the ActionWorkflow technology, a business process is automated and managed as a network of workflows.

ActionWorkflow technology can be applied within virtually any work situation and is especially strong in providing the following functions:

. Automating standard procedures within a group.
. Notifying users about actions that need completion.
. Providing users with specific tools and information to complete their tasks.
. Managing reminders, alerts, follow-ups, and other aids that maintain the flow of work.
. Giving users a bird's eye view of their business process, and detailing how their tasks fit into the overall process. (A simplified and structured access is provided to all information.)

. Providing managers with overviews of the state of work, both on demand and on a scheduled basis.

ActionWorkflow technology creates a systems framework for integrating networks of people, and it supplies and manages the actions that drive work to completion.

2 ARCHITECTURE

ActionWorkflow technology serves as both a blueprint for redesigning organizations and as a means to automate work within computers. Enabled as a complete ActionWorkflow Management System™, the technology fuses together people and computers. At its core is the ActionWorkflow Server™. Here events (actions taken by a person or by an electronic agent on behalf of a person) are represented as transactions within workflows and are operated and maintained at this level of abstraction. Each event is maintained as a specific instance within a workflow, and a complete process is maintained as a group of such instances arranged into a series of workflows. In other words, the workflow structure is replicated again and again to form a network of workflows that constitutes a complete business process. This simplification is a key to the architecture's success.

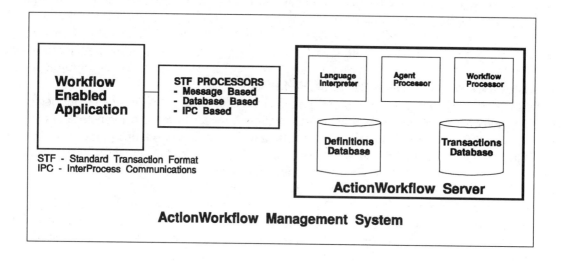

The architecture is platform independent. The ActionWorkflow Management System utilizes and integrates the following components of a computing platform:
- *User interface,* to let users interact with the system in a familiar and natural way,
- *Communications,* to tie people together to participate in business processes, even if dispersed at multiple locations within the organization, and
- *Databases*, to store business process definitions and the records of work transactions.

In a message-based environment, ActionWorkflow technology transcends messaging. Messaging as such involves connectivity and the ability to send, receive and store messages; but ActionWorkflow technology adds the design and automation of business processes, plus managing and recording the work transactions that constitute these processes. In effect the technology converts a traditional messaging system into an "action messaging system" wherein messages are associated with specific acts within workflows. In other words, in an action messaging system, the messages do not reflect the state of information flows but rather the state of workflows.

In a database environment, ActionWorkflow technology transcends the traditional database function. Database technology as such is concerned with the storage, sorting, retrieval, and maintenance of information.

But ActionWorkflow technology adds the design, automation and management of business processes, plus the coupling of the information contained within the databases to the new business processes. The technology converts a traditional database system into an "actionbase system" wherein the individual records are associated with particular acts within workflows. In such an actionbase system, the stored records do not reflect the state of stored data but instead reflect the state of dynamic workflows.

ActionWorkflow technology can also be implemented within an inter-process communication environment whereby the ActionWorkflow Server provides functions to client applications. But instead of simply handling information (sending and receiving messages or modifying shared databases), ActionWorkflow functions are delivered through mechanisms such as remote procedure calls.

The technology is an integrating force that complements the existing messaging and database systems. Two other key components of the architecture are the ActionWorkflow Language and the Agent Processor. The ActionWorkflow Language provides both the linguistic constructs to express the relationships between business processes and workflows and the constructs to integrate existing information systems. The Agent Processor automates recurring actions and the notifications that signal when actions are overdue.

The ActionWorkflow Management System includes tools to facilitate the analysis and design of business processes (that get placed into a definitions database) as well as reporting tools to track workflow transactions, monitor the status of workflows, and display profiles of individual and group performance. The technology also provides a complete set of standard development tools. These start with a series of educational and training materials for designing and redesigning organizations and include the reporting tools. These aids address the divergent needs of three classes of users:
 . *Designers,* who create the business process designs,
 . *Managers,* who track the progress of work, and
 . *Workflow participants,* who participate in and are integral to the workflows.

3 EXAMPLES OF BUSINESS PROCESS APPLICATIONS
 Action Technologies has developed a series of applications enabled with ActionWorkflow technology within the Lotus Notes™ environment. These applications have been developed for the consulting division of a large software company, a large money-center bank, an international consulting company, one of the largest advertising agencies in the country, and for several key government agencies.

The applications include the following administrative and management processes common to all businesses:
 . Automating and managing the hiring process
 . Automating and managing ad hoc projects
 . Automating and managing the ordering and delivery of products and services

In addition, several mission-critical applications have been created specific to individual businesses. The following typify these demanding applications:
 . Automating and managing the billing process in a major consulting firm
 . Automating and managing the development and introduction of new products
 . Automating and managing the communications and functional integration of a service organization with
   its customers
 . Automating and managing a quick-time response to customer queries

This diversity demonstrates the adaptability of ActionWorkflow technology within real-world situations and operating conditions.

WORKFLOW AS GROUPWARE: A CASE FOR GROUP LANGUAGE?

Geoffrey Bock
Project Manager for Collaborative Systems
Office Systems Applications Group, Digital Equipment Corporation
110 Spit Brook Road, Nashua, N.H. 03062

At first glance workflow systems and groupware applications appear antithetical to one another. Workflow systems seek to automate formal policies and procedures, enabling the reengineering of basic business processes. Groupware applications seek to facilitate informal group interactions by enhancing communications, coordination and collaboration of task teams. Both attempt to improve organizational effectiveness, beginning with different definitions of work.

In fact, workflow concepts *may be* part of a groupware application in surprisingly new ways. I would like to make the case for first discovering and then enabling **group language** in order to build **coordination environments**.

1   ENVISIONING WORKFLOW SOLUTIONS

Workflow systems create create a software environment to encode and enforce business practices. One can readily envision systems to expedite insurance claims processing, medical records tracking or equipment purchasing--reengineering business processes and "radically" improving productivity along the way (Hammer and Champy, 1992). Typically these are transaction-oriented activities, based on forms processing metaphors. More often than not, they begin by automating operational activities and clerical work.

Key components for workflow systems include:

- Electronic forms or other documents (including scanned images of paper documents) for collecting and displaying relevant information;

- Tasks performed by people with varied roles in an organization, contributing to the business process through interactions with the electronic forms;

- Rules or standard operating procedures to determine who performs what tasks on which kinds of information--in effect making determinations on behalf of the organization.

Users have defined roles. For instance the insurance industry includes (a) customer-oriented brokers who write and sell policies; (b) specialists who have the knowledge at hand to resolve particular issues; and (c) line managers who assign tasks and manage the process. The software environment links these users to their tasks while also providing the capacity for tracking their work activities.

Most importantly, systems analysts or designers have key roles for implementing and managing workflow systems. While their actual job titles and skill sets may vary, and their authority may span different layers of an organization, these people provide the links to integrate the software environment with the operational setting. They design the electronic forms, describe users' roles, specific the processing rules and define the workflow. In effect they first capture and then encode organizational knowledge about a particular business activity.

2   ENVISIONING GROUPWARE SOLUTIONS

Groupware applications, by comparison, are designed to address the needs of knowledge workers. With changes in organizational structures and flatter organizations, team solutions are essential. Groupware applications "support interactions within groups of two or more people" compared to "*major systems* designed to support entire organizations" (Grudin, 1989)*. For example, a groupware application might help a task team sort and manage group information so that individuals will get the information they need, as they need it, and then track requests, action items and documents generated as part of the team's activities.

Knowledge workers seek environments that will enable them to do their current jobs better, and permit them to accomplish new kinds of tasks with less effort. Key components for groupware applications include:

- A networked infrastructure (such as electronic mail) for communicating information within a task team, including the ability to effortlessly reach others in the enterprise wherever they might actually reside, in a consistent fashion.

- Highly adaptable repositories (such as electronic file cabinets or libraries) to organize, store, retrieve and browse shared information in a networked environment;

- Personal assistants or filters enabling knowledge workers to prioritize and manage their interpersonal communications in personalized ways;

- Intelligent agents that have the capability of monitoring general information streams such as news wires, network news groups and the like for relevant items of interest.

Knowledge workers typically have multiple roles within a task team; encoding specific privileges and corresponding access rights is difficult to enforce. Moreover, users place a premium on coordinating activities in a rapidly changing environment; successful groupware solutions must be flexible, adaptable and extensively modifiable.

Nevertheless, without careful planning and design, groupware applications can grow in scope and become chaotic. By their very nature, managing groupware applications is often a decentralized and distributed effort, emphasizing democratic values. Unlike workflow systems, experts external to the task team, such as full time systems analysts, rarely get involved with scoping the solution or managing the environment.

---

* Grudin goes on to explain that a:

> group is either small to moderate in size, or is narrowly focused, as in the case of an electronic bulletin board or electronic mail interest group. Thus electronic mail, co-authorship programs and voice annotation are examples of groupware, whereas computer integrated manufacturing or order-and-inventory control systems are not, even though they share many of the same properties and are subject to many of the same analyses.

3   THE PROMISE OF GROUP LANGUAGE

The emerging generation of groupware applications must solve a difficult problem: how to represent the varied and diverse activities of a task team in ways that advanced information technologies can readily interpret and compute. In theory, one might decompose group work into a set of component (and autonomous) parts. The activities of a task team become complex instances of workflow systems, with multiple branches, parallel actions and complicated rules. But knowledge work often requires ad hoc judgements and subtle interpretations, activities that are not readily encoded by formalized policies and proce- dures. Frederick Taylor to the contrary, it is difficult to imagine defining an electronic form and rule set for every kind of informal group activity. System analysts can hardly antici- pate, much less design, the multitude of interpersonal interactions in a high performing work group (Cole and Cole, 1992).

I believe new groupware applications will enhance coordination by promoting structured conversations and group language, democratizing the design process and encompassing key attributes of both workflow systems and groupware applications. Knowledge workers in task teams must develop an awareness of their primary activities, the core competencies that comprise their basic work tasks, and the kinds of information they need to fulfill these core competencies. Second, they must define a common set of terms, a group vocabulary, about what these core competencies are--much as physicians have defined an extensive set of diagnostic related groups (or DRG's) to catalogue medical conditions. Third, knowl- edge workers need to be able to combine and recombine these terms in multiple and highly flexible ways. That is, they need to view their environment as a set of multiple conversations, where individual members take personal actions on a known set of group activities.

In the near future I would anticipate **coordination environments** as mail-enabled groupware applications. These kinds of environments will capture and represent the group language of a task team, encoding structured lists of key terms that describe the basic at- tributes of group activities. Knowledge workers will have easy access to this lexicon of group terminology through pop-up menus and other highly visible user interface paradigms (many of which have yet to be invented). Terms may be interrelated or linked to higher order concepts through a thesaurus that captures the group culture. The coordination envi- ronment will disseminate knowledge of the group language to all task team members. Individual knowledge workers will be able to engage in structured conversations with one another by developing their unique personal assistants, or ad hoc individualized proce- dures, about how to handle each of the varied group items.

References

Cole, P. and Cole, J. 1992. Primer on group dynamics for groupware developers. *Groupware: Software for Computer Supported Cooperative Work,* D. Marca and G. Bock (eds.) , New York: Computer Society Press.

Grudin, J. 1989. Why groupware applications fail: problems in design and evaluation. *Office: Technology and People* 4:245-264.

Hammer, M. and Champy, J. 1992. What is reengineering? *Information Week-- Bonus Issue* May 5, 372:10-24.

GROUPWARE: BUREAUCRACY BUSTER OR ONE MORE EXPENSIVE LAYER?
(Economic Design Architecture Can Make a Difference)

Peter Dolan, Ph.D.
PhDesigns Group
VFD Consulting, Inc.
Suite 2000
541 South School St.
Ukiah, California 95482
FAX (707) 485-8299

ABSTRACT

"Productivity" increases are often claimed, but seldom demonstrated in workgroup software. Automated electronic bureaucracy can equal or exceed the waste of resources consumed by conventional bureaucracy because it works faster and uses more expensive tools. How can we know if our convenient tools are good or bad for the bottom line?

Whether your groupware implementation is a cost-effective business management tool or yet another layer of bureaucratic overhead depends on its economic design architecture. Effective groupware designs should have sufficient intelligence to eliminate duplication of effort, cut communication costs and other "paper shuffling" types of management activity. Economically productive groupware should be a proactive "bureaucracy buster," not just another hazard in an administrative maze.

1   WELCOME AND INTRODUCTION

Greetings to all, and welcome to the Conference. For those of you who have travelled great distances to be here today, please allow me to extend to you a special welcome to California and to the United States. I hope that you will be rewarded for your effort to attend.

Since time is short for this session, we must first get down to basics. Obviously many of you are already believers in, or developers of, the concept of groupware, or you would not be at this conference. Some of you are probably curious and/or skeptical about the overall value of groupware, and this session is addressed to you.

This will not be an evangelical sermon, because there is nothing to sell or preach. Today's presentation is not concerned about whether groupware or groupware products are good or bad, desirable or undesirable, but is focused on some important underlying principles of designing group-oriented software. These principles may affect the value of groupware for your organization or your product.

The material presented today should be taken as an economic interpretation, rather than scientific fact. Some of the illustrations are based on statistical analyses published elsewhere, and others are based on my practical experience. There will be a few whimsical items thrown in for their entertainment and educational value.

You are invited to listen with a critical ear to this interpretation, and there will time for questions later. No one has advanced groupware software development to the level of a science yet, and with a bit of luck everyone will learn something today, myself included.

2   WORKING DEFINITIONS

First, there is not yet a standard definition for groupware. Lacking a standard, we will use the following two statements as today's working definition.

1. Groupware consists of a computer-based work environment which enhances the productivity of a group of people.

2. A group consists of two or more persons working toward a common goal, typically a business goal.

These two sentences are deceptively simple. The definition of elements which are relatively less controversial from the first statement include "computer-based" (which we assume for this discussion), "work environment" (there are exceptions, and varying definitions of work), and "enhances" (we assume that this means making something better). We will not spend time elaborating the definitions of these elements of the statement.

Similar elements from the second sentence include "group" (many definitions exist) and "typically business" (other categories such as recreation and creativity are equally valid bases for groupware). We will not spend time elaborating the definitions of these elements of the statement, either.

Having thus swiftly disposed of much potential nitpicking, we come to the core of the most controversial aspect of groupware as we see, touch and envision it today, namely the nasty term, "productivity."

3   PRODUCTIVITY: SOMETHING VERIFIABLE

Productivity has been a controversial "hot button" with respect to information systems for many years. Nearly all of what is said, presented, represented and published regarding the productivity of information systems is anecdotal, meaning that it is not based on systematic, replicable analysis of reliable data.

Despite a longstanding interest in productivity by business and industry, until recently there has been little verifiable data and virtually no standardized method for evaluating the economic productivity of systems.

This situation changed in late 1990 with the publication of the research results of

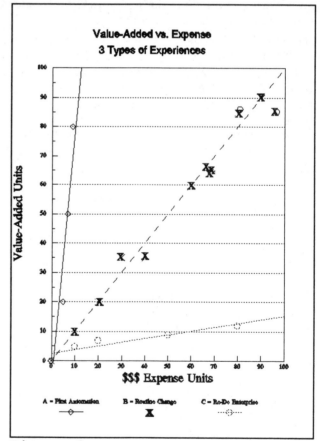

Figure 1

Professor Paul Strassmann.[1] This work provides us with a systematic analysis of economic and information system data from a sample of 292 companies of all major industry types. It also gives us an appropriate methodology and substantive results. The point which I wish to make in this presentation does not necessarily depend on using Professor Strassmann's methodology. Any economic analysis which uses systematic and replicable methods should produce similar results.

Figure 1 shows a grossly simplified version of Strassmann's results by plotting the correlation of value-added versus expense. This is a "fast and loose" display of three types of economic outcomes for information systems which he describes in his analysis. In order to "keep it simple," I have abstracted the results of over 500 pages of economic analysis of data from 292 corporations into three or four graphs. I have taken the further liberty of inserting coordinates in the graphs that allow the regression lines to clearly show the three types of outcomes.

First, looking at the horizontal axis in Figure 1, note that it is labelled "$$$ Expense Units." This represents monetary expenditures for information systems. The monetary units in the graph are generic and linear. They do not represent literal amounts of dollars, but the relative amount of dollars which are spent. For the purposes of today's session, it does not matter if the units are dollars, yen, or deutchmarks, nor if the units are single dollars, thousands, millions or billions.

The vertical axis of Figure 1 represents "Value-Added Units." Now you may ask the question: "What is a value-added unit?" A value-added unit is something that I have created to represent the economic value of information systems to a company. This designation is not something fictional; it represents a "hard dollar, bottom line" value, not a theoretical productivity gain. Following Strassmann's methodology, this type of number is obtained from corporate financial reports, not theories. Once again, it is not necessary to accept Strassmann's numbers, for any financially quantifiable, replicable and verifiable method should produce similar results.

4   WHAT VALUE-ADDED IS OBTAINED FROM INFORMATION SYSTEMS?

Thus far, we have set the scene and defined the "playing field" for economic value. We have talked about relating the expense of information systems (horizontal axis) to the "hard dollar, bottom line" results (vertical axis).

Now, lets look at the results. I am sure that you will find them surprising, as I did when I first saw them.

My fast and loose interpretation shows three types of outcomes. The "A" group of companies shows that very substantial value is obtained from relatively small expenditures on information systems. I have noted that this group of companies typically might be doing "first time" automation, where they convert from "doing things manually" to computers. This high productivity would especially apply to companies which move directly from old fashioned manual operations to generic low cost commodity personal computers without using mainframes or minicomputers. Unfortunately, this group of companies is relatively small in number. Either a unique situation such as first time automation, or perhaps a very unique set of business and market circumstances permit an outrageously high value return. This type of situation and company is extremely rare.

[1]Strassmann, Paul A., *The Business Value Of Computers*, The Information Economics Press, New Canaan, CT 06840-0284, 1990. (800) 800-0448; FAX (203) 966-5506. Library of Congress Catalog Card Number 88-80753, ISBN 0-9620413-2-7.

Moving to the "B" group of companies, we see what is the mainstream, typical situation. The surprising result represented by this group is that most companies do not get very much value for their information system expenditures. The linear plot shows that, on the average, most companies just break even on information system expenditures. This means that, on the average, a dollar spent on information systems yields about a dollar's worth of value to the company. I have inserted a label of "Routine Changes" here to indicate that this type of company has already automated, and probably tinkers with systems continually without necessarily taking a quantum leap in either a positive or negative direction. We will look more closely at this group later in this presentation, since most of our companies, most of the companies in the world, and most of the potential market for groupware sales is in this category.

Finally, there is the "C" group. This collection of companies consistently gets a negative return on information systems expenditures. For every dollar spent on information systems, the company gets a negative return. Unfortunately, there are a substantial number of companies of this type, and many different reasons for the low value return on information systems dollars. I have put the label "Re-Do Enterprise" on this group, indicating that they are typically in need of major system work, spend substantial amounts for it, and are way beyond the "tinkering" category of expenditures to adjust information system problems.

Since this is a groupware meeting, and most of you are interested in this aspect of economic analysis, we will spend the remainder of the session looking more closely at the "B" group of companies, the ones which are in the vast majority, probably your company and mine, and certainly the primary marketplace for present and future groupware.

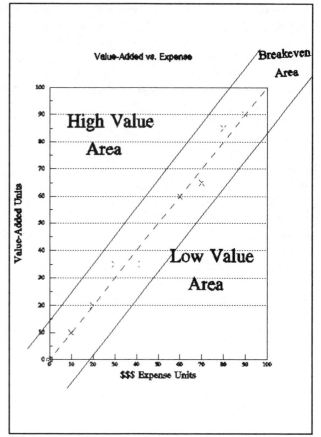

Figure 2

5   TYPICAL INFORMATION SYSTEMS
       OUTCOMES

Moving to Figure 2, we see a closer look at the line indicating typical information systems economics for most companies. These companies have been represented by the "X" plots showing how many "Value-Added Units" each company gets for each unit of expenditure on information systems. The dashed line represents an average (regression) line, and the X's represents individual companies which fall above, below, and on the regression line.

What this figure indicates is that the typical result for most companies is they often do not get much value-added for information systems expenditures. However, they often do not lose a lot of money either. One way of interpreting this situation is that the dashed "average" line shows a one-to-one relationship between expenditure and value-added. This means that the average represents a "break-even" point, where a company gets a dollar's value for each dollar expended on information systems.

But the real world is not so simple. In fact, most companies do not land on the "average," they are either just above it or just below it. The "average" is simply a concept used for comparing results.

6   WHAT HAPPENS TO MOST OF US

So, if the average is not typical, how can we characterize the economic value of information systems expenditures for this mainstream group of companies that is the primary groupware market? I have provided a couple of lines running parallel to the average, just above and below it. These lines represent what I will call the general "breakeven" area for information system expenditure. In this area, companies do not get either spectacularly good or bad results for their information systems expenditures. The area above this "breakeven area" is labelled "High Value," because each unit of expenditure brings a high return in value. The area below breakeven is the "Low Value" area where information systems expenditures go into a black hole that never returns positive value.

OK, fine. We have now defined a "playing field" for sorting out companies on the basis of economic value received for each unit of information system expenditure. But we know that groupware is not bought or sold by groups of companies, it is a one-at-a-time proposition, with each company making its own decisions. What is needed is some way to relate the aggregate statistics to the case of an individual company, and in turn relate those results to the productivity of groupware design and use.

7   SHIFTING FROM AGGREGATE STATISTICS TO A SINGLE COMPANY

Figure 3 provides an interpretation which I have supplied for this situation. The straight lines represent the "Breakeven Area," and the curved line shows how an individual company's information systems relate to economic value-added.

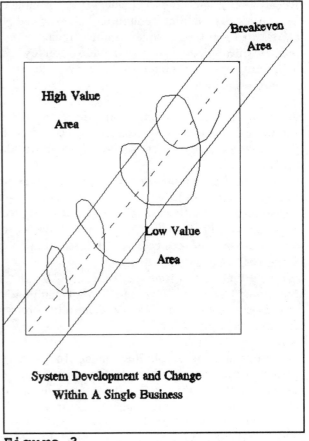

Figure 3

We have made a shift in perspective to show this relationship. The straight lines show the same economic boundaries as they did in Figure 2, but the curved line represents "changing and evolving" systems, something that is typical in most corporate environments. Thus, when we consider the curved line, we are looking at a "track record" of economic value-added for a single company's systems as they change over time, and as they are modified to meet changing competitive and business situations.

At first glance, the curved line may seem puzzling. Obviously it tracks economic value-added through positive, negative and breakeven ranges, but if it is "tracking," there must be a time base. If there is a time base, do the loops imply that time moves backwards? How do we interpret this?

There is an easy way out of this one. Although the curved line has been represented in two dimensions, if we add a third dimension it becomes a spiral, rather than a line that loops back on itself. Look again, and think of the curved line as being a "snapshot" of a spiral that tracks value-added relative to information systems expenditure in a single company.

Now I will offer a reality check. Consider your own company's experience with information systems expenditures and systems development. Was development and results clean, linear, straightforward, profitable and economically trouble-free? If it was, your company is in the "A" group described earlier, and does not represent the typical situation we are trying to portray.

8   NAMING THE PRODUCTIVITY CURVE

Recall that something whimsical was promised earlier in this session. When working on a way to graphically depict economic value-added for a single company, there were several failed attempts to use traditional, more linear economic charts. After experimenting with various curves, the spiral shape seemed to convey the point quite nicely. In effect, we cheated by projecting a three dimensional curve over the two dimensions classically used in traditional economics.

So now, without worrying what the third dimension represents, another dilemma arises. What should we call this newly-emerging economic curve? As we work through this problem, we will get closer toward the groupware economics that we are seeking.

The name for the shape should somehow reflect what it depicts, which is the meandering of economic value-added from information systems among positive, negative and breakeven ranges. It would be especially helpful if we could use a name which helped us to better understand these fluctuations, and how we might design software and systems to keep our companies in the positive (or at least breakeven) ranges.

The economic performance indicated by the curve is characteristic of most systems used by business. The curve represents what happens in most companies: systems require continuous attention, consume resources, generally break even, and are not either huge winners or losers for the business.

The first and most obvious name for a curve having these characteristics would be "The Bureaucratic Spiral." This would accurately convey the types of things which affect system development within a company, while at the same time providing a readily acceptable explanation for the meandering nature of business system economics.

The problem with this label is that the term "bureaucratic" has come to have a negative connotation, and that is not a very good place to begin a positive effort at understanding.

We spent some time researching and considering the possibilities for naming this curve. As it turns out, this was not the first time that this type of curve had been used to enhance understanding and recognition of a relatively dull situation. The origins of one earlier use of such a curve can be found in the work of D.R. "Doc" Rice some 42 years ago. Rice successfully applied a very similar curve in a product redesign situation in 1950.[2]

---

[2]Acknowledgment and thanks are due to Ms. Cindy Borkowski of the Continental Baking Company Research and Development Laboratories of St. Louis, Missouri for providing information regarding D.R. Rice and his use of the squiggle curve. Rice began

Thus, in honor of Rice's earlier work, the curve in Figure 3 has been called the "Cupcake Curve" rather than the "Bureaucratic Spiral." Since multimedia presentations are known to be much more effective than simple audio and visual ones, we are now passing out sample exhibits of Rice's application of the curve for you to consider as we continue. We hope that you enjoy this mnemonic device.

9   UNDERSTANDING THE CUPCAKE CURVE

Now that we have defined and named the Cupcake Curve, there comes the task of understanding how it works, and how it might affect groupware design and acceptance.

Figure 4 shows an annotated version of the Cupcake Curve that labels key events which cause the curve to take its characteristic shape. These events are familiar to most of us who have participated in corporate information system design, development and implementation.

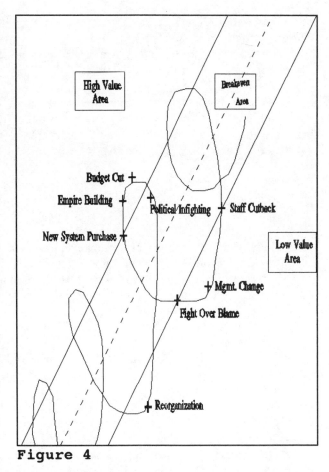

Figure 4

A cursory examination of the events marked with crosshairs on the curve shows that they seem to be located in appropriate places relative to information systems lifecycles: Empire Building occurs when things are going well and new systems are purchased when there is budget money. Fights, Reorganization, Management Changes and Staff Cutbacks occur when things are not going well. Political Infighting occurs at any time.

10   KNOWING HOW SOMETHING WORKS DOES NOT NECESSARILY FIX IT

Now we have outlined the overall economic "playing field," provided an interpretive Cupcake Curve that relates individual company system lifecycle to the economic value-added, and put a few milestones on the Cupcake Curve to elaborate its nature. Where does groupware design come in, and how can it help a company at least "stay between the lines" of breakeven, or approach higher value-added?

One answer is provided in the aggregate by Professor Strassmann's work. Paraphrasing his study results, he strongly indicates that there are never computer system failures, only failures

---

his career with the Hostess company at the age of 17 as a cake dumper, and added the squiggle design to their trademark chocolate cupcake in 1950 as part of a post World War II product redesign project that included adding a creme filling similar to the one that had been used in the Twinkie product since 1930. The squiggle stripe was added to differentiate Hostess' chocolate cupcake from the competition.

of management. Look at the events marked on the curve in Figure 4, for the nature of their presence tend to illustrate and reinforce the point. It is surely the job of management to keep track of the value-added of information systems expenditures and to keep company systems "on target" in an economic sense.

Since we now have strong indications that most companies do not receive substantial economic value-added from information systems expenditures, the task of groupware designers, buyers, implementers and managers would seem to be making sure that companies get appropriate value-added for their groupware investment.

But how can groupware help to "straighten out" the Cupcake Curve? If the responsibility rests with management, and most workgroups are local or departmental, what can be done to set things on the appropriate value-added path?

It is likely that the groupware marketplace is now contemplating just this question. The slow acceptance of groupware by the market strongly indicates that Professor Strassmann is correct, and that groupware is no exception to the value-added approach. There seems to be no obvious and dramatic economic benefit from introducing groupware into business systems.

11   BUILDING VALUE-ADDED INTO GROUPWARE

There was an initial claim that this session would not be evangelical, and that is true. Neither is it intended to be a doomsday message for groupware.

Groupware has what may be a unique potential for adding value to a business enterprise that clearly does not exist in most current information systems. Remember that Professor Strassmann's data is almost five years old, and the groupware concept as a distinct market is about the same age. Although many of the companies in the statistical sample had strongly integrated vertical systems, it seems unlikely that groupware as we now know it had any influence on the outcome of the value-added studies described.

So, back to the question of the role of management. It seems to be true that management is responsible for keeping the company on track for value-added systems. But there is another aspect of the Cupcake Curve (Figure 4) that points in a different direction that is uniquely addressable by groupware, and that is people.

12   INCORPORATING INTELLIGENT MANAGEMENT PRACTICES

A bureaucracy is not built only of technology or information systems, it is made up of people who cooperate (or don't cooperate) in a systematic, predictable manner. Groupware, if it is to be something which enhances the value-added of work groups, must therefore take on some of the characteristics of intelligent and enlightened management in its design and implementation. This intelligence should focus the workgroup on achieving management-defined value-added for the business.

"Focus" is a gentle word, but do we really mean that groupware should take on the role of Big Brother by spying on individual workers' activity? No, the type of intelligent design necessary to keep workgroups productive is something more fundamental than that. Spying, browbeating and similar activities are reactive behavior that can only attempt to fix something that has already gone wrong. Groupware design can deliver a much better solution, by positively and proactively guiding workgroup behavior and avoiding mistakes in the first place.

Is this some magic bullet? Not quite. The elements of intelligent groupware design are so fundamental that it seems amazing that they have not long since become a standard part of software design. So we go back to basics, and here they are.

First, the Cupcake Factors that retard value-added:
- Vague business goals
- Overstaffing
- Inattentive management
- Disincentives / Lack of incentive
- Politics
- Empires
- Personality clashes
- Divided authority and responsibility

All of these things are certainly the province of organizational management, and most tend to coincide with poor management. But these things are not an explicit part of the organization for they are hidden from view. When was the last time you read an annual report which said that last year's earnings were down because political infighting had paralyzed the company and a better organized competitor stepped in and took away market share? Probably no one has seen an admission like this in print, but most of us have certainly experienced the reality of such a situation.

Groupware as a workgroup-oriented concept is in the unique position to provide value-added to business organizations by explicitly addressing those "people problems" which reflect poor management behavior.

How can this arise without browbeating individual workers? The answer is that groupware should incorporate as an integral part of its design the explicit capability to logically and structurally incorporate management and business objectives. These types of management guidelines for running the business form a counterpoint to the Cupcake Factors listed above. Some of them are familiar:
- Clear business goals
- Clear communication within the organization
- The ability for each worker to "see" goals and economics
- Positive incentives

13   BUILDING IN POSITIVE MANAGEMENT CAPABILITY

Building these positive management goals into groupware will not be an easy task. It will involve drastically expanding our current notions of the scope of workgroup software to include a capability to explicitly model all positive management factors that would guide the group software operation.

For openers, this means that what are now commonly accepted as CASE (Computer Assisted Software Engineering) tools need to be expanded to include explicit motivational guidelines which are integrated into groupware designs. Worse still, the explicit modeling capability must be changeable "on the fly," to accommodate changes in business and management direction. Further into the abyss: the management-specified positive goals should be overlaid on each business process so that every data element, transaction and business function can be "seen" in its proper business and value-added context. There should be a simulation capability for asking "what if" questions regarding proposed changes to business processes and procedures, so that the results clearly show what will happen to value-added if such changes are implemented.

A question arises here: who will "see" these processes and simulations? This is a good question, and reflects a further step in the discussion. It is not sufficient for system designers, programmers, or even management to "see" the business context of system processes. The individual worker should be able to query the system regarding the business and management goals of each and every aspect of day-to-day activity. This becomes a final "point of delivery" quality test that will allow the individual worker to clearly understand his/her place in the enterprise, and to intelligently suggest changes and improvements.

Along with this ability to perceive value-added at the lowest levels of the enterprise should be a built-in incentive to ask such questions, and to receive bonuses based on worker-initiated suggestions that provide better value-added to the enterprise.

So, does this sound like a browbeating approach? Quite the contrary, the underlying intent is that every worker in the groupware environment should be able to obtain from the operational software a clear understanding of each and every business and organizational process that is implemented in the system. This sort of groupware implementation will not "put the heat" on individual workers but on management, which is where such scrutiny belongs.

There is a final touch to be put on the type of design outlined above. Groupware should be completely definable, implementable, changeable and maintainable by those managers and employees who conduct the day-to-day operations of the business. If it becomes necessary to add "artificial intelligence" interpretive functions to teach or interpret the workings of the system, then those should be included in the groupware design as well.

14   BUT WHERE DO THE POSITIVE MANAGEMENT GOALS COME FROM?

Since we have just come up with a series of sweeping design requirements which would have the effect of making groupware something with demonstrable value-added, it seems fair that we ask about the source of these allegedly wonderful and positive management ideas. Where do they come from? Out of a can? Are they built into the software?

Oddly, it does make some sense to supply workgroup software with at least rudimentary "default" values that reflect an appropriate focus on value-added for the business processes of the group. This basic knowledge should be a point of departure for the most competitive of managers, and an educational tool for novice managers. The more experienced could use the "default" management values for comparing (in the online simulation mode, of course) the effect of using their own management process instead of the "default" values supplied by the software.

It is just such an educational function that has been lacking in most business software, and which could represent the most substantial underlying value-added component of our future groupware products. The level of the "default values" supplied with the basic software should be consistent with conservative return-on-investment analysis and accounting methods.

If this approach sounds like the intent is to provide a complete online college level course in value-added analysis at the touch of a "help" button as part of the groupware, then the message has been received clearly.

15   WHAT SHOULD BE THE CONTENT OF GROUPWARE INFRASTRUCTURE?

It is fairly easy to prescribe a solution that is comprehensive, pervasive and general. It is another matter to actually build a working model. The dynamics of the marketplace will ultimately shape the product characteristics, but here is an outline of some architectural requirements that will probably be necessary to deliver an assured value-added to business.

1. A capability to perform economic analysis of the business unit should be present. This should include recent history, present financials, and competitive positions.

2. The ability to capture a clear business plan. This means that there should be a default plan outline, and that it should include a range of risk and value suggestions for consideration by inexperienced managers.

3. There should be extensive capability to capture and calculate data on the economic value of information handling specific to the business unit. This would include costs of data capture, storage, processing and disposition. It is critical that this costing and value framework include "people cost" for every information related transaction in the company. This includes computer related items, telephone calls and sales activities. This structure should have a "place" for every individual member of the group, and every group in the business. All financial data should be consistent with current and historic company data.

4. There should be a very extensive capability to make return-on-investment calculations of many types. These would be used in testing "what if" questions, and for tracking value-added.

5. It is critical that there be a mechanism for relating workflow and data flow to financial data on a worker-by-worker basis, for all groups and the entire enterprise. This mechanism should also be used to create online simulations of what will happen to value-added if changes are made in staffing levels or workflows.

6. An educational perspective should be an integral part of the groupware infrastructure. It should include extensive explanations of "why" certain things are appropriate or not, and should require such "why" answers to be inserted as documentation for changes in workflow or business processes made by managers.

7. An incentive component should be an integral part of the groupware infrastructure. Incentives should be firmly based on value-added, and should be calculated for each individual participating in the enterprise. The educational and investment return capabilities should be linked to the incentive component as an encouragement to all workers to ask questions and learn more about value-added. It might be desirable to combine the incentive and educational components in such a way that workers receive bonuses for "completing" value-added exercises and suggestions.

16   HAVE WE THROWN IN EVERYTHING, INCLUDING THE KITCHEN SINK?

The above outline of groupware infrastructure suggestions might be criticized as an extensive shopping list that bears little relation to the groupware products of today. Such features would be complicated to develop, difficult to integrate, would have to break in new product development and sales support, and require substantial changes in the role of software in the business environment. Is this for real?

It is not only for real, but these are only the entry level requirements for groupware designs which will succeed, prosper and proliferate in the world business marketplace. The logic of this argument is very simple, and can be summarized as follows.

Unless there is demonstrable value-added, there will be no incentive for businesses to attempt to implement groupware concepts. No incentive means few sales, which is much like today's worldwide groupware market situation.

Thanks to people like Professor Strassmann asking difficult questions and publishing potentially embarrassing answers, value-added increasingly will have to be demonstrated for specific business and workgroup software acquisitions.

The emphasis on value-added means that the software infrastructure must have extensive capabilities for information-related cost accounting (including people costs), ways to simulate workflow and process changes and illustrations of the resulting financial impact. The business world has already learned that software simulations are generally much cheaper than real-world testing, and the market will require that this knowledge be put to use.

There is already growing evidence that (in the U.S. certainly, other countries possibly) educational infrastructure has not kept pace with technological development. There will have to be an effective means of "on the job" training for managers, and for enhancing worker skills related to competitive business situations. Groupware is a nearly ideal vehicle for delivering such results, even though relatively little is being done at the present time.

Current software development for business has been noticeably lacking in the areas of group dynamics, and its ability to relate financial consequences to workgroup behavior. CASE tools have given us a false sense of control, but they are typically static-prescriptive rather than dynamic-interactive. CASE tools do not necessarily learn from experience or prevent disasters. Whatever we use for building business group software in the future will have to be much smarter than the CASE tools that we are using now. Groupware can provide an excellent "platform" for integrating the essential ingredients of technology and human teamwork.

17   WHAT'S NEXT ON THE AGENDA?

In summary, what have we gotten into? First, a relatively recent work strongly indicates that most businesses do not get much value-added for information system expenditures. Word of this finding is gradually spreading, and it will make an already tough groupware market much tougher. The same managers who might consider a groupware option are precisely those who will be demanding demonstrable value-added.

The proposed remedies for this situation appear to require a fundamental revision of groupware infrastructure, rather than just a few enhancements.

The market potential for groupware products is substantial and will take many years to develop and mature. We are fortunate at this time to have the availability of abundant inexpensive hardware and mass storage resources which are capable of supporting much more sophisticated groupware infrastructure than that offered in the current marketplace.

For developers of groupware and related software, a value-added approach leaves a clear message: there is substantial opportunity for systematic market development and exploitation by providing demonstrable value-added capability to groupware infrastructure.

For groupware consumers, there is an equally clear message. They must demand from developers and publishers that the value-added perspective be an integral part of any groupware environment. The perspective should encompass individual workgroups, inter-related workgroups, and the entire enterprise.

For groupware users, there is a great opportunity to influence your work environment in the coming years. Do not be satisfied with the traditional prescriptive order of "packaged" software. Insist that your workgroup software have the capability to answer "why" questions online, and to give you a clear perspective of your place in the group software context.

In closing, I'd like to thank you for your attention today, and your patience in helping me develop this early perspective on groupware development possibilities. The rest of the session is open to your questions.

Principles of Secure Information Systems Design with Groupware Examples

GroupWare'92 Conference and Exposition -- San Jose, California
3-5 August 1992
by Charles Cresson Wood
Independent Information Security Consultant
Information Integrity
P.O. Box 1219
Sausalito, California 94966 USA

Introduction

For the most part, computer systems designers and analysts are acutely aware of and genuinely concerned about information systems security. Ironically, in many instances they do not manifest their concern by incorporating specific control measures into the systems they create, enhance, and maintain. The reason for this is that they lack a set of principles of secure information systems design, that may be used when selecting or devising control measures. Such principles can constitute a foundation for thinking about information security, assist in the proper categorization of controls by type, and facilitate prudent selection of appropriate controls from amongst these categories. Responding to the need, this article provides an overview of security principles for information systems design. These principles may also be used by those who are evaluating the security features found in commercial information system products. Specific examples from the new field known as "groupware" are also provided. For purposes of this article, groupware is defined as any product using computer and communications systems to facilitate the collaboration of teams of workers.

Building Controls into Systems

Various studies performed at SRI International[1] and other organizations have clearly indicated that it costs up to ten times more to add controls after a software application system has gone into production, than if such controls are added during the system's development. Because software maintenance costs constitute a very large portion of the data processing budget at many organizations, better design of controls into application systems is likely to significantly reduce software maintenance costs.

---

[1] For additional information, contact Bruce Baker, manager of the Information Security Consulting Group, SRI International, Menlo Park, California, USA.

Given the significant financial benefits in favor of building controls into systems, an uninvolved and unbiased observer would think that a considerable number of controls are being built into applications now under development. As a consultant who has performed information security work for more than 80 different organizations, the author is regularly dismayed to learn about the large number of application systems now being developed that continue to be unduly vulnerable. Likewise, there are many groupware products now on the market that lack rudimentary control measures.

What is missing in many instances is the involvement of concerned users, enlightened developers, experienced EDP auditors, experienced information security specialists, or other parties who understand how to incorporate controls into systems while the systems are still in development. Given that those who know the technical side of controls often do not directly work on development teams, <u>developers themselves must assume responsibility for controls design</u>. This is particularly called for when end-users are developing departmental or personal computer production applications. A number of groupware products, such as Beyond Mail from Beyond Inc., support end-users in the development of systems. Since it is not safe to assume that the vendor has built sufficient security into the underlying operating system (such as Microsoft's DOS), developers as well as users who are acting in the capacity of developers must shoulder responsibility for building appropriate controls into their systems.

The information security design principles discussed below are offered to support developers with this responsibility—which should be explicitly assigned and documented to ensure understanding and proper performance. The principles can be used most successfully during the feasibility analysis, systems analysis, and general design phases of the traditional development life cycle. Even if developers are using prototyping development methods, these principles should still be considered early in the effort to minimize costs, rework, and future problems. A quick scan of the following principles will efficiently refresh developers or the information security practitioners with the reasons for incorporating controls into systems. These principles are also quite useful to auditors reviewing the controls in systems, as well as to those responsible for evaluating the merits of various commercial offerings.

Barney Oliver, head of Hewlett-Packard Labs, once said "... the only difference between theory and practice is that practice takes into account all of the theory." Mastery of the many different principles (theories) of controls design will provide the analyst, designer, auditor, or purchaser with the ability to build truly robust information security systems.

Architectural Placement of Controls in Groupware Systems

When information systems are "right-sized" (down-sized) from mainframes to groupware systems, often the involved applications must be redesigned. In an effort to control costs and to make information more readily accessible, many organizations are tempted to dispense with the controls that were previously found in the mainframe environment. Rather than abandoning these proven controls, we should transfer much of this functionality to groupware systems. The need for controls in groupware systems is further evidenced by the special threats that were never a part of the mainframe world: connectivity to outside organizations through a wide variety of communications systems, wide dispersal of sensitive information (most notably on the desktop), relatively naive users who have taken on many roles (operator, programmer, database administrator, etc.), inhospitable conditions for computing (cigarette smoke, coffee spills, etc.), lack of generally accepted security measures and products, a historical tendency of computer and network vendors to ignore security, and a widespread user practice of altering the hardware and software internals of personal computers.

The push toward interoperability and interconnectivity means successful groupware systems must interface with or run under a large number of local area network and workstation platforms. Since groupware systems bring together the functions found in a number of different applications—such as scheduling, document management, electronic mail, and project management—groupware systems also run as applications rather than systems software. For example, like an application, Lotus' Notes runs on top of existing operating systems and network operating systems. This means that groupware systems have a choice: either rely on the underlying platform's security measures (which are often lacking), or add other security features for new groupware functions and the information sharing that goes along with these functions. In the absence of adequate security at the platform level, Lotus has appropriately chosen the latter approach for Notes. Other successful groupware products (such as Higgins from Enable Software) have followed suit and included supplemental security measures, such as additional access control granularity and data encryption.

1. Cost effectiveness

A control's cost should be less than the resulting reduction in expected loss. This idea is dramatically indicated by the caveat—"one should not kill a fly with a sledgehammer." If you do, a control may be effective, but it will not be efficient. Although the expected reduction in loss that a control will occasion is often unknown, this fact should not be used to invalidate the principle of cost effectiveness.

As an upper bound on the amount to be spent on a control, it is often appropriate to say that the cost of a control should always be less than the value of the asset protected. For example, one should not spend $10,000 per year to protect a groupware-supported database that could only fetch $2,000 on the free market. This example assumes that the database does not have some significant use within the organization, that would indicate it indeed has a higher value.[1]

Some say that the cost to compromise a control[2] (a cost to be borne by a potential system penetrator) should be greater than the value of the compromise to the penetrator. While this rule-of-thumb has some theoretical justification in the military arena, it is seldom used in the commercial sector. Its validity is particularly suspect when one appreciates that system penetrators often act irrationally[3]. This cost-to-the-penetrator view of cost effectiveness is additionally suspect because it takes the analyst or designer away from the proper perspective to be used in control decisions— that of the owner (sometimes called sponsor) of the information. The cost-to-the-perpetrator view of cost effectiveness may be used, however, as a useful check on the owner-of-the-information view; this gives the decision maker greater assurance that all important aspects of the control environment have been included in the analysis.

With respect to groupware, the combination of an organization's existing applications and a groupware toolkit (such as Twin Sun's COeX) may suffice. Such toolkits can add a menu to existing applications so as to improve the productivity of workgroups. The toolkits also come with already-written code for certain controls, such as mediating simultaneous updates to a shared document made by two or more users. The toolkit software may cost a few thousand dollars rather than the tens of thousands of dollars that a groupware package may cost.

---

[1] A new methodology for valuing information will soon be issued by the Information Systems Security Association's Information Valuation Working Committee, on which the author sits. Contact the ISSA, P.O. Box 7367, Newport Beach, California, USA 92658, for further details of our work.

[2] This is traditionally known as the "work factor," i.e., the total financial amount required to circumvent a specific control measure.

[3] This is particularly true for system penetrators who are religious fanatics, deranged, or seeking revenge.

2. Simplicity

The less complex a control is, the less effort will be devoted to its design, implementation, operation, and the like. This will in turn improve its likelihood of being cost effective. Users and managers want to get their job done, not spend time attending to control measures. Accordingly, a control is more likely to be successful the less real-time dependence on people it requires. In many instances, simpler controls are stronger than complex controls because they can be thoroughly understood and tested, and because loopholes or trap-doors[1] can be more easily detected. Surprisingly, simpler controls are often better able to withstand the tests of time because they are understood by management and others who must support them. For example, the notion of having people sign their name to identify themselves is fundamentally very simple and for many years has been widely used. In the information security area, the notion of passwords to identify users likewise is simple and has been used for a long time.

Groupware products are generally considerably more complex than the software systems they have integrated such as electronic mail, document management, teleconferencing, scheduling, and project management. If a simpler product will meet your current and known future needs, it is preferable to groupware products. For example, if one of the major objectives of a proposed groupware implementation is accessing archived documents, then the reader might consider a product like Verity Inc.'s Topic system—a distributed full-text retrieval product with sophisticated indexing and query capabilities. This may meet the organization's critical needs, and in the process reduce the chances of security problems.

3. Override

Many of us have probably seen the ubiquitous fire alarm systems that include the instruction "break glass in event of emergency." Like these instructions, override measures are steps to be taken when ordinary procedures fail or when they are inappropriate. Under normal operating conditions, controls should not be subject to override. Only in special circumstances (such as when the control is materially interfering with business activities) should people with proper authority be allowed to stop, or otherwise interfere with, the operation of a control. The IBM systems programming product called Superzap is an example of an override control that should be used most judiciously. This program allows the user to modify and/or examine any file on a large mainframe, regardless of previously defined access control rules. If made generally available to all users, Superzap can quickly be used to overcome the constraints imposed by password-based access control packages such as IBM's RACF.

---

[1] A "trap door" is a specific segment of program code that allows programmers or other cognoscenti to defeat a control or obtain some privilege and/or service not otherwise available.

When one does not provide a failsafe or override mechanism, the resulting information system is likely to be unduly inflexible. For instance, it is highly desirable that access control restrictions be overridden so that a system may be rebuilt on different hardware in the event of a fire or some other disaster. Without this override capability, the entire recovery effort may be jeopardized.

It is important to remember that reset mechanisms should be provided to allow the reinitialization of a control. Reinitialization will be necessary to get the control back to the normal operational state. For example, if special access control related system privileges have been granted to a systems programmer so that he or she may fix a problem, these privileges can be defined to expire in a few days. In this way, the probability that these "godlike" privileges will be used for unauthorized activity is reduced.

With respect to groupware, consider how Lotus' Notes handles concurrent document updates. When two or more versions of the same document are modified, the most current version is selected as the "main" document to be replicated across the network. The documents that were not used to update the "main" document are archived to ensure that no information is lost. If one user is late in posting his or her changes, this algorithm for maintaining currency may break down. In this case, an older version will be adopted as the "main" document. Human involvement is then required to roll-back to a "previous" version of the document, i.e., the procedure must be overridden.

4. Overt Design and Operation

Overt design and operation of control measures is to be preferred to secrecy in and of itself. Although it may enhance security when combined with other controls, by itself, secrecy is not a strong approach to securing systems. For example, if an unusual and secret communications protocol is used for dial-up lines, that protocol alone should not be relied on to keep unauthorized persons off the system. To achieve a higher level of security, additional mechanisms, such as user identity tokens,[1] should be employed.

---

1 Identity tokens are smart cards or other hand-held devices that provide additional security in the user identification area. One of the most popular of such devices is a smart card offered by Security Dynamics of Boston, Massachusetts. With this system, one-time challenges issued from the host computer are encrypted by the token using a secret encryption key, and then returned to the host; only an authorized token will be able to perform this cryptographic transformation correctly.

The strength of a control depends primarily on its design and proper operation, and to a lesser extent on the secrecy surrounding it. Thus, the National Institute for Standards and Technology (NIST) subjected the Data Encryption Standard (DES) to public scrutiny and comment prior to endorsing it as a standard. The widespread analysis of the DES and the openness surrounding its operation have given those in the security community greater confidence in its ability to protect information and processes. If an encryption algorithm, such as the STEN algorithm used by the Society for Worldwide Interbank Funds Transfer (SWIFT), is kept proprietary to a vendor or organization, then the users or customers do not know whether it is indeed sufficiently strong to appropriately protect their information and processes.

Secrecy has its own hazards. If control measures and related activities are kept in secrecy, then incompetence, laziness, and illegality may be readily concealed. As the popular movie "The Snowman and the Falcon" illustrated, the encryption communications "code room," into which nobody but a select few were allowed, was a haven for activities that were in direct opposition to management policies. As another example, it was the cloak of secrecy that allowed certain high ranking officials in the Reagan White House to circumvent United States law and to support the Contras in Nicaragua. As the former President found out, overreliance on secrecy may lead to a loss of control.

Accordingly, while confidentiality of design and operation may be helpful, significant reliance should not be placed on these measures. For instance, the specifics on the configuration for an access control package such as RACF should not be readily available to all who wish to examine them. To a much greater extent, reliance should be placed on the access control rules enforced by RACF.

In the groupware arena, consider the rendering of digital signatures—an encryption-based process whereby a user can definitively show that a message was sent by a certain person and that the message has not been altered. NIST has announced that it will endorse an obscure method to generate digital signatures (called ElGamal). Meanwhile, Lotus' Notes already uses the widely-endorsed and widely-tested RSA public-key encryption approach to providing digital signatures. While the security of both of these digital signature techniques depends on the secrecy of encryption keys, NIST has taken a questionable position because RSA digital signatures have already been widely deployed, licensed by many influential computer vendors, endorsed by international standards organizations, and subjected to extensive strength testing. The ElGamal technique has none of these and is additionally considerably slower than the RSA approach.

5. Least Privilege

The concept of least privilege involves what the military calls "need-to-know." It indicates that access to information, the ability to execute certain programs, and other system privileges should be restricted to those who can demonstrate or make a case for a business- or mission-related need. When applied to standard file-oriented access control packages such as RACF, the least privilege concept involves the distinctions known as "subjects" and "objects." Only those objects (files, databases, application programs, terminals, etc.) required for the performance of a task or the execution of a computer program are granted to specific subjects (users, application programs, networks, etc.). When applied to modern system integrity theory, this concept involves the distinctions of data, programs, and users.[1] Integrity of data is preserved by allowing only certain programs to access such data; integrity of the processes supported by programs is preserved by allowing only designated users to affect the processes.

Least privilege is a very powerful security principle, but when used to excess has significant adverse side effects. For example, if employees do not know what others are doing or how they are doing it, there is scant opportunity for them to make suggestions to improve the organization's operations. Likewise, the assembly-line specialization inherent in the least privilege approach is often demoralizing for workers and often leads to boring and unrewarding work.

In the groupware domain, packages such as Lotus' Notes employ "views" (like database subschemas) to show only the information that a certain user can access, not all of the information on the system. Notes also uses access control lists (ACLs) to define user and process privileges. These ACLs are defined with new document-oriented distinctions that were previously unnecessary in the mainframe world. For example, a Notes administrator can define users as "depositors," i.e., users who may submit documents but not read or edit them. In addition, the granularity of access controls under Notes has been refined so that administrators can specify user access to fields within a document, rather than access to a document as a whole.

---

[1] For further information on the Clark/Wilson model, see NIST Special Publication 500-160, entitled "Report on the Invitational Workshop on Integrity Policy in Computer Information Systems (WIPCIS)," edited by Stuart W. Katzke and Zella G. Ruthberg, January 1989. This publication is available from the US Government Printing Office, Washington, DC 20402; code number NSPUE2.

6. Entrapment

Entrapment refers to the process by which someone is lured into performing an illegal or abusive act. One way to establish controls that use entrapment is to set up an easy-to-compromise "hole" in the access control system and then log or otherwise observe those system penetrators who attempt to exploit this hole. Entrapment has been used successfully to lure juvenile systems hackers into performing certain acts, such as playing games over dial-up lines, in turn allowing their calls to be traced or other incriminating evidence to be gathered. Entrapment may be one of the few means available to gather information about unknown penetrators already accessing an organization's systems. It may also be useful in the gathering of evidence for prosecution or punishment of system penetrators. Note that entrapment related controls may violate local laws, regulations, or ethical standards, and may therefore be contraindicated. Prior to installing entrapment-related controls, consultation with one's attorney is advisable.

With respect to groupware, consider NCR Corp.'s Cooperation groupware package. Using the Business Information Monitor features in Cooperation, managers can monitor, maintain, and report the status of information contained anywhere in a network. Likewise, this software can extract information automatically from a wide variety of databases including those created by 1-2-3, Excel, Oracle, SQLBase, DB2, dBASE, R:base, Paradox, DataEase, and AS/400 Data Manager. The data may be local or remote, and it may be accessed directly without conversion or filtering. Besides being used for executive information systems and other groupware needs, such facilities could be used for monitoring an entrapment situation. The power and flexibility of this software underscores the need to rigidly restrict access to authorized personnel.

7. Independence of Control and Subject

The person charged with designing, implementing, and/or operating a control should not be the same person who is to be controlled thereby. For example, a conflict of interest would exist if the individual who designed an encryption system is at the same time controlled by that system. Likewise, management should not expect to exclusively control systems programmers who installed an access control package such as RACF with that same package. Other control measures, such as peer review, should be used to control these systems programmers. As another example, the Information Security function should not report to the EDP Audit Department because EDP Audit will then be unable to perform an unbiased review of the work performed by Information Security. In overall terms, this principle is a variation of separation of duties, with specific focus on who is controlled by which measures.

In the groupware area, consider the access controls that come along with Lotus' Notes. Access control lists (ACLs) may include individuals, groups, and groups within groups. Furthermore, Notes uses "deny lists" as an additional barrier to unauthorized accesses. These "deny lists" specify which people (such as former employees) are not to have privileges. In this environment, it would be inappropriate for a Notes administrator to grant himself or herself significant operational privileges, such as the ability to write paychecks. Although certain small organizations may be forced to do this, it is a violation of the notion of separation of duties. If it is necessary to grant the administrator such privileges, compensating controls like increased supervision should be employed.

8. Universal Application

Universal application refers to the consistent and all-embracing usage of a control measure across the spectrum of environments, computers, or people to be controlled. Each exception in this spectrum weakens a control. For example, if top management is not required to wear badges when in the computer room, then an interloper may likewise be in the computer center, and the operations staff may stay out of his way, regarding him as a new member of the top management team. As another example, if the only people who need to wear identity badges are visitors, a curious visitor who wanted to take a look around could easily masquerade as an employee simply by removing his badge. If badges must be worn by every person in a controlled area, the status of visitors and others in need of escorts or special treatment can be easily determined and consistently enforced. The concept of universal application is properly manifested in the design approach to password-based access control systems called "complete mediation." On computers where this approach has been implemented, every user or process request for service must first be checked against a list of authorized privileges; if access has been explicitly permitted, only then is the request granted.

In the groupware area, Lotus' Notes is a good example of a product that treats remote and local users the same way. Groupware products should apply the same access controls to all users, no matter what type of a workstations are employed, and no matter what operating system runs on these workstations. Unfortunately, many groupware systems rely on the underlying workstation operating system(s) to provide security services. This means that differences in operating system access controls will affect the extent to which groupware controls may be inconsistently applied. Under these circumstances, it may be necessary to use a workstation-based groupware package such as OASIS from Knowledge Network Systems. OASIS extends the server controls found in Novell NetWare to the workstation. With OASIS, workstation local drives can be locked, software running on a workstation can be metered, and certain server access controls can be extended to the workstation.

9. Acceptance of Control Subjects

If controls are not acceptable to users, or to others who are affected by such controls, these people (collectively called "subjects") will invariably find a way to overcome or ignore them. The interpersonal communications needed to garner support for new controls are often forgotten in the effort to patch up an inadequate control system in the wake of a major loss. Management often treats the involved people as though they are just another part of the system, without feelings, concerns, and other uniquely human attributes in need of special consideration. Without investing time to gain acceptance from those involved, without training these same people, and without otherwise obtaining cooperation and support, management invites sabotage, work slow-downs, and other rebellious responses. For example, at a well-known computer manufacturer's facility in Italy, a plastic card-based physical access control system was installed on nearly every door in the data center. Every time employees went into the hall, into the washroom, into the lunchroom, or into other areas, they were forced to insert their card into a wall reader. The employees considered the system an unwarranted invasion of their privacy, and soon after it was installed, they went on strike.

The performance impact on both involved humans and involved computers is an important element of garnering acceptance of control subjects. If there is an adverse performance impact, given no dispensation for the changed circumstances, acceptance will be most difficult to obtain. For example, if data entry personnel get paid based on the number of transactions they enter, and if management introduced a control that slows their data entry work, the staff would be likely to object, unless there was a corresponding adjustment in the pay rate.

One of the primary reasons why groupware has not caught on with more organizations is the concern about its effects on the business. These effects include inadvertent disclosure of information to those who should not have access to it, invasive monitoring of employee behavior, business interruptions caused by the unavailability of groupware systems, and other security matters. Before groupware will be wholeheartedly supported by management, the promoters of the technology must demonstrate that security will be adequately handled.

10. Sustainability

Controls should not only be resilient, they also should be able to stand up over time and under a wide range of adverse circumstances. Sustainability is intimately tied to both flexibility and adaptability. For example, self-healing packet switching networks now automatically re-route message traffic over communications lines that are working when other lines are no longer available. Likewise, neural networks use hardware redundancy so that they are able to produce a certain result in spite of an internal fault. The successful "continuous-processing" redundant computers made by Tandem and Stratus demonstrate that sustainability is an exemplary and marketable systems design principle.

Sustainability implies not only that controls should be resistant to intentional efforts to compromise them, but also that unintentional acts should not jeopardize the proper functioning of controls. For example, software that incorporates a digital signature checking routine is able to detect intentional as well as unintentional alterations in messages and/or files. Using processes much like hash coding or check digits, MACs are sustainable despite deliberate fraudulent activities or hardware-induced errors in data.

More generally speaking, to be sustainable, controls should be designed to accommodate the most significant threats; they will thereby also be able to accommodate many lesser threats. For example, if a system is designed to withstand a wide range of intentional attacks, it most likely will be able to withstand operator-induced errors and omissions. If the same system was first designed to accommodate only errors and omissions, and controls for intentional attacks were added later, the total cost would ordinarily be significantly greater because two separate control systems would be required. A sustainable design that handles a wide variety of circumstances is often also an integrated system system that, in overall terms, involve lower costs.

Groupware can be considered as the next level of integration beyond network computing. Since it brings several application systems together, often on an organization-wide or inter-organizational basis, groupware is likely to present a significant contingency planning challenge. If groupware is used and a software fault is encountered, a large number of applications may be down; in a traditional environment with relatively unintegrated applications, only one application would be down. Thus more in-depth contingency planning may be required to reflect the tighter integration of applications that groupware provides. Simply moving to an alternate site and loading last week's back-up tapes may no longer be sufficient.

11. Auditability

Auditability requires that controls generate sufficient evidence to show that they have been operating correctly.   This evidence may take the form of logs, audit trails, reports, blinking lights, or other forms of obvious or hidden feedback. One of the most salient examples involves password-based access control systems, which can generate voluminous logs showing when users logged-in, when they logged-out, the programs they ran, and the requests for access they submitted (whether approved or denied).   Without evidence that a control is operating properly, management cannot be confident that the control is in fact doing the job it is intended to do. Without such evidence, management is unable to make adjustments so that the control does its job better. Auditability, therefore, does not merely apply to the auditors; it is an essential part of day-to-day management.

A more proactive view towards auditability involves what is sometimes called instrumentation. Instrumentation refers to specific lights or other feedback that a control provides such that if it fails, or if it is being attacked, those responsible for the control are immediately notified. The notification allows these parties to promptly take corrective or defensive actions. Thus, some commercially available personal computer access control devices have audible alarms which announce that their "tamper-proof enclosures" have been compromised. Similarly, some password-based access control systems like IBM's RACF notify the operator on duty if someone is attempting to gain system access by guessing passwords. In the latter example, a more proactive design allows attempted as opposed to actual unauthorized system access to be reported.

Lotus Notes provides a number of laudable ways to achieve an auditable groupware system. For example, the authenticity and source of documents can be checked with digital signatures. Similarly, Notes uses user-IDs, passwords, and encryption to create "certificates" that reflect the identity of the users interacting with a groupware system. This information is then used to create logs reflecting system activity.

12. Accountability

Accountability is one of the most fundamental internal control principles. It refers to a specific individual being answerable, responsible, or liable for specific activities. For example, a user-ID and a password serve as the means of identifying users on the Higgins groupware system from Enable Software Inc. A user-ID and a unique password make such users accountable for the activities they perform. If mechanisms like user-IDs and passwords were not available, there would be no way of tracing specific activities to the initiating parties. Without such accountability, a forensic (fraud-oriented) audit would be impossible. Without accountability, computers could not support electronic mail or groupware systems where message recipients have confidence that the senders indeed are who they are alleged to be.

The operation of control measures should also be assigned to specific individuals, i.e. at least one individual should be explicitly accountable for the proper functioning of a control. The explicit assignment of this accountability is very important to motivating involved parties to support specific control measures. For example, assigning accountability for the use of a specific user-ID to each individual to whom user-IDs are issued is an important part of ensuring that the user does not share his or her password, choose a password that is easily guessed, or otherwise behave in a way that compromises the security provided by password-based access control packages.

Rather than just using user-IDs and passwords, Lotus' Notes goes one step further by employing public-key encryption to authenticate both individual users and servers. While most computer literate people are familiar with the process of authenticating their identity to a computer, they are not familiar with a remote computer authenticating itself to the user, nor are they familiar with a remote computer authenticating itself to another computer. As incidents of masquerading nodes and hosts become more prevalent, such encryption-based computer authentication to both users and other computers will become standard practice.

13. Defensive Depth

Greater security is achieved with defensive depth, that is, when multiple overlapping controls protect a single asset. We see this for instance at nuclear power plants where a fence is used in conjunction with motion detectors and other physical access controls. If one of these controls is compromised or circumvented, the other controls provide a safety net to ensure that, in overall terms, a penetration is not successful.

Defensive depth is also found in the redundant use of a single control measure. For example, nuclear power plants sometimes use several concentric fences to protect the facility. If an attacker gets through one fence, he or she still must go through the others. This same approach is found where two layers of passwords are required in groupware systems such as Close-Up LAN from Norton-Lambert Corp. For instance, a first password might be used to log-into a local network node; a second password may be required to get special privileges. Whether single or multiple types of controls are used, the fundamental idea pointing to the principle of defensive depth is the old adage "don't put all your [control] eggs in one basket."

The defensive depth principle should be applied with the understanding that a strong system is created when controls are connected in parallel rather than in series. Controls configured in parallel must both be compromised before the protected system can be compromised, while controls configured in series may either be compromised for the system to be compromised.

14. Isolation and Compartmentalization

Unlike defensive depth, the principle of isolation and compartmentalization does not focus on layers or redundancy of controls. This principle instead argues for the splitting up, diversifying, and/or dispersing of assets. By segmenting assets into separate groups, one increases the overall ability of a system to withstand shocks and adverse events. For example, data centers may have multiple backups of critical files and programs stored at different sites. If a fire destroys one copy, computer operations can be recovered with the other copies. Similarly, a groupware package like Lotus' Notes supporting a distributed database may have multiple overlapping backups at different sites. Unavailability or corruption of the database at any one site can be overcome by using the portions of that one site's database stored at other sites. Another groupware example involves Notes' use of separate encrypted areas for each user. These areas prevent Notes administrators from reading the electronic mail of a particular user.

As with the defensive depth principle, the "don't put all your eggs in one basket" adage underlies the principle of isolation and compartmentalization. The latter, however, is concerned with assets whereas the former is concerned with controls. With isolation and compartmentalization, the compromise of a control will not jeopardize the entire asset because the asset has been separated into parts. Such separation can be either logical or physical. Although they are stored on a single same computer, information assets can be separated logically, for instance, with an access control package. Information assets can be separated physically as mentioned above by locating them at different sites.

15. Least Common Mechanism

The principle of least common mechanism seeks to minimize reliance on a central system component that may become unavailable. For instance, if a local area network (LAN) has a bus or a star configuration, failure of either the bus or the central star node will mean the network is unavailable. But failure of any one link on a LAN with a ring configuration will not render the LAN unavailable; in this case, traffic will be sent the other way around the ring. Thus the ring structure is the best of these three configurations from the standpoint of least common mechanism. Implementers of groupware systems would be well-advised to reconsider the stability of the central LAN components supporting their groupware system.

The least common mechanism principle implies that the effectiveness of controls should not, to the extent possible, depend on the proper operation of other controls. For example, if an organization uses automatically generated terminal passwords[1] but no user-IDs or passwords to control system access, it is implicitly relying on physical measures to control who may gain access to a computer. If unauthorized physical access is obtained, unauthorized system access may also be easily obtained. A more secure way to design this system would be to have two separate and independent systems, one for controlling physical access, and one for controlling computer access.

Seen a bit differently, the design principle of least common mechanism indicates that systems should minimize the number of mechanisms shared by different users for their mutual security. For example, if all the banks who used an electronic funds transfer network relied on the network to perform authenticity checks of the data sent over the network, then the compromise of the network's data authenticity checking process (such as a digital signature) could lead to similar compromises for each of the banks. It would be preferable to have the banks separately perform their own authenticity checks, thereby eliminating reliance on a shared control. As was mentioned in the section dealing with sustainability, there is reason to be concerned about the resilience of centralized controls provided by a groupware system.

---

[1] Terminal passwords are known by various other names, such as location-specific system passwords and hardware-linked passwords. Terminal passwords allow anyone knowing such a password to access the system, as long as the person is using a predetermined terminal, workstation, or personal computer. That the correct hardware is being used is often checked by random number challenge/response dialogs, or by a special chip containing a unique parameter implanted in the involved device. Properly speaking, terminal passwords are lockwords, not passwords. Lockwords are secret strings of characters that allow anyone who knows them access to a system resource. Passwords are uniquely associated with a single user, whereas lockwords are shared among users. Automatically generated terminal passwords do not require user interaction; they are handled entirely by the computer system.

16. Control the Periphery

The notion of a fence or wall is fundamental to security for good reason. If an unauthorized agent is able to get into a castle or a computer system, significant damage could be done. Accordingly, strong computer systems focus on detecting and preventing intrusion at the point of attempted break-in or control compromise rather than after the intruder has gained entry.

An example is provided by password based access control systems which prevent unauthorized persons from gaining any system access whatsoever. The groupware package known as BRAINSTORM from Mustang Software includes such passwords. When implemented in a secure fashion, these systems do not allow unauthorized persons any system privileges and do not disclose any information that might assist in a break-in effort. They do not allow the display of user names or telephone numbers, and they do not provide information that might be useful to an attacker intent on guessing passwords. Another example of the control the periphery principle is provided by new computer virus detection packages that will immediately alert the user to the fact that an infected floppy disk has been inserted into the machine. This alert allows the user to avoid running the software on the disk, and thereby prevents infection of the software resident on his or her machine.

17. Completeness and Consistency

Strong controls are completely specified, completely tested, and consistently operated. Recognizing the mathematical proof problems inherent in complete specification of all possible conditions that might be faced by a system, "completeness" as used here refers to all conceivable conditions. While developers will never have true closure on specification or testing, they can at least strive to be comprehensive in their efforts. This approach to specification and testing has been quite popular within the US Department of Defense and has in fact spawned a class of computer systems called "provably secure systems."

Likewise, regular and conscientious operation of controls will provide significantly more control than infrequent application. Regular operation need not preclude the element of surprise that so often reveals control conditions in need of changes. Regular operation can refer to twice a quarter, or some similar quota rather than a specific time and date. As a time-specific example of consistent operation, commercial banks provide a good example. At the end of each day, tellers must reconcile their transactions and balance their accounts.

In the groupware area, Lotus' Notes 3.0 is expected to include a spreadsheet package called Chronicle that will allow users to send part of a spreadsheet to another user without exiting the spreadsheet program. Although the author does not know how this feature will be implemented, there is reason to be concerned about the proliferation of multiple communication channels for the movement of information in groupware systems. For completeness and consistency reasons, we need standard information highways over which all information travels. Only when all information is using the same highways can we apply standard "rules of the road" to this information, thus ensuring that it is adequately protected (for instance via communications encryption).

18. Default to Denial

When a control fails—and designers should anticipate such failure—the control should deny access to users and other entities requesting service. As an example, many encryption devices will shut-down completely if they are being tampered with. This control prevents the devices from being used by unauthorized parties to decrypt wiretapped incoming messages, prevents an unauthorized person from using the devices to masquerade as though he or she was an authorized sender of messages, and prevents the devices from revealing secret key and internal operational information that might be used to compromise other encryption devices.

Designers should appreciate that it is most often easier to turn a control off than it is to circumvent it. For example, some systems programmers simply turn the password-based access control system off when they want additional privileges. If the control is designed such that turning it off does not compromise security, additional operational flexibility can also be obtained. In those instances where circumstances require the control to be deactivated (such as recovering from a computer virus), management will be able to rest easy because deactivation of the control does not imply that the assets protected by the control will be made unduly vulnerable.

The default to denial principle is manifested another way in password-based access control packages. If access to a "resource" (file, database, application program, etc.) is not explicitly granted to a user, some access control packages, such as Computer Associates' ACF2, will deny access rather than permit it. The opposite approach was taken by a popular groupware package that had best go nameless. Thanks to a software bug, this groupware package allows multiple users on a network to edit a document simultaneously. Normally simultaneous access means that the first user has both read and write privileges, while subsequent users have only read privileges. The bug allows all simultaneous users to have write privileges. Under this principle, the groupware package should have denied write privileges to everyone rather than provide them to everyone.

Future groupware packages can benefit from a timeout feature in which user privileges expire if they were not used for a certain period of time, such as 60 days. Thus, machine to machine communications links, document access privileges, and the like would automatically default to denial in the absence of active usage.

19. Parameterization

The principle of parameterization indicates that controls are more effective and flexible if variables, rather than constants, are used. For example, if a retail point-of-sale system were to have a floor limit that changed daily, criminals using stolen credit cards would not know at what total amount their purchases needed to be authorized by a central database. The criminals would thus be discouraged from engaging in credit card crime because today might be the day when they would get caught. If the same system had a stable $100 floor limit, below which purchases did not require authorization at the time of purchase, criminals would be sure to keep their purchases below this level. Beyond discouraging criminals and other abusers of a system, parameterization also allows management to more readily reconfigure controls to better suit a changed business environment.

In the groupware world, Lotus' Notes provides dynamic encryption session keys for the protection of all communications travelling over a channel. The key is assigned for each session, and thus provides only a small volume of information that could be used by an attacker attempting to recover the encrypted information. Since only a small volume of information is available, a solution that allowed recovery of the encrypted data would be of limited value, therefore reducing the incentive for such an attack. Other security parameters that can be modified in groupware systems include passwords, pseudo-random number generator seeds, and encryption initialization vectors.

20. Hostile Environment

Until proven otherwise, controls should be built with a hostile environment in mind. Designers should build systems such that they are able to accommodate the worst user intentions, the lowest user capabilities, the most horrendous of user errors, as well as the occurrence of other unfortunate and/or adverse circumstances. Assumptions about a high level of user education, a certain modicum of intelligence, basic clear thinking, quick reaction time, or other desirable attributes should NOT be made. Therefore, designers should consistently incorporate all important controls, and should refrain from thinking that user characteristics will make up for the absence of a control. For example, designers should not omit an important control, believing that users will compensate for the control's absence after they read complicated instructions found in accompanying documentation.

This design principle, which embraces Murphy's Law,[1] is exemplified by some of the equipment used by the US Department of Defense. Known as "ruggedized" equipment, these computers are able to withstand very high humidity, extremely dusty conditions, etc. While such extreme conditions are not likely to be encountered in the typical business data center, thought about the hostile agents the organization faces is very much in order. These include disgruntled employees, employees under the influence of drugs, and "acts of God" such as earthquakes. The designers of Lotus' Notes have thought about such things; they have reflected their concern in the system's extensive use of encryption to protect both information in motion and at rest.

21. Human Involvement

The principle of human involvement requires the intermediation of a human being in every critical or very important decision. Although impressive strides forward have been made in the domains of artificial intelligence, expert systems, neural networks, and other "thinking machines," complete reliance should not be placed in the omnipotence and comprehensive vision of the programming behind these systems. Inevitably there will be circumstances where the answer provided by the machine is wrong, inapplicable, or unreliable. Contemporary computer systems cannot appreciate all the possible circumstances and cannot be counted on to exercise common sense. Accordingly, there should always be a human being acting as a double check on the system.

A good example of this is the nuclear missile attack warning system used in the United States. Considerable discussion among computer scientists is devoted to how much we can rely on the computer to accurately understand the circumstances and take corrective action. Many, including the author, believe that the only tenable approach is to require the involvement of humans (in this case more than one) before any retaliatory missiles are launched. Other less potentially catastrophic decisions are made every day in the data center: should a disk be reformatted, should a system be powered down, and should a computer operator get a raise? Computers have a long way to go before we can rest assured that they are making appropriate decisions for these and other questions.

---

[1] Although there are many corollaries, the basic version observes that "anything that can go wrong, will go wrong."

In the groupware arena, an innovative product called Beyond Mail from Beyond Inc. includes the ability to define agents that automatically take action based on the content of electronic mail messages. For example, such agents can scan the wire service feed from Dow Jones looking for keywords, extract certain stories, sort these, and forward them to the appropriate individuals. The package also allows electronic mail users to define rules to create work-group applications without the intervention of an administrator. While it is a suitable replacement for human clipping services, such end-user programming of these agents should be prohibited for critical or very important business activities. These end-user programming privileges also highlight the need for appropriate user training on security as well as other matters.

22. Secure Image

Whether or not reality bears it out, an image of security and orderly operation should always be presented to the public. To look vulnerable is to invite attack and exploitation. It is for this reason (and others) that many organizations choose not to disclose the fact that they have been victimized by a computer criminal. Image applies to systems as well as to organizations. Preventing the revelation of inconsistent or disorderly controls, whenever they exist, is an important part of maintaining customer confidence. Many people have changed banks because a bank computer generated statements that had incorrect balances and the resulting error resolution process did not convince them that their bank in fact is well-controlled.

From a systems design perspective, if an internal fault is detected, it should not be communicated to the customer, but to some employee who is in a position to take corrective action. If it is necessary to communicate an internal fault to a customer, it is very important that the customer maintain confidence in the organization's systems of internal controls; this might be accomplished by informing the customer, in general terms, about the mechanisms used to detect and resolve problems. In general, it is a poor idea to rely on customers or other external parties to alert an organization to control problems.

Some groupware systems, such as Higgins from Enable Software, allow end-users to create information resources and set up rules for sharing these resources. If the end-user departments are writing their own applications, it becomes the end-user department's duty to convince management that the system they are creating will include adequate security measures. Although it may sound rather traditional, this is another situation where software development change controls are needed. Even in end-user departments, management should review and test such in-house systems to give themselves assurances that these systems have both an image and the reality of security.

23. Low Profile

The principle of low profile applies to both assets and controls. The existence of significant assets should not be thrust into the public eye. The practice of displaying expensive computer equipment through a large window is ill-advised and old-fashioned. To do so invites terroristic attack and informs passers-by that this is where the computer center is located. Instead, computer equipment and related activities should be inconspicuous or preferably not noticeable. As a good example of the latter approach, newer computer machine rooms are placed in windowless rooms without any sign designating the activities carried on therein. Servers supporting groupware systems should likewise be locked in closets or other physically-inaccessible locations.

Application of the principle of low profile is also appropriate to controls. It implies that the very existence of control measures may in fact be withheld from employees and other subjects to whom the controls are applied. Alternatively, the details of how certain controls work may be withheld. Either of these approaches discourage attacks from knowledgeable insiders who might otherwise reason that they know how to defeat the controls. In general, it is a good idea to restrict access to documentation about controls.

Summary

Very rarely will all of the control principles discussed above be applicable to any one system being developed, enhanced, or maintained. However, by examining and understanding how these principles might be applicable to a proposed system design, the systems developer will be likely to generate many ideas for better information security. By keeping an open mind and by not immediately dismissing a control principle, the developer will be able to generate an even larger number of proposals for improved control. The same applies to the auditor and the system purchaser.

Some of the above-mentioned principles may point to contradictory system designs. This should not be cause for concern or loss of confidence in the principles; it is instead evidence of the real-world need to make decisions about tradeoffs. For example, an extreme application of the principle of least common mechanism would mean that all users should have their own machines, complete and current copies of every database they might need, copies of all programs they may ever need, etc. This approach would be inconsistent with the principle of hostile environment, which indicates that the end-user may in fact be an unauthorized person. Another systems design that embraces others of the principles is likely to be more-user-friendly and in other ways preferable.

Inconsistencies between the implications of the different control principles should not preclude the use of multiple controls. Strong systems are made up of a well-designed fabric of many controls, which, in overall terms, synergistically work together. The real challenge for the systems designer is to understand the synergistic, antagonistic, and symbiotic relationships among controls, and to incorporate this understanding into systems.

About the Author:

Charles Cresson Wood is an independent management consultant specializing in computer and data communications security. His practice involves risk assessments, secure systems design, tailoring application controls, policy and standard writing, and end-user training. In the information security field since 1978, he has been a computer security management consultant at SRI International, and chief data communications security consultant at Bank of America. He has done information security work for over 80 organizations, many of them Fortune 500 companies and/or information security vendors. Mr. Wood has also been a keynote speaker at several conferences. He is the author or co-author of several information security software packages, over 75 technical articles, and three books. He additionally serves as the Senior North American Editor for Computers & Security magazine. His work has taken him to Australia, Austria, Belgium, Brazil, Canada, England, Finland, France, Holland, Ireland, Italy, Norway, Portugal, Saudi Arabia, and Sweden.

TRACK 2:
Technology and Groupware Development

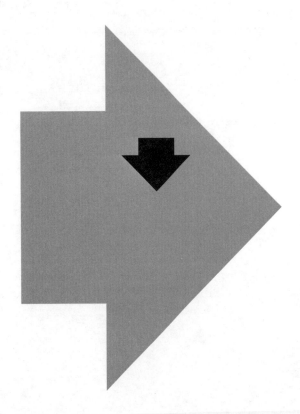

Glueware

This panel, called Glueware, will address some of the issues surrounding the layer of software that falls between applications software and operating systems software. Glueware, sometimes referred to as middleware, consists of network services, connectivity software, application programming interfaces, and other elements that provide a structural framework for the implementation of distributed applications.

Vendors and researchers on the panel will outline the requirements for this glueware layer in today's emerging distributed networks. In addition, there will be a discussion of active groupware functions such as mail and integrated groupware applications, toolkits, and prescient agents that can monitor and anticipate user needs.

Panel Moderator

Timothy O'Brien
West Coast Bureau Chief, Network World

Panelists

Hub Vandervoort, Horizon Strategies, Inc.
Yaron Goldberg, The Weismann Institute of Science
Scott McGregor, Atherton Technology
Dorab Patel, Twin Sun, Inc.

Glueware: The Evolution and Feasibility of Distributed Applications In a Multivendor Network

by

Timothy O'Brien and Hub Vandervoort

Over the past five years the vision of fully interconnectible, open systems, has been at least partially realized with the advent of sophisticated, internetworking transmission equipment and cost effective carrier-based networking solutions. These ascending technologies have enabled users to construct high bandwidth private networks which provide reliable "any-to-any connectivity" between computers, which means physical access to the computing resource no longer presents the technical or financial challenge to wide-spread computer availability.

Further, the vast selection of emerging standards has, at least in part, helped guide the provider and user of transmission equipment toward insured "plug-and-play" compatibility with new and existing transmission equipment allowing any computer in the organization to "get on the corporate backbone and have its data ride upon a common medium.

Yet with all of this progress, benefits to the end-user continue to lag far behind, as there is still something lacking in the integration of all of this communication and computing technology across all of the human and business processes pervasive to daily corporate life. Simply put, the computers are communicating but the applications are not.

The reasons for this dilemma stems from two areas: Protocols and application interoperability methodologies. On the one hand, the compatibility between device protocols remains elusive, and on the other hand the technologies and methodologies for interchanging information between computer applications has remained largely vendor, and even application specific.

Many enterprises are finding that a more cost effective way to support business applications is to "downsize" selected applications from the corporate mainframe computer to a mid-range system, workstation, or LAN-supported servers and clients workstations. These new (and smaller) platforms for the application are not only proving to be more cost effective, they are providing the required (or greater) performance and usually more flexibility in growth and application support. Many enterprises are going the distance and dismantling the corporate mainframe computer altogether, completely distributing the processing power.

All of the above computing relationships, including file transfer, can be grouped into one broad category called distributed computing. The market for solutions in the distributed computing environment is rapidly growing. This is evidenced by the wave of new product announcements specifically addressing the various modes of distributed computing, such as client/server, Remote Procedure Call, or distributed objects.

In other instances, the mainframe system remains as the "workhorse" for high volume transaction processing, or the repository of the enterprise database (which may not be portable to smaller computing environments because of size). The mainframe might remain as the political anchor that the enterprise just can't eliminate. In these instances, access from the new distributed applications to the mainframe presents the new challenge.

Earlier attempts at decentralized computing offerings (and there have been several) were, by and large, specific to a vendor, with proprietary protocols, devices, limited applications, and few tools to manage the distributed application network. Currently, many enterprises are struggling to adopt an interconnect strategy that will guide computing equipment and software investments in the future.

In recent years, numerous vendors and standards committees have put forth guidelines and specifications that all computer vendors can adhere to in developing their products so that interconnection with other brands of computing equipment can be achieved with minimal pain. The guidelines are really being developed for the user in response to increasing demand for interoperability between manufacturer's offerings. More and more, vendors are being forced to offer some type of standards compliance (or statement of future compliance) in order to compete.

Many of these standards attempts are still in finalization stages but examples of these open systems are the International Organization for Standards' (ISO) reference model, the Open Software Foundation (OSF), Distributed Computing Environment (DCE), the Defense Advanced

Research Projects Agency, Transmission Control Protocol/Internet Protocol (TCP/IP), and to a certain extent International Business Machine's (IBM) Application Program-to-Program Communication (APPC), Advanced Peer-to-Peer Networking (APPN), and Common Programming Interface for Communications (CPI-C).

This movement towards open systems is visibly evident. Scores of software vendors are offering products that support one or more of the above interconnect methodologies. And, most major computer equipment vendors offer at least one methodology for integrating their computer(s) with other manufacturer's offerings.

Importantly, all of the above methodologies address only part of the concern. All provide for some common protocol for computing systems to employ when communicating with one another. All provide for some interface to the user's application (typically referred to as an Application Program Interface, or API). The APIs are generally complex, with numerous application verbs, hundreds of verb parameters, and hundreds of error conditions that he "business" application programmer has to deal with. Additionally, these APIs (even within one vendor's array of offerings) will present inconsistent interfaces, from one computing platform to another, for the programmer to "hook" the business application to. This not only complicates the development and maintenance of applications, but greatly limits the portability of completed applications from one computing platform to another.

Even with an application API, the actual "business application" is lacking. In other words, the processing rules, data structures, and data flow still need to be developed or purchased to sit on top of these interconnect methodologies.

The term client/server seems to be applied very loosely to a broad variety of offerings. One type of offering, called CASE (Computer Assisted Systems Engineering) tools, actually generates (writes the code) client/server application software for a specific user need based on higher-level parameters that are input to the process. The result is the desired application, complete with Graphic User Interface (GUI), and communications capabilities to other supported computing platforms.

In providing these tools, the vendor will typically embed one of the interconnect methodologies mentioned earlier (APPC, TCP/IP), as the basis for communication with the participating computing platforms, into their specific offering which rides on top of the interconnect methodology. The user is shielded from the intricacies of the communications protocol, and given a framework for development of an application specific to the business need.

The trend in interconnection is shifting away from gateway-like connections, and towards connections that provide for transparent access, or seamless operation with networked computing platforms. This seamless operation calls for freedom from device specifics and formatting information that is typically required for control of the device and user presentation. Newer deployments of technology allow the "local" computing platform to perform all of the front-end functions, such as presentation (menus, screens, or graphic user interface) and editing (checking that entries are numeric, of the proper length or range, etc.), while shipping only the application specific data to the remote computing platform where it performs its functions. This defines "client/server" computing, where the "client" initiates processing by performing front-end functions, and then requests back-end processing from a "server". The server typically files or retrieves data, performs some calculation or response screening (filtering out undesired information) and returns the results or requested information to the client. This client/server model is often used in decision support applications, where data needs to be retrieved quickly from a central database, and presented in a useable form to the user that may be responding to a customer inquiry or problem.

The client/server offerings (for the most part) support access to databases, with the predominant database methodology referred to as SQL (Structured Query Language).   SQL defines a standardized format for queries or updates from a user (or client) to the database (residing on a server).   Most of the major database vendors support SQL compliant interfaces and communications links to various computing platforms.   There can be tremendous advantages to supporting a network-wide database and access strategy.   Upon deployment, users retrieve and file data using a standard interface, regardless of computing platform type.

However, even after implementation, SQL methodologies have several limitations which can leave the user with the residual need for some peer-to-peer methodology.   Distributed SQL databases and SQL gateways (a bridge from a computing platform without a resident SQL database and a platform where the database resides) support the client/server mode of operation only, i.e. one-way request and deliver.   Two-way exchanges of data and commands that trigger some subsequent process, whether on the original requesting platform or some other platform in the network, are very limited.

Another variant of the client/server model is called Remote Procedure Call (RPC).   In this model, the client calls on a server for execution of part of a program that they both are responsible for completing.   This is similar in concept to procedure calls in a program, where a required routine is accessible by other portions of the program when needed, with the whole program being resident on the same computer.   An RPC extends the call on the procedure to a remote computer over some network and interconnect methodology, thus Remote Procedure Call.   This client/server model is often used in high volume, heavy calculation environments, where the primary computer needs to off-load part of the processing burden to "partner" computers to accomplish the overall task.

Another computing relationship, peer-to-peer (or cooperative processing), provides for two-way interaction between intelligent processes, where either participating computing platform can act as client and server as the specific application might require.   Some method of messaging is typically employed that carries the application data and commands to be processed between the participating computing platforms.

An origin application (running, perhaps, on a PC)   might send a request with the necessary data to a destination application (let's say, running on the mainframe) to generate a sales order.   The destination application might respond with results (maybe a completion notification with sales order number).   The destination application might now assume the new role of origin application for the next in the chain of events.   The next sequence might involve subsequent requests (perhaps a manufacturing order to fill the sales order) to the original application platform for execution or to an application (that handles manufacturing materials requisitions) on a third computing platform elsewhere in the network.

Applications that require event-driven processing, spread across similar or dissimilar computing platforms, can benefit from this approach.   Some industry experts are referring to this model as Distributed Object Computing.   In a sales order example, the application rules, procedures, and data associated with generation of the sales order would constitute an application object. With function specific application objects strategically positioned in the network on the appropriate platform, the term distributed object computing fits the bill.

There are definite limitations in each of the various modes of distributed computing (none of them can solve all requirements).   For example, using file transfer as a means of getting data to a customer service representative who is on the phone assisting a customer with an account question, or placing an order, would undoubtedly prove ineffective.

Movements of large amounts of data to facilitate the servicing of a request for a specific record, introduces a time delay that can negatively impair customer satisfaction. Perhaps more appropriate for solving this problem would be a real-time client/server relationship between the customer service representative's PC (which prompts for customer number, date, verifies input, and presents a graphic image to the representative to aid in productivity) and the mainframe (which is home for the continuously changing customer database).

Conversely, for month-end movement of financial summary records to the corporate computer, file transfer might be the appropriate solution, as there is less sensitivity to time delays in getting the data there. It depends on the business need and the availability and flow of information required.

Another key consideration is that existing, or legacy applications, that were developed to support the business need and network device population as it existed at one point in time, may still be appropriate to today's needs. These client/server, GUI, and CASE tools have little regard for the legacy application or the installed terminals. Perhaps most impacted is the tremendously large population of IBM 3270 (or look-alike) family of terminals and printers. Enterprise networks struggle to get to the next evolutionary step in distributed computing, while still supporting their investment in these equipment resources. It's not easy.

Unfortunately for the user, the vast majority of tools available for making the next evolutionary step towards distributed computing focus largely on the desktop and the user interface. Integration with the enterprise computing infrastructure seems to take a back seat, though is perhaps the most important consideration in the endeavor.

Currently, the market is in need of tools, that facilitate development and management of networked applications, in the various modes of distributed computing. These tools need to reside between the functional layers responsible for communications between computers and the business application. This tools are making up the emerging area sometimes referred to as "middleware" and is what will become the glueware of the next decade.

Horizon Strategies, Incorporated

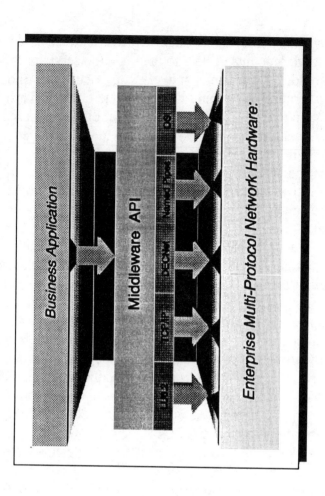

Middleware:
A Checklist for Migrating
to Distributed Computing

Hub Vandervoort
President, Principal Consultant
Horizon Strategies, Incorporated
75 Second Avenue, 4th floor
Needham, Massachusetts 02194
(617)444-7575

What is Hindering TRUE Distributed Application Development?

7 Application
6 Presentation
5 Session
4 Transport
3 Network
2 Data Link
1 Physical

- ## Complexity of Programming to Different Communications APIs

- ## Existing "Middleware" Tools are Too Narrowly Focused

- ## Downsizing & Demand for Desktop Services are at Odds with One Another

Need for "Middleware" Solutions

- **Enabling Layer of Software Between the Business Application and Network**

- **Simple, High-Level API**

- **Insulates Programmer from Underlying Protocol Stack(s)**

- **Delivers a Discrete Service** (i.e. File Transfer, Data Query/Update, Remote Computation, Message Delivery)

- **Protocol, Platform, Network, Data and Language Independent**

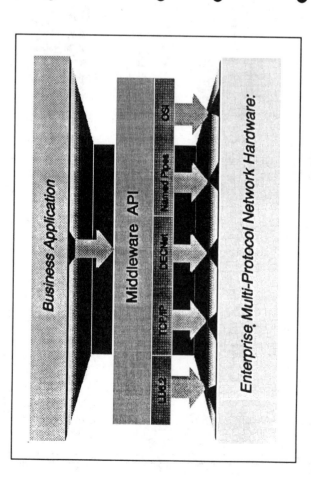

Middleware = "Meta-API"

a higher level representation of the underlying communications services that are provided

Distributed Computing: Environments & Industry Position

Distributed File	Distributed Database (SQL)	Distributed Function (RPC)	Distributed Object (Messaging)

Typical Environments

	Distributed File	Distributed Database (SQL)	Distributed Function (RPC)	Distributed Object (Messaging)
	Workflow Control Processing (File Transfer/Batch)	Transaction Processing and Inquiry (OLTP)	Compute Intensive Environments (Manufacturing/Engineering)	Workflow Control Processing
	Decision Support (Extract & Download)	Decision Support	Process Control	Event Driven Control
				Enterprise Integration

Industry Position

Distributed File	Distributed Database (SQL)	Distributed Function (RPC)	Distributed Object (Messaging)
Mature... Falling out of favor for many applications.	Reaching Maturity... Now coming into vogue in numerous industries.	Reaching Maturity... but behind SQL. Vogue in certain sects.	Still in Infancy... Users still learning. Limited tools available.

Broadening the Focus of Middleware Solutions

- **Common and Consistent Interface to Multiple Modes of Interoperability :**
  - File Transfer, SQL, RPC, Messaging

- **Extended Service Capability/Features:**
  - Naming & Distribution Lists
  - Trusted Partner Management & Security
  - Guaranteed Delivery & Recovery
  - Deferred Delivery & Synchronization
  - Flexible Session & Data Management Controls
  - Network Administration & Recovery

- **Vendor Independent Solution Improves:**
  - Developer Training Overhead
  - Cross-Application Integration
  - Delivery Time of Distributed Applications
  - Application Maintenance Overhead
  - Network Management and Administration

Business Application

FILE SQL RPC Message
Composite Middleware - Meta API
LU6.2 TCP/IP DECNet Named Pipes OSI

Enterprise Multi-Protocol Network Hardware:

Corporate API

Satisfying the Need for Delivery of Services to the Desktop as well as the need for Enterprise Integration

Checklist & Criteria for Migrating to Distributed Computing

Tools

- Transparent Protocol, Platform and Network Support
- Language and Data Independent
- Provides Multi-Modal Support
  - Distributed File
  - Distributed Database (SQL)
  - Distributed Function (RPC)
  - Distributed Object (Messaging)

- High Degrees of Error Control
  - Insulation/Isolation
  - Guaranteed Delivery
  - Forward Error Recovery
  - Distributed Object (Messaging)

- Provides Deferred Delivery and Message Level Synchronization
- Conformance & Commitment to Standards & Future Technology

Installation

- Supports Existing Platforms
- Supports Existing Protocols
- "Fits" with Organizational and Development Culture

Administration

- Capacity Planning Tools Provided
- Security & Partner Management
- Diagnostic & Fault Management
- Cross-Architecture Name Service

Design

- Simple and Easy to Learn
- Easy to Develop and Test With
- Promotes Object Oriented and Event Driven Architectures

Active Mail: A Framework for Integrated Groupware Applications

Yaron Goldberg, Marilyn Safran, William Silverman and Ehud Shapiro
Department of Applied Mathematics and Computer Science
The Weizmann Institute of Science, Rehovot 76100, Israel

Abstract

What do conversations, legal contracts, technical papers, meeting schedules, and the game of Tic-Tac-Toe have in common with electronic mail? How can a multi-user application cause a new user to "get on board" in a way which is non-intrusive, can tolerate delayed response, and require little effort on the user's part?

A system for computer-mediated interaction, Active Mail provides a solution to both questions. Receivers of *active* messages can interact with the sender, with future recipients, and with remote, distributed multi-user applications. Persistent active connections are maintained in hierarchical, notifiable folders.

Our presentation of applications implemented within this framework includes a text conversation tool, a collaborative writing facility with a floor passing protocol and revision control management, an interactive meeting scheduler — and some distributed multi-user interactive games.

1 Introduction

Active Mail is a framework for implementing groupware, designed to support more effective computer-mediated interaction. Active Mail extends ordinary electronic mail with *active messages*, which are active entities that contain communication ports. An active message, manifested as a window on the user's screen, contains facilities that allow communication and cooperation with other users. In particular, it allows its receiver to interact with its sender, with other users to whom a copy of the message was sent, as well as with remote, distributed multi-user applications connected to a communication port in the message.

2 The Different Views of Active Mail

An Extension to Ordinary Electronic Mail

Electronic mail is convenient for human interaction because of its non-intrusive, informal nature, its ability to support both asynchronous and more immediate communication needs, and its ability to interoperate with other computer-based tools. It assumes no predefined roles for its users, both sender and receiver gain from using it, and no rigid format is required [4]. The universal nature of electronic mail is the source of its power, but also prevents it from supporting the specific needs of the two main modes of interaction for which it is used: computer-mediated conversations, and document exchange.

When electronic mail is used for computer-mediated conversation, users often find it hard to maintain continuity. To which message does the current one respond? What was the sequence of messages exchanged on a particular topic? When participants join a conversation, how can they be brought up to date?

When Active Mail is used, an instance of its *conversation agent* supports an ongoing asynchronous discussion among a dynamically changing group of users distributed across a network of client processors, and maintains a conversation log. A user can initiate an *active conversation* which can be sent to others (by the originator or by any of the current participants) at any stage of the discussion. When new participants join in by opening the relevant *active conversation* message in their input folders, they receive a copy of the log which (by definition) details the history of the conversation.

When electronic mail is used for exchanging documents, users often find it hard to maintain document consistency. What is the most recent version of the document? How can one distribute an update and maintain previous versions? How are multiple authors coordinated?

When Active Mail is used, an instance of its *document agent*, like a conversation agent, allows a dynamically changing group of users to collaborate by creating, sending, and modifying automatically updated *active documents*. A current *floorholder* status and queue of pending floor requests are maintained, and revisions are managed by interoperating with a Revision Control System (RCS) agent.

A Protocol for Computer-Initiated Interaction

The problem of computer-initiated interaction is of fundamental importance to groupware; the design of any groupware application must provide an answer to: *How can a multi-user application cause a new user to "get on board" in a way which is non-intrusive, can tolerate delayed response, and requires little effort on the user's part?* Active Mail offers a protocol and a user interface to achieve just that. When users of its *meeting scheduler agent*, for example, wish to schedule a meeting, they simply send an active "meeting scheduler" message to desired participants. The system places it in the appropriate input folders, and recipients can choose to interact whenever they wish. The interaction mimics the usual human meeting scheduling process by supporting negotiations between expected participants[1]. Note that these same people can discuss the meeting agenda on-line, and/or collaborate on related documents without leaving the Active Mail environment. The conversations, documents, and meeting scheduler itself are all simply specific instances of active messages.

A Tool for Maintaining Persistent Interactive Connections

When handling passive messages in electronic mail, two kinds of storage facilities are involved: the user mail-spool (or *in-tray*) where incoming mail resides, and the local file system, where old messages are saved in *folders*. Both forms are persistent, in that they survive logging out or computer shutdown.

Maintaining active messages is more of a challenge, as the messages can still communicate with the outside world. Active Mail provides a hierarchy in which the user's persistent *active* connections are maintained. Thus users may hold multiple connections to various agents in their private folders and yet not lose them when logging out. Each user's folder system consists of two components: the *input folder* where incoming active messages are placed—with a functionality similar to the user's ordinary mail-spool—and a folder hierarchy which functions like a private file system hierarchy.

In contrast to electronic-mail, active messages *change*, and the user should be alerted about those changes (e.g., a new contribution to a conversation has arrived, or the user's opponent in a chess game has moved). Hence the Active Folder system incorporates a *notification mechanism* [6]. An agent becomes *notified* after a modification has occurred; if its window is closed, the icon changes and beeps. A folder becomes notified if any of its member agents (including subfolders) becomes notified. Thus the modification of an agent may reach the root folder (and hence change the Active Mail icon if it is closed). Notification also affects open windows.

3   Active Mail Architecture

An Active Mail *configuration* consists of *agents*, interconnected via two-ported bidirectional *communication channels*. There are two types of agents: *users* and *applications*. An example of an Active Mail configuration is given in Figure 1. We say that a user is a *participant* in an application if there exists a port connecting it to the application. Figure 1 shows two users, *User A* and *User B*, participating in two applications *Application 1* and *Application 2*. *User B* participates in an additional application not shown in the figure, and *Application 2* has an additional participant, also not shown in the figure.

An Active Mail agent with a given set of ports may change the configuration it is in by creating a new application agent, by sending a copy of one of its ports to a user, and/or by discarding one of its ports. It may also send messages to, and receive messages from, any of its ports. A participant in an application (*i.e.*, a user with a port *p* to an application) may initiate another user into the application by sending that user a copy of its port *p*. A user can leave an application by discarding its port to it.

Similarly, an application *A* having a port to some other application *B* may initiate an interaction between a user and the application *B* by sending to the user a copy of its port to *B*. Abstractly, users interact with applications via a bidirectional communication port. This abstraction is realized via windows on the user's screen. Each application comes with one or more application-specific windows, and all support a uniform way to view and interact with participants. Users are provided with an interface that allows them to spawn new application agents, as well as with a folder system, to manage their application ports.

---

[1] One of the main criticisms [4] of existing meeting schedulers is that they require all participants to maintain their schedule on-line using the same tool, and let various algorithms search through their calendars for vacant slots. Many consider this to be a breach of privacy, quite bothersome, and of little benefit to anyone but the meeting coordinator.

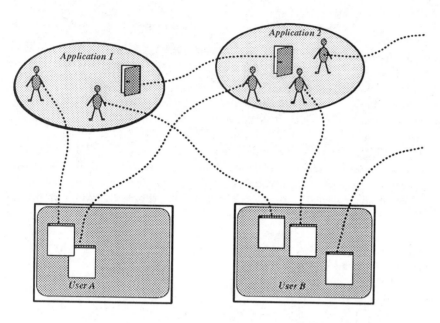

Figure 1: An Active Mail Configuration

4 Implementation and Future Directions

Active Mail is implemented under the Logix [7] distributed programming environment in a subset of the concurrent logic programming language FCP [7] which employs directed logic variables [5]. Its main aspect which requires support from the language is the need for communication ports to migrate. Concurrent logic languages are particularly suitable for supporting dynamic port migration, and the Directed Logic Variables (DLV) algorithm described in [5] provides a practical implementation of this capability over the datagram communication protocol of the Internet [1].

FCP has been interfaced with the X window system using the XView library (conforming to the OpenLook standard). An FCP transformer was also built to convert the output of an interface design tool (Sun Microsystems's Dev-guide) to FCP, enabling semi-automatic creation of new applications.

Active Mail can accommodate a wide range of applications. We are planning to refine the currently available applications and to provide additional ones.

The implementation of Active Mail is based on a single server. Although the DLV algorithm [5] may support a multi-server implementation, the lack of a recovery protocol that can sustain server failure prevents us from using it. We are working on such a recovery protocol, following ideas from [2].

The Active Mail architecture provides a powerful generalization of electronic mail, but does not provide a similar generalization of shared file systems. Its folders are private, and it has no notion of public, or shared, folders. We are working on a more general abstract architecture which supports such a notion of sharing.

References

[1] Comer D., *Internetworking with TCP/IP*, Prentice-Hall, second edition, 1991, pp. 434-435.

[2] Gaifman, H., Maher, M.J., and Shapiro, E., Replay, Recovery, Replication, and Snapshots of Nondeterministic Concurrent Programs, *Proc. ACM Conference on Principles of Distributed Computing*, ACM, 1991.

[3] Goldberg Y., *Active Mail: A Framework for Implementing Groupware*, M.Sc. Thesis, The Weizmann Institute of Science, November 1991.

[4] Grudin J., *Seven Plus One Challenges in Understanding Social Dynamics for Groupware Developers*, CHI Conference, Tutorial Notes, 11, 1991.

[5] Kleinman A., Moscowitz, Y., Pnueli, A., Shapiro. E., *Communication with Directed Logic Variables*, In ACM conference of Principles of Programming Languages, 1991.

[6] McCarthy J. C. et al, *Four Generic Communication Tasks Which Must Be Supported in Electronic Conferencing*, To appear in acm/SIGCHI Bulletin, January 1991.

[7] Shapiro, E. (Editor), *Concurrent Prolog: Collected Papers*, Vols. 1 and 2, MIT Press, 1987.

A Toolkit for Synchronous Distributed Groupware Applications

Dorab Patel and Scott D. Kalter

Twin Sun, Inc.
360 N. Sepulveda Blvd, Suite 2055
El Segundo, CA 90245-4462, USA
dorab@twinsun.com   sdk@twinsun.com

Abstract

This paper describes a framework, based on an extensible and application-neutral collaborative toolkit, for the development of concurrent distributed groupware applications. Features common to all groupware applications, like communications, notification, and management of sharing, are distilled into the toolkit without imposing a sharing policy. This leaves the developer free to concentrate on higher-level collaborative interface and functionality issues. Although the toolkit addresses some issues, developers must address other issues like maintaining consistent state, displaying reserved objects, and handling asynchrony. Applications that handle requests gracefully, separate data from views, and separate validation from execution of operations, are easier to make collaborative.

1   Introduction

Groupware [1] covers a wide spectrum of software—from extremely loosely coupled asynchronous software like electronic mail and databases, to tightly coupled synchronous software like shared editors. Here we concentrate on groupware applications that allow multiple users to edit the same document at the same time. The developers of such applications are faced with many issues such as session identification and management, event notification, and multicast communication.

COeX™ is an application-neutral, platform-independent, extensible groupware toolkit which provides a framework within which collaborative applications can be developed. Features common to groupware applications are factored out into the COeX toolkit so that developers can use these features directly without having to re-implement them for each application. By providing tested solutions

to low-level communications and sharing problems, COeX glues individual instances of an application together to form coherent distributed groupware.

2   Common problems

Groupware developers and researchers face many problems [2]. This section describes some of them. The first problem is that the term "groupware" means different things to different people. Groupware consists of a wide spectrum of applications from which developers must choose the subset they are interested in. This then provides a basis for addressing other issues. For example, this discussion is focussed on tightly-coupled, synchronous, distributed groupware applications like collaborative editors.

Developers must solve the "discovery" and "rendezvous" problems. How do users find out what is available to share? How does the system realize that two users have asked to share the same thing? One solution is to uniquely identify shared resources in a way that is independent of their location on the network or the path through which they are referenced. Sessions, which are groups of users sharing a resource, form and dissolve dynamically. Groupware applications have to maintain a consistent view of these dynamic sessions in the presence of races and failures.

Communication among sharing applications is an integral part of groupware. Data are converted back and forth between a form understandable to the application and the form on the network. These data often need to be multicast to all the members of the session. The delivery order of messages is important in constructing correct and efficient consistency algorithms.

One of the hallmarks of groupware applications is that they provide their users with active notification of events of potential interest. For exam-

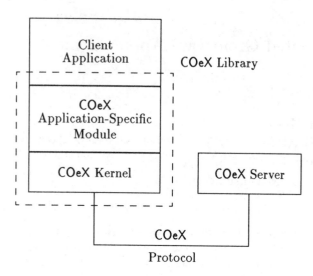

Figure 1: The COeX framework

ple, users must be notified when group membership changes or when members modify shared data.

The state information maintained by all application instances must be consistent. Different distributed consistency algorithms are available to achieve this. The most appropriate choice will depend on the demands of the application.

Solutions to the above problems must work correctly across heterogeneous hardware and software platforms. Often, system support is lacking for implementing complete solutions.

Other problems, including those dealing with user interfaces, social theory, and multiple channels of human communication, are not addressed here.

3   The COeX framework

The framework provided by the COeX toolkit addresses the above-mentioned problems. It consists of an application-specific module, a kernel, and a server as shown in Figure 1. COeX clients communicate with a COeX server using the COeX protocol over a TCP/IP network.

The *server* manages groups of client applications sharing the same document. All multicast messages to the group are sent via and serialized at the server. The server handles different kinds of applications at the same time, ensures the mutual exclusion of conflicting messages, and uniquely identifies shared resources. Identification involves deciding whether two clients requesting access to a shared file or other resource are referring to the same item.

COeX provides a *protocol* for reliably exchanging

information among multiple application instances that are sharing the same document. The delivery order of messages is guaranteed to be the same for clients in a session. *Exclusive messages* ensure that only one such message is active in the system at any time.

The protocol handles the creation, modification, and dissolution of sessions. The protocol is asynchronous, fail-safe, application independent, and extensible. The asynchronicity allows user actions (e.g. scrolling, editing in another buffer) while COeX operations are in progress. The failure of either clients or the server is handled safely, ensuring that the rest of the system can function correctly. Application independence allows many different applications to use the same protocol. Client applications can define and send their own application-specific messages via the protocol.

The library *kernel* handles the low-level communication between a client and the server. The kernel sets up and monitors the connection to the server, and translates between client and COeX message formats. It provides information to the server allowing it to identify the resource to be shared.

The *Application-Specific Module* (ASM) provides high-level sharing and consistency-maintaining functionality that is specific to a class of applications, e.g., text editors. The ASM uses the extensibility features of the kernel to provide an application with the ability to define, select, and manipulate regions (pieces of a shared document). Since a sharing policy can vary with the application, only a minimal policy is implemented, allowing developers to tailor the details of the policy as required.

4   Application integration

A toolkit only provides a partial solution to building effective groupware applications. The remaining effort is in building the application and integrating it with the toolkit. Developers must choose which operations to multicast and the appropriate ordering of the multicast to ensure that the states of each application instance remain consistent. Other decisions are the units of sharing and the display of sharing information. A discipline of integration, such as that provided by COeX, is useful in providing a structured framework in which to develop groupware.

Though COeX can be integrated into almost any application, applications with the following characteristics are significantly easier to integrate.

- Event-driven applications are easier to integrate because they already have a structure capable of handling asynchronous events. For example, applications using the X Window System fall into this category.

- Request-oriented software, which handles denial or partial granting of requests in a reasonable way, is easier to integrate.

- Applications that cleanly separate their data from views they provide to users, are easier to integrate.

- Applications that separate the validation of operations from their execution are easier to integrate because collaboration involves more checking. For example, new failure modes and restricted operations in shared mode need to be checked.

5 Comparisons

Like other toolkits, COeX abstracts common features from a variety of potential applications and provides a general interface to that functionality. This general interface insulates the application from platform dependencies. Performance and reliability enhancements to the toolkit are transferred to the applications simply by relinking. A good toolkit implements flexible mechanisms on which application programmers can impose their own policies. Thus, code reuse is a major benefit of toolkits.

Well-designed toolkits are beneficial to end users, programmers, and software managers. Developers benefit from canned solutions to parts of their problem allowing them to concentrate their efforts on application-specific problems. Managers benefit from the lower risk of using existing solutions, improved reliability, and shorter time-to-market. End users benefit from more consistent and reliable software.

Other toolkits, like Sun's ToolTalk [3] and HP's SoftBench [4], also offer communication among applications by providing a "software backplane" for applications to connect to. However, both are oriented towards dissimilar applications using loosely-coupled communications. The ISIS toolkit [5] provides communication mechanisms for fault-tolerant distributed computing with multiple processes. COeX is tailored for tightly-coupled synchronous distributed groupware applications. The ASMs provide high-level sharing and consistency support for a wide range of application classes. COeX is independent of any particular vendor's

platform and runs on wide range of UNIX platforms ranging from PCs to Crays.

6 Conclusions

Groupware developers face many problems. A toolkit that provides canned solutions to common problems is one approach to addressing these issues. This provides developers with features common to all groupware applications, avoiding the need to re-implement the same functionality repeatedly.

The COeX toolkit provides platform-independent, application-neutral facilities that aid in communication, notification, sharing management, and synchronization control. The toolkit consists of a library that is linked in with applications and a single server that can service different client applications. COeX thus glues together multiple application instances forming distributed synchronous groupware.

This approach is particularly suited for applications that are modular, event-driven, and have a clean separation between data and views. The discipline of using a toolkit framework provides a structured approach for developing groupware.

References

[1] Irene Greif, editor. *Computer-Supported Cooperative Work: A Book of Readings*. Morgan Kaufmann Publishers, Inc., San Mateo, CA, 1988.

[2] Clarence A. Ellis, Simon J. Gibbs, and Gail L. Rein. Groupware: Some issues and experiences. *Communications of the ACM*, 34(1):38–58, January 1991.

[3] SunSoft, Mountain View, California. *ToolTalk 1.0 Programmer's Guide*, September 1991.

[4] Martin R. Cagan. The HP SoftBench environment: An architecture for a new generation of software. *Hewlett-Packard Journal*, 41(3):36–47, June 1990.

[5] Kenneth P. Birman. ISIS: A system for fault-tolerant distributed computing. Technical Report TR 86-744, Computer Science Department, Cornell University, Ithaca, NY, April 1986.

Prescient Agents

Scott L. McGregor
Prescient
3494 Yuba Avenue
San Jose, CA 95117
mcgregor@netcom.com

ABSTRACT

Past systems have been largely passive, acted upon by the user, but new systems are becoming more participative. Instead of having systems which act as mere slaves that do only precisely what they are told, we are entering an era in which systems will participate more like clerks or secretaries in a "team of two" with the user. This leads us toward interfaces that monitor actions and anticipate needs, automatically reconfiguring themselves to facilitate future actions. "Prescient agents", as they are termed in this document, can improve the productivity of both individuals and groups. They represent the confluence of many research areas such as UI design, agents, database technology and Computer Supported Cooperative Work (CSCW) into the applications of tomorrow.

1.0 What are Prescient Agents?

Most computer systems today begin execution at the same state each time. When you start up a PC or Unix box, you typically begin with a directory prompt for your home directory. It doesn't matter if the last time you were using the system you were working in a different directory. A few systems, such as the Apple Macintosh Finder, remember the state from the last time you used the system. This saves you the effort of having to re-establish your previous working context. Only a few systems, such as the MIT Media Lab's NewsPeek system, actually learn about your preferences from previous sessions. Prescient computing systems derive from this last approach.

Prescient computing systems learn about your work patterns by monitoring your use of the system. They simplify future work by creating and managing agents or other forms of accelerators that simplify those changes. While this is possible due to the habitual nature of much human work, we observed that it still can be pleasantly surprising to users.

Heightening this feeling of prescience is that these agents not only support an individual user but also actively support work groups of collaborators. Part of the surprise aspect comes from the fact that the system agents can not only learn your own work artifacts, contexts and habits, but also those of your collaborators. The system simplifies access to contexts and artifacts (created by collaborators) that are germane to current work, including those previously unknown to you.

Current systems are often confusing for users because they require the user to remember and specify details that are peripheral to their tasks. My project team at Hewlett-Packard and I collected a large sample of Unix shell history files and found that 25-66% of each user's commands just navigate around to search for and use related artifacts in the file system. A primary cause of this problem is that most of today's computer systems do not manage the context in which you are working. This forces you to remember how the file system stores your work contexts (for example, by local naming conventions). You must then continually manage any translations or navigation implied by this mapping. These overhead tasks compete for short term memory with your goal directed work. As the number of things to be remembered increases, cognitive performance suffers, leading to increased errors, decreased task performance and decreased productivity. We believe this was particularly true for the task areas we were studying (software development), which are characterized by an extremely high number of artifacts to be managed.

2.0 Theory of Prescience

Having recognized some cognitive aspects of current systems that were not well matched to the user's capabilities and tasks, my team and I sought to develop a model for how computer systems might better simplify personal work and collaboration with work partners. We found that having a model of a human agent accomplishing such work was helpful for discussing how our computer agents could facilitate such work as well. One type of agent we envisioned was that of an administrative assistant, in particular, we referred to the character of Radar O'Reilley, the company clerk in the movie and TV show M*A*S*H.

2.1 Radar O'Reilley - A Human Prescient Agent

Radar O'Reilley exemplifies the way changes to the user interface can support management of complexity and interaction with others. We frequently saw the colonel heading into the outer office to tell Radar to take care of something only to be greeted at the door by Radar, who already held not only all the files and forms the colonel was about to request but also files he hadn't yet even realized he'd need. Other times we'd see Radar finding out what was going on elsewhere in Korea by talking on the phone with Sparky, the local radio telephone operator. Later we might see Radar telling everyone to get ready for incoming wounded before anyone else heard the approaching helicopters. In the TV series, Max Klinger later replaced Radar as company clerk. In contrast with Radar, Klinger was rarely able to find requested files and often suggested that officers rummage through the files themselves. This is how most computer interfaces are today.

Now let us look at a theory for how computer agents can simplify users' work, and how computer agents can offer some of the behavior of a Radar O'Reilley.

Imagine you are Radar's commanding officer. Radar augments your memory by remembering where all the files are kept and having them ready when you need them. You don't need to remember their names or storage locations. Radar improves your communication by keeping in touch with Sparky and the other clerks around Korea. He can find out things that will help you, that others have forgotten to mention to you. He also knows about other people who have interests that intersect with your unit's, so he can help with bartering and other exchanges that begin with communication. Lastly, he can enhance your reasoning by allowing you to stay focused on the task, while he manages the communication and data storage details. He can help you anticipate outside changes (such as incoming wounded) which will alter your current work tasks, so you are always ready to proceed to the next task.

It is important to notice that Radar gains this knowledge of what you will need next just by watching you at work. Radar has realized that when you are working on something you also are likely to need related files. He is able to anticipate what files relate to your current work based on what files you used together before. He used that information to "pre-fetch" the handful of files. Then a one or two word cue is sufficient for him to choose just one from the handful. Radar also can anticipate what work will require interaction with others by noting where it came from, who it might be shared with, etc. But he does this unobtrusively without having to ask constantly or having to be told. How different from most computer systems today where flexibility necessitates explicit programming!

3.0 Why Prescient Agents are Coming Soon

The technology necessary to deliver this level of apparent prescience does not require sophisticated programming and tricky artificial intelligence reasoning. Rather, it requires only a few very simple things. Remember, it relies only on the fact that people are creatures of habit, and that if you can monitor and remember what they have done in the past, and communicate this to others, you can help the users. Thus the major inhibitors are the increased processing power required to cover the extra monitoring activities, the increased storage required to keep the records of past activities, and the increased communications links and band width available to join individuals. The dramatic price reductions and performance increases in all three of these areas suggest that prescient agent technology can be delivered affordably and with acceptable performance.

4.0 Implications for Groupware Developers

This is especially good news for those who are interested in the growing popularity of groupware focussed applications. A recognized problem leading to the failure of many groupware systems has ben the lack of balance between the relative benefits of the groupware system for each individual, compared to their individual costs. Even where the group benefits have been substantial, if individual benefit has been low, people have often not used the systems in a sufficiently timely or committed manner to make them successful. Because prescient agents have an extremely low cost (most data is collected automatically) and provide a significant benefit even for the individual, they are able to avoid this typical problem. And once there are sufficient users, the cross-user communications benefits go up substantially with little effort on the individuals' part, other than allowing their associations to be shared with their collaborators.

Groupware: Systems Support and Glueware

Dennis Allison
HaL Computer Systems
Campbell, CA 95008

March 1, 1990

1.0 Introduction

Groupware is software which facilitates group efforts whether it be decision making or the joint development of complex systems. Effective groupware must be tailored both to the needs of the particular task to which it is being applied and to the culture of the organization using it.

All groupware systems require a underlying base of systems support: networks, data bases, file transfer mechanisms, and the like. These are elements of the enabling technology for groupware applications.

Integrated groupware packages are effective in some environments. They are designed to provide cradle-to-grave support which meet the need of most business organizations. They have major advantages because they present a standard interface and a uniform tool set.

Another approach is to provide a collection of tools which interoperate with one another using a combination of glueware and applications programs. When flexibility is needed to support the organization's requirements and culture, this is often the better choice. Glueware is the software which holds together the various component elements in a groupware system including the underlying system elements.

2.0 Culture, Communication, and Computers

Groupware effectiveness is predicated upon several cultural and technical models.

First, everyone in the organization is presumed to perform their work on a workstation or personal computer. This means that everyone has on his or her desk a computer and that the processing of symbolic information is the primary concern of everyone from clerks to CEO. It also presumes that everyone know how to keyboard (today's jargon for typing).

Second, all of the members of a workgroup (that is, the a collection of individuals within the organization) are presumed to be connected with a high bandwidth network. Current network technology (for example, ethernet) rapidly become a bottleneck. Moreover, workgroups are unlikely to work autistically isolated from the rest of the word. High bandwidth communications with a global span is increasingly necessary to access data, communicate with others in the field, and to track recent developments.

In a groupware based environment, participants immerse themselves in cyberspace and use the computer with its specialized software and communications mechanisms as their primary mechanism for interpersonal communication. It's a major cultural switch and one which makes many uncomfortable. But, once mastered, it provides access and efficiencies otherwise not possible

The technical base today is still limiting. Most organizations utilize an inhomogeneous collection of workstations and PCs interconnected by a moderate to low bandwidth network. To be effective and generally useful, groupware software needs not only to provide the proper context to support the group's work culture, it needs to interoperate on a variety of different machines communicating transparently across a number of different networks.

3.0 Groupware Systems Components

Groupware makes substantial demands upon normal system components. As with most systems organizations, it is advantageous to re-use standard system components rather than create a special purpose product which may not interoperate as well, or which may not have the same level and degree of support.

The three primary components of systems services groupware systems require are communications, data base access, and user interface.

Communications has a direct impact on what is possible. For example, if the backbone network has adequate bandwidth, it becomes possible to consider using the network to support voice communications, interactive shared graphics (a shared whiteboard) and other multi-media whizbang stuff. There is also the issue of what level of communication access should be used. Some systems require access at a low level (say a datagram) while others can function using the electronic mail interface.

Data base systems have become a standard tool whose existence can be assumed. Groupware tools need to be able to interoperate with a variety of different database systems and, in fact, across a complex of potentially incompatible systems. Nonetheless, it's an advantage for the groupware system to use the local database system rather than one of its own.

User-friendly graphical user interfaces have become what people expect. Tools are beginning to appear to make it easy to build a seamless system out of diverse components which will interoperate, share data, and provide a single consistent interface. When a groupware system is constructed out of diverse components, this kind of a glueware system is highly desirable.

4.0 Authentication, Access Control, Recoverability, Security, and Privacy

In the autistic development world, each person is responsible and accountable for their own information. In a groupware world, much information is shared. The groupware system must provide protections for private information, arbitrate possible conflicts between modifications, and ensure that changes can be recovered. Not all the needed features are common components of workstation and PC systems.

For example, access to data may require that the user have appropriate authorization and that the user be appropriately authenticated by providing an appropriate password or by some physical device such as a smart card.

Mail may be considered private and maintained and transmitted in the system using an encryption system. Public key encryption systems provide an effective way to share data privately between users. Use of a trusted server to audit and authenticate transactions between users can add to the security of the system.

Most groupware operations may be characterized as transactions on a data base. As in most data base systems there must be a mechanism to back out and recover from an error. This is a difficult problem strongly tied to the task at hand and the culture of the organization using the system. To be accepted, this must work.

Shared data needs to be protected to prevent simultaneous updates. Again, the way in which this is managed by the groupware system will control its acceptance. The interface needs to be natural within the context of the workgroup. Some groups would not mind a checkout procedure while others would find it unacceptable.

5.0 Constructing A System

Groupware systems are constructed both by software suppliers and by users to meet their specific problems. In each case, the groupware component of the system is a layer placed over other systems services and provided to the group in a specialized fashion which improves their productivity and enhances communication.

User addressed communication can be overlaid on the local mail system. Mail provides a convenient and effective mechanism of transferring information to identified individuals. Mail files have a highly formalized organization which is easily searched for complex patterns using, for example, the Unix `grep` and `agrep` commands.

Information of all kinds can be stored in data bases and retrieved using standard queries. The interface to the query language can be augmented by specialized commands or a menu driven interface.

GUIs (Graphical User Interfaces) are difficult when the systems to be supported are inhomogeneous. For the workstation environment there are a variety of tools, mostly hosting the X-Windows system, which can be used. In the personal computer world, the choices are more constrained. Apple has it's own standard interface; the PC has Windows. When portability into inhomogeneous environments is important, a system such as Objectworks/Smalltalk makes sense as programs look and function identically in different environments.

6.0 Conclusions

The computer and communications technology necessary to support groupware is evolving rapidly. It's a question of "what to do".more than "can it be done" or "how to do it" that drives groupware today.

Changing Development Environments through the use of Groupware

Douglas J. Hawn
MCI Telecommunications
Engineer-Planning Technology
2400 N. Glenville
Richardson, TX 75080

Richard W. La Valley
MCI Telecommunications
Sr. Manager-Planning Technology
2400 N. Glenville
Richardson, TX 75080

ABSTRACT

Groupware has allowed developers to tackle a new class of problems that are beyond typical end-user computing applications. Enterprise-wide applications require the integration of desktop computing and decision support applications using multiple platforms across multiple LAN/WAN/GANs. Groupware development capabilities within this environment are evolving and include server replication, fully functional administrative support, and imbedded performance metrics. This provides high-performance, distributed, industrial strength applications that meet traditional IS standards.

INTRODUCTION

The development of local area networks (LANs), wide area networks (WANs) and the recent concept of a global area network (GAN) creates the need for a new class of applications known as groupware. The LAN/WAN/GAN allows for work groups to share information resources and information processors, while groupware allows people with common interests to cooperatively use these resources to accomplish common goals and objectives. Although groupware can be seen as a new application class of software still in its infancy stages, the Systems Planning department of MCI is currently using groupware applications to break down the traditional IS role. The most successful groupware products allow for rapid prototyping, continual refinement, integration and simplified administration.

RAPID PROTOTYPING

One factor leading to successful groupware deployment is the ability to rapidly prototype applications. This provides solutions to today's problems. Tom Peters states that as new technology becomes available doing things fast will be the main competitive advantage in the 90's. Just as business groups convene around short-term projects, so must groupware. Applications must be made readily available with minimal development cycle-time.

One way to achieve instantaneous solutions to problems is allowance for end-user application development. Who better to create an automated card catalog system than an information specialist? The end-user must not be required to be a technologist; the groupware software should buffer the end-user from the complexities of the software.

CONTINUAL REFINEMENT

Rapid prototyping is essential, but it leads to another technical requirement of groupware products. Applications created must remain easy to modify and transform. Rarely is the first attempt to provide a solution accepted as the right solution. Gathering requirements is simplified when a working prototype is used. The prototype can serve as a strawman to distinguish perceived requirements from actual requirements. This approach will also allow for the identification of hidden requirements not perceived in the original applications design. Successful business tools will allow end-users to add additional feature/functionality and eliminate unnecessary feature/functionality. The iterative process and continual refinement will make success of applications virtually guaranteed.

Business groups typically perform diverse activities. Groupware should not dictate how a group interacts; group interaction should mandate how a particular group utilizes groupware applications. Groupware applications attempting to strictly mimic group processes may translate into success today, but will prove to be unsuccessful in the long run. Just as business processes change, so does the interaction of people. Successful groupware applications should change as the dynamics of the business group changes and actually serve as a catalyst for cultural transformation and improved business processes. Had Alexander

Graham Bell tried to strictly model people's communications processes, he would have invented voice mail not the telephone. The telephone is a good example of a technological innovation that served as an agent to transform and revolutionize the way people communicate.

INTEGRATION

No groupware package can provide all of the functionality to satisfy all organizations within the enterprise. Certain packages may offer a majority of functionality needed for effective enterprise-wide collaborative computing, but it is likely that the out the box solution will be missing some major pieces. In an attempt to be all things to all users, products may prove to be unsuccessful by shallowly providing certain functionality. For example, a groupware application might attempt to provide for group calendaring, but be missing the necessary security levels. Other products might attempt to provide a built in word processor, but lack a spell checker. It is far better to allow for the integration of other products rather than superficially provide essential groupware functions.

The amount of integration achievable is largely dependent on the platform used to run the application. The smoothest integration is provided in multi-tasking environments such as OS/2 or Unix. Windows can provide DDE and OLE to move data between applications, but the groupware vendor must provide full support for these facilities to make integration successful. In Windows the users should be shielded from the complexities of the DDE/OLE processes.

Effective groupware solutions are built around multi-platform architectures. Groupware applications utilizing multi-platform architectures allow the business solution to be the factor in determining the appropriate platform. It is a pull approach rather than a push approach. The push approach requires an organization to work in the confines of a particular platform and does not provide for a migration path. The pull approach allows for the business and computational needs of the organization to determine the platform. This empowers the organization to use MIPS wisely.

ADMINISTRATION

The underlying factor allowing for the creation of groupware applications is the client/server architecture and more recently the distributed architecture. Particularly in distributed architectures the boundaries indicating whether IS or another organization should manage and control an application becomes clouded. Groupware should allow for distributed management and administration of applications while also allowing for IS to remotely monitor and trouble shoot the system. Organizations should have access to performance information allowing them to solve minor problems, leaving IS to solve the more difficult problems. The same flexibility needed to make groupware applications successful is necessary in the systems management paradigm.

Distributed architectures allow for the dissemination of information across the network. Sharing information across a distributed platform requires that the information be up to date and consistent. In order to provide this necessity, groupware applications must allow for distributed content administration and timely replication of information throughout the network. The content or data comprising an application should be kept up to date by the individuals or organizations requiring the data. Done properly, replication requires complex underlying algorithms to resolve the conflict imposed when a single object is being updated by more than one person. Conflict resolution should be savvy enough to indicate changes down to the most basic element of an object.

Performance information is the key to providing adequate management and health monitoring of the system. Groupware applications require detailed performance matrices allowing systems administrators to monitor the components down to a micro level.

CONCLUSION

Successful implementation of groupware unleashes the power within an organization by flexibly modeling the way people and organizations interact. Groupware changes the traditional development paradigm to actively include the user in development and content administration. Groupware has the potential to be more of a change agent to information technology than spreadsheets were in the 80's. Those individuals and organizations recognizing the potential value in harvesting the synergy of group dynamics will be successful groupware users.

REFERENCES

Briere, Daniel. Sep 1991. Groupware: a spectrum of productivity boosters. NETWORK WORLD pp. 1,33-34,36,46.

Flynn, Laurie. Aug 1991. The Year of the LAN arrived and it was nothing like I expected. INFOWORLD pp. 41.

Gillin, Paul. Nov 1990. Group(ware) therapy: Tips for success. COMPUTERWORLD pp. 109-111.

Herman, James. Jul 1991. Distributing the wealth. NETWORK WORLD pp. 53-59.

Mercilliott, Marc and Nelson, Fritz. Nov 1991. Lotus Notes: Some Insights Into Replication. NETWORK COMPUTING pp. 98-100.

Morse, Stephan. Nov 1991. Where Is Groupware? A Guide to the Options. NETWORK COMPUTING pp. 53-55,58,60.

Data Access in Workgroup Environments

Richard Schwartz, Borland International, Inc.

As workgroup computing becomes more pervasive, the technology supporting workgroup environments will need to address many of the issues that today are associated primarily with personal productivity applications. One of the principal areas of concern will be how data is stored, maintained and accessed in workgroup settings.

Increasingly, data is becoming central to the idea of workgroup collaboration. In earlier models, the only technologies that provided specific support for collaboration were based on interpersonal messaging models. In the past several years, the notion of interpersonal messaging has been expanded to encompass the idea of bulletin boards, which provide on-going support for discussions about specific areas of interest to collaborating parties. More recently, the concept of bulletin boards has itself been extended to include the notion of discussion databases, which not only provide the ability to conduct on-going group discussions on specific topics of interest, but also allow users to store and reference documents or other materials relevant to the discussion at hand.

Organizations need to access and share the tremendous wealth of structured data that exists in strategic applications and enterprise databases. Because messaging systems are typically the only way to provide broad based connectivity throughout an organization, many large organizations are looking for ways to use these systems not only as vehicles to support interpersonal communication, but also as a cost-effective way to deliver the organization's mission-critical data to those who need to access this information. In addition, it is anticipated that there will be more demand for workgroups to be able to use existing or future versions of today's personal productivity applications in collaborative settings.

Such requirements raise some fundamental questions about data access in workgroup or collaborative environments, including:

-- Underlying database technology: should workgroup systems be based on existing database models, or do we need to develop new models specifically to support the needs of workgroup environments?

-- Scalability: can the same architecture and tools be used in small workgroups as is used across the enterprise, or must new approaches be adopted as the number of users increases?

-- Data delivery model: what is the best architecture to move data from place to place within a collaborative environment?

-- Access and security controls: what support does there need to be at the system level for controlling access to the data?

-- Searching capabilities: how do users find out about the data that is available for them to access in the system?

-- Use of multiple transports: what types of transports can be used to move data between the various members of a workgroup?

-- Supported data types: what kinds of data need to be able to be stored and delivered within workgroup environments?

Underlying Technology

A basic question in building workgroup database technology that supports broad data storage and delivery capabilities is whether the underlying data model and database engine can be based on existing models and technologies, or whether these models are not sufficient to support the special demands of workgroup environments.

Some vendors have in fact decided that the demands of coordinated information delivery among users scattered in many different sites requires the development of new proprietary database models whose architecture does not conform to traditional database models. Others are attempting to extend existing models to support these special demands.

The adoption of proprietary models raises some important questions concerning overall compatibility and integration into existing application environments. For example,

-- Can standard access methods and languages, such as SQL, be used to access data stored in workgroup databases?

-- Is it possible to easily access data and information and to interface existing applications with the workgroup database?

-- Are access and security controls provided at the database level, or must these be maintained by higher level applications?

Data Delivery Models

There are several different architectures that may be employed to make data accessible to members of workgroups. Among these choices, three are of special interest: client/server, replication and peer-to-peer.

Client/Server

In the client/server model, data is maintained centrally in a database server, and each user's workstation is established as a client of that server. Because all data is centrally managed, it is potentially easy to establish security and access controls and to provide support for efficient searching of the contents of the database.

However, the client/server model has some potential drawbacks in a workgroup setting. For example, members of a workgroup may not all be available through a common communications link. In addition, traditional transaction and concurrency models may need to be modified to provide the appropriate type of support for collaborative computing especially when group members are geographically dispersed.

Replication

The replication model can be thought of as an elaboration of the client/server approach that is specifically tailored to support workgroup computing. In a similar fashion to the client/server model, each user's workstation is connected to a server that manages all of the data to which that user has access. However, all users are not connected to the same server, but rather to a specific designated local server. In turn, all of the servers are connected to each other at the backend and maintain consistency of state by "replicating" their data between themselves.

When a user makes a change by adding new data or altering or deleting an existing value, the change is first propagated to the server to which that user is directly connected, and then must be replicated across all other servers supporting users who need to access that piece of data.

In contrast with the highly centralized pure client/server model, the replication approach requires the maintenance of multiple copies of the same data across the system. In addition, both the client/server model and the replication approach require significant resources to install, configure, maintain and administer the system. Because of this administrative overhead, systems based on replication may not be appropriate to serve the needs of smaller or ad hoc workgroups.

Peer-to-Peer

In systems based on peer-to-peer architectures, each workstation communicates directly with other workstations in the workgroup. At base, there is no centralized point in the system where all data is managed and maintained. It should be noted, however, that certain database architectures may allow individual workstations effectively to be configured as servers so that they can manage data for multiple workgroup members.

The lack of the need to set up and maintain centralized server machines as well as the distributed nature of peer-to-peer systems makes them more suitable to support smaller ad-hoc workgroup collaboration sessions in addition to larger more persistent groups.

Summary

Today, there is a tremendous stockpile of strategic information that organizations have generated using PCs, minicomputers and mainframes. Though computers have enabled us to create a wealth of information, we are still struggling for a way to share it with others so that we may get the maximum benefit from our technology investment, and most importantly, maintain a competitive advantage.

The category of workgroup computing is expanding rapidly and there are a variety of workgroup solutions to choose from in order to improve an organization's data access and sharing capabilities. It is important to understand the wide range of issues surrounding this new area and to carefully evaluate an organization's data access and sharing needs before selecting a solution. Close attention should be paid to the underlying technology and the data delivery models each approach uses so that there is a close fit with the data needs and the level of maintenance an organization can support.

Performing Search and Managing Change in Groupware Applications

Clifford A. Reid
Verity, Inc.
1550 Plymouth Street
Mt. View, CA 94043

ABSTRACT

Groupware applications are faced with managing large collections of data. In some cases, groupware applications must perform only a small subset of traditional database management tasks; in other cases, they must go beyond traditional DBMS capabilities. This paper examines two major areas of groupware database services: performing search and managing change.

1. INTRODUCTION

Database management system perform two fundamental tasks: performing search and managing change. Groupware applications typically require a subset of the change management facilities in a transaction processing system, but require a new generation of the search capabilities not yet available in traditional DBMSs.

2. PERFORMING SEARCH

The characteristics of the search problem faced by groupware applications include:

- The text data type is dominant.

- The databases are large, distributed, and potentially stored in multiple repositories (file systems, RDBMSs, etc.).

- The form and content of the data is irregular, generated by multiple authors using different applications.

- The users are predominantly novices at searching electronic documents.

These characteristics render traditional text search (Boolean retrieval) ineffective. Typical users do not have enough knowledge of the form and content of the data to formulate good queries, and do not have the skills or commitment to find documents by iterating and successively refining arcane Boolean queries.

Groupware applications need a subject search capability that allows a user to search for all of the documents that discuss a subject of interest, without relying on each user to describe the subject in detail. A powerful subject description accounts for all of the different ways different authors discuss the same subject. Relying on each user to create author-independent subject descriptions is unrealistic.

2.1 CONCEPT SEARCHING

There are two ways to provide users with subject search capabilities. The first is to add keywords, or concept tags, to all of the documents. An editor reads each document, decides which concepts the document discusses, and tags the documents with those concepts. Users can then retrieve documents by their concept tags. The drawbacks of keywording are cost, consistency, and flexibility. For most applications, the cost of reading and keywording each document is prohibitive. Requiring the authors to keyword their documents (an unreliable approach) creates a consistency problem -- different authors assign different keywords to similar documents. Finally, users who want to search for concepts not included in the list of keywords are out of luck.

The second approach to searching groupware database applications is knowledge-based retrieval. Knowledge-based retrieval is the integration of a thesaurus-like knowledge base with a search engine. The knowledge base consists of a collection of concepts, each consisting of a list of words, phrases, or other subjects defined elsewhere in the knowledge base. Users performs searches by selecting one or more concepts from the knowledge base. The search engine translates the user's concept search into a search for a collections of words, phrases, fields searches, etc., that span the different styles and vocabularies of the documents. In addition, users have the ability to tailor searches by adding special search terms of their own.

In the absence of a powerful knowledge-based retrieval capability, groupware applications rely on users create from scratch the relevant parts an author-independent knowledge base each time they want to perform a search. Some expert users can do this, but most users will find the search capabilities lacking.

3. MANAGING CHANGE

A key problem in managing changing data is handling conflict -- two users simultaneously changing the same data. There are two basic approaches to managing conflict: preventing conflict, and resolving conflict.

An application that prevents conflict must centralize the control of change and manage permission to change via a locking scheme. An application that resolves conflict can allow distributed, uncoordinated change, but must periodically consolidate the changes and resolve any conflicts. Neither approach is inherently superior, and an application should select an approach based on an analysis of the cost of managing conflicts.

There are two primary costs of preventing conflict:

- Autonomy: Users may be prevented from performing some tasks by the (possibly unexpected) actions of other users.

- Infrastructure: The instantaneous coordination requirements of a conflict prevention system are extreme, and require infrastructure such as guaranteed high-bandwidth connectivity and high-availability computing systems.

Similarly, there are two primary costs of resolving conflict:

- Negotiation: Whenever a conflict is detected, some negotiation among the conflicting parties must take place to resolve the conflict.

- Integrity: During the time the conflict exists, there is a data integrity problem -- two conflicting changes exist simultaneously.

3.1 CLASSES OF APPLICATIONS

Based on the costs described above, groupware applications can be divided into two classes: high cost-of-conflict applications, and low cost-of-conflict applications. Examples of high cost-of-conflict applications are transaction-oriented systems and group authoring systems (programming teams are group authors of source code, and conflict prevention systems like SCCS and RCS are popular and effective). Examples of low cost-of-conflict applications are email (virtually no cost of conflict) and conversation applications (popular Lotus Notes applications).

4. CONCLUSIONS

Different types of groupware applications need different approaches to conflict management, ranging from absolute conflict prevention to periodic after-the-fact conflict resolution. Because of the heterogeneous nature of groupware data and users, groupware applications require search facilities that provide a new level of power and usability. Knowledge-based retrieval offers this new level of search capabilities.

Collaboration and Document Databases

Bruce Duff and George Florentine
Information Dimensions, Inc.
5080 Tuttle Crossing Blvd
Dublin, OH 43017

1. Introduction/Abstract - Collaboration

As connectivity between user desktops continues to improve and document objects continue to increase in size and complexity, users will increasingly share documents at the subcomponent level — chapters, titles, tables, etc. The set of problems presented by sharing document components within a distributed system are well suited to the capabilities and features provided by a distributed document database. But to maintain simplicity and ease-of-use these databases must present information to users based on their logical view of document universe, not a view driven by rows and columns or the physical location of data stores.

2. Sharing - Potentials and Pitfalls

Throughout the last decade the increase in desktop computing speeds and graphical interfaces, together with a decrease in hardware costs, has resulted in an explosion of electronic documents. Although desktop users were excited by the freedom and flexibility of having their own personal computers, the sharing of information, in particular of documents and document components, became much more complicated. As users increased their personal productivity through use of electronic spreadsheets, graphics and presentation packages, and sophisticated word processors, they wished to share documents with their peers. Clearly the infamous "sneaker-net" of the early 1980s, although actually possessing fairly good bandwidth, was not a viable long term solution.

At the same time, document creation began to demand more sophistication and specialization. Although it is common for a single user to author a simple ASCII mail message or document, it is rare that one individual will have the talents or tools on their desktop to be able to create a complex compound document that contains tables, images, vector graphics, audio, presentation graphics, etc. Consequently, users started to share document components, using compound document architectures to create these complex documents.

As these complex documents were developed, users attempted to use existing distributed file systems to coordinate access. However, because complex documents can contain hundreds of pages with dozens of different object types, sharing at the document level proved impractical and unusable. What was needed was an n-writers/n-readers model where multiple users could have concurrent read and write access to document components. But existing file system locking protocols and transaction semantics were insufficient for such complicated distributed concurrency schemes.

At IDI we realized that these types of problems could be addressed by database technology. Databases excel at providing:

- Strong transaction semantics
- Fine grained locking and concurrency control
- User defineable attributes and schemas
- Physical and logical integrity of data through use of journaling and referential integrity constraints.

3. The Myth of "Unstructured Text"

Over the last ten to fifteen years the relational database model gained preeminence in academics and industry as the defacto standard for database models. At the core of this data model is the assumption that fields in a record are fairly small, and that data can be represented as rows of tuples, where each element in the tuple is of a predefined data type. Traditional RDBMS have had a single record size limit of 16-64kb. When users demanded database technology to coordinate access to large textual and compound documents, RDBMSs extended their data models to incorporate the notion of a BLOB, or Binary Large Object. Traditional RDBMSs manage BLOBs as single elements, with no knowledge of the internal structure of these elements.   The first generation of text retrieval engines used a variety of brute force methods to extend the BLOB model, and indexed either at the word level or the individual byte level to support free-text searching. However, this approach was somewhat a case of "You can't see the forest from the trees." By focusing only on words or bytes, all understanding of larger document components such as headings, introductory paragraphs, chapters, sections, summary points, and tables of contents was lost.

Both the full-text indexing and BLOB approaches contributed to the idea of "free text", or "unstructured text" searching. Looking at the problem not as database developers, but rather as electronic publishing developers, we easily see the fallacy of considering documents unstructured. One of the fundamental tenets of the electronic publishing industry is that documents have well defined structure. The amazing increase in desktop publishing capabilities over the last decade is the direct result of manipulating both the logical and the layout structure of documents — understanding paragraphs, running headers, running footers, frames, text flows, etc.   From this perspective it becomes obvious that there exists a better way to combine database technology and documents then either the BLOB handling or simple full text searching. This new approach utilizes the inherent structure in complex documents to improve search precision, system scalability, sharing granularity and the overall usability of the system.

4. The Non Linear Document Model

We have proposed a new model for representing documents. This model is a hybrid incorporating components of traditional relational database management systems (Codd 1970) as well as document grammars such as those that can be defined using SGML. A complete review of this document model can be found in (Gawkowski 1992).

To begin our definition of this new data model we will use Dyson's (Dyson 1990) classification of data into two types:

1.)   **Content Components.** Content components consist of components within a document that the user deems worth managing at a structural level. This means that the document database will manage this component as a separate entity, maintaining its relationship to children or ancestors within the document. Components of this class may be searched, retrieved and updated as entities.

2.)   **Criteria components**. Criteria components are components whose content is not interesting from a structural perspective, but whose value is interesting when considered as an attribute of a content component. For example, an author component may not in itself be interesting, but certainly is meaningful when considered as an attribute of a book or technical manual content component. Criteria components can be managed using traditional RDMBS mechanisms, ie., selections, projections, etc.

Given these two definitions, we then define a non-linear document (NLD) as being a hierarchical textual record representing content elements with a set of record-oriented critera elements associated with each content element. The legal structure for content elements within an NLD is defined by a context free grammar associated with the NLD. The grammar defines the allowed relationships between content elements. An NLD is content with an explicit structure. This structure is typically represented as a set of tagged components where the syntax of those tags conforms to a context-free grammar (Gawkowski 1992). This grammar may support inheritance of criteria attributes, multiple parents and children of a content component, versioning of documents and document components, and so on. The results of this new document model are improvements in collaborative sharing of documents in a distributed systems environment. These improvements may be characterized as follows:

1.) **Improved search precision.** Rather than searching a document database for all references to ASTM, a user can search for ASTM in Appendices, or ASTM in chapters that are a part of a repair manual.

2.) **Improved logical integrity of the document collection.** Referential integrity constraints can be applied to document components to enforce rules such as "Don't delete this chapter if more than one book references it," or "Mark this appendix as out-of-date if its last modification date was greater then one year from the current date."

3.) **Improved scalability.** When documents are managed at the document level, a user may need to load a 10 Mbyte document into his editing program simply to correct one spelling mistake on the last page. By managing documents at the component level, a user can get quicker access to individual document components. This improves both the latency of the system as perceived by the user (time taken to perform an individual action), as well as the overall scalability of the system, as measured by overall system throughput. The reduction in disk i/o and computation for any one request results in more requests being serviced by a given server over a set period of time.

4.) **Improved collaboration of workers.** Multiple workers can be updating multiple components of a document concurrently, since documents are managed at the component level, rather than the document level.

5. Distributed and Replicated Databases and NLDs

The development of distributed and replicated databases is driven by several key user requirements:

1.) **High performance across wide geographical areas.** Despite the improvements in routers, gateways, and network bandwidth, database performance is still strongly a function of how physically close a user is to a data store. As corporations become more global in scope, and document sharing crosses local work group boundaries, it is becoming more prevalent for users to need access to widely distributed data. Performance can be improved in these configurations by replicating data, so that, for example, users in Boston and London can both access local copies of a database table.

2.) **High availability.** Many organizations are moving towards 7x24 operation of their document management systems wherein replication of database information and RPC-based fail-over mechanisms can assure that users have uninterrupted access to documents, regardless of individual system hardware or software failures.

3.) **Improved collaboration**. Users need to be able to share document components without regard for the physical location of the data store. In general users wish to consider their document management systems and document databases from a logical perspective—either based on the organizational structure of the company ("I'd like to look at all work being done by the software services group"), or on the logical structure of their documents ("Show me all documents edited by Fred during the last two weeks in November"). Users do not want to *have* to think about their documents based on the physical topology of their network— although they may be forced to do so if poorly implemented distribution or replication decisions result in poor performance.

Distributed database technology should allow application developers to build applications using a logical view of document structures which can be shared across machine and network boundaries without consideration of these boundaries. A distributed database mechanism based on horizontal or vertical partitioning of relations (which underlies most existing RDBMS) is not the best distribution model for today's work environments; rather, a distribution algorithm based on document components and structure is more naturally suited to the work patterns of collaborative document authors/coworkers.

6. Automation of System Management

One problem with distributed and replicated database systems is the significant system management cost associated with them. Most commercial distributed DBMSs today require explicit guidelines for replicating and distributing data. Depending on the robustness of the algorithms used, there are a myriad of error conditions that may occur— ranging from incomplete replications, to recursive loops in replication, to poor performance on distributed updates. Current work in the area of *object migration systems* may help with this problem. Object migration systems have heuristics built into the distributed system that automatically move objects closer or farther away from users, based on how often they use them. In other words, objects automatically migrate topologically according to usage. Whether or not object migration systems are readily adopted, the ability to automate system management will be a critical factor in how distributed and replicated databases are accepted in the general market.

7. Federated Databases and Desktop Browsers

Over the last several years there has been a significant amount of research done in the area of federated databases (Hsiao 1990, Scheuermann 1990, Sheth 1990, Du 1989). A review of the work done to date in this area is beyond the scope of this paper. However, the end result of this work has been the commercialization of several 4GL and windows-based application development environments that allow users to access data stored in multiple databases, using a single-user interface. Many of these applications use SQL as the common query language for accessing federated databases. However, SQL in its current form lacks the semantics necessary to do effective content and structure based queries of document databases. Consequently, other standards have emerged that are focused on providing a query language that is well-suited to accessing full-text and hierarchical document data stores. These standards include ANSI Z39.50 (NISO 1991) and SFQL, which is being developed by the Airline Transport Association.

Position Summary

In many applications, ranging from simple file system browsers, to user interfaces that query chemical databases using chemical compounds as query values, to JCALS components that assemble technical manuals on the fly, there is a common theme: *End users wish to be presented with a simple and consistent data model and user interface for accessing documents and document components from a variety of data stores.* This reinforces our previous observation that to maintain the simplicity and ease-of-use of collaborative systems, information must be presented to end-users based on their logical view of the document universe—not a view that is driven by the physical structure or location of underlying data storage systems.

8. Future Directions

We anticipate that as users continue to increase the complexity and extent of their document collaboration, more applications will be brought to market that support sharing documents at the component level. Distributed system technologies such as Microsoft's OLE, Apple Events in Macintosh System 7, and the Object Location Broker as defined by the Object Management Group, will help in defining the standards necessary for applications. There are several characteristics of NLDs that lend themselves well to object-oriented databases, including attribute inheritance, considering content components as objects, etc. We will be exploring ways of extending the object oriented paradigm to model NLDs.

References

D.K. Hsiao, Magdi N. Kamel. Heterogeneous Databases: Proliferations, Issues and Solutions. Computer and Administrative Sciences Departments. Naval Postgraduate School. Monterey, Ca. 1990

Du, W., et. al. Effects on Local Autonomy on Heterogeneous Distributed Database Systems, MCC Tech. Report ACT-OODS-EI-059-90. E.F. Codd, A Relational Model for Large Shared Data Banks. Communications of the ACM, 13, 377-387, 1970E.

Dyson. Release 1.0 - EDventure Holdings, 30-April 1990

Gawkowski, John A. & Raudabaugh, George E. The Design and Development of a Database Model to Support Non-Linear Document Management, Proceedings of Symposium on Document Analysis and Information Retrieval 1992, Information Science Research Institute, University of Nevada, Los Vegas.

National Information Standards Organization. ANSI/NISO Z39.50-1992 (Draft)

Scheuermann, Peter et. al. Heterogeneous Database Systems, Report of the NSF Workshop on, December 11-13, 1990

Sheth, Amit and Larson, James. Federated Database Systems. ACM Computing Surveys, Vol 22, No 3, September 1990

Groupware Applications Interoperability

Mitch Shults

Intel Corporation

ABSTRACT

Commercial groupware applications today are closed environments. The data storage mechanisms are unpublished, the development-tool internals are unavailable. The only mechanism provided for enabling interoperability, typically, is a limited-function API. Important value-added applications have been constructed with these API's, but it's not enough. The theme of this presentation is that what is needed for groupware interoperability is a standard set of services that developers can use to create their own groupware applications. These services are in the areas of front-end development, interprocess communications, and data management.

The three panel members offer products in these areas, and will address the general concerns of building groupware applications based on these services.

Introduction

So, you've decided to implement groupware?! Congratulations! Today, you have two basic choices:

1.   Buy a groupware vendor's packaged solution off the shelf, and hope that

    a.   It fits most of your needs today, and

    b.   The vendor will enhance the package on a timely basis to meet the rest of your current and future requirements,

- OR -

2.   Build your own groupware application.

In which case, you face a major challenge in terms of building in the basic capabilities of a robust groupware system.

It's the same situation you've always faced with software in the past: build or buy.

'Groupware' is not a product. It is a concept. Groupware capabilities can be incorporated into any application. It just takes the right design concepts and productive implementation tools.

This presentation is concerned with the tools and techniques to make this possible.

The Current State Of Affairs

The first 'groupware' application, in a very real sense, was the first multi-user on-line transaction processing system. No doubt it ran on a mainframe somewhere, probably with a TTY-based user interface. Nevertheless, the fact that one individual in a company could input information that was immediately accessible to others made this a 'groupware' application.

Today, of course, no one describes groupware in these terms. To a large extent, products such as Lotus' Notes have defined the groupware market in their own terms.

It is certainly true that Notes is a groupware product. Many companies have used its toolset to build powerful information-sharing applications. Third-party software companies have created some amazing applications to add value to the default Notes environment.

Very few, however, have used Notes to create an effective business-critical transaction-processing application. Why? Because products like Notes and other groupware offerings on the market today are not designed to build such applications. When developers attempt to use them for that purpose, they are inevitably disappointed. They quickly discover that the tools

- do not easily support access to existing data resources within the enterprise

- do not support access to existing applications and validation routines, or require that someone write large amounts of C code to do it

- do not provide the highly reliable integrity-management schemes that transaction processing requires

- do not scale well for enterprise-level[1] usage

Tools like Notes, Workman, and the rest are great at what they do. However, they are limited in their capabilities, and they do not interoperate well, if at all, with other systems. Such tools are adequate for relatively simple, limited function, limited-scale groupware applications. More is needed in order to realize the full potential of groupware. Specifically:

- The ability to create classic transaction-processing applications that fully utilize groupware concepts in their implementation.

- The ability to tie groupware applications directly to existing 'legacy' databases and applications.

---

[1]   A note on the term 'enterprise'. Simply stated, it means a heterogeneous, geographically dispersed collection of computing resources. It includes all of the individuals internal to an organization, and their external business partners. It includes numerous existing applications that perform the day-to-day work of running the company. An enterprise solution must provide mechanisms for addressing each element of this environment or it really isn't enterprise-class. "Use my stuff everywhere" isn't the right answer.

The ability of multiple groupware applications, each with a different purpose, to effectively share data and logic.

Providing these abilities requires tools. That's the subject of the next section.

Technology Developments

The technology of groupware is essentially the technology of distributed computing. This technology is today far advanced from where it was five years ago. When Lotus set out to build Notes, the only real standard was NetBIOS. Everything else they had to build themselves. The result is a product that works well, but does not interoperate directly with other systems.

The world is different now. International standards exist for communications interfaces, distributed database management, directory services, and others. Standards are emerging for object management and complex-document representation. Combine these standards with the tools to use them effectively, at a high level of abstraction, and it becomes possible to consider constructing customized applications that incorporate groupware.

What tools are needed?

Communications Technology

Network nodes today are separated by a veritable alphabet soup of communications protocols. SNA, TCP/IP, OSI, IPX, XNS, the list goes on. Of themselves, these protocols provide basic **connectivity**. It's up to the application developer to establish **communication** between network nodes using these protocols.

Development at the native network protocol level is a nasty, dangerous business. It's also very expensive to provide a high degree of portability in an application written to this level. Most enterprises have more than one protocol in use. End users don't care about protocols. They care about the results that effective communications can provide. Without robust communications, groupware is meaningless.

PeerLogic has world-class tools for building communicating applications. These tools are well-suited to an object-based, message-passing development approach. Their product allows developers to build communicating applications that utilize a single, very high-level interface across a wide range of platforms and protocols.

Object Management

Fundamentally, groupware is concerned with the management and distribution of loosely structured, highly interrelated data. Add the problem of managing the programs that act on the data to the picture, and you've got object management.

Pure distributed object management is a developing standard. It has numerous advantages for general-purpose systems development, but there's one drawback:

- Because they are so generalized, groupware implementation using object management systems is challenging. The developer must extend the object manager to include many of the higher-level functions of loosely structured data management.

'Loosely structured data management' is another term for hypermedia. The Xanadu Operating Company, a subsidiary of Autodesk, has been working on the hypermedia problem for some time. Their product will offer an API-based approach to the problem of hypermedia management. Front-end developers will be able to utilize the Xanadu server to build a wide variety of applications that include hypermedia functionality. The object-manager extensions required to do effective hypermedia come built-in with their product.

Database Interoperability

Information that drives groupware functions often resides within existing databases. Interoperability and connectivity to these databases is important. Groupware developers must be able to directly incorporate existing corporate data sources in a seamless fashion into their applications. Tools exist to provide this level of operability. The panelists do not directly focus on this market, however.

Development Tools

The world of the application developer. Developers want the best of both worlds: highly abstracted and productive tools that also provide direct access to the lowest-level system functions when necessary. Shrink-wrapped groupware front-ends allow development, but only within a pre-defined and limiting framework. What's needed are general-purpose development tools, designed to build production-quality systems, that can also access groupware-oriented services.

Configurex understands the challenges of building custom transaction-processing applications that take full advantage of a distributed approach. They provide front-end tools that can be used to more-easily create serious business applications that also exhibit 'groupware' characteristics. Applications built with their product are inherently distributed, and are able to take advantage of any API-based service in the environment.

Configurex will address the issues involved in building a distributed application that effectively incorporates groupware functionality.

Ending

Groupware is more of a concept than a specific product. There are as many ways to do it as there are inventive minds to think about it. Services can give developers the ability to build groupware facilities into what used to be thought of as 'conventional' applications. The mass-market groupware vendors should follow suit by opening access to their internals and allowing third-party tools developers to add value. Vertical industry add-ins are not sufficient to address the requirement.

Rich, scalable, and interoperable service-based approaches are more viable in the long run. The developer's challenge is to use these tools to build next-generation applications that can take full advantage of the potential that groupware and distributed computing offer.

Businesses today are emphasizing process re-engineering as a means to achieving lasting competitive advantage. Information systems support this process. Information systems that combine both transaction-processing capability and integrated support for groupware functionality will best address the business need in the long run. There's a place for closed, limited-function groupware applications. But there's more to the groupware story than that.

But I Don't Talk TCP/IP:
Solving the Interoperability Problem

Julie Lepick Kling
Vice President, Marketing
PeerLogic, Inc.

The Problem

It is a cliche that organizations are made up of different individuals, different workgroups, and different computing cultures. Yet it is equally commonplace to acknowledge that local workgroup cultures must be respected. True groupware will treat the network, the resources on that network, and most especially, the human resources as a single, dynamic system facilitating the ad hoc formation and dissolution of cross-functional teams. Interoperability will be a key requirement of such applications, enabling machines, as well as people, to work together.

Issues of price, performance, and portability are encouraging the distribution of computing functions across varying platforms. In the distributed model, each platform performs the task for which it is best suited: the desktop performing pre-processing and presentation, specialized servers supplying much of the real application processing, and the mainframe serving as a data respository (from the PC perspective, an enormous hard disk). But the lack of a consistent set of systems-level services across these platforms seriously impedes the expansion of groupware.

The Choices

To develop groupware that spans today's complex enterprise-wide computing environment, developers have basically four choices:

1. Develop for a single environment, then port the application to additional platforms.

2. Develop a distributed groupware application by coding to each desktop environment (GUI or not), operating system, and network.

3. Try to enforce a homogeneous environment, for instance, by adopting TCP/IP.

4. Wait for products based on standard specifications such as those proposed by OSF.

Alternatively, developers can look for enabling technology that addresses the issue of interoperability at a layer residing between the application and the network.

Architectural Requirements for Enterprise-Wide Groupware Development

We should make it clear that we assume any enterprise-wide groupware application will be, by necessity, a distributed application. And any form of distributed application, including groupware, will best be built on a common communications infrastructure that addresses the problems of interoperability, reliability, and flexibility. Whether we call this layer "enabling technology," "middleware," or distributed systems software, it must provide applications with a robust set of network services. In the most simple terms, it should enable applications to treat the network as if it were a single virtual computer.

Most obviously, just as disk, video, other peripheral I/O has been abstracted away from the underlying hardware, these services should virtualize all network I/O on behalf of the application. But applications will require additional services beyond a virtual transport.

True groupware applications will consist of resources, or objects, distributed throughout the network. The software enabling communication among these objects will allow any resource to request or offer services to any other resource. It will present a logical network to the application, providing session management, routing, error detection and recovery, monitoring, and performance optimization, among other services.

The ideal platform for distributed applications must provide for change. It should accommodate not only change, but the migration to standards, if and when migration occurs. And it should simplify the developer's task, reducing development costs and reducing the time from design to implementation. Finally, it should encourage the reuse of common components.

PeerLogic believes this platform is best provided by an object-oriented, message-based solution. We have implemented this solution as a distributed operating system kernel that runs on each machine, regardless of its native OS. PIPES Platform provides the services of a distributed operating system, isolates the application from the dirty details of local OS and transports, and provides a common API in all environments.

The design and development of groupware applications should increasingly be the province of the users of the system. Groupware will only proliferate throughout the enterprise when it becomes possible to easily write applications that span varying GUIs, OSs, and network OSs. Making the network transparent to the application and the user is a major step in this direction.

Richard A. D. Vincent - Configurex Inc.
White Paper for "Groupware in the Enterprise"
- ENTERPRISEWARE - a reality

"One of the most powerful trends in the computer industry today is the conversion of large, centralized applications into networks for decentralized, front-end systems. As part of this downsizing process, organizations are retiring old host-based applications and are re-building them using networks of host computers, departmental machines, terminals, and workstations. The overall objective of the downsizing process is to move critical processing and database functions closer to the end user."

Pieter Mimno
CASE Trends
February 1992

Although Groupware may be a reality today - "Enterpriseware" is a more appropriate term for the Application Development Systems that address the centralized needs of the enterprise as a whole, while supporting the diverse needs of workgroups and individuals. Enterpriseware needs to handle the issues that have been traditionally been the responsibility of MIS, such as:
- Security & Integrity
- Backup & Archive
- Change & Copy Management
- Performance & Availability Management
- Problem Management
- Audit Trails
- CASE Analysis, Maintenance & Documentation
Enterprise-wide systems have to be "Industrial-strength".

Configurex believes that workgroup integration and interoperability at the application level should be approached through the use of objects. Objects and their messaging protocol provide a natural way to approach groupware integration.

"Enterpriseware"

Enterpriseware is positioned to be a replacement for older technologies and for building departmental applications on networks and cooperative processing systems. The products are differentiated from each of the other classes of application development products by one or more of the following features:

- Total application development using only "point and click", so users do not need to learn a new language
- True OOP development environment
- Built in peer-to-peer network messaging, which is not found in other products
- RDBMS-resident application code, which is shared across the network for instant release of updates
- MIS control and analysis of the system at a high-level, graphical abstraction
- Support for client/server and cooperative processing environments

Distributed computing is the natural way to develop enterpriseware applications. For real distributed computing, peer-to-peer communications between PC's is required. Applications and sub-applications must be able to communicate cooperatively between PC's across the network. To accomplish this, the application platform must support transparent peer-to-peer communications. At the application level, the best way to support transparent communications is through the use of objects and messages between them. These application objects lend themselves naturally to solving the security and integrity challenges inherent in industrial-strength applications. Application objects provide the benefits of extensibility, reusability, encapsulation, inheritance and polymorphism. Application objects can also help realize the promise of true user-defined applications. Since objects are encapsulated, the user need only have contact with that part of the object that is user-definable -- the internals of the object and its relationships with other objects remain hidden and protected.

Product Capabilities Required in Enterpriseware Systems

Enterpriseware should have the following product capabilities:

- **Support of Standards**
  Current standards are DDE, OLE and Open Systems/OMG CORBA (Common Object Request Broker Architecture). There are also some mail-based standards being developed, such as VIM (Vendor-Independent Messaging) standard, supported by Apple, Borland, Lotus and Novell, and the MAPI (Message API) being driven by Microsoft.

- **Object Oriented Programming (OOP)**
  Enterpriseware should provide the OOP benefits of simplicity, reusability, extensibility, and scalability. Object building blocks make object-oriented programming accessible to users. Programming a building block should be no more difficult than creating a formula in a spreadsheet. Applications are built by grouping building blocks into windows and then connecting selected building blocks together.

- **Centrally-Resident Application Code**
  Enterpriseware should maintains its internal application code on a central database. In business systems, this is usually a relational database. Although the application runs on the client, it is stored on the relational datbase. This means the application code can be protected using the same RDBMS security features as the data. MIS can also access the application code with analysis tools or other programs. The Enterpriseware architecture should support RDBMS-based stored procedures, which are essential to efficient client-server transaction programming. Products cannot provide these functions when the internal application code is client-based.

- **Graphical User Interface (GUI)**
  Enterpriseware must provides CUA-compliant interfaces. Users must be able to quickly put together a complex display of information with little training.

- **Point and Click Programming**
  The predominant design goal of Enterpriseware should be that no programming operation be more difficult than operating a modern spreadsheet or word processing product. All programming should be accomplished with "point and click" methods.

- **Peer-to-Peer Communications Built In**
  While many systems support communications between client PCs and central servers, almost none support application-level peer-to-peer communications without complicated programming. This feature is required for the development of distributed applications.

- **CASE**
  Provides "real-world" CASE technology to enable MIS to analyze the system as a whole and to track and control change. Object-level CASE can be used to keep a 'directory' of the thousands of objects created using Enterpriseware.

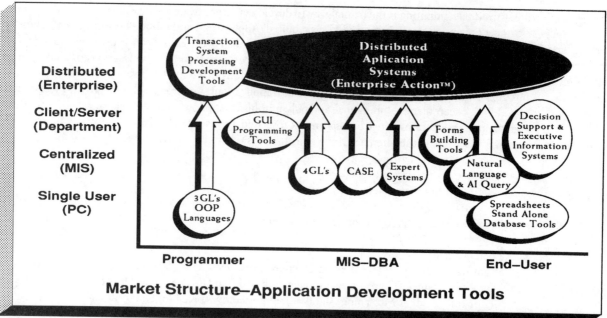

Market Structure—Application Development Tools

Market

Enterpriseware systems are targeted across users, across the Enterprise (see above). The target market for Enterpriseware products is comprised of organizations with 500 or more employees, cross-industry. These companies should have networked PCs attached to relational databases, and run OS/2, Windows, or on MAC's. Industry estimates indicate that the number of sites of this type will be 15,576 in 1991, and will grow to 60,372 such sites by 1994[1].

The demand for these products is being driven by several major market trends:

- Increase in use of client/server technology.
  The percentage of client PCs connected to file servers and database servers on LANs is projected to increase from 34% in 1990 to 65% in 1994[2].
- Increase in use of graphical user interfaces (GUI).
  The worldwide GUI installed base for Windows, OS/2 PM, and Macintosh is expected to grow from 13 million in 1990 to 57 million in 1994, a compound annual growth rate of 45%[3]. The market for GUI tools is projected to grow at a 40% compound rate from 1990 to 1993[4].
- Increase in the acceptance of relational databases.
  Relational databases are increasingly replacing hierarchical and network databases in operational systems. They also are the foundation for the new distributed database technology, which is presently being introduced. The following table shows the actual and projected increase in the market share for relational and distributed databases[5]:

Year	Hierarchical/ Network Databases (%)	Relational Databases (%)	Distributed Databases (%)	Flat File Databases (%)
1988	31%	61%	0%	8%
1994	10%	71%	17%	2%

- Increase in the demand for object oriented programming (OOP).
  OOP had a revenue base in 1990 of $50 million, and is projected to grow at a compound annual growth rate of 50%[6]. Many new user- and GUI-oriented tools are based on OOP technology.

1 Source: MIRC study on Sales Automation Software Markets, 1988.   3 Source: International Data Corp., 1990   5 Source: MIRC study on DBMS Markets, 1988
2 Source: Dataquest, 1991   4 Source: Case Studies IV, Volpe, Welty and Company, 1990   6 Source: Case Studies IV, Volpe, Welty and Company, 1990

Target Applications and Industries

Major strategic and operational MIS systems can be built using Enterpriseware. Examples of the kinds of applications best suited for this kind of development are:

- Accounting
- Customer Service and Support
- Employee Benefits
- License, Claim, and Credit Processing
- Order Entry and Management
- Process and Production Control
- Sales and Marketing Information

Enterpriseware can be used to develop a broad range of production business applications. Configurex is pursuing a horizontal approach to the market since their product - Enterprise Action™, can be used by a broad class of users that span across many vertical markets.

BUILDING THE APPLICATION

Using the example of Configurex's Enterprise Action™, applications are developed by interactively creating, moving, and modifying application "building blocks". These building blocks are graphical representations of the common screen elements used in business applications today: fields, lists, spreadsheets, documents, graphical images, and menus. Building blocks are combined into windows that are used much like the screens in current business applications.

These "building blocks," for example, lists, fields, menus and buttons, are intelligent "objects" that form the application itself. Enterprise Action provides an easy-to-use point-and-click interface for defining these building blocks. Writing an application is as easy as defining a series of spreadsheet cells. Transactions are initiated by user actions such as clicking on a menu, pushing a button, or by other external events. These events are routed to the appropriate building block(s), whether on the user's client machine, another client machine, or a server.

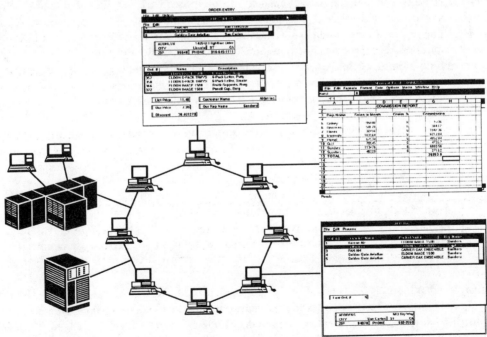

In the example above, a salesperson using the "ORDER ENTRY" window clicks the "Enter..." selector on the "Orders" menu. This initiates a transaction that is routed to the "SHIPPING" window at a client PC in the shipping department. The "SHIPPING" window adds the order to its list and to the underlying relational database on the appropriate server. This order can then be selected and processed by the shipping department, using the "SHIPPING" window. After the order is processed, the application updates a commission report running under Microsoft Excel. This commission report update is an example of the Dynamic Data Exchange (DDE) linking provided by new application development systems. Users define these links using simple point-and-click operations. No DDE coding is required. Once defined, each DDE link is automatically maintained by the application development system. DDE linking is available for Lotus 1-2-3, Microsoft Excel, Word for Windows, and WordPerfect.

Windows and all other building blocks can be copied and re-used in new windows. Any window can be copied or updated at any time if the user has update authority. This feature enables the application to change and grow as the users' business changes and grows.

MULTIPLE PLATFORMS & OPERATING SYSTEMS

In the Application Example (above), the reality of a business's Enterprise, could be that the Mainframe (with DB2), is linked by LU 6.2 to multiple networks (LAN's & WAN's) to multiple servers, with client platforms that could be a mixture of OS/2, Windows, MOTIF and MAC. This Application Development System allows development on any of the platforms, and will then run on any other, transparently to the users. The flexibility allows companies to choose the right technology for their environments - and also allows the development on a single focussed platform - or multiple platforms, as there organization warrants it. Those simple changes can also be completed by the end users themselves, reducing the MIS load.

Groupware Application code is retained in the relational database as "object classes", which are extracted and activated by user PCs as needed. This architecture makes it possible to bring PC-based point-and-click programming to the line organization, while providing support to MIS (such as CASE methodologies) to maintain the application system as a whole.

Configurex - Company Overview

Configurex markets and develops Enterprise Action™, a rapid development system used to create and modify industrial strength, distributed, transaction-based applications. Enterprise Action provides point-and-click programming at hierarchical levels that are suitable for MIS programmers, database administrators, and sophisticated end users. Using Enterprise Action, line organizations can quickly respond to changing information needs, yet MIS can maintain the security, integrity, and configuration of the underlying application and data. Because Enterprise Action uses a "point and click" methodology, no programming language must be learned. This methodology, combined with the windowing interface, greatly decreases the learning curves at all levels of use. Encapsulation of other "legacy software" may be utilized, and standards "migrated" to object orientation from more traditional MIS application development methodologies.

Enterprise Action is used to develop a broad range of production business applications - independent of RDBMS vendor. Enterprise Action:

- Brings object technology to relational database applications
- Supports distributed applications on networks and cooperative processing systems
- Enables users and database administrators to modify and extend applications
- Provides MIS with the tools to maintain the system's configuration, security, and integrity
- Provides easy-to-use links between Enterprise Action and popular end user applications, such as spreadsheets and word processors

Richard A. D. Vincent is Co-Founder and Vice President of Marketing and Sales. Vincent has more than 22 years experience in international software sales and marketing, holding senior management positions for the last 15. He has worked for IBM, International Computers Limited (ICL), Data General, Hewlett-Packard, Co-Cam Computer Services (an Australian software company that he grew from $6Million to $28Million in under two years), XA Systems, and Boole & Babbage. Prior to joining IBM in 1970, Vincent spent eight years as an engineering officer in the Royal Air Force. Mr. Vincent was educated in England at Dean Close School in Cheltenham, and holds a masters degree in electronics & aerodynamics from Cambridge University (UK), while at the Royal Air Force Technical College.

TRACK 3:
Groupware in the Commercial Marketplace

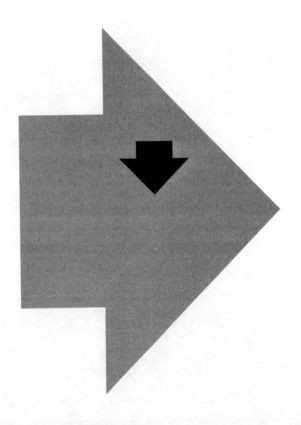

Creative Networks

Nina Burns
President, Market Development Services

Creative Networks
*Dedicated to helping businesses succeed
in the '90s through the effective use of technology.*

- 1 -

Creative Networks

Electronic Messaging: A Platform for Collaboration

- 2 -

Corporate Computing Dynamics

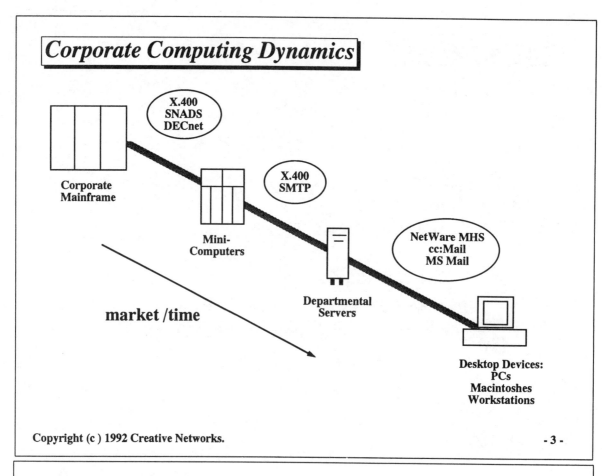

market /time

- 3 -

Messaging vs. Electronic Mail

- **More than just E-Mail.**

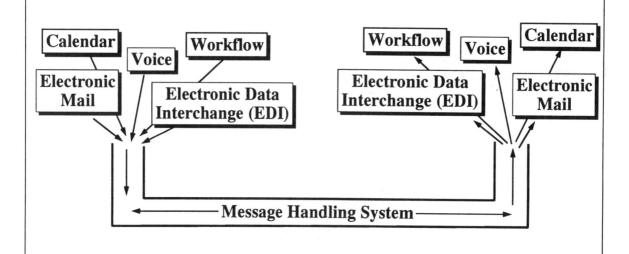

- 4 -

Engines vs. Applications

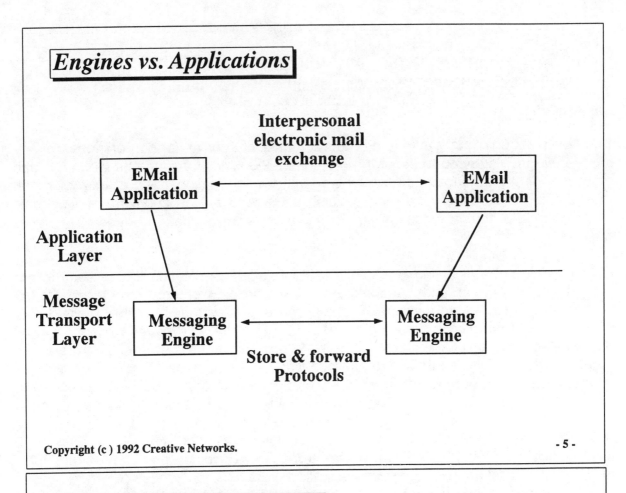

Interpersonal electronic mail exchange

EMail Application

EMail Application

Application Layer

Message Transport Layer

Messaging Engine

Messaging Engine

Store & forward Protocols

The New Messaging Model

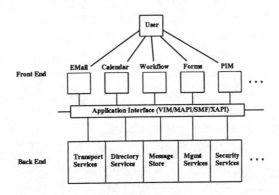

User

Front End

EMail   Calendar   Workflow   Forms   PIM   ...

Application Interface (VIM/MAPI/SMF/XAPI)

Back End

Transport Services | Directory Services | Message Store | Mgmt Services | Security Services   ...

MAILbus 400™

New Generation of Electronic Messaging Solutions

Debra Murphy, Kevin Miles, Geoff Oades, and Audrey Augun
Digital Equipment Corporation

Introduction

Effective electronic mail systems are now a matter of survival for corporations, reflecting in their growing need to transfer more complex business documents internally, and among trading partners worldwide. As a result, the international acceptance of X.400 messaging standards is increasing, placing a demand on the suppliers of electronic mail systems for further functionality, performance, ease-of-use, and ease of management.

Digital's vision of messaging is to provide a cost-effective solution that is easy to deploy, manage and use, and that scales from the smallest workgroup to the largest extended enterprise. Digital's vision is global -- messaging with no borders. Digital views the world of messaging as one logical network of dissimilar systems and one logical directory service, all interconnected. Digital is unique among systems integrators and other vendors in our breadth and depth of messaging experience. This experience has been gleaned from our own diverse 100,000+ user worldwide messaging network that is used for electronic mail, EDI and FAX. Digital has been a leader in electronic messaging networks for many years, providing multivendor connectivity dating back to 1987 when the Message Router/X.400 Gateway, Message Router/SNADS Gateway, and Message Router/PROFS Gateway were introduced. Building upon our leadership in networking, Digital brings a unique combination of being a full service provider, as well as integrator of electronic messaging solutions, from the laptop to the backbone.

International Standards

Digital has a long history of incorporating international, national, and defacto standards into its products, and of actively participating in the formation of standards. Digital was the first company to ship a standards-based messaging product -- Message Router -- in 1981, based on the 1980 National Bureau of Standards (NBS, now NIST) standard. Digital was the first to deploy a commercially available 1984 X.400 product and now is one of few vendors delivering a 1988 X.400 Message Transport Agent with 1992 extensions. Digital is the only vendor that has integrated international standards into the heart of their networking environment. Our ability to provide and implement solutions across multiple vendors' platforms is made possible by conforming to international standards. Corporations demand industrial strength products that they can depend on to run their business. Digital meets that demand through ADVANTAGE-NETWORKS™ and MAILbus 400.

Our involvement and leadership in standards is not only a demonstration of our commitment, but also of our respect for the international community. Yet, meeting a standard is only the beginning. Our experience in deploying these standards makes Digital unique in its ability to address the business issues associated with deploying a global messaging system. Digital offers well-architected solutions, that not only work, but provide business benefits and a competitive advantage for those who choose to deploy Digital's offerings.

Digital's History of Electronic Messaging

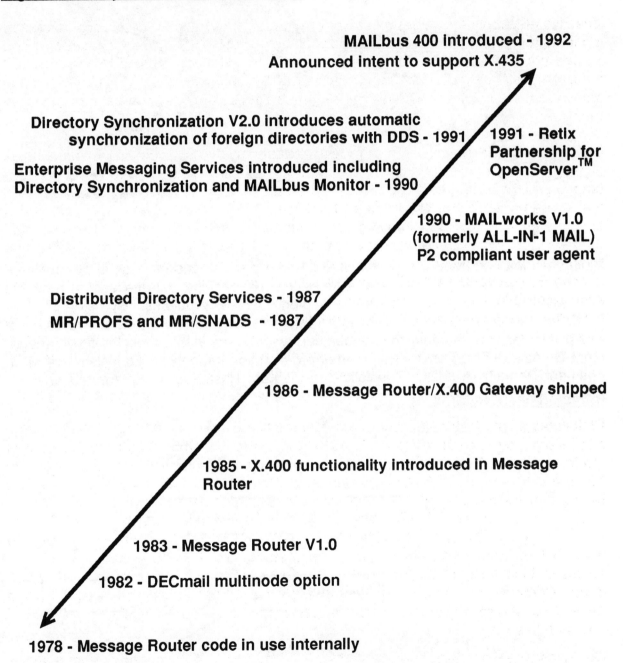

MAILbus 400 introduced - 1992
Announced intent to support X.435

Directory Synchronization V2.0 introduces automatic synchronization of foreign directories with DDS - 1991

1991 - Retix Partnership for OpenServer™

Enterprise Messaging Services introduced including Directory Synchronization and MAILbus Monitor - 1990

1990 - MAILworks V1.0 (formerly ALL-IN-1 MAIL) P2 compliant user agent

Distributed Directory Services - 1987
MR/PROFS and MR/SNADS - 1987

1986 - Message Router/X.400 Gateway shipped

1985 - X.400 functionality introduced in Message Router

1983 - Message Router V1.0

1982 - DECmail multinode option

1978 - Message Router code in use internally

Multivendor Mail Network Problems

Many corporations have built a messaging environment that is comprised of multiple proprietary mail systems. Now they are faced with the task of tying them all together into one cohesive, integrated messaging system. The following picture illustrates a typical environment where "islands" of mail systems have grown.

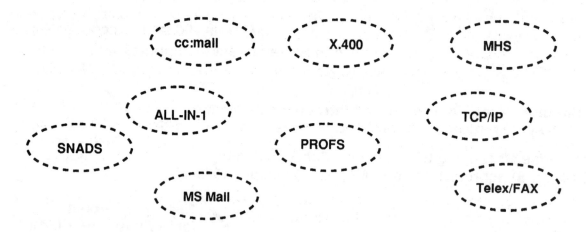

Digital has learned from experience what it takes to install and manage large multivendor mail networks and knows what it takes to build best-in-class messaging products and services that solve customers' messaging business problems. By using Digital's MAILbus 400 products, you can build an integrated environment that allows users of any proprietary mail system to communicate with others within their Private Management Domain (PRMD) or external to their organization through an Administrative Management Domain (ADMD). The following diagram illustrates the integrated environment.

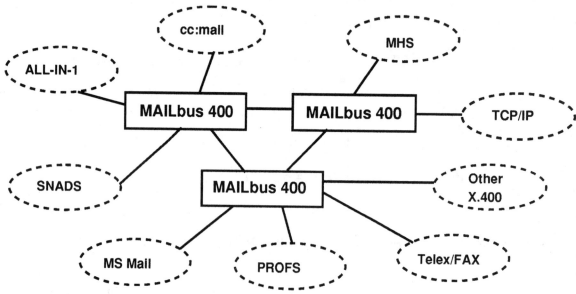

Introducing MAILbus 400

MAILbus 400 is a landmark in Digital's ongoing leadership of providing its customers with cost-effective, messaging solutions that integrates islands of electronic mail systems. Present MAILbus customers can extend their MAILbus messaging networks to include new standards and features provided by MAILbus 400, while retaining their investment in their current technology. Those now considering how to build a corporate messaging system have available an extensive set of solutions that provide not only a messaging backbone, but also connectivity to popular PC LAN mail systems, the Internet (TCP/IP) environment, IBM, plus Digital's own extensive set of mail user agents.

MAILbus 400 is a product set of electronic messaging offerings built on the CCITT 1988 X.400 standard, that provides customers the infrastructure in order to build messaging backbones for their evolving business communications needs.

The MAILbus 400 Message Transfer Agent (MTA) is the first of several electronic messaging offerings that prove Digital is the leading provider and integrator of Enterprise Messaging Systems; building the infrastructure for customers evolving business communication needs.

MAILbus 400 Product Set

The MAILbus 400 product set is comprised of products based on the CCITT 1988 X.400 electronic messaging standards. MAILbus 400 incorporates high performance, extensive management features, international standards, and a low cost of ownership. There are three initial product components available on ULTRIX:

- MAILbus 400 Message Transfer Agent (MTA)
- MAILbus 400 Application Program Interface (API)
- MAILbus 400 SMTP Gateway

MAILbus 400 MTA incorporates the 1988 X.400 Message Transfer Agent (MTA) with an X.500-based directory component that enables the MTAs to share routing information. It provides a messaging service to applications such as user agents and mail gateways. The MAILbus 400 MTA will be available initially on ULTRIX/RISC, with VAX/VMS to follow.

The operational management of the MAILbus 400 MTA conforms to the Enterprise Management Architecture (EMA), enabling it to be managed from any DECnet/OSI node with an appropriate EMA director (for example, the NCL utility). It is supplied with default settings making installation easy, reducing set up time and costs.

The X.500-based directory routing information allows all the MAILbus 400 MTA's in a network to have the same picture of how to route messages. This achieves consistency throughout the domain by reducing the management overhead as routing information does not need to be duplicated at each MAILbus 400 MTA. Subsequent versions of the MTA will use the full X.500 Directory Service for this purpose.

The MAILbus 400 MTA can exchange messages with other vendors' MTAs that conform to either the 1984 or 1988 X.400 standards. It can perform conversions on the content of a message, based on which data formats the recipient of a message is capable of processing.

The MAILbus 400 Application Program Interface (API) provides application developers access to the messaging services of the MAILbus 400 MTA. The MAILbus 400 API is an implementation of V2.0 of X/Open CAE Specification (November 1991) and provides both the Application and Gateway interfaces.

The MAILbus 400 SMTP (Simple Mail Transfer Protocol) Gateway provides a bridge allowing mail to be exchanged between the traditional UNIX mail community and the X.400 mail community. The gateway is able to utilize the backbone management facilities and to handle address translations through the X.500 based routing directory. It provides conversion of messages, envelopes and content as described in RFC 987. This gateway can transport both text and binary message contents.

Why is MAILbus 400 the best solution to the Multivendor Mail Problem?

The MAILbus 400 MTA has been designed to provide an Enterprise Messaging backbone, and as such, it incorporates many features that are not addressed by the X.400 standards, notably:

* Conversions
* X.500-based directory
* EMA management

Conversions

The international telephone system allows anyone to call any subscriber in the world. However, making a connection with another person's telephone does not necessarily result in conversation unless both subscribers speak the same language. Similarly, X.400 will also offer global interconnectivity, but not only must sender and recipient 'speak' the same natural language, they must also use a mutually acceptable encoding for the documents they exchange.

There are probably hundreds of document encodings in use today, ranging from simple, such as ASCII text, through to complex, such as ODA. As X.400 joins up islands of computerization, many people will find that the only document encoding scheme they have in common is an unacceptably simple one.

The X.400 standard allows the Message Transport System (MTS) to perform an automatic conversion of a document where it recognizes that its current encoding will be unsuitable for the recipient. This can permit subscribers to exchange messages using complex document encodings even though they do not share a common one, provided it is possible to convert between them. However, the X.400 standard does not, as yet, address this area in a number of ways.

- X.400-1984 only defined a small set of document encodings with no agreed means for adding support for additional encodings, except by updating X.400 itself or by bilateral agreements between management domains. X.400-1988 changed this and provided a scheme making the registration of new encodings independent of X.400. Anyone, including vendors and customers, can invent a new encoding, assign it an unambiguous identifier, and X.400-1988 will then be able to carry it.

- X.400-1988 does not describe how automatic conversions are performed in a distributed environment - it does not say either where or how they should be performed. MAILbus 400 MTA performs automatic conversions and will be delivered with the following features:

  — The conversion capability of the MAILbus 400 MTA is extensible, allowing appropriate converters to be added as necessary. MAILbus 400 MTA will allow for the ability to integrate third-party or customized converters as they become available.

  — X.500 is used to indicate both the encodings acceptable to each recipient, or group of recipients, and their order of preference. This information is then used in conjunction with information in the message to determine if a conversion is necessary and to select the conversion to be performed.

  — Any MAILbus 400 MTA in the network can perform conversions. Conversions are normally performed as early as possible on the route taken by the message. If a MAILbus 400 MTA on the route does not contain the appropriate converter, the message is passed along the route until a MAILbus 400 MTA with that converter is reached, or the message arrives at the destination MAILbus 400 MTA. This allows companies to distribute, or centralize converters anywhere they choose on their network.

Implementing an X.400-1988 MTA allows Digital to transport any encoding, and removes the constraint of X.400-1984 of a small predefined set.

Digital provides the integration between islands of proprietary electronic mail which have data connectivity but are lacking either common encoding or the means to convert.

X.500 based directory

The MAILbus 400 MTA uses the X.500 directory as a central repository for naming, addressing, routing and address translation data, and is an enabler for many value-added features. Using the X.500 directory in this manner ensures consistency across the messaging environment. Some of the value added features available include automatic conversion of character sets and document types and powerful routing capabilities.

The X.400 specification does not currently standardize routing. Most MTAs performing routing use a proprietary local table. Tables are difficult to maintain since different tables must be kept manually synchronized if routing loops and 'black holes' are to be avoided. Manual synchronization gets progressively more difficult the larger the domain and the more distributed the management.

In the MAILbus 400 MTA, a single, shared database is employed to hold routing information. It is the same database used for naming people for other purposes: X.500. There is no need for manual synchronization of different databases since there is only one network-wide database. The manager(s) have control of the routing policy and it is fully expressed in the X.500 directory. A domain can start operation with just the default routing policy and then add more sophisticated policies over time. The advantage of taking control over message routing is that expensive bandwidth can be used more cost-effectively by reducing the number of copies of a message sent over the same wire.

EMA Management

The messaging backbone is a critical service to companies that build their competitive edge based on the timely availability of information. In order to keep the backbone running, its behavior has to be monitored, the messaging network manager needs to be warned of impending problems, and tools need to be available to fix problems when they arise. Without excellent management, a messaging backbone will be very costly to operate.

MAILbus 400 management was designed almost before the MAILbus 400 MTA product itself was designed. Digital's MAILbus 400 provides a consistent management architecture across the entire networking environment using the Enterprise Management Architecture. This enables cross-platform management to be carried out in a consistent manner and allows any management structure to be supported from fully centralized to fully distributed. By using EMA, MAILbus 400 capitalizes on the many years of software development effort that has been undertaken to understand enterprise network management. In addition, the MAILbus 400 MTA provides a message accounting capability, whereby any envelop fields of a message may be captured on disk for later use by accounting report generators..

A command line or windowed interface is used to manage the MAILbus 400 from any node, or series of nodes throughout the network. The interface may be customized to add new features, status indicators, etc., but most importantly, EMA provides consistency across products, for both MAILbus 400 and non-MAILbus 400 products. Someone already familiar with managing products built using EMA will easily be able to learn MAILbus 400 management, and vice versa, thereby reducing the cost of management.

Some of the additional features MAILbus 400 offers are:

- minimal set-up on installation
- 24 by 7 by 52 operation without requiring regular housekeeping tasks
- remote management
- regional management
- accounting
- message trace

We also offer the ability to have multiple MAILbus 400 MTAs function as one "set", appearing to the Message Handling System as one entity. If one MAILbus 400 MTA node is unavailable, another MAILbus 400 MTA node will automatically take over for that node, thus allowing the continued flow of messages through the network and even out to another PRMD or ADMD.

Conclusion

MAILbus 400 is a major part of Digital's software efforts to deliver solutions that promote multivendor interoperability through standards. For over 17 years, Digital has provided messaging and network infrastructures for customers with diverse needs and problems. With over seven million users of Digital mail products, customres look to Digital as the most experienced vendor to deliver on the promise of open systems and international standards with a wolution set that is solid, efficient, and truly open.

Trends in the LAN E-Mail Market
Groupware '92 Panel Presentation
J. Robert Martinson, President and CEO
Futurus Corporation

LAN-based electronic mail is one of the fastest growing segments within the personal computer market. International Data Corporation (IDC) predicts that in 1992, there will be a total of 9.2 million LAN mailboxes installed in the US and in 1994, the number will increase to 19.6 million mailboxes. This represents such a phenomenal growth trend that larger applications software vendors such as Lotus and Microsoft have recently entered the market. In addition to providing endusers with more product choices, a "legitimization" of the market has resulted.

Network operating system companies have also recognized the importance of E-mail. Novell, for example, acquired Message Handling System (MHS) technology and the company has demonstrated that MHS is an important part of their strategy. Even vendors in the peer-to-peer market know that their starter kits must include E-mail or their starter kits cannot effectively compete. In addition, Microsoft's "Sparta" will most likely include E-mail, scheduling and chat. Once again, the E-mail market is further validated.

The Local Area Network Dealer Association (LANDA) estimated that in 1991, 50% of networked PCs had E-mail. By extrapolating this curve, we believe that by 1995, greater than 80% of networked PCs will have E-mail. This demonstrates how much different E-mail is than other LAN applications such as menuing, back up software, or network utilities. E-mail is no longer an "afterthought" type of purchase and it is beginning to drive LAN sales in the market today. In other words, E-mail is what provides the basic foundation of LANs. After all, the whole point of LANs is to exchange information!

Another trend in the E-mail market is the inclusion of groupware functionality in E-mail software. While a few companies such as Futurus haveoffered integrated scheduling for quite some time, it is only recently thatothers (DaVinci, Lotus, and others) have realized the benefits of providingtheir customers with scheduling. In fact, within the next year or two, inorder to effectively compete, most every E-mail package must contain acombination of the following standard features: Scheduling, networkfront-end menuing, forms management, network utilities, personal information management (PIM), and group productivity.

As the E-mail market matures, more and more standards are evolving (MHS and NGM are among the first), and as E-mail vendors adhere to these standards, many connectivity issues are beginning to be resolved. As a result, customers are choosing E-mail software based on each products' feature set.

Beyond Incorporated

"Mail-Enabled Applications:Beyond Interpersonal Mail"

GROUPWARE '92

August 3-5, 1992   San Jose, CA

Eugene Lee
Director of Product Planning

Beyond Incorporated

Development of the Electronic Mail Market

1st Generation	2nd Generation
Host-Based OA	Proprietary LAN E-mail
• Highly functional	• Much cheaper
• Customizable	• Essentially a port of the mail function to the LAN
• Enterprise-wide	• Lost functionality
• Expensive	

Beyond Incorporated

The Third Generation of Electronic Mail:

Value-added, next-generation clients providing
new levels of functionality for users,
workgroups and enterprises.

BeyondMail Applications

Personal Productivity

- Filter, File, Sort, Prioritize
  Messages from my boss are urgent
  I was copied
  Phone calls I have to return
  Distribution lists
  Project tracking

- AutoTickle

- Out of the Office
  AutoReply
  AutoForward
  AutoDelegate

BeyondMail Applications

Interpersonal

- Boss/Secretary relationship

  - automatic delegation

  - secretary reads, boss doesn't see

- Status report consolidation

- Issue tracker (PCR, ECN)

Mail Script Wrapper

- Application already exists
- Goal is to provide access to this application across the network
- Use BeyondMail as the "launching pad"
- Email with forms becomes a window into applications on your network

Mail Script Wrapper

Application Mailbox Uses

- Intelligent redistribution
- Topic-based archiving
- Process controllers (intelligent switches)
- Process monitors/trackers
- "Office Robots"

BeyondMail Application Model

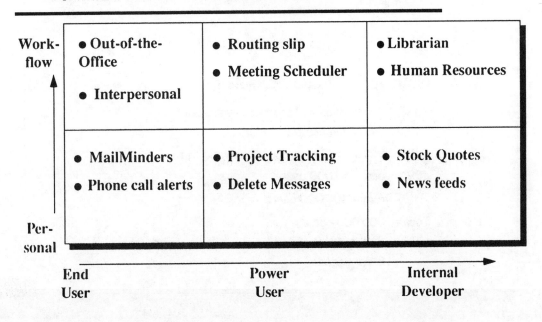

Work-flow	• Out-of-the-Office • Interpersonal	• Routing slip • Meeting Scheduler	• Librarian • Human Resources
Per-sonal	• MailMinders • Phone call alerts	• Project Tracking • Delete Messages	• Stock Quotes • News feeds
	End User	Power User	Internal Developer

Notework

John Rizzi

Notework Corporation, Who are we?

Incorporated 1985 to make and sell TSR programs for PCs

Makers of "EXACT"

TSR to add complex math typesetting to documents

Sold to NASA, Government, Research and Academia

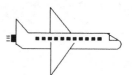

Notework

Notework Product Evolution

1987	Began two year product development, evaluation and test period
1989	Introduced Notework at Networld Dallas
1991	Jan – 40,000 users
	Aug – 100,000 users
Today	200,000+ users
	Sold in 42 countries
	8 languages

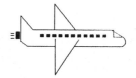

Notework

Notework and Groupware

- MHS Compliant
- Developer's Toolkit
  - Create forms
  - Mail enable your apps
- Optimize each task

Notework

Notework Fundamentals

- 5K TSR
  - Accessibility
  - Notification
  - Speed
  - Reliability
  - Automated Installation
- Twin DOS/Windows
  Interfaces

Notework

Notework Fundamentals

- Address Book
  - Reads bindery
  - Wide area
- FAX
- Notework Remote

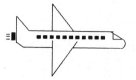

Requirements for Workflow Products

Ronni T. Marshak
Editor-In-Chief
The Office Computing Report: Guide to Workgroup Computing
The Patricia Seybold Group
148 State Street, Suite 700
Boston, Massachusetts 02109

Abstract

Both users and vendors are targeting workflow as the next hot area to automate. The panel on Workflow Products will present four different vendor approaches to the workflow market. This paper provides background information which I believe will be useful to the attendee by providing a context for workflow as well as a set of criteria against which the products presented can be measured.

1. Buying Into Workflow

Even though workflow (in the guise of procedural automation and image management) has been around for years, 1992 looks like the year when workflow, as a software product category, will hit its stride. All the major vendors have indicated that they plan to "address" the workflow market, either with their own products or with partnerships with ISVs. Lotus, for example, has announced a pilot project to investigate ways to enhance Lotus Notes with Action Technologies suite of workflow methodology and design components. AT&T, NCR, HP, among others, have all made workflow and workflow building tools a strategic part of their product directions. Workflow, at last, is hot!

However, the concept of workflow builders is not all that easy to grasp quickly. Oh, people have no trouble understanding the idea of sending information along to others in a prescribed order, but the idea of defining what data goes to which person under what conditions and with what security, etc., is not like the idea of word processing--electronic typing, only prettier. Thus, I doubt that workflow builders will be successfully sold on the retail shelves or through mail order--at least not until the product category is better defined and the market better educated.

Most likely, most workflow products will be bought though VARs or other vendors who will provide a mission-critical customized application for the customer. Ideally, this initial application will be co-developed by the vendor and the customer, thus helping the customer understand how the workflow builder works. And, again ideally, the customer development team will consist of one or more members of IS, plus at least one member of the business department--someone who may not be very technical, but who does understand the business problem being addressed. The technical developers, though, will probably be in command, as is true in the traditional application development model.

Once the strategic workflow application is up and running in the customer organization--and it begins to prove its value--the organization's IS department may well choose to use the workflow tool on its own for application development. I anticipate that these IS-developed applications will probably be complex, interdepartmental, mssion critical, and time consuming (though less time consuming than applications written in third, or even fourth generation languages). The original development partnership with the vendor may continue for quite a while as more strategic workflows are developed for enterprise-wide use.

I also anticipate, though, that the bulk of follow-on workflows built with the workflow development tool will come from the departmental business users. These users, initially, will automate less complex procedures, such as travel voucher requests or expense reporting. And I believe that ad hoc workflows will remain the province of the departmental business user.

Ultimately, workflow applications will be developed jointly by IS and business users; the end user will prototype the application, determining the flow and the forms to be used; the back-end operations--such as sophisticated database access and complex routing rules--will be scripted by in-house developers. As end-user workflow development tools become more robust, the role of IS in departmental workflow building will decrease.

Until that time, however, workflow development will be a partnership between business user and IS developer-- one that is mutually beneficial; the business user can have control over how the application will look and how the information will flow, and the developer needs only provide specific scripts for well-defined actions, rather than having to spend time learning the entire process from beginning to end. After all, the most time-consuming elements of application development is probably not the coding process, but rather the tedious back-and-forth interviewing process where the developer attempts to understand all the ramifications and convolutions of the existing business procedure.

2. Functionality Requirements

Like many technologies, workflow will cease to be remarkable as a separate entity as it becomes simply the way this type of application is developed. (I believe the same can be said about object orientation and distributed computing. No one will be talking about them in 10 years because that's just the way it's all done!)

WHAT'S NEEDED NOW. The road to that end, however, begins today, with the first generation of modern workflow tools (as opposed to procedural automation and image management tools). I have done a great deal of thinking over the past few months and have come up with a list of features that I believe define workflow and should be included in a competitive workflow product:

- **Rules-based routing.** Workflow must provide electronic routing of information, images, documents, files, or any other object. The routing can be sequential (when one person is done with the object, it automatically goes to the next person on a predefined list) or rules-based (dependent upon certain criteria--including, but not limited to, if-then-else logic).

- **Routing data.** Certain systems only route specific types of data, such as documents or forms. To really compete in the market, a system must be able to route a variety of data objects, including documents, spreadsheets, forms, mail messages, etc.

- **Parallel tracks.** Usually, routing is sequential, running on one of several paths (for example, a "yes" response to an action sends the object on one sequence of steps, while a "no" response triggers a different set of steps to be followed). A competitive workflow system however, must also support parallel route, where after a specific step on a path, the object can be sent to two or more different steps. Different, but not contradictory, actions are taken on the object (e.g., one route would go through a credit checking process while another would check inventory). At some point, both paths converge, and the object continues on its original, single path route.

- **Tracking.** Every workflow system must provide a management layer where the status of any object in a workflow can be monitored.

- **User notification of tasks and deadlines.** A system must notify users of their tasks. This can take the form of a To-Do list, be integrated into the standard E-mail inbox (in, for example, a separate folder), appear on a menu of action items, etc. A user should be able to view his or her action items in a variety of manners--by deadline date, by project, by type of action--and these views should be able to be defined by the user.

- **Alerts and notifications of problems.** Managers and users (with proper permissions) should be alerted when actions are overdue or have been pending (awaiting certain other actions) for a specified amount of time.

- **Role definition.** Actions should be able to be assigned to either a specific person (or persons) or to a role, such as claims adjuster.

- **Sets deadlines.** Each action should be able to be assigned a deadline, usually expressed as a duration of time (i.e., this step must be completed within three days). Ideally, you could also set a specific date (must be completed by April 15) or a recurring date (must be completed by the first Monday of every month). The system should also support certain rules based on missed deadlines (i.e., if a deadline is missed, send action back to previous step).

- **Security.** A permission structure must be in place to allow access rights and modification rights. Permissions should be assigned by workflow (i.e., a user with modification permission for one workflow may only be able to be a user in another workflow). Permission should also extend to management reports, again by workflow and, ideally, by report. For example, a user may be allowed to view a report which shows the deadline dates on all actions assigned to a workgroup but may not view a breakdown of which users have failed to meet deadline. Security must also be addressed in the steps of a workflow. The developer needs to specify who can see and/or modify certain fields in a screen form, for example. These permissions should be able to be set by individual user, role, or group.

- **Graphical front end to workflow definition.** A successful product must provide end users with an easy to use graphical front end for defining the workflow steps (what action is to be done), sequences (the order in which actions should be done), routing (who should do each action), and conditions (what rules should the process follow when routing the actions).

- **Forms definition and routing.** Even though a forms-based paradigm isn't the only method necessary for flowing data through a process, certain steps will require creating forms. These forms must be easy to create and modify. In addition, a trained end-user (as opposed to programmer-level person) should be able to include variable field information for straightforward applications.

- **Ability to modify workflow.** Once a workflow has been developed, it should be able to be copied and modified or modified directly by any end user with the proper permissions.

- **Support for non-electronic steps.** Not every step in a process is computer-based. For example, a step in a personnel procedure could be to call and check references. This step requires a telephone--not a computer--and the action itself is very subjective. The workflow should allow the person assigned the step to indicate that the step has been initiated and/or completed and what the results are.

- **Assignment to a group (rather than a role).** In addition to assigning actions to individuals and roles, actions should be able to be assigned to members of a specific group, even if these group members have different roles.

- **Ability to claim role or group action.** When a step is routed to a role or group, there needs to be some mechanism which notes that an individual has claimed the action, who that individual is (for tracking purposes), and that notifies the other members of the role or group that the action is being handled. For example, once an action is claimed, it could disappear from the To-Do list of all other users. Or else, if a user attempts to open an action that is already claimed, a message is displayed indicating who is working on that step.

- **Support for customer's applications of choice.** If a step requires creating a document, any word processor on the network should be able to be used, etc.

- **Graphical flow chart creation.** The graphical tool for designing the workflow front end should include an easy-to-use flow chart generator which assists the user in visualizing the application.

WHAT WILL BE NEEDED SOON. The following items will quickly become necessary to remain competitive, but, for now, you can consider them to be longer-term requirements (i.e., put it in version 2.0):

- **Flowing data from step to step.** A key benefit of workflow is the integration (or flow) of data from application to application in the process. For example, an insurance application includes the type and amount of insurance requested as well as the demographic information on the applicant. When the underwriter performs some "what if" scenarios in her spreadsheet, the appropriate information—age, salary, amount of insurance, etc.—would automatically be inserted into the correct cells in the spreadsheet. Similarly, when the letter of acceptance and invoice are sent, the address, amount, and cost as determined by the underwriter, would be automatically merged into the appropriate documents.

• **Remote user support.** Users should be able to remotely access the workflow applications, including launching a new instance of a flow.

• **Integration with agents and other workflows.** Workflows should be able to launch agents or other workflows. Similarly, an agent should be able to launch a workflow application.

• **Ability to modify workflow on the fly.** It would be useful if a user could modify the forms, rules, or add steps from within a workflow process, rather than having to go back to a development facility. This, of course, assumes the proper permissions.

• **Reusable components.** A key to end-user application development is the ability to reuse steps and rules from other workflows. This could either operate on a library model (preferable) or by going into a workflow definition and copying a step into a new application.

• **Graphical flow chart as front-end to application development.** When users create a flow chart, the workflow system should automatically generate steps and routing information, based on the chart. Conversely, as each step or route is defined in another manner, it should create a corresponding flow chart. Users need to be able to switch between these two methods of workflow definition freely as they define a workflow.

• **Integration with mail inbox.** Users typically do not want to have to check a variety of locations to read all their messages and action items. Allowing workflow actions to appear in the standard inbox, perhaps in a separate folder or identified with a workflow icon, would be a great benefit. Users should also be able to view just a workflow To-Do list if they prefer.

WHAT WILL BE NEEDED EVENTUALLY. Ultimately, the following capabilities should be included in a competitve workflow product:

• **Integration with other group applications.** Other workgroup applications, such as document management systems, project managers, and calendaring/scheduling tools, should be able to be integrated with the workflow development tools. The integration should be completely transparent to the user.

• **Meta-Management reports.** In addition to simple tracking reports (e.g., Anne Sheehan's credit application is currently on Martin's desk at the "check credit history" step and has been for three days), systems should provide more sophisticated higher-level reports, such as how many actions were handled by each user in a week (productivity), how many exceptions to the basic routing rules are being handled each day, and how many times is a specific type of request coming in. These reports are more than tracking the flow of information, but are actually providing data that might not be able to be captured without the workflow system.

• **Provide the proper tool with the proper data.** A sophisticated system should automatically call up the proper application tool to complete each task. For example, in a sales ordering scenario, if a regular customer places an order, the order form would usually go to the assistant credit manager for approval. However, if, say, the customer is already at the top of its credit limit, the form is sent to the credit manager. In addition to the order form, the system brings up the customer's credit history, its Dun & Bradstreet rating (the latest one), and a Lotus worksheet already loaded with the appropriate formulae for calculating the interest on the extension of credit.

• **Allowing users to see where tasks fit.** While this doesn't necessarily help complete a task, it does help the user understand the importance of his role and the consequences of a task poorly, or well, done. The user can begin to see the interdependencies inherent in every process. For example, by looking at the entire process, a user can see how missing a deadline effects the other members of his team. In addition, by looking at the process as a whole, users are more likely to discover innovative modifications that could significantly improve the procedure.

- **Integration with local name service.** When defining roles, groups, or routing, the local name service should be invoked. Similarly, you should be able to use defined E-mail groups as workflow groups.

- **Integration with personal to do list.** Many users already have implemented some sort of PIM or personal To-Do list application. Ideally, workflow action items can integrate with this list.

- **Assignment to role to enable load balancing and/or next available.** Currently, products must allow an action to be routed to a role, and then permit an individual with that role to claim the action. In the future, assignment to individuals within a role should be able to be determined based on a variety of rules: load balancing would assign an action to the next person due one (to ensure that all individual role members are being assigned an equal number of actions); or assignment to the next available role member (for the quickest response).

- **What-if process modeling for workflow modification and redesign.** It would be extremely valuable to be able to, for example, delete a step or change a rule and see how the process would run.

3. Enabling Applications--An Era of Tools

Two years ago, I came up with a redefinition for office computing based on a model of enablers. Enabling platforms underlying enabling technologies underlying enabling applications all used to provide customized business applications. We are coming to the realization, if we haven't already, that the underlying platform doesn't really matter. And the enabling technologies, such as distributed computing, object orientation, and graphical interfaces, are pretty well in place. We are now working on the enabling applications layer, and this is evidenced in the number of tools being released and enhanced with which customers can quickly build applications that uniquely reflect how each organization does business.

Providing tools requires a lot from the people making the tools. Unlike personal productivity applications, the vendor can't sit back once a sale is done and interact with the user via a help desk. Vendors have to form partnerships with their customers to help them build something useful with the tools and to ensure that the tools are, indeed, useful. Most vendors have always offered some form of consultancy to their customers; we see this area of vendor business growing exponentially.

When I talk to users, they invariably say that what they want is a seamless system which does everything they need to do. They are willing to work hard to design and build it, but, once built, they want a single piece of work, flawlessly flowing together. Currently, the enablers they have frustrate them--they can see bits and pieces coming together, but they have yet to find the magical seamless tool.

In the next few years, workflow development systems will encompass features of document management, scheduling, email, and many of the other technologies that are also hot today. I see workflow as becoming an umbrella under which all these workgroup technologies fit. Each can be used separately, but when developing a workflow application, all the capabilities of these types of systems must be available. So, though we have not yet reached a world where our systems can be put together seamlessly, workflow builders will, hopefully, will make sure the seams are strong and hard to see.

FileNet

Groupware '92

Workflow Products Panel

Jordan Libit

Vice President of Marketing

FileNet Corporation

FileNet

Paper Triggers
the Business Process

FileNet

The Manual Effort in Paper Flow

- Log in/log out documents

- Sorting and routing

- Suspense file management

- Staff load balancing

- Control of elapsed time

- Training of new staff

- Quality control of the business process

FileNet

Why Image Applications are Natural for Workflow

Paper-based business processes are inefficient:

- Forces serial work process rather than parallel

- Process problems
    - tracking transaction status
    - monitoring productivity
    - managing priorities

- Too much effort to make information flow

FileNet

What is Workflow?

- "Workflow"
  - a set of software functions that assist the processing of work packages, primarily composed of an image (or folder) and its associated transaction screens, that must be forwarded to a series of users for completion

source: BIS Strategic Decisions; August, 1991

FileNet

Workflow Software Elements

- Work package routing
  - activity processing logic
  - routing logic

- Work distribution

- Work prioritization

- Work package tracking

- Management reporting

FileNet

Managing the Workflow

- Moving work from desk to desk
  WorkFlo Queue Services

- Automating the process for the worker
  WorkFlo Scripts

- Keeping track of results
  WorkFlo Reports

FileNet

WorkFlo is a Tool to:

- Tailor each screen's appearance

- Define document-image flow from workstation
  to workstation

- Prioritize document-images

- Rendezvous multiple documents

- Set time limits on work in progress

- Provide management reports

..... a high-level language for defining events,
document-image flow, and information integration

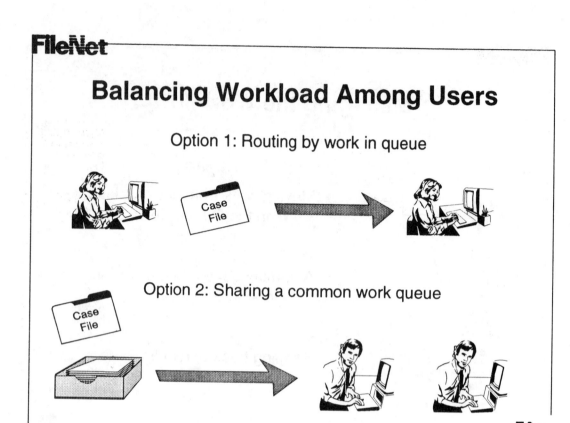

Balancing Workload Among Users

Option 1: Routing by work in queue

Option 2: Sharing a common work queue

Managing Work in Process

- Monitor queues to manage time limits
- Assign and adjust priorities
- Identify exceptions - notify supervisor

User	User	Supervisor

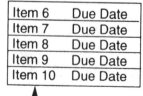

Item 1	Due Date
Item 2	Due Date
Item 3	Due Date
Item 4	Due Date
Item 5	Due Date

Item 6	Due Date
Item 7	Due Date
Item 8	Due Date
Item 9	Due Date
Item 10	Due Date

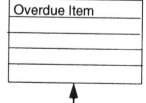

Overdue Item

Queue Monitor Script

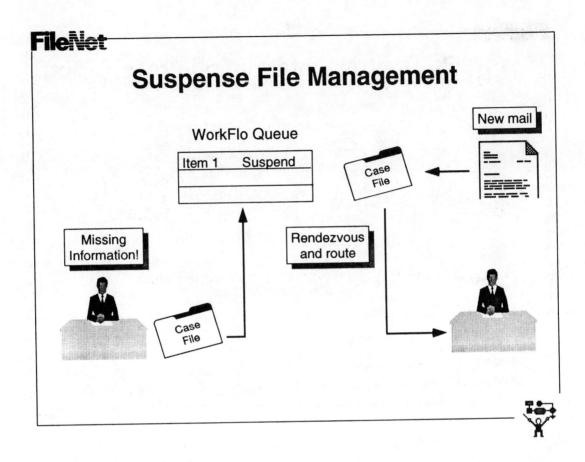

Suspense File Management

WorkFlo Queue

Item 1   Suspend

Case File

New mail

Missing Information!

Rendezvous and route

Case File

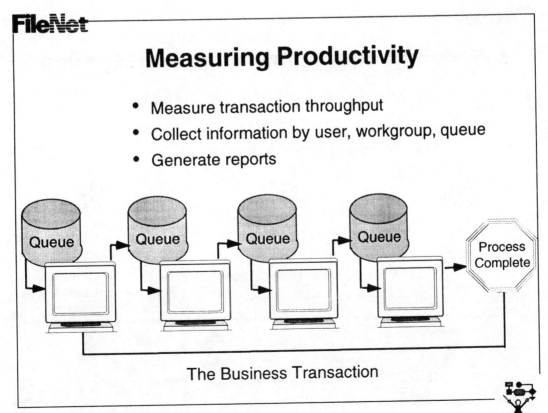

Measuring Productivity

- Measure transaction throughput
- Collect information by user, workgroup, queue
- Generate reports

Queue Queue Queue Queue Process Complete

The Business Transaction

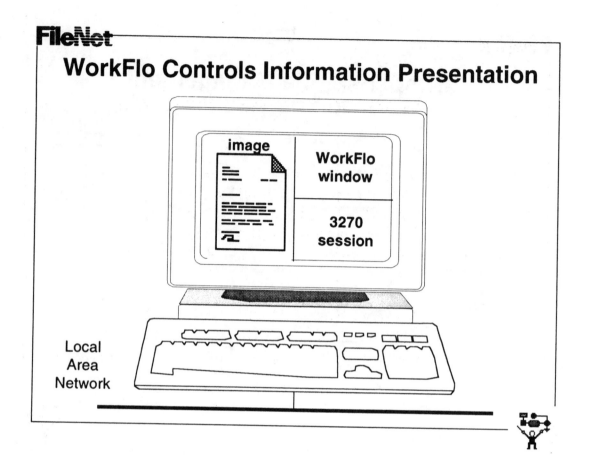

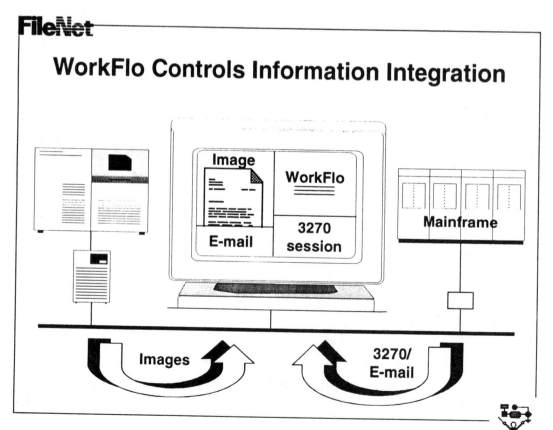

FileNet

WorkFlo Software Products

- WorkForce Desktop
  Image Display for Windows
  WorkFlo Script Runtime for Windows
  AutoForm Runtime for Windows
  FolderView

- WorkShop Development Environment
  WorkFlo System Development Kit for Windows
  AutoForm System Development Kit for Windows

FileNet

Workflow Software Benefits

- Cost justification from increased productivity

- Shorter elapsed time to handle transactions

- Ability to adapt process and control results

A systematized approach to transaction throughput

Reach Software Corporation

Anand Jagannathan

REACH Mission

To be the leading provider of workflow applications platform software for PC LANs

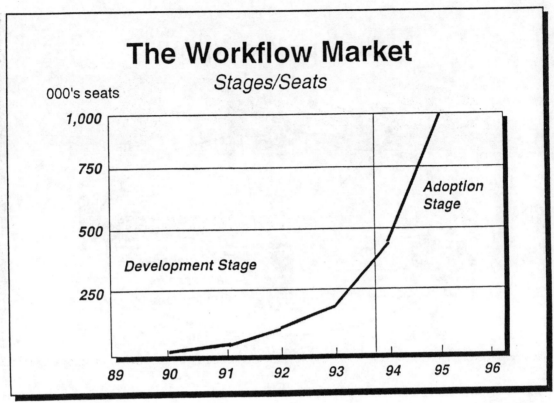

The Workflow Market
Stages/Seats

000's seats

Development Stage

Adoption Stage

Projections - Forrester Research '91

Workflow Today...

Software which manages the flow of work between users

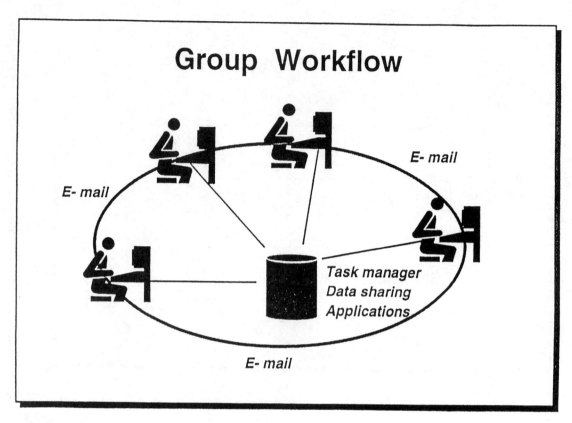

Group Workflow

E- mail

E- mail

Task manager
Data sharing
Applications

E- mail

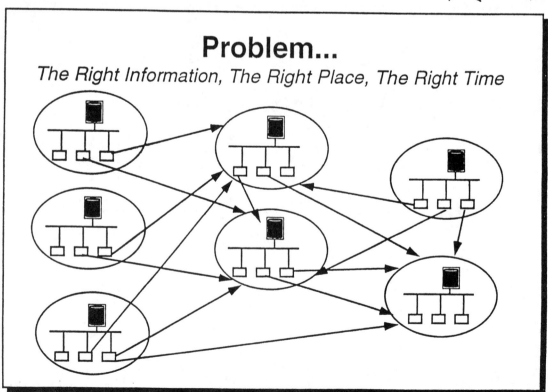

Problem...
The Right Information, The Right Place, The Right Time

The Solution: WorkMAN

The e-mail Enabled Workflow Management Application Platform

What Workflow Really Is...

*Software which **actively** helps manage the <u>flow</u> of information and the <u>processing</u> of business tasks within an organization.*

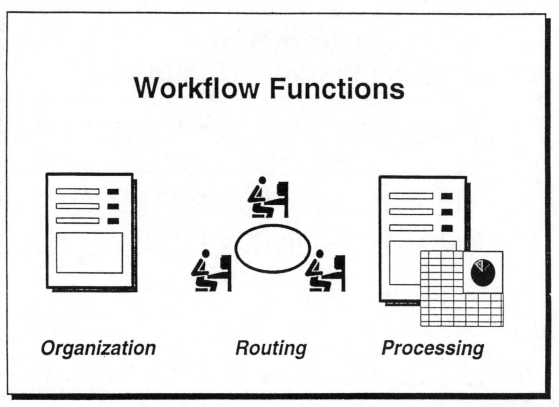

Workflow Functions

Organization   *Routing*   *Processing*

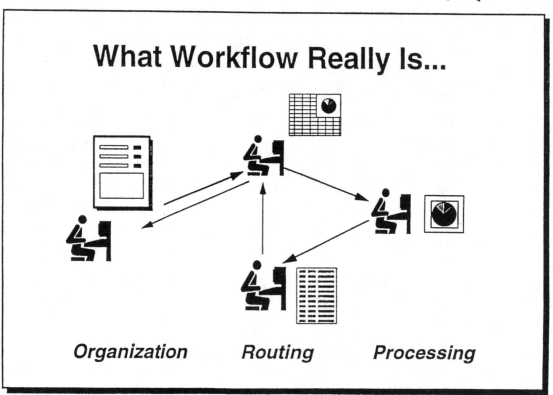

What Workflow Really Is...

Organization   *Routing*   *Processing*

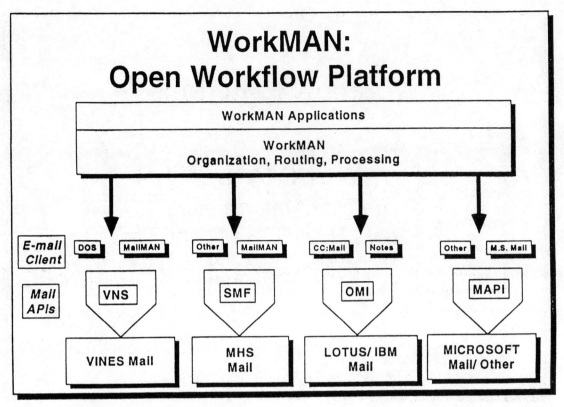

WorkMAN:
Open Workflow Platform

The Intelligent Data Highway

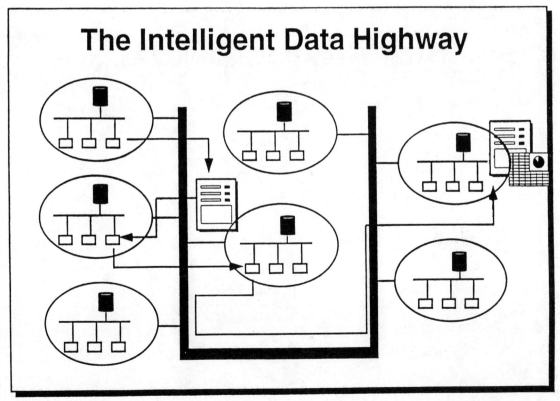

WorkMAN...

The Right Information,
The Right Place, The Right Time.

Work Process Automation

Beyond Traditional Workflow

An Evolution to Enhanced Business Productivity

Dean Cruse

Work Process Automation

◆ Definitions and Examples

◆ Categories and Areas of Focus

◆ Evolution

◆ Productivity Examples

◆ Creation and Development Approaches

◆ Benefits

◆ Future Directions

◆ Summary

Work Process Automation

Objective

Coordination of Tasks, Data, and People to Improve the Effectiveness and Efficiency of Organizations

PLEXUS

Work Process Automation

Business Process Example

PLEXUS

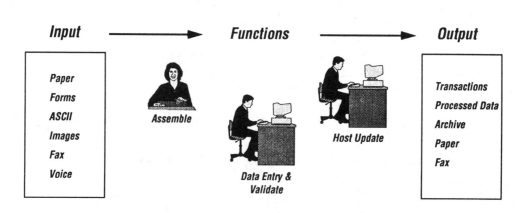

Maximizing Results through the Most Efficient Use of Resources and Skills

Work Process Automation

Types of Workflow

TRANSACTION-BASED

◆ Procedural Task Automation

◆ Manages Routing of Work between Activities or Users

◆ Monitors Who Has Work, Needs Work, Owes Work, Etc.

Examples:
   – Credit Card Enrollment
   – Health Care Claims Processing

INFORMATION-BASED

◆ Ad Hoc Automation

◆ Allows Groups of Users to Share Ideas and Data

◆ Generally Supports Group Work, But Does Not Manage Its Processes

Examples:
   – E-mail
   – Integrated Office Systems
   – Ad Hoc Queries

 Plexus Focusing Efforts on Transaction-Based Automation

Work Process Automation

The "Value" River

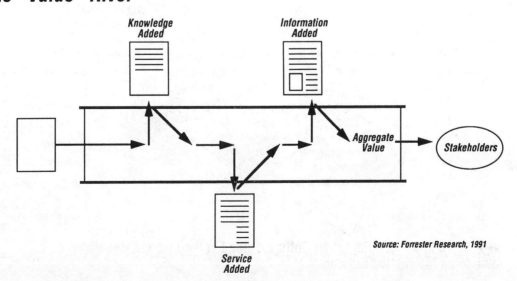

Source: Forrester Research, 1991

Work Process Automation

PLEXUS

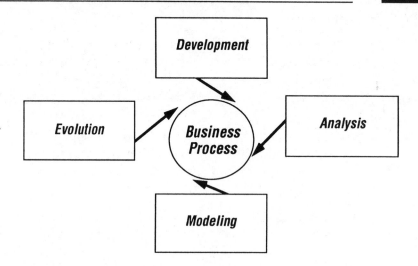

☑ Focusing on Re-Engineering Your Business

Evolution of Work Process Automation

PLEXUS

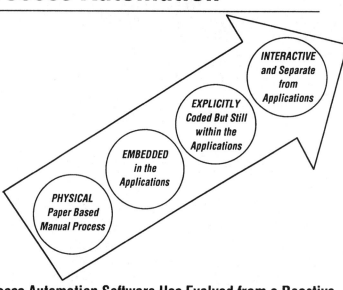

☑ Work Process Automation Software Has Evolved from a Reactive
to an Interactive Service

Work Process Evolution

PLEXUS

Physical — 1st Generation

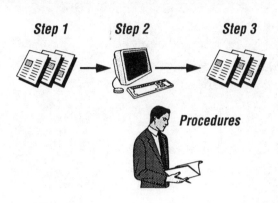

Step 1   Step 2   Step 3

Procedures

- ◆ Collage of History
- ◆ Things Happen Because They've Always Happened This Way
- ◆ Paper-Based, Manual Process
- ◆ Heavy Reliance on End-User Training for Following Procedures
- ◆ Automation Has Perpetuated Current/ Historical Efficiencies

 Manual Process Begins to Be Automated

Work Process Evolution

PLEXUS

Embedded — 2nd Generation

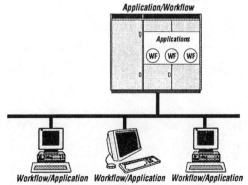

Mainframes & Minicomputers

Application/Workflow

Applications

(WF) (WF) (WF)

Workflow/Application   Workflow/Application   Workflow/Application

Workstations & Terminals

- ◆ Work Processes Are Automated, But Are Embedded as Part of Data Processing Applications
- ◆ Supports Physical, Paper-Based Workflow
- ◆ Process Changes Require Application Changes (Programmers)
- ◆ Perpetuates Corporate Inertia — No Time to Optimize, Just Trying to Keep Up
- ◆ Automates Transactions, Not Relationships

 The Physical Flow Is Automated

Work Process Evolution

Explicitly Coded — 3rd Generation

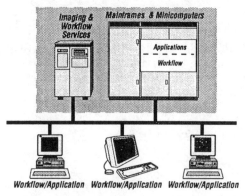

Workstations & Terminals

 Workflow Is Application Dependent

◆ Work Processes Are Explicitly Defined But Are Still Part of the Application (e.g., Document Imaging)

◆ Processes Remain Static (Snapshot in Time) and Application Dependent

◆ Changes Easier, But Programmers Still Required

◆ Allows Business to Begin to Understand the Dynamics of Their Workflows and Relationships — Inefficiencies Begin to Become Obvious

Work Process Evolution

Interactive — 4th Generation

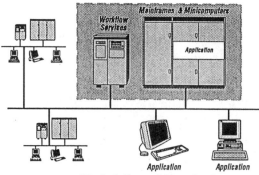

Workstations & Terminals

 Business Processes Are Redesigned and Optimized

◆ Work Processes and Applications Are Separated — Workflow Becomes a Network Service

◆ Business Processes Redesigned to Maximize Efficiency and Effectiveness

◆ Profound Productivity and Monetary Benefits Realized

◆ Impact Goes Beyond the Department — Enterprise-Wide Effects

◆ Work Processes Automate Relationships between People

◆ Work Processes Evolve Interactively — Applications Are Not Affected

Work Process Automation

Productivity Examples

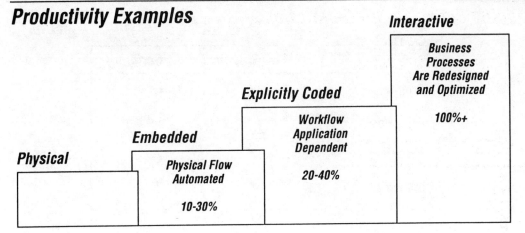

✓ Maximize Benefits from Business Process Redesign

Work Process Development

PLEXUS

The Evaluation Process

- ◆ Define Inputs, Tasks, Functions, Outputs
- ◆ Relate Manual Processes to Existing Applications
- ◆ Evaluate Workflows in Existing Applications
- ◆ Identify the Critical Path for Data Flow
- ◆ Identify Value-Added Components of Data Flow
- ◆ Identify Exception Processing Paths
- ◆ Design Workflow

✓ Effective Evaluation Is Needed Prior to Workflow Development

Workflow Development

	Graphical	Scripting
Creation	✔	✔
Evolution	✔	✔
Modeling	✔	?
Analysis	✔	?

☑ **Optimization of Business Processes Will Require Modeling and Analysis Tools**

Work Process Automation

Approaches

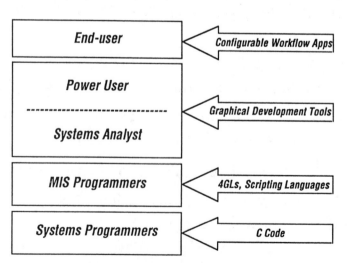

☑ **Work Process Automation Tools Should Support Non-Programmers as Well as Programming Tools for Extensibility of Applications**

Work Process Automation
Modeling & Analysis

- ◆ Evaluate Exception Processing Paths

- ◆ Optimize Workflows through Simulation and Iteration
  - – Test Workflows Prior to Implementation
  - – Manage Economics of Bottlenecks

- ◆ Provide Feedback for Continued Workflow Evolution
  - – Real-Time Status Monitoring
  - – Dynamic Load-Leveling, Work Balancing

- ◆ Set Realistic Goals for Business Productivity

 Optimization Requires Ability to Simulate Business Processes

Work Process Automation

Evaluation, Development, Modeling Summary

- ◆ Different Approaches Are Appropriate for Different Environments

- ◆ Most Alternatives Solve the Basic Problem — Workflow Creation and Development

- ◆ Investigate the Limitations Associated with Evolving Beyond the Basic Problem:
  - – Evolution to Interactive Workflow
  - – Modeling and Analysis

Next Generation Must Be Interactive and Include Modeling and Analysis Tools

Work Process Automation

PLEXUS

Benefits

- ◆ Explicit Examination of Productivity and Quality
- ◆ Consistent Policies and Procedures
- ◆ Improved Control
- ◆ Less Training; More Specialization
- ◆ Focus on Costly Exceptions
- ◆ Optimize Intergroup Relationships

 **Maximizing Productivity of Groups Is the Key to Organizational Efficiency**

Work Process Automation

PLEXUS

What's Next

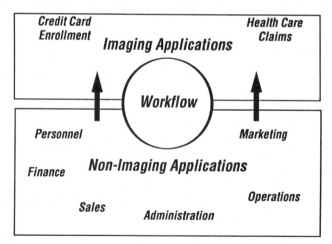

 Work Process Automation Software Is Evolving to Also Address Non-Imaging Applications

Work Process Automation
PLEXUS

Future Direction

- More Graphical Development Tools
- Statistical Simulation Tools
- Organizational Modeling (CASE Tools Integration)
- Self-Evolving Intelligent Workflows
- Expert System Integration
- Heterogeneous Application Integration

☑ **Committed to Be the Leader in Providing Evolution-Based Work Process Automation Software for the Enterprise**

Work Process Automation
PLEXUS

Summary

- Evolutionary Process
- Must Evolve Past Simple, Procedural Routing and Queuing
- Analysis Should Result in Redesigning Business Processes for Improved Effectiveness and Efficiency
- Increasingly Requires Less Sophisticated Users
- Address Requirements for Evolution to Interactive Workflow

☑ **Evolution of Business Processes Will Be Aided by Interactive Workflow Tools**

Lotus Notes Implementation Factors

Kenneth E. Norland
Distributed Systems Solutions International, Inc.
5655 Lindero Canyon Road, Building 100
Westlake Village, CA 91362

Abstract

For a successful implementation of Lotus Notes®, a number of critical factors have been abstracted from experiences with several customers. The factors relate to technology base, organizational culture, participation and expectations vs. reality.

1 Introduction

From a number of application and system implementations of Lotus Notes in organizations of varying sizes and structures, a number of experiences bearing on the success or failure have occurred. This discussion focuses on some of the key factors that affect both success and failure. The most important factor observed is a focus on concrete business related benefits in a reasonable time. Without that focus and expectation, the Notes learning efforts get shifted to other areas, and then languishes.

2 Technology Base

In evaluating a situation for the potential success of Notes, the state of the current technology base is often overrated. It helps if the organization is currently using a LAN and some email package. This area yields to a sincere desire to accomplish business goals, the equipment will be obtained. Some examples will be provided in the discussion ranging from full tooling of companies to support Notes to just adding it into an "optimal" technology complement. Differences in timing and logistical activities will be highlighted.

3 Organizational Culture

Two major areas have affected projects with Notes in recent experiences. The first is the attitude towards and acceptance of technological assistance. The second is the already existing cooperative environment.

The experiences in organizations that have an inclination to use technology just because it is there are not significantly better than those with a more cautious approach. If anything, the technology oriented organizations sometimes have a more difficult time to see the real benefits of Notes. These benefits are often obscured by long comparisons with other "similar" technologies and attempts to put Notes into some pre-existing category. In some situations, these processes have held back the timing of the end users' viewing and understanding of the potential for Notes in their environment. The initial installation of Notes may occur more quickly, but the spread to other areas may be slower as the technical dissection of the product proceeds.

For the less technologically current organizations, Notes can provide the impetus to update their environment to a GUI and possibly other features. The upside of this is the enthusiasm and commitment it generates. The downside is the difficult cost justification often required. This justification and subsequent updating of the software and hardware for an organization can take quite some time, which delays the Notes implementation. Although this delays the process, it does not seem to affect the eventual success rate.

The other area of cultural consideration is how the organization works together before Notes arrives on the scene. If it is already functioning in a collaborative way, but is looking for ways to improve the information flow and timeliness, Notes will fit smoothly into the operation. If Notes is looked upon as the "solution" to bring cooperation into an organization, it will either fail or take much longer than is usually expected. For these organizations, Notes can help a cultural change, but it will not cause it to occur unaided. Strong direction and attention to the desired results are essential.

4 Participation

The group participating in the first Notes efforts in an organization is crucial to its eventual success. The people do not have to be PC literate as much as they need a sincere desire to use the best tools for the task. The technology is easier to learn than the attitude. They must also be actual users, not just technology voyeurs playing with the latest toy.

The composition of the group takes some attention. The group should be one that is held in esteem, and tends to want to do reasonable things rather than being a fringe group. The focus should be on a major business area, where the impact of the group (using Notes) will be visible.

The other key to success is an interested and committed sponsor within the organization. A senior, respected person who can provide an umbrella for the effort and who is understanding of the amount of time and effort really needed speeds the effort immensely. This person will publicize the successes and advise on the shortcomings of the integration of Notes into the organization. Notes can succeed, at low levels, without such a person, but s/he is essential for long term success and propagation of Notes applications.

5 Expectations vs Reality

The most common misperception is that Notes will be installed on Monday and be integrated into the pilot organization by Friday of the same week. Managing the expectations of both the management and the participants is one of the most difficult tasks the Notes sponsor has. Notes alone will solve few problems, although it often gets viewed as the latest "silver bullet."

The cycle in organizations is fairly typical of new technologies. First is the understanding phase, where the organization is struggling with what it can do. This is often followed by a phase where Notes can do "anything" and is the *de facto* solution for all problems the organization, whether it is appropriate or not. The normal let down (or adjusting to reality) is then a trough the organization goes through. Finally, the organization learns how Notes works in their environment, what its limitations are and how it can be most effective.

The length of time for this cycle is typically 6 months or more. I dislike calling an initial assimilation of Notes either a success or failure in less time. The steps have to be gone through before a normal operating mode including Notes can be assessed. The orientation of Notes to group activities also prolongs the process. Notes can not be reasonably evaluated by a single person who then passes on it (or not) as an organizational standard. It must be experienced in a group situation of several people (usually at least a dozen) and those reactions absorbed and corrective actions taken. All this takes time, so those looking for quick fix inevitably become disappointed. Once again, the human dynamics prevail, not the technological ones. Humans still take longer to adapt than machines for this type of situation.

6 Optimal Environment

As a summary, the ideal environment (that I have never run into in real life) for Notes success would be an organization that:

- Is fully state of the art with GUI workstations, working on a supported LAN
- Works cooperatively today, but wants to work more effectively
- Has no political participants
- Is focused tightly on business solutions and improvements
- Effectively communicates today with phones, faxes, email, etc.
- Is managed in a participative way
- Relishes the challenge of turning new technologies to their advantage.

Having more, rather than less, of these characteristics will not guarantee success, but will improve the odds a bit.

A Case Study of Integrating Advanced Communication Technologies into a High Technology Organization

A Directed Research
Project Submitted by:

Theresa G. Havton
I.S. Project Leader
Graduate Student, MHROD
Professional Studies
University of San Francisco

Dr. Charles E. Grantham
Graduate Advisor
Professional Studies
University of San Francisco

Background Of The Issue

Since the early 1980's, business organizations have invested large sums of money in personal computers in order to keep up with the many demands of a fast-paced market. Businesses have made these investments with the anticipation of a return of investment similar in proportion to what was realized in the factory when manufacturing automation was deployed. The deployment of personal computers was successful in the amplification of the *labor* produced by the white-collar worker.

The introduction of Local Area Networks (LANs) in the 1980's provided the necessary physical links among personal computers that allow the sharing of common resources, like printers & programs, within a workgroup. Additionally, they provide for a high-speed, electronic means of communication: electronic-mail (e-mail) and file transfer (Johansen 1988).

In general, LAN applications focus on the concept of individual productivity. This includes e-mail. E-mail is a LAN electronic messaging system designed to send messages from: one individual to another, one individual to other individuals or groups of individuals. Unfortunately, the "one worker-/one product" model does not apply to most of what goes on current marketplace. (Brown and Newman, 1985)
Today's market place demands that many business organizations have networked computers that do more than process electronic mail and speed up information processing. It calls for an electronic medium that can harness the activities, dynamics and information gathered within the organizational workgroup. This medium must also be able to process and transmit information at extremely high speeds, regardless of the users' physical location(s).

Workgroup computing, addresses todays market place demands for the business organization. It is a new discipline that focuses on "computer-supported cooperative work" through local area networks using a class of programs known as groupware.

Computer-supported cooperative work, CSCW, is a discipline that highlights concepts such as "office automation", the "paperless office", and the "office of the future" by emphasizing office work as inherently cooperative, involving both reciprocal and serial interdependencies among often diverse individuals and groups (Grantham, 19XX). Groupware can therefore be defined as software products that address group communication needs with the benefits of networked personal computers.

Statement of the issue

Once an organization commits itself to workgroup computing, it faces two major challenges. Its first challenge is to take into consideration all of its workgroup computing needs - for the present, as well as, the future. This will allow the organization to best select and/or plan a method to integrate groupware into its existing systems.

The second challenge is to understand and to address the underlying issues that influence the acceptance and usage of advanced communication technology. This is based on the assumption that technology is only an asset when it is used *and* used properly. After all, what is the sense in purchasing advanced technology to keep up with the market unless it is used? Questions to keep in mind and to address include: Was the current technology readily accepted when made available? To what degree was it was accepted and utilized? How was it implemented? Was it perceived as an asset or a liability? Was training available or necessary? How much training was required? What was technology's life span? Did it meet the users' perceived needs and expectations?

Normative Definitions Of Relevant Variables

Logitech Incorporated, is a major electronics firm headquartered in Fremont, California, has completed the first challenge. Its Information Systems and Communications Department setup a taskforce that was committed to research and provide its computer users the ability to electronically work in groups. Among the different groupware packages available, one was selected for consideration. The consideration criterion had many requirements, such as, its ability to meet Logitech's present and near future needs, its development & upgrade plans, and its previous reviews and recommendations from other sources. The selected groupware medium is Notes™ from the Lotus Development Corporation. The implementation process at Logitech was therefore dubbed "The Notes Project".

Notes™ was selected as because of its ability to allow for personal computer users who are connected to LANs to create and access shared information in an environment that is conducive to two categories of users: the individual(s) and the workgroup(s). On the individual category, the users can write and file sales contact reports, draft evaluations and documentations, record customer service contacts, complete requests such as: service, vacation/sick leave and purchasing, as well as, electronically send messages to individuals or to groups.

On the workgroup level, activities include the integration of electronic communication and document-management functions. This means that the document-management functions automatically fit the documents into a structure giving them identifiable types so they can be retrieved and shared, for instance: electronic mail, discussion topics or responses. Additionally, specialized forms used within applications may be identified by name, such as: Client Information, Product Evaluation, Monthly Activity Report. Another important feature is that the workgroup will also be able to share information back to the individual.

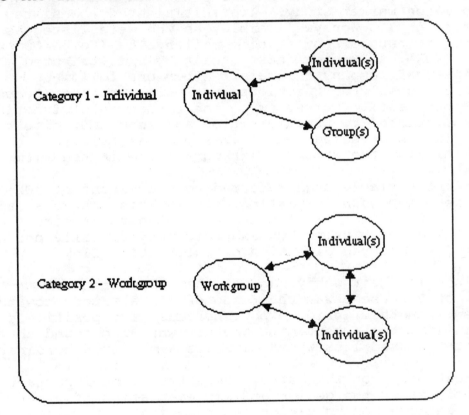

Presently, Logitech Inc. is in the early stages of Notes groupware deployment to all of its worldwide offices and is ready to undergo the second challenge - Understanding the issues that will ultimately affect the return on investment. To understand the issues surrounding the Notes project, a systematic investigation of the variables that mediate the relationship between technology and behavior is required (Eason 1983, Waterworth, 1984).

This paper will examine the individual and combined effects of three categories of variables as related to the usage of groupware as integrated with its present communication systems: electronic- and voice-mail. The variables include the individual's attitudes toward the technology, their prior experience with voice message systems and the direction in which information flows between communicating parties (e.g.: laterally between peers, upward to superiors or downward toward subordinates). These variables, as suggested by previous studies (Clendening et al. 1981, Kielser et al. 1984, Trauth et al. 1984), independently describe the usage of advanced communication technologies.

A study by Grantham and Vaske (1985) examined the combined effect of these factors on behavior. The data collected was part of a large market study. Its initial study consisted of a population of 306 Honeywell employees who were listed as subscribers to the company's voice mail system (Voice Output Exchange - VOX). A 12-page questionnaire was distributed through internal company channels. After one follow-up reminder, 279 completed questionnaires were returned (response rate = 78 per cent). The review of the respondents' functional activities, span of control, position and length of time with the organization revealed that the sample was fairly representative of the white-collar work force in the firm.

The dependent *variable* used referred to the extent of VOX usage. *The independent variables* used in this analysis fall into three categories: [1]-Attitude, [2]-Length of time respondents had been using VOX and frequency of daily phone usage and [3]-Measured direction of information flow

The findings in their study suggest that the strongest predictor of VOX usage was the respondent's attitude toward the system. Length of prior experience was also positively associated with the extent of usage. It was also found that the system was used less when communicating with subordinates.

The implications from this study suggest several important considerations for the design and implementation of computer-mediated communication technologies. First, the physical access to technology needs to be combined with other means of to promote usage. Second, the strongest predictor of VOX usage was the respondent's attitude toward the system. This implies that the individuals who have been predisposed to hold positive beliefs about technology will be more willing to experiment with new communication channels. The third point to consider is the human-computer interaction. It is because beliefs about technology are linked together to form an overall attitude.

The present project is an extension of the above by Grantham and Vaske (1985). However, a more advanced computer mediated communication situation will now be analyzed.

The three variables which will be examined in this study group themselves into two specific focii: attitude structure and situation context factors.

Attitude structure:

> Attitude structure refers to the combination of different beliefs that leads to a particular conclusion. The specificity and strength of these beliefs influence the attitudes of the individuals toward computer-mediated communications and their behavior patterns relative to the technology.

Situation context factors.

> Situation context factors refer to: (1) the amount of time the person spends communicating via electronic systems, and (2) the length of time the person has used the systems.

Understanding the focii, in relation to the acceptance and use of a new technology, will be an asset towards the planning and implementation of future technology. Previous studies have shown that attitudes learned from direct experience with an object correlate better with behavior than do attitudes learned without direct involvement (Regan and Fazio 1977, Fazio and Zanna 1978). Additionally, Clendening et al. (1981) and Gould, and Boies (1984) speculate that the direction in with communication flows (e.g. superior to subordinate) may also influence the modality of the communication.

Specifications Of The Research

The purpose of this study is to examine the individual and combined influences of these indicators on the use of groupware. The following relationships were hypothesized: (1) people with a more positive attitude toward advanced communication technologies will use the available systems more frequently; (2) length of prior experience on the system, the amount of daily usage and training will be positively correlated with the current usage; and (3) the status of the two communicating parties and the direction in which the information flows between them will be related to usage patterns.

This study's groundwork is based upon the methodology and the 12-page questionnaire developed for a previous research project (Grantham and Vaske, 1985) and is modified to reflect the specifics for Logitech, for example: technology availability.

The questionnaire will be distributed twice to all Notes™ subscribers, at Logitech, regardless of site. The first distribution of the questionnaire will be to the available subscribers during the first wave of Notes installations. The second will be of those who have Notes™ subscriptions during the second wave of installation.

The measures used in this study are adapted from those defined by Grantham and Vaske.

Dependent variable

The dependent variable in this investigation refers to the extent of current communication technologies. Questions regarding the use of electronic- and voice mail were embedded in a larger matrix of items relating to a wide range of communications technologies. Respondents were asked to indicate how frequently they used groupware (and the other technologies) to plan, coordinate, assign responsibilities and report on the status of projects. Each of the four behavioral variables will be coded on a six-point Likert scale ranging from "no access" (0) to "always user" (5). Specific statements were adapted from previous work of Grantham (1982) which has shown that scaling self-reported behaviors avoids the problems of single-item indicators.

Independent variables

The independent variables used in this analysis fall into three categories. The first category refers to an attitude scale constructed from six Likert statements coded on a four-point scale (i.e., strongly disagree (1) to strongly agree (4). Each statement evaluated the extent to which respondents believed Notes improved their communication capabilities. Similar to the behavior scale, an item analysis was conducted on the attitude scale to determine the best combination of variables. A second set of independent variables examined the length of time respondents had been using Notes and their frequency of daily Notes usage. These variables were coded from open-ended responses and on a nine-point scale (i.e., "zero" to "almost all day"), respectively. The final group of independent variables measured the direction of the information flow (i.e., upward, downward or laterally in the organization hierarchy). Individuals were asked to estimate the percentage of their business communication that occurs with superiors, peers and subordinates. Answers were coded from open ended responses.

Importance of the study

The importance of this study is to examine the findings that could ultimately assist in the design and implementation of advanced communication technologies in the business organization , predict the usage of newly implemented technology and provide information about the issues that may enhance or inhibit acceptance of non-traditional channels of interaction (i.e., electronic- or voice-mail). This study will also see if the technology does indeed impact productivity of social relationships in the work place.

Limitations of the study

This research is limited to the number of questionnaires returned from the Notes user population at Logitech Inc. This is because the user population will not approach 100% until December 1992.

Another limitation would be the company's electronic work culture and environment. The fact that Logitech introduces new technologies on a frequent basis (1-2 major changes per month) and because it has a distinct cultural undertone that encourages change and diversity, the attitudes towards technology may not be applicable to all other environments.

Results

To date, a total of 30 questionnaires were distributed within Logitech internal channels (first wave). 21 questionnaires were returned. Only one follow-up reminder was issued. After the collection of questionnaires, an examination of the respondents functional activities, span of control, position and length of time with the organization revealed that sample was representative of the white-collar employees of the company.

Table 1 demonstrates that in the present sample the attitude among all users is generally very high. However, the usage of Notes™ is very variable - with a span of some individuals with a more limited usage of this software to those with a vary extensive usage of Notes.

Due to the current early stage of the Notes™ Project, all current users are considered as "new users". It is at present date too early to access whether the length of prior experience with Notes™ would effect usage. This important issue needs to be re-addressed at a later time when the company will consist of a mixture of new, intermediate and more senior experienced Notes™ users.

Tables 2-4 demonstrate that the most preferred form of communication, to supervisor to peers & subordinate is personal , on either 1-1 or 1-many, basis. With regards to computer generated forms of communication, the most frequently used form is elec. mail in communicating with the 3 types of categories of employees This is followed in popularity by the recently implemented Lotus Notes" , which already in usage has surpassed both telephone and telephone voice mail. This preference of forms of electronic communications appears independent from whether the independent party communicates to peer, subordinate or superior.

Discussion

The overall high attitude towards Lotus Notes" after a short period of initial implementation together with a very variable usage may be explained by different factors. Further analysis is required whether the differential usage of Notes" maybe related to level of training or work description (manager vs. employee, salesperson vs. engineer, etc.). However, due to current limited sample, a later follow-up investigation when the project is fully expanded may explain these discrepancies.

Although e-mail is more frequently preferred over Lotus Notes" as a electronic means of communication, the Notes Project has only been in effect just over 4 months, whereas the e-mail system has been in place between 5 and 6 years. It is of interest, however, that Notes has already in its short time of usage passed in popularity other well established forms of communication, such as the telephone and voice-mail.

It will be of interest to follow up on the usage of Lotus Notes after, for instance, 1-2 years when a larger group of people would be connected to the system and had more experience to use it. Will Notes, for instance, surpass and replace electronic mail - both in usage and popularity?

References

Brown, J.S., and Newman, S., 1985, Issues In Cognitive and Ergonomics: From Our House To Baughaus, Human-Interaction, 1: 351 - 391.

Clendening, J.L., Munson, V.M, and Sutherland, D.B., Jr., 1981, Office communication: A study of networks and impediments. Research report. Advanced Systems Laboratories. Wang Laboratories Inc. Lowell, Massachusetts.

Eason, K., 1983, Methodological issues in the study of Human Factors in teleinformatic systems., Behavior & Information Technology, 2: 357-364.

Fazio, R. H., and Zanna. M.P., 1978, Attitudinal qualities relating to the strength of the attitude-behavior relationship. Journal of Experimental Social Psychology, 14: 398-408.

Gould, J.D., and Boies, S.J., 1984, Speech filing - An office system for principals. IBM Systems Journal, 23: 65-80.

Grantham, C.E., 1982, Social Networks and Marital Interaction (Palo Alto, CA: 21st Century).

Grantham, C.E., 199X, Manuscript

Grantham, C.E., and Vaske, J.J., 1985, Predicting this usage of an advanced communication technology. Behavior And Information Technology, 4: 327-335.

Johanson, R., 1988, Groupware, New York: Free Press.

Regan, D.T., and Fazio, R.H., 1977, Self-focused attention and the experience of emotion: Attraction, repulsion, elation and depression. Journal of Personality and Social Psychology, 35: 625-636.

Waterworth, J.A., 1984, Interaction with machines by voice: A telecommunications perspective. Behavior & Information Technology, 3: 163-177.

TABLE 1

Subj	Usage Scale				Attitude Scale						Weeks Notes	% Communication with:			# Subord
	Init Tasks	Coord Tasks	Report Tasks	Assign Tasks	Redcs time to get inf to other	from others	Privacy	Promotes cohesive	Decr. ass to comn	Convey Context		Subord	Peers	Superiors	
AVG	2.42	2.29	2.53	1.93	3.20	3.05	2.59	3.53	2.83	3.37	5.38	17%	58%	20%	0.9474
SD	1.63	1.60	1.61	1.16	0.81	0.86	0.84	0.50	0.83	0.67	4.55	24%	24%	12%	1.7614
N	19	17	17	14	20	20	17	19	18	19	21	17	18	17	19
	Scale 1-5				Scale 1-4										

TABLE 2
Form of communication used -

To Supervisors

	1-1	1-Many	Written	Tele-phone	Voice Mail	Electronic Mail	Lotus Notes
AVG	4.14	2.64	2.53	2.07	1.93	3.30	2.13
SD	0.91	1.23	1.41	0.85	0.70	0.85	0.99
N	14	11	15	15	14	15	16

TABLE 3

To Peers

	1-1	1-Many	Written	Tele-phone	Voice Mail	Electronic Mail	Lotus Notes
AVG	4.12	3.50	2.00	2.53	1.93	3.83	2.83
SD	0.76	0.94	0.79	1.19	0.80	0.76	1.12
N	17	16	16	17	14	18	18

TABLE 4

To Subordinates

	1-1	1-Many	Written	Tele-phone	Voice Mail	Electronic Mail	Lotus Notes
AVG	2.08	1.73	1.50	1.50	1.09	1.77	1.25
SD	1.49	1.42	1.19	0.96	0.51	1.12	0.83
N	13	11	12	12	11	12	12

Scale: 1 to 5
1 = Never
2 = Seldom
3 = Sometimes
4 = Frequently
5 = Most of the time

Notes on Information Technology

Michael A. Goulde
The Patricia Seybold Group
148 State Street
Boston, MA 02109

Abstract

Although electronic deliver of information services is nothing new, using Lotus Notes to deliver the Industry Reports produced by the Patricia Seybold Group has enabled recipients of the reports to interact dynamically both with the authors of the reports, and with one another. Notes' unique architecture has also made interactive electronic distribution an integral part of the publishing process.

1. Introduction

Patricia Seybold's Notes on Information Technology is a Lotus Notes database which includes all of the information published in the printed versions of this Boston-based research and consulting firm's four research newsletters--the *Office Computing Report, Unix in the Office, Network Monitor,* and *Paradigm Shift.* The database also includes Special Bulletins and analyses written specifically for the Notes-based readership by the Group's analysts.

Notes on Information Technology is available either through individual licenses, server-based licenses, or enterprise licenses for multiple Notes servers.

2. Description of the Service

As a part of its comprehensive services, the Patricia Seybold Group publishes four research newsletters--the *Office Computing Report, Unix in the Office, Network Monitor,* and *Paradigm Shift.* The first three of these newsletters are published monthly, and the latter is published six times a year. Each of these newsletters contains feature-length articles, news, analysis, editorials, and product assessments.

Notes on Information Technology is a Lotus Notes-based services that provides the full text of these newsletters to subscribers. Once replicated at their local site, subscribers may search, browse, read, and print the newsletters or sections of the newsletters as needed based on their information requirements.

Customers may respond to points in the newsletter and their responses are available for all other N.o.I.T. subscribers as well as the Seybold analysts to view and respond to in turn.

We selected Notes as the delivery vehicle because 1) it enables the direct electronic delivery to and shared use by the customers, 2) it allows a high level of interactivity with the customers, and 3) because it allows the customers to use the information within their current (Notes) environment, rather than having to leave it to, for example, dial out to an on-line information service.

3. The N.o.I.T. Publishing Process

All Seybold research reports are prepared in a networked Microsoft Word for Windows environment, making transfer of the full text of reports into the Notes database a trivial matter. However, Notes does not support the full range of formatting options used in the printed version of the reports, so some adjustments have had to be made in the way reports appear in the database. In addition, Notes has limited support for different vector graphic formats. Customers do not want bitmap versions of illustrations because of the disk storage they require, so illustrations are currently not provided. We plan to address this in the short term by using Lotus Freelance as much as possible for illustrations, although we would like Notes to directly support more graphics formats.

After the text as been inserted into the database, each article is indexed according to Publication, Article Type, Author, Technologies, Companies, and date of publication. Subscribers can then select the way the want to view the database sorted according to those criteria. Word searches can be performed within selected documents or across the database as a whole, but with the current Notes technology searches are extremely limited and slow. Lotus' planned addition of the Verity engine to Notes Version 3 should greatly enhance this capability.

Once a report is opened, the subscriber can print or copy selected portions. While this opens us to some risk of plagiarism, the same risk exists with our printed reports. The basic assumption we make is that our subscribers are all professionals and will use these capabilities appropriately.

The delivery mechanism is the Notes replication process. It allows the database to be easily synchronized between the Seybold Notes servers and the subscribers' Notes servers, giving the members of the service next-day access to the analysis and discussions. Because the information is being delivered electronically, subscribers to the service receive the analysis up to three weeks faster than the printed newsletters.

4. Notes Provides Access

Using the Notes "response mechanism", subscribers to the service can respond to the articles, giving their own views and experiences or asking for more information. Subscribers may also raise their own topics for discussion among the Seybold analysts or other subscribers. These discussions enable subscribers to gain a greater understanding of the information that is presented and to use the analysis to meet their specific needs.

We anticipate that as subscribers become more comfortable with Notes, they will become more "vocal" and express more opinions, give us more feedback, and make requests for future research to include in our publications. In this way, N.o.I.T. will become an important bi-directional means of communication between the Patricia Seybold Group and its customers.

GroupWare for Document Management Panel

George Rossmann, XSoft

Chairman

XSoft

Agenda

- Introduce Panel Members

- Introduction to the Document Management Marketplace

- Presentations

- Questions and Answers

XSoft

GroupWare 92   **XEROX**

Panel Members

- George Rossmann, XSoft

- Chris Bowman, Adobe

- Stephen Conkling, Kodak

- Darelene Mann, Verity

- Alvin Tedjamulia, SoftSolutions

XSoft

GroupWare 92   **XEROX**

Market Overview

- $2 Billion Market by 93

- The Decade of the 80s' Focused on Personal Productivity
    - White Colar Productivity Declined

- The Decade of the 90s' Will Focus on Group Productivity

- Document Management Definition Still Unclear

- But, Everyone Understands Documents

XSoft

Document Management Basics

- Document Management <u>Manages </u>the Entire Document Life Cycle

  - Creation and capture, revision, translations, share/route,search, retieve, store and archive both as individual documents as well as network objects

  - Document Management Must be supported with WorkFlow Automation independent of the file structure

Document Management Basics

- Document Management Services Should be Independent of the Underlying:

  - Platform
  - Network
  - Application Format
  - Operating System
  - GUI
  - Data Base
  - Printing and/or Scanning (Image)

Document Management Components

- Document Profiling
- Document Location/Tracking and Version Control
- Group Access Control
- Compound and Image-Based Documents
- Full Text Searching and Retrieval
- Check in/Check out Services for Workgroups
- Text Translation
- Network Configuration and Archiving Management
- File Management
- Document Data Base Management
- WorkFlow Automation Tools
- Data Base and Retieval including Image Integration

XSoft

3/24/92

XSoft
The Big/Little Company

- **Independent Business Division of Xerox**
- **Full-featured Software Company**
- **Research and Technology Rich**

XSoft's Strategic Intent

- **Focused on the Commercialization of Pioneering, Document-Focused Software for Key Business Process Productivity**

Leading Technology
XSoft Today

- Object-Oriented
- Compound Document E-Mail
- Distributed Document Services
- Agents/Job Assistant
- Tokens in DocuBuild
- Information Visualizer (Rooms)
- Paper Clients
- ODA
- Native SGML
- • • •

World Class Research

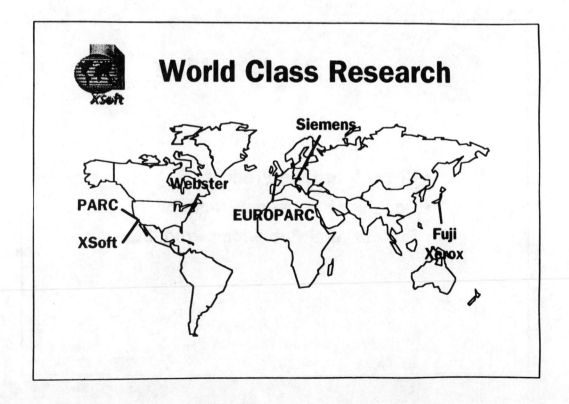

The XSoft Advantage

Focused on Document Management

- **We Understand Documents**
- **Pioneered Client/Server**
- **Ease Of Use**
- **Collaboration**

XSoft Product Line

- **Client Interface Products**
- **Document Services Products**
- **Professional Publishing Products**

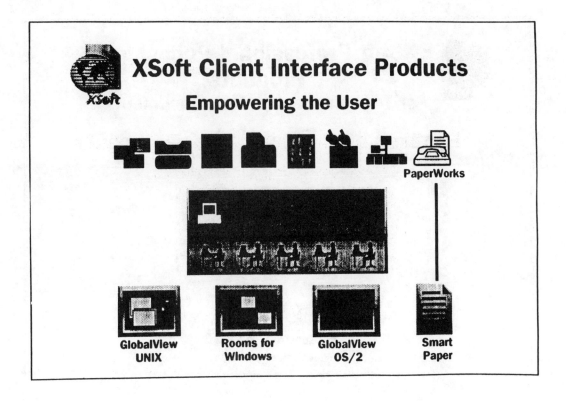

XSoft Professional Publishing Products
For Technical and SGML Documents

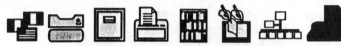

Workstation   **PC**

Near-Term from XSoft

**Additional
RISC Platforms**

**Additional
Interoperability**

**GlobalView Client
Under X Windows**

**Rooms for
X Windows**

**ConnX for
Windows**

XSoft Direction

- **Modular Document Services Independent of:**
  - Network
  - Platform and Operating System
  - Graphical User Interface
  - Document Format

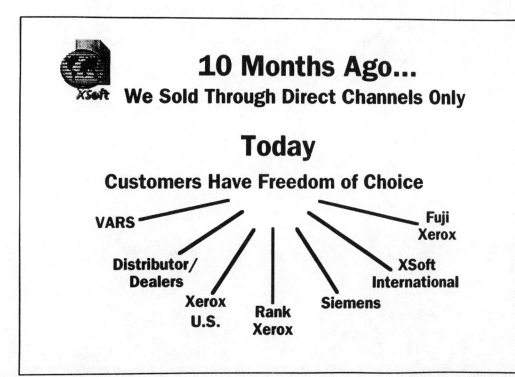

10 Months Ago...
We Sold Through Direct Channels Only

Today
Customers Have Freedom of Choice

VARS

Fuji Xerox

Distributor/ Dealers

XSoft International

Xerox U.S.

Siemens

Rank Xerox

So...

When You Think
Document Management

Think XSoft

A Leader In Document
Management Software

Stephen L. Conkling
Director, Desktop Document Imaging
Integration and Systems Products Division
Eastman Kodak Company

Environment

The proliferation of LANs, proven effectiveness of workgroup communication software, and growing popularity of the client/server model, are ushering in a new phase in the information revolution — one in which electronic information can be shared by workgroups and distributed seamlessly across organizations. For end-users, these advances introduce the ability to act on incoming information quickly and efficiently, spurring improvement in their productivity and ultimately their company's competitive position.

The Challenge

Networks are only as valuable as the information they can communicate. Despite the advantages caused by the aforementioned trends, only five percent of all business information resides in electronic form — the other 95 percent remains on paper. The challenge is to create one information source that incorporates information from both the electronic and paper worlds.

Traditional Document Imaging Systems

Some industries such as insurance and banking, must process enormous amounts of paper. It is these companies who first realized the value of document image processing.

High-end document management systems were the first solutions for document image processing. Such systems allow users to quickly process high volumes of images among designated workgroups. The systems were designed to provide a very specific, mission critical solution and for that reason are often expensive and proprietary in nature.

Companies adopting such imaging solutions are reaping the following competitive benefits:
- improved productivity and communication at the individual, workgroup and enterprise-wide levels;
- improved customer service;
- improved security and;
- reduction of time spent on file and sorting.

Kodak's DDI Solution

While dedicated document image management systems are fostering enormous productivity gains in image-intensive applications, their high cost (typically thousands of dollars per seat) precludes their acceptance by the general, desktop-computing market. To realize the benefits of improved productivity, service and organization that document image management systems provide, businesses need to integrate an affordable, full-featured imaging solution as part of users' traditional desktop-computing environment. Kodak DDI Group's goal is to bring the productivity benefits of high-end document imaging systems to the mainstream computing market.

With this goal in mind, Kodak has developed a strategy which takes advantage of the installed base of applications and networks. The focus of its solution is twofold: to provide an open network imaging infrastructure as well as front-end, image-enabled applications. Such an infrastructure takes advantage of the client/server model and makes imaging functionality available to the desktop user, while retaining document management and storage on the server level. Imaging functionality is introduced to users on a network through existing applications which have been image-enabled. With image-enabled applications, images are treated as another data type and integrated as a natural extension of desktop network applications and tools.

Kodak, leveraging its expertise in imaging software, is delivering to its partners a variety of Application Programming Interfaces (APIs) to image-enable their product. The APIs include functionality to support document, folder, and workqueue services, as well as a system's mass-storage devices.

<u>Kodak's Partners</u>
To date, Kodak's Desktop Document Imaging Group has collaborated with three partners:
Lotus, Novell and IBM.

Kodak/Lotus
Kodak has provided its imaging technology to create Lotus Notes: Document Imaging
available from Lotus Development Corp. Scheduled to ship in July, 1992 — Lotus Notes:
Document Imaging (LNDI) —is an add-on product allowing Notes users to access paper
and film-based information. This solution provides a cost-effective means for users to
integrate paper information into their electronic data mix, reaping the benefits of improved
productivity and communication at the workgroup and enterprise-wide levels. The goal is
to transform users' desktops into a single source for all their critical information.

Kodak/Novell
Kodak is working with Novell to develop image-processing, mass-storage and object -
management technology to add to NetWare 3.2. Kodak is providing Novell with APIs and
NetWare loadable module (NLM) tools that allow systems and applications to handle
images more efficiently on NetWare networks. The software services from Kodak are
tightly coupled with NetWare's operating system and provide open platform support for
front-end applications, database products and NLMs. The services provide developers
with an opportunity to create specialized applications that send, store, and manage image
files over a NetWare LAN.

Kodak/IBM
Kodak has applied its application expertise in document-image management systems to
provide a graphical user interface, extensive indexing capability and workflow management
for IBM/s SAA ImagePlus/2, the newest member of IBM's ImagePlus family of
products.

<u>The Impact of Desktop Document Imaging</u>
Kodak's present and future partners are creating an imaging revolution. Document images
will soon be included in all types of applications, from databases to electronic mail. This
new information phase will evolve to where computers can seamlessly process and
integrate data and documents in any format in a manner completely transparent to the
end-user.

With document-imaging capabilities integrated into their desktop computers, casual business users will be able to capture, store and share documents electronically as a routine activity at their desks. The desktop PC will become a single point of reference for information from *all* sources — online, an external or internal paper or fax document, a voice message, etc. By integrating document-imaging capabilities into line-of-business and desktop applications that run on standard platforms, Kodak's DDI strategy will provide every general-knowledge worker easier access to more information and greater power to communicate. The result will be a significant increase in office productivity at all levels.

The DDI strategy is part of a larger Kodak initiative to leverage its imaging and color expertise to enable efficient access to and management of all types of images, from microfilm to high-resolution color photographs, all within a common desktop environment.

###

A Knowledge-based Approach to Information Access in Document Management Systems

Darlene Mann
Director of Product Marketing
Verity Inc.
1550 Plymouth St.
Mountain View, CA 94043

Abstract

1. Introduction

Document Management systems provide storage, control and access to large information repositories for one or more workgroups in an enterprise. Unlike traditional databases, the information contained in a document management system is highly unstructured. It consists of different data types, created by multiple authors, in different styles and formats. Depending on the type and breadth of the information under it's control, a document management system may need to provide access to information to virtually anyone within a workgroup or company. As these information repositories grow, users will judge the value of a document management system by the simplicity and accuracy of the information access methods available.

2. Current Methods of Information Access

Most document management systems treat "documents" as individual data objects. Typically, a document management system will register the information about a data object that is available from the operating system's file system, such as filename, user name, file size, file type, etc. In addition, as the documents are registered with the system there may be required attributes which must be recorded before the document will be accepted -- information like department name or type of document. Once objects are registered in the document management system, end-users of the system may access the documents based upon these attributes. However, in large repositories with hundreds of thousands of entries, attribute-based search is unsatisfactory unless the user knows exactly which document is required.

If a user is searching for a document or set of documents which contain particular information, but that information is "inside" the document and not in the attributes, then the user needs a content-based method of retrieving information. Since document management systems are dominated by documents which consist of text (combined with image, graphics, and other data types), full-text indexing is the most common method of identifying document content. Unfortunately, these traditional content-based methods (Boolean retrieval systems) are insufficient to meet the needs of most users; they require too much training and expertise for effective use by the casual user of a document management system.

3.   A Knowledge-based Approach to Information Access

To provide effective methods of accessing information to a wide audience of casual end-users, a document management system must provide the end-user with a means to retrieve the documents which are about their subject of interest. In other words, the system must be able to convey knowledge about the content of the documents to the end-user.   There are two methods currently available for conveying knowledge about the documents in a document management system:

     1. Keywording
     2. Knowledge-based retrieval

3.1   Keywording

Most document management systems provide the ability to keyword documents as they are registered with the system.   Using keywords to identify the content of a document, an author or editor will "tag" or *keyword* a document with words representing the concepts discussed within the document.   End-users may then retrieve documents which are associated with particular keywords.   Keywording can very effective for small, highly controlled repositories, however for large collections of information with multiple authors and readers, a keywording system quickly proves impractical.   In a large document management system, it is too resource intensive to maintain full-time editors to read and keyword each document.   Using authors to keyword their own documents reduces the cost, but causes problems with consistency -- authors use different keywords to mean the same thing or use the same keyword to mean different things.   And using either editors or authors, once a document is keyworded it is very expensive to return to the document to update or add additional keywords.

3.2   Knowledge-based   Retrieval

A second approach to capturing and conveying knowledge about documents to end-users is to use a knowledge-based retrieval system.   Knowledge-based retrieval systems define concepts by structuring groups of words and phrases relevant to particular subjects into meaningful organizations(*See Figure 1 below*).

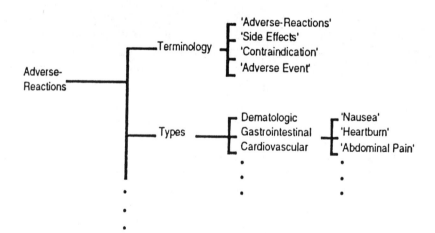

These "thesaurus-like" structures are named, saved as an entry in the knowledge-base, and then shared among end-users for use with an integrated search engine. When an end-user chooses one of the concepts represented, the search engine retrieves all the documents which contain information represented in the structure of the subject matter. More advanced forms of knowledge-based retrieval systems provide advanced algorithms and term weighting. These advanced features allow documents to be returned in an ordered list such that with the most highly weighted terms are presented first to the user first.

The benefits of a knowledge-based approached to information access are three-fold:

1. Casual end-users can easily access information with both accuracy and completeness. Since they are simply choosing among a set of concepts, they may perform content-based retrieval without learning an arcane retrieval language. In addition, they may retrieve documents about a particular subject are without possessing deep knowledge of that subject.

2. Documents may be added to the system without a laborious or rigorous keywording effort. Entries in the knowledge-base are created a single time, unlike keywording which requires reading and assigning keywords to every document in the system. In addition, multiple documents do not have to retrieved and updated each time a keyword is changed or added. Instead, the concepts may be modified to retrieve a broader or narrower set of documents.

3. Organizational knowledge is captured and shared through the entries in the knowledge-base. As concepts are structured and defined, a collection of expertise is created for subjects of importance to an organization. This collection of subject-matter expertise can be used and extended by other members of an organization.

4. Conclusion

Content-based retrieval is essential for information access in document management systems managing large collections of documents. Traditional content-based retrieval methods offer insufficient capabilities to casual end-users unfamiliar with Boolean syntax or with limited subject-matter expertise. By using a knowledge-based approach, the costs of extensive keywording are eliminated, a flexible approach to updating search criteria is established and the efficiency and effectiveness of casual end-users performing searches can be dramatically improved.

Alvin S. Tedjamulia
VP, Technology

**SOFTSOLUTIONS
TECHNOLOGY CORP.**

Groupware 92

**Evolution of
Document Management**

August 1992
San Jose, CA

Document Management

*Managing Documents from
"Cradle to Grave"*

*Creation - Retrieval - Editing -
Searching - Archival - Restoration*

Unique Doc Numbering
Long Document Names
Document Profiling
Directory Structure Enforcement
Document Echoing
Activity Log
Archival & Purging
Archival Restoration
Billing
Security Enforcement
Version Control
Report Writer
Management of External Documents
Automatic Indexing of Full-Text
Auto Drive Mapping

Text vs Document Mgmt

- Historical Approach -

TEXT MANAGEMENT

1. Locates sentences/paragraphs within text
2. Manages Selected Documents
3. Deals with Static Texts
   (Publications, Court Proceedings, Manuals)

DOCUMENT MANAGEMENT

1. Locates Documents within WAN
2. Manages All Documents
3. Deals with Dynamic Texts
   (Letters, Contracts, Budgets, Minutes)
4. Launches Applications
5. Provides Administrative Support

Advanced Document Management Features

Text Management & Concept Searching

Portable Mode
Reaching Documents Not on the LAN
Redundancy
Information Portability

Multi-Protocol Support
Heterogeneous Networks

Work-Flow & Process Control

Compound Document Management

Operating System Awareness

Global Searching

Object Management

Image Management Systems

- *Historical Approach* -
Process Control
Format Conversion
High-Volume Scanning
Compression of Data
Expensive Hardware Requirements
Archival on Optical Devices

- *Features Lacking*
Searching Features
Wide Area Support
Access Control
(Activity Logs, Security, Versions)
Integration with the Image
Creation Process
Redundancy

Document Mgmt System
+
Image Mgmt System
=
Object Mgmt System

Combining Images and Text Documents into a Single System

Other Objects:
Text & E-Mails
Bit-Mapped Images
Presentation Graphics
Spreadsheets
Faxes
Voice & Sound
Motion Picture

Factors which Contribute to Object Management Proliferation

Industry move to Distributed Processing

Windows facilitates "Middleware" Approach

Multitasking & Better Operating Systems

Groupware Aware

Market Forces Rewarding Efficiency

Quality Initiatives

Global Scope of Information Sharing

DocuFLOW, AN OBJECT-ORIENTED, DOCUMENT MANAGEMENT, WORKFLOW SYSTEM

Kenneth M. Santoro
Director of Development
INVENTA Corporation
3080 Olcott St., Suite 230C
Santa Clara, CA 95054

ABSTRACT

Over the last decade, little has been done to automate the processing of paper. As documents and forms are manually routed through an organization, they prompt manual actions and manual management techniques. With thousands, sometimes even millions of pieces of paper involved, organizations are finding this paperwork maze to be a costly, labor-intensive nightmare. Database solutions for cataloging, archiving and searching are only part of the answer. More important is automating the processes themselves. This demands capabilities for the intelligent routing of documents and forms and the transparent intercommunication with data contained therein.

This paper proposes an object-oriented, workflow approach to these document management issues and describes one product, INVENTA Corporation's DocuFLOW, designed specifically to automate document intensive activities for organizations.

1 INTRODUCTION

Organizational service functions (customer service, sales, purchasing, engineering etc.) share many characteristics across organizations. In general, these service functions can be characterized by:

- A large proportion of knowledge workers;
- A broad spectrum of applications implemented to automate specific tasks;
- Costly, labor-intensive paperwork requirements;
- A wide variety of manual processes.

In spite of all the advances (not to mention the investment) in data processing technology, productivity increases for these functions have been essentially nonexistent. Peter Drucker, the famous economist, has called this the major challenge of the 90s, increasing productivity for service functions and knowledge workers.

Until now classical data processing methods offered nothing new. But a new approach to software programming promises to change all that. Object-oriented programming builds applications in a revolutionary new way. By thinking of processes in terms of the real world entities (purchase requests, claim forms, managers, originators, customers, etc.) that make them up, applications are written using software objects to mimic the actual process. This approach brings a number of significant benefits: 1) efficiency in application development 2) the ability to adapt to changing requirements and 3) reusability of software.

With all the publicity surrounding this approach, organizations have yet to understand the implication it holds for solving their problems. Workflow technology will dramatically change that perception. Workflow uses these object-oriented techniques to closely model whole, manual processes. Electronic form-like objects (built with easy-to-use graphical tools) are created, and then intelligently routed over networks like mail messages. Along the way they are efficiently accessed by users and applications, analogous to products on an engineering production line. This dramatically reduces cycle times. Moreover, complex software development goes away, making the ultimate solutions not only simple to build but cost-effective as well. This can finally set organizations free from the chains of their manual methods. The potential for productivity is so high that workflow has become an immediate priority for many organizations.

2 OVERVIEW: WORKFLOW TECHNOLOGY

Workflow: The path by work as it is processed within a community of users.

To gain a perspective on workflow automation, think about the activities associated with the purchasing process. An "object", in this case a purchase request document, (PR) is first originated by incorporating requirements and specifications. It is then maneuvered through a complex internal review and approval process, requiring the close cooperation of individuals and departments. Next, it is passed to purchasing which checks sources and suppliers using the PR to generate new documents, request for quotes (RFQs) or request for proposals (RFPs). These documents are merged with existing procedural boilerplate, published and distributed to suppliers. Along the way, these objects gather multiple attachments (memos, redlines, diagrams, etc.), chart unique "paper trails" (approvals, mainframe updates, ad hoc queries, etc.) and undergo constant revision. Ultimately, they spawn a new generation of documents, purchase orders and contracts that will have their own flows. In general, these methods have no facility for real-time reporting and generate documents that are difficult to track and have a maddening collection of revisions.

A large percentage of work in many organizations is made up of processes like this, activities surrounding the movement of some object. These objects extract information and update databases as they travel, require intelligent routing and demand interaction between co-workers. Up until now, these processes required manual approaches and used computer applications merely to automate specific tasks within the flow. Software which could easily automate the whole dynamic process could save light years of work for organizations starved for productivity.

Actual implementation of such software has proved to be a daunting task. Until very recently, attempts to provide this functionality were database-oriented and/or proprietary in nature. In addition, heavy information and communication requirements, significant user interface issues and the lack of a universal platform made success difficult. Major building blocks were needed: graphical user interfaces (GUIs), LAN operating systems with message routing functions and "store and forward" application support and most importantly, the object-oriented programming techniques.   The availability of these "enabling technologies" in the PC LAN world have finally made it possible to produce simple and cost-effective workflow packages.

3 DocuFLOW

One practical example is DocuFLOW, workflow software available from INVENTA. It is based on the concept of a self-routing intelligent workflow "objects", which use an underlying LAN E-Mail capability as the transport for information. These objects contain information which is augmented and shared with users and processes as it is routed across the network according to the rules maintained in the workflow application. Users see these objects as electronic forms. These forms present "action buttons" at each stage, permitting the user to invoke powerful scripts which automate complex background activities, such as database access, mail message generation, document access, application launching and data display. The object has a defined underlying data structure and can access the data in this structure for the exchange of selected information with other applications. These other applications could be shared network applications running on PC LAN servers or pre-existing applications already running on minicomputers and mainframes e.g. databases, imaging, MRP, accounting etc. Requirements for detailed text messages, documents or images are supported as attachments with the electronic form serving as a "cover sheet". The system works directly with popular electronic mail services for user addressing and transport functions and with standard LAN services for security, connectivity, peripheral access, wide area network (WAN) support, and integrated administration.

INVENTA's DocuFLOW provides:

1. Automated "front-end" tools for the customization of electronic user interfaces.
2. The ability to easily script an intelligent route, e.g. if this purchase request is more than $500 it goes to the Director level, if not it goes to the Manager level.
3. Object tracking and real time report generators, e.g. Who is processing claim #17615? How much in unreconciled claims are in the system? How long does it take to process a claim?
4. Application hooks for transparent communication with minicomputers and mainframes.
5. Document management back-end (Saros Mezzanine) for naming, cataloging, version control, audit trails, key word and full text searches..

Now the power of this approach should start becoming clear: easy to customize applications for modeling established methods, the ability for this application to transparently receive and refresh data from other applications, performance measuring for managing activities historically difficult to measure and document management facilities for tracking, storing and retrieving.

4 CONCLUSION

Document management is as much about automating the processing of documents as it is about cataloging, indexing and retrieving them. The marriage of object-oriented, workflow techniques with document management engines promises to revolutionize the way work is accomplished in organizations and finally bring productivity to huge corporate and government sectors drowning in paperwork.

May 22, 1992

Panel Session:

GROUPWARE FOR DECISION SUPPORT

Jay F. Nunamaker, Jr., Chairman
Ventana Corporation
1430 East Ft. Lowell
Suite 301
Tucson, Arizona 85719
602-325-8228

Panelists:

David Friend
Pilot Corporation
617-350-7035

Gene Pierce
NCR Corporation
803-739-7737

Arnie Urken
Smartchoice
201-379-2306

This session will provide a state of the art description of decision support. This session will discuss recent advances in systems architecture GUIs, executive information systems, collaboration tools and field studies in decision support. Insights and the theoretical foundation that have emerged over the past 10 years will be described along with the grand challenges motivating the work. The panelists will explore the lessons learned and the insights gained from building decision support systems experimenting with them and observing their use.

Experience concerning decision support is entering its second decade. In its broadest context, decision support has been around for a long time. We are merely attempting to improve that process. The objective of decision support is to develop ways in which information technology can be used to make organizations more productive.

It is becoming increasingly obvious that decision support is changing the way people work and establishing a new paradigm for group communication and decision making. Advances will take place in both the architecture of the technology and application of the technology.

Components to the technology architecture of the future will include:

- Any time/any place (all combinations) systems to support the individuals, groups, projects and entire organizations.

- Organizational Memory which involves the integration of individual, corporate and executive information.

- Boardroom/meeting room technology that makes use of portable (notepad) sized computers with wireless LANS.

- Multi-media; multiple public screens with audio and video support.

- Multiple input devices such as keyboards, mouse track balls and styluses.

- Software designed specifically for small and large teams.

- Multi-cultural/multi-lingual systems that enable participants to communicate in their native languages.

- Graphics support in addition to the text based support.

Future applications will include support for:

- Re-engineering with an emphasis upon work flow analysis, concurrent engineering and re-design of business processes.

- Negotiation

- Quality Improvement Teams

- Better use of human resources in terms of evaluation and review activities

- Project Management

- Marketing focus groups

- Planning; strategic and operational

We are moving from the familiar world of face-to-face communication and decision making into an entirely new world where we will depend upon technological resources to achieve a level of interaction we can scarcely imagine. The promise of the application of technology to the breaking down of barriers of time and geographic location is spectacular, but we have barely begun to explore it. The applications being explored today will in the future seem relatively primitive.

The panelists will share their experience about the development and use of decision support tools. We will discuss the opportunities and problems facing decision support systems, the barriers to implementation and usage and prospects for the future.

Executive Information Systems and Groupware

Jeff Flowers
Pilot Software, Inc.
Groupware '92 Presentation

Pilot Background

Pilot Is Leader In Executive Information Systems (EIS)

First To Market, Product Innovators, Highest Customer Satisfaction Ratings

Focus On Visual Information Access

Intuitively Easy to Navigate Data

Fast Response Times

Rapid Development

Executives and Groups

Executives and Knowledge Workers Function In Groups

Generally Manage A Group

Information Providers Are Often Groups

Communicate With Large Groups

Deal With Both Internal and External Groups

View Themselves As A Group

Group Communications

Group Communication Important Since The Start of EIS

Information Is Often Annotated With Interpretation

Executive Reviews Comparisons of Different Groups: Functional, Industry, Economy

Request For Information Using Electronic Mail

Interfaces To Groupware Products Such As Notes

Pilot and Notes

Pilot LightShip and Notes Interface

LightShip Provides Easy, Visual Interface For Viewing and Navigating Data From Many Data Sources

Developed Interface Allowing LightShip Screens To Be Mailed and Entered As Discussion

Future Release Allows Retrieval And Update Of Notes Database

Future Of EIS And Groupware

Interactive Discussion Of Issues

Ability To Track Critical Issues and Actions

Call Attention To Exceptions

Monitor Data And Generate Exceptions

Providing Data Warehouse Function

Query and Locate Specific Information From Vast Storage

Coordinated Organizational Decision Support

Eugene A. Pierce
Coordination Technologies
NCR Corporation

Introduction

Decision Support is effectively the concern or focus of almost every business, manufacturing and general IT application or tool today. The focus, of course, is helping a knowledge worker make the best decisions possible for the purpose of making organizations more productive. When a problem confronts a knowledge worker it is very desirable to bring to bear the most appropriate resources to solve that problem in a just-in-time way. Such resources may involve enterprise database access, organizational/process context of the work item(s), ad hoc discussions with other people, expert systems or access to local spreadsheet/document information. All of this, of course, should be presented to the user in an optimal presentation style with appropriate context.

Making decisions today solely on an individual basis with little or no concurrence or input from co-workers or subordinates is extremely dangerous ! The health of any business is dependent upon making the most logical and risk free business decisions possible. Achieving this involves the leveraging of organizational memory and organizational reasoning power. Problems are becoming more global in nature and they require organizational team context and group decision making for the best possible decision.

Decision support tools today are primarily standalone. They empower individuals in accessing databases (sometimes enterprise) and provide some form of graphical interface . They do not provide any organizational process control and context and they provide little, if any, coordinated group discussion support with other co-workers for the purpose of bringing organizational memory and reasoning to bear for making the best decision. It is agreed that decision making, as a partial result of re-engineering organizational processes, is being pushed down the organizational chart to those who can make the most timely and most correct decisions. But this poses the following questions.

1. What Information technology mechanism should exist to empower decision makers, at the lowest level of the organizational chart ? What decision support applications and tools are needed when an organizational process must be followed based on organizational policy in order to achieve clear objectives ?
2. Who is the most appropriate person within an organization to make a decision and why ? Also, what should the mechanisms be to help determine who that person is ?
3. Does the most appropriate person have all of the key information at his or her fingertips to make the best decision for every case ? Many times other co-workers possess this information. What mechanisms should exist to help access this information from other co-workers for direct decision support usage ?

Here we will concentrate on the description of a proposed architecture to help provide a solution to the questions above. Then, a list of benefits will be provided regarding this architecture with concluding remarks.

An Architecture for Coordinated Organizational Decision Support

Before addressing the questions directly let us first describe an architecture that establishes the relationship between the following three modes of group work in terms of achieving office goals and objectives through group decision support tools. These three modes are:

- Same Time/Anyplace Ad Hoc mode   (e.g. telephone, video conference, face to face, Electronic Meeting Rooms, etc)

- Different Time/Anyplace Ad Hoc mode   (e.g. Email, Discussion Support tools, Extended Email, Voice Mail, etc)

- Different Time/Anyplace Process-based Mode   (e.g. Workflow (human & computer))

The first mode is very familiar to us and we use it everyday in an ad hoc fashion, meaning there are usually no rules or procedures regarding its time of usage. We make phone calls and use video conferencing tools for the purpose of achieving some goal in support of other goals at any point in time. This is effectively any real time communication mechanism. The second mode is one that is somewhat familiar and we again use it in an ad hoc fashion but it is non real time in its usage. We may establish an electronic discussion group to seek an answer to a question but not expect an answer until several iterations of discourse. Again this is usually in support of other goals. The third mode is one that is non ad hoc and this implies the adherence to a process structure with organizational constraints applied for the accomplishment of a goal. For example, after filling-out a travel expense form the form will follow a travel expense process structure for the purpose of achieving the goal of accounting for the travel expenses incurred. This is done by routing the form to people or applications that play a well defined role in the process structure such that each person or application activity in the process performs a specific decision support role that contributes to the accomplishment of the process goals.

Coordinated organizational decision support applications may utilize all modes of working described above. Technically integrating the tools that support each mode can seamlessly provide an infrastructure to establish an organizational memory. This implies the capture of information during each working mode with explicit links established between information instances across working modes. The links connecting different working mode information instances effectively define a semantic net structure that describes a particular group decision. For example, capturing the decisions and information via phone conversations, electronic mail and at each process step for the processing of a travel expense form and providing the appropriate links between each type of information establishes an organizational memory structure for the processing of that travel expense instance. Such a structure can easily be referenced for process audit, measurement and management.

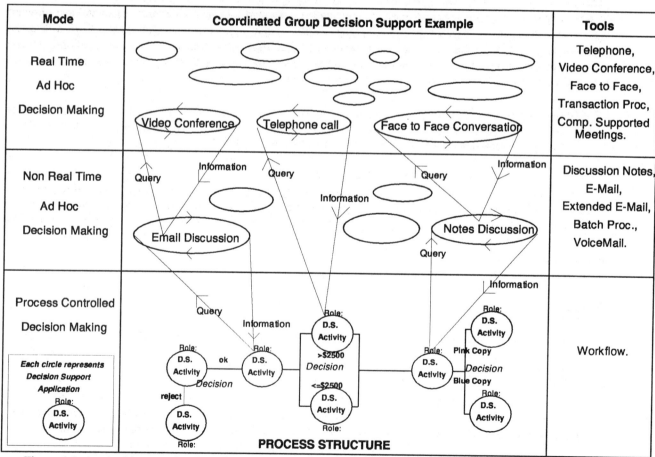

Figure 1.0 An Architecture for Coordinated Organizational Decision Support

Figure 1.0 describes an architecture for coordinating organizational decision support applications along with how ad hoc interactions impact decision support. The information-passing links, shown between working modes, indicate how information is passed to a decision support activity from an email discussion as well as how information is propagated via a process map to each decision support application within a process structure. The capture of these links can be the basis of an organizational memory.

Let us now return to the set of questions posed at the beginning of this paper.

1. What Information technology mechanism should exist to empower decision makers, at the lowest level of the organizational chart ? What decision support applications and tools are needed when an organizational process must be followed based on organizational policy in order to achieve clear objectives ?

Figure 1.0 suggests how workflow information technology could be applied to support a coordinated set of decision support applications that follows some organizational process map. This approach implies that decision support process knowledge is separate from decision support application knowledge. This is useful in that decision support applications can change without having to change the process policy and the process policy can change without having to change the decision support applications.

2. Who is the most appropriate person within an organizational to make a decision and why ? Also, what should the mechanisms be to help determine who that person is ?

The answer to this question is dependent upon the role a person plays within an organization and the skills that person brings to that role. Such information concerning a person is usually not explicitly defined and easily leveraged within an organization. A possible mechanism to support this is an electronic organizational directory that defines the roles and skills a person may have in the context of an organizational chart. Such a directory would have interfaces for decision support processes and their associated decision support applications. Having access to such information can improve decision support in that the chance of having the most appropriate person assigned to the right decision support function is much higher.

3. Does the most appropriate person have all of the key information at his or her fingertips to make the best decision for every case ? Many times other co-workers possess this information. What mechanisms should exist to help access this information from other co-workers for direct decision support usage ?

Figure 1.0 shows the relationship between 3 modes of interaction for the purpose of providing information for making decisions from either an ad hoc or process standpoint. When a person is interacting with a decision support application in support of a decision support process and key information is unknown for making the decision then that person may choose to use an ad hoc tool to obtain that information as quickly as possible. The information may be accessed via a telephone call or it may require a discourse with four other people via a discussion notes tool.

Benefits

The following are benefits derived from the architecture discussed in the previous section:

- Anytime/Anyplace information access to support individuals and organizations.
- Integration of Ad Hoc and Process methods for achieving organizational objectives.
- Workflow provides ability to redesign and evolve organizational decision support processes and policy.
- Provides infrastructure to establish an Organizational Memory (links ad hoc decisions with process decisions)
- Workflow Separates Decision Support Process from Decision Support Applications for easier change.
- Infrastructure exists for on-going Decision Support workflow analysis for optimal tuning.

- Support for the following types of decision support teams and their associated applications:
  - Negotiation teams,
  - Quality Improvement teams,
  - Marketing/Product Teams,
  - Concurrent Engineering Design Teams,
  - Effectively any team utilizing a process structure to achieve goals.
- Optimal usage of human resources via role/skill management.
- Fundamental base for breaking down barriers of time and location for higher productivity.

Conclusion

As discussed earlier, decision support tools today do not effectively support organizational decision support processes very well, if at all.   The architecture presented here will help establish a basis for providing organizations an infrastructure for decision making on a process level with integrated ad hoc ability. Such an approach also provides the ability to respond to change quickly by allowing modification of the decision support process without having to modify decision support applications.

Enabling an organization to leverage its entire organizational reasoning and memory resources via a process approach with integrated ad hoc behavior enhances its ability to react quickly to change. This provides a business a tremendous advantage over its competition.

References

Singh, B. 1991. Role Interaction Nets: A Coordination System Model.
    Software Technology Program, MCC, STP-91

Bullen, C., Johansen, R., 1988. GROUPWARE: A KEY TO MANAGING BUSINESS TEAMS ?
    CISR WP No. 169, Sloan WP No. 2012-18
    Center for Information Systems Research, MIT Sloan School

Crowston, K., Malone, T., 1987. Information Technology and Work Organization.
    CISR WP No. 165, Sloan WP No. 1960-87
    Center for Information Systems Research, MIT Sloan School

For additional correspondence please use the following electronic mail address: *gene.pierce@columbiasc.ncr.com*

Rationality, Voting, and Group Decision Support Systems

Arnold B. Urken
SmartChoice Technologies
614 River Street
Hoboken, New Jersey 07030

ABSTRACT

The choice of a voting system affects the likelihood that groups reach their objectives. But voter attitudes about voting and choosing voting systems usually prevent groups from recognizing options. Group decision support tools, as generic as e-mail, can reverse this behavior if they are tailored for network decision tasks.

1 INTRODUCTION

"Voting" is a very common technique for making group decisions, but people have an uncommon ability to treat the choice of a voting system as neutral even though it is not! This attitude is not altogether surprising. Voting is a metaphor for many different ways of expressing or communicating information. So although voting with one's feet or by a show of hands may come to mind, the complexity of choosing among metaphors may leave us more indifferent than neutral. In fact, such indifference about the problem of choosing a voting system is reinforced by the negative connotation that the term "voting" has in our culture. Here the term connotes manipulation, deception, and other undesirable aspects of public elections.

Despite these attitudes, voting continues to be used for making collective choices about what objectives a group should have (normative rationality) and/or how these objectives should be pursued (instrumental rationality). But the underlying ambivalence voting leads us to rely on words such as "polling" or "surveying" to describe the activity.

If a choice process is defined as a voting problem, possibilities for controlling the process become apparent and normative or instrumental rationality is facilitated.

2 VOTING CONTROL MECHANISMS

Social scientists have outlined mechanisms for controlling the collective behavior of individuals by designing the ostensibly noncontroversial rules for communicating or representing information about their preferences and judgments. These mechanisms make it possible to control the probability that voters reach a decisive outcome, produce a tie or indecisive outcome, or make one or more "optimal" choices, where optimality is well defined.

An important theoretical problem in the design of choice mechanisms is "incentive compatibility." Simply put, this means that the users of a system must be motivated to act according to the requirements of the mechanism if the predicted collective outcome is to occur.

This is not a new problem for developers of group decision

support systems. Traditionally, support has involved building systems for improving access to appropriate information for improving individual formulation of preferences and judgments. If the support is not usable, the system "fails." Now we are providing support by analyzing what happens or what can happen once voter preferences and judgments have been formed. This conception of support allows us to accept the complexities of individual choices and see if and how the choice mechanism can be designed to affect the collective outcome.

In principle, understanding the theoretical possibilities for building systems of support is straightforward. Computer-mediated communication becomes a means for identifying options and guiding the user in selecting the "best" system. Here com- puters are more than super-adding machines; they are tools for intelligent guidance through a decision making process.

3 ISSUES IN DESIGNING SUPPORT SYSTEMS

Although the growth of networked personal computers and work-stations has opened up new options for designing decision support for voting processes, software vendors have only begun to move away from the decision room mode for delivering support. Although changes in costs have made it possible to provide computer-mediated guidance for a fraction of the cost of decision rooms, much remains to be done to exploit opportunities for building tools for modern distributed network environments. In particular, three issues stand out.

3.1 Complexity and Facilitators

In the traditional decision room and its more recent reincarnations, facilitators play an important role in helping users cope with complexity. But facilitators addressing the choice of a voting system would be hard pressed to play the same role even if they were well trained in voting theory and could provide advice based on computer analysis. For as noted in section 1, users will be resistant to abstract advice about something that is not a problem for them. Moreover, since one rationale for investing in group decision software is to save time and money, the facilitator could have an incentive compatibility problem if he or she allows messy ties or indecisive outcomes to occur.

This issue is important for voting processes such as brainstorming, which is normally conceived as a synchronous rather than an asynchronous activity. In a synchronous mode, the work of facilitators seems to be judged exclusively on reaching a consensus very quickly. But the quality of the consensus, whether or not it accurately or strongly represents group opinion that is eventually translated into action, is not normally considered. Yet if tasks such as brainstorming were carried out asynchronously, the quality of deliberation and access to information might be improved to produce more accurate representations of group opinion.

A challenge to designers of networked group decision software is to make facilitation unnecessary by adapting the system to the user rather than relying on a facilitator to make the user adapt to the system. This can be done by developing software tools that can be configured to produce templates for different types of decision tasks. These templates can be designed so that users can easily modify them for their needs. In fact, user-system dialogue can be developed as a basis for tailoring new templates.

3.2 Rethinking Polling

One of the greatest opportunities for group decision software is to change the way polls are done. Polls are typically used to provide feedback from internal and external organizational clients, but getting people to see that polls involve the problem of interpreting voting information is difficult. Professional pollsters have standard techniques that rely on statistical procedures which are normally poorly understood by users, who are not aware that the statistically blessed representation of group opinion may not be the only way of looking at the collected data.
   Often, the conception of polling can be changed when a "crisis" occurs when predictions and observations are dramatically and unconstestably inconsistent. Then polling can take on the character of exploratory data analysis and decision support software can make a contribution toward enabling users to understand and deal with complexity. Of course, as organizations develop and restructure their computer networks, the drive to distribute processing and make efficient and effective use of resources may also induce a sense of crisis that leads users to rethink what is going on in polls.

3.3 Integrating Decision Support Software

The movement to provide support by developing templates for decision tasks makes it desirable to design decision support software so that it can be easily configured or reconfigured for different applications. This strategy for software development suggests that group decision support can become a generic tool, like electronic mail, that is accessible and tailorable within a menu. This type of tool will be developed to complement software for collective decisions in project management, scheduling, group editing, and other tasks.

References

Jessup, L.M. and J.S. Valacich (eds.). 1993. **Group Support Systems: A New Perspective**. New York: Macmillan Publishing Company.

Urken, A.B. 1988. Social choice theory and distributed decision making. **Proceedings of the IEEE/ACM Conference on Office Information Systems**. R.B. Allen (ed.).

Urken, A.B. 1989. Voting in a computer networking environment. **The Information Web**. C. Gould (ed.). Boulder: Westview Publishers.

How Do I Sell Groupware and Still Make Money?
A Position Paper for GroupWare '92
Groupware Licensing, Pricing, and Distribution Panel,
David Coleman (Panel Chairperson)

It has been said that there are no distribution channels for groupware and that the only ones buying groupware are courageous corporate "pioneers." As groupware technologies and markets mature, new distribution channels for groupware are emerging. This panel, composed of a hardware vendor, a software vendor, a large corporate user, a VAR, and a retailer, will call upon their experiences and perspectives of groupware to discuss issues of channel viability, customization, support, network licensing, and much more.

The groupware market (if there is such a thing) is projected by WorkGroup Technologies, Inc. (Hampton N.H.) to be a $2 billion industry by 1995. This requires over 30% growth each year for the intervening years. One of the impediments to this rapid growth is the distribution channels for groupware software.

One of the first major groupware packages to sell into Fortune 500 accounts and be financially successful was Lotus Notes. Lotus started selling Notes initially only to corporate accounts for about $60,000 a license. Over the last year, their strategy has changed to include the VAR channel. Al Stoddard from Lotus Development Corporation will give us Lotus' views on distribution channels for groupware and what new channels Lotus is opening up. Kevin Brown from Corporate Software is a Lotus VAR and can provide their point of view on how well Notes and other groupware packages sell in this channel.

Kevin can also give a VAR's perspective on whether shrink-wrap groupware will be the next major channel of distribution, or will customization always be required for these complex products?

Digital Equipment Corporation (DEC) has been selling groupware (All-in-1) for almost ten years. Lindy Brandt of DEC will give us their perspective on distribution channels, pricing, and licensing of groupware in the VAX/VMS, UNIX and DOS environments. Her talk will detail the administrative costs and overhead for software licensing and distribution, current licensing options, and the unrest amongst MIS managers on current licensing policies. Lindy proposes two solutions for groupware licensing: site licensing and active license tracking. She recommends an industry-endorsed API to aid software license tracking across the distributed, heterogeneous systems we see in corporations today.

Action Technologies (ATI), with their Coordinator Product, was one of the first commercial groupware packages available. They penetrated many corporate accounts, yet chose to get out of the business of selling groupware. Fritz Dresler of ATI will talk about their experience, distribution channel pros and cons as well as their decision to become a groupware/workflow consulting group called Business Design Associates.

Finally, there is John Holliwell, with Ziff-Davis Publishing. John and I as independent industry observers and groupware users provide these perspectives to this session.

My perspective on groupware, having been a group product marketing manager for Oracle Corporation, is that the level of complexity in pricing, licensing, and distribution of database (RDBMS) products is very similar to groupware. Although not all database run on a LAN (just distributed databases), most groupware runs on a LAN, insuring the complexities of versioning, security, views, input conflict resolution, etc. Both database and groupware require training, support and maintenance, and often customization to provide a complete solution to the business challenge.

I make the analogy of groupware and database software, because databases have been sold successfully into mainstream corporate MIS for over a decade. Many of the issues such as licensing simultaneous users on a network, maintenance pricing, bundling consulting with the price of the product have been delt with in this environment. Can the same solutions apply to groupware?

Some of the questions to be answered by this panel include: Who will distribute and support groupware products? What channels are most appropriate for corporate accounts, small groups, or geographically distributed groups? What pricing and licensing schemes are appropriate, should groupware be licensed by the desktop or on the host/server? What if there is a multi-platform network in the enterprise? How do you license across heterogeneous networks? How are licenses tracked and who should track them? Can the software industry as a whole do anything about these issues? Will the sales cycle change as shrink-wrapped products enter the market? As groupware becomes more mainstream will the consulting or applications development services necessary today for a groupware sale still be required? How will customers determine the value of groupware in relation to its price?

This two-hour panel should be a lively discussion with vocal panelists and plenty of time for questions and audience participation.

Groupware Licensing & Distribution

GroupWare '92

Lindy Brandt
Software Licensing Technologies Marketing Manager
Digital Equipment Corporation

d i g i t a l ™

Groupware Licensing & Distribution

- **Groupware Environment**
- **Licensing and distribution issues**
- **Factors that influence licensing preferences**
- **Solutions**

d i g i t a l ™

Groupware Environment

- **Diverse systems connected with peer-to-peer networking**

- **Client/server architecture to take advantage of desktop power**

- **User interface to emulate manual activity involving departments, task forces**
  - **logical representations (pictures, object orientation)**
  - **"intuitively obvious"**

... Groupware licensing issues are the complex software licensing issues most customers face

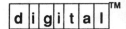

Licensing and Distribution Issues

- **Who knows what's out there?**

- **Few or no tools to inventory, control, purchase and manage software in a distributed environment**

- **Needs vary among installations; no single solution fits**

- **Little knowledge of the magnitude of the issues**

- **"Small potatoes" attitude: How much *did* you spend?**

Costs of Licensing, Renewals, and Distribution

- On average, large companies utilize 1-5 people for licensing and administrative tasks

- Administrative overhead for software distribution accounts for under 10% of software cost

- Current licensing options increase the cost of administration

- . . . but decentralized purchases hide the total cost

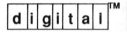

The Agony of Licensing

- Distributed software and groupware licensing policies have not caught up with distributed hardware and networking capabilities

- License-compliant companies subsidize all software use

- Those "in the know" about software licensing issues are buried

- 31 of 50 IS Managers are unsatisfied with software licenses*

* Forrester Research, 1992

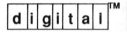

Vendor Relationship Issues

Barriers to partnership between customers and software vendors

- Unsuitable licensing for the way that software must be used
  - licensing does not fit needs
  - confusing policies go unenforced

- Pricing for software support, upgrades, and new platforms

- Lack of consolidation of PC software purchases

- Quality of products and timing of correctiive releases

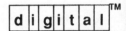

Factors that influence Licensing Preferences

- Application use within the organization: Application investment

- Influence of IS and Info Centers with user populations

- Mechanisms to track users who have purchased applications

- Ease of implementation

Types of Licenses

- **Personal Use**
- **Concurrent user**
- **System capacity**
- **Locked (by node or domain)**
- **Transaction- or consumption-based**
- **Demonstration**
- **Embedded**
- **Packaged product**
- **Site**
- **Multi-site**

What Users Want

- **Simplicity and consistency**

- **Flexibility and choice**

- **Fair pricing**

- **Ease of administration**

Only 2 Solutions!

- **Active software asset and license tracking**
  - **- yields stronger negotiating position**
  - **- licensing costs reflect usage**

- **Site licensing**
  - **- easy to implement**
  - **- requires no management resources**

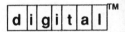

Common Client License API

License Service Application Programming Interface

- **Industry-endorsed API**

- **Software developers incorporate simple calls that tie to multiple license servers**

- **Software managers administer all applications from a single license management**

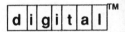

Licensing Options of the Future

- **Flexible licensing options**

- **License management as foundation for asset management**

- **License management as part of larger solution**

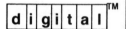

Cost Control Measures

for Software Licensing, Renewals, and Distribution

- **Track software usage and costs**
- **Centralize purchases; use transfer costs**
- **Incorporate a distributor model in-house**
- **Encourage use of centralized purchasing by providing end user services/benefits**
- **Collect single-user applications from departed employees and terminated projects**

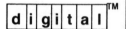

Partnerships with Service Providers

- Assistance with licensing, management, distribution of software

- Help with divisional organizations

- Auditing capability and asset protection

- Manageability

Creative Solutions

Administration
- Appoint a software manager
- Consolidate purchases
- Maintain a software log

Licensing
- License management servers
- Automated tools for asset management
- Value-based pricing

Distribution
- Electronic distribution
- "License-only" options

Groupware Licensing, Pricing and Distribution Issues
Kevin G. Brown, Director Strategic Sales, Corporate Software Inc.

As groupware software products evolve in the market, a variety of issues have surfaced that raise the following questions:

1.   *Who will distribute and support these products?*

2.   *What pricing and licensing schemes are appropriate?*

3.   *Are these products more like host-based products than traditional desktop products and should they be procured, maintained and upgraded similarly?*

Distribution
It is becoming apparent that the distribution of groupware products will require unique methods and hybrid channels for the following reasons:

1.   *Long and complex selling cycles with multiple levels within a corporation.*

2.   *Consulting and applications development services requirements.*

3.   *Integration of LAN/WAN technology with client/server platforms.*

Pricing and Licensing
Groupware software often appears much more like host-based software than the software traditionally found on the desktop. This is forcing publishers and corporate customers to explore the rules for pricing and licensing. The following questions arise:

1.   *How do publishers recover their significant R&D investments in groupware software?*

2.   *How do corporate customers reconcile price and value?*

3.   *What licensing schemes are appropriate: server-based, client-based, or usage-based?*

4.   *What maintenance and upgrade pricing is appropriate?*

These and other issues indicate the need for fresh perspectives by publishers, channel participants and corporate customers. The success of this technology is inextricably tied to the establishment of new rules for pricing, licensing, and distribution.

Delivering Groupware in the 90s

Fritz R. S. Dressler
Action Technologies, Inc.
Alameda, CA 94501
510 521-6190

Abstract

This talk presents the view that without a complementary and richly-developed delivery channel, groupware can never be more than gropeware — a blind and stumbling search for application niches. The talk outlines such a delivery channel and shows that the beginnings of this channel already exist and are growing rapidly.

1 INTRODUCTION

Groupware has come to mean many things to many people, and, because of its slippery something-of-everything nature, it will probably always be hard to pin down. Settled firmly into its low end are the emails, a class of popular software tools that have brought low-cost communications to the desktops. At the high end are the emerging workflow applications with their powers to reengineer entire organizations and to automate the flow of work. Emails can be readily shrink-wrapped and delivered through the existing channel of network dealers and retailers. For the relatively simple emails, most of the value added by this channel is providing the right products at the right places and selling them for the lowest prices. There is some capacity to add more value because there is a modest need for hand-holding and systems integration. To be fair, hand-holding and systems integration can swing widely from case to case and can be extensive.

At the upper end of the groupware spectrum, and in particular within the new workflow products, there is a critical need to have a high value-added capability within the channel. This capability is now being created in sync with the new workflow products. It is not monolithic or simple; instead, like the workflow products themselves, this new channel is rich and varied. How should it function? How much and what kind of value should it add? Here are some answers to these questions as they apply to workflow applications.

2 THE SEARCH FOR PRODUCTIVITY

The need for companies to re-invent themselves, to become ever more competitive in global markets, is now the overriding concern of business. All the rushed activities that this entails are often lumped together into a general overhaul called "reengineering." The reengineering process can take the form of radical change in which the new and single driving force is to "do whatever it takes to satisfy the customers." In fact this notion itself is so new it's radical. But reengineering can also be an evolutionary change in which a series of incremental changes are used to achieve specific goals, such as reducing cycle times and improving the quality of products and services.

Either way, radical or evolutionary, the search for ways to improve productivity is the central activity of business today.

As a corollary, MIS departments are working hard to produce ever-more-flexible systems that can be quickly aligned to their company's business goals. This is shown clearly in the annual surveys of CSC/Index, the polling company in Cambridge, MA that tracks MIS departments in Europe and North America. For the past five years, MIS managers' top concern has been to align their information systems with corporate goals.

What systems are available to help perform these alignments?

We believe that workflow-enabled applications have both the power and the flexibility to continuously align computer systems to changing organizations, both for small incremental changes and for radical leaps. In fact, we have purposely designed our ActionWorkflow™ technology to accommodate both kinds of alignments.

We see the future as very rosy for workflow. Why not? Chip-based hardware continues to develop at its traditional break-neck speed, still doubling in power every twenty months or so. Right on schedule have come the workflow applications. These powerful yet flexible applications can focus the power of chip-based hardware and use it to increase productivity.

However, an appropriate delivery channel is at the moment still immature. What is needed is a robust channel that delivers not only the familiar emails but one that contains the talent, the peopleware, to design and install workflow applications for specific and varied organizations.

3 WORKFLOW CHANNEL

We believe that a useful model for the development of a workflow channel is the LAN industry where market leader Novell ignited and fostered the larger LAN industry. Still, getting there from here with workflow products is the classic chicken & egg dilemma, a situation which requires that one company take a leadership position.

We envision a groupware delivery path that straddles both high and low channels. On the low side there is already today's channel for networks and related software products. The high side is evolving and can be seen in the likes of the consulting and service groups within Lotus Development Corp.; in Delphi Consulting Group, a consultancy for imaging systems; within Arthur Andersen and Nolan, Norton & Company; and also in broad-based consultancies such as McKinsey & Company. These consultants are advising their clients on the art of business restructuring, and they are also advising their clients on the use of technology to carry out the restructuring. These various groups are the beginnings of the high value-added channel for groupware, a channel that can be rightly called the workflow channel.

We believe it is now timely and necessary to develop a standard business reengineering methodology to help consolidate and accelerate the evolving workflow channel. To this end we have established a Workflow Institute. The design methodology taught at the Institute is both application and technology independent, and can, we believe, be a catalyst to consolidate and accelerate a high-end workflow channel.

Our goal is to help evolve a total delivery capability as summarized below.

Delivering Groupware In The 90s

Low End
Network dealers and retailers

High End
Business Specialists
- VARs
- System Integrators
- Consultancies

Channel Specialties
- Software platforms (DOS, OS/2, Windows, Unix, Host O/Ss, Notes)
- Application platforms (Imaging, Data Mgt., Communications, Databases)
- Markets (Manufacturing, Distribution, Retailing, Banking, Government)

Although Action's focus is on the workflow high end, our Workflow Institute features a reengineering methodology that is vendor independent and can be employed by all levels and specialties within the total groupware channel.

References

Craumer, M. A., et al., 1992. *Critical Issues of Information Systems Management for 1992.* A survey by CSC/Index, Cambridge, MA (617) 499-1855.

TRACK 4:
Combination Track

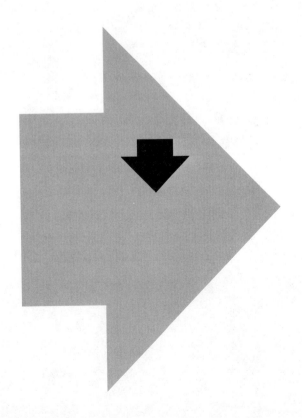

Technology

Making the Right Connections™

Conall Ryan
President & CEO
ON Technology, Inc.
Groupware '92 panel presentation

Theme: Group scheduling - the next big workgroup application?

Why Group Scheduling?

E-Mail is the first groupware product that has reached standard application status in corporations. While it's fine for a two-way conversation, or for broadcasting out a message to a lot of people, it starts to bog down as you move from just sending a message to coordinating a group effort that might evolve over time.

Helping people work more effectively together is a function of automating common, everyday workgroup tasks, like trying to set up a meeting which drives people nuts. We spent a great deal of time talking to the people who were setting up meetings on e-mail. When we asked the secretaries and the people who actually lead meeting-intensive existences, we found out that e-mail was inadequate for the job because they would send out a request into the void, to ten people, to see if they could get together at ten o'clock on Friday morning and get nine different responses. They would end up in negotiatiaion hell in trying to transact a meeting, spending more time trying to get it put together than actually attending it -- and then no one would know what the meeting was about. We decided that there was a real opportunity for a product that make this common task much simpler.

An Example -- Meeting Maker version 1.5

We developed Meeting Maker to solve this problem. After listening to potential customers, we incorporated a set of group scheduling features, unmatched by any other product. It includes a personal calendar for blocking out activities, meetings, and recurring weekly or monthly appointments. You can call up full details about any activity or meeting on your calendar, navigate to any day of any year, or zoom to a full monthly or daily view.

ON Technology, Inc.
155 Second Street • Cambridge, MA 02141 • Phone (617) 876-0900 • Fax (617) 876-0391

The Propose Meeting feature allows you to schedule a time and date, select required guests, reserve rooms and resources, and prepare agendas. Auto-Pick finds the first available time for all required attendees. Meeting Maker tracks responses to a meeting proposal automatically by sending a message to you when someone responds to your proposal.

Meeting Maker displays the current status of each proposed meeting as fully confirmed, partially confirmed, or cancelled, and also follows up automatically on schedule changes. If you need someone to schedule meetings for you, Meeting Maker has a Proxy feature that allows another user to act on your behalf. Proxies can manage your schedule from their own machines. You can print your Meeting Maker calendar in popular appointment book formats, or export it to the Sharp Wizard, Casio B.O.S.S., and HP 95LX.

Target Markets

Like electronic mail, a group scheduler requires a departmental buying decision.

There are three primary targets for group schedulers:

1.   The people who actually schedule and attend meetings in Fortune 2000 corporations (as well as medium-to-small businesses).

2.   The administrative and secretarial people who manage and coordinate meetings and resources in these companies.

3.   The network administrator, or MIS manager, who manages the computer network.

The meeting attenders (#1) and meeting arrangers (#2) generate the demand for group schedulers, but the network administrator (#3) is almost always the key player in the buying decision.

To grow a corporate account into the hundreds and thousands of seats, vendors must keep the IS person happy.

You must also begin to focus on direct sales to small and medium businesses where there is no such thing as an IS department. Using direct mail and telesales, software companies can get these businesses to buy sooner in smaller volumes.

Who else is in the market?

Other vendors working on group scheduling fall into two basic camps:

1.   Email vendors, who develop scheduling products to sell to their existing customers.

2.   Calendaring vendors, who add group functionality to their existing stand-alone products.

Calendar-based products like Now Up-To-Date (for Macintosh) and On Time (for DOS and Windows) have a distribution advantage: they can be sold one-at-a-time and connected at a later point. It's a low-friction sale: no IS involvement, no backed-up evaluation queue, and no standards list to worry about.

Three things differentiate these products in a head-to-head evaluation versus a true group scheduler. The first is that they are miserable at scheduling. The second is that they don't scale well to multiple-server configurations. The third is that eventually, IS always gets involved in any sizeable account.

In the strict group scheduling market, a product like Meeting Maker wins big versus the competition because its functionality, interface and ease-of-use are consistently rated as far superior to Schedule+ and Word Perfect Office.

1.   Printing - Polished output is a big part of a scheduler. We've discovered that customers still find value in their day planners, and in the current product, we offer a wide range of printing options to satisfy the most finicky user.

2.   Scalability - Corporate customers rapidly become addicted to group schedulers and have started to push over 1,000 seats. We have learned a lot over the last year about installing and administering these sites. Group Schedulers must support multiple interconnected servers with connections into Wide Area Networks.

E-Mail Message Transports -- The Issues

The strength of email-based solutions is unified administration and transport. Customers who already own Microsoft Mail can add Schedule+ at a nominal cost per user. As a consequence of this, the email vendor must focus on selling email first -- they have two things to sell; and the scheduling tool must operate within the limits of the email client.

Customers are telling us it's important to add new messaging and transport capabilities to Group Schedulers (for example, using MHS to send meeting requests to networked users who don't have the scheduler), and it's equally important to align products with directory services standards like Apple's Open Collaborative Environment. Transport "platforms" like Novell's global messaging server could become the off-the-shelf engine for future products.

These formative technologies are attractive (and probably inevitable) future options, but it's a good thing that they aren't immediate necessities for running workgroup products.

Future Directions

Two things will determine the direction of group schedulers in the future:

1.   Personal Data Assistants. The Sharp Wizard and the HP-95LX are the harbingers of newer products -- some of which will be pen-based.

2.   Networking. Increased networking means a demand for interoperability across platforms. This means Macs, Windows, and UNIX platforms will all require solutions, and these solutions.

Personal Calendaring & Group Scheduling:
An extension of the electronic mail system

Eldon Greenwood
Technical Marketing Manager, WP Office
WordPerfect Corporation
1555 N. Technology Way
Orem, UT 84057

ABSTRACT

WordPerfect Corporation (WPCorp) is the provider of WordPerfect Office, an electronic mail, calendaring and scheduling product for various platforms. This position paper examines the background of WP Office, its current functionality, and its strategic direction with regard to personal calendaring and group scheduling.

INTRODUCTION

With the widespread implementation of LAN technology in the 90's, many organizations are turning to computer-based time and resource management tools. What benefits are derived from such tools? What obstacles might an organization expect during such a transition?

Some of the benefits of utilizing the computer for time and resource management are that users can:
- Automate repetitive tasks
- Easily enter recurring events
- Carry "to-do" items from day to day
- Transfer information to/from other computer applications
- Easily share information with co-workers
- Rely on the software to find available times and resources for a scheduled event—rather than the "telephone tag" or "sneakernet" approach
- Have scheduled events automatically entered into the user's personal calendar (when accepted)

A few of the obstacles that must be considered before time management and resource scheduling can be successfully moved to the computer are:
- Lack of portability
  - Home, personal, and non-business use
  - Remote access
- User education
- Privacy and data security
- "Culture" (resistance to computers, paper-based planner habits, etc.)

While with today's technologies we still cannot reasonably approach the "paperless" office, networking technology and the associated advances in applications software are bringing this idealized goal closer to reality. Personal calendaring and group scheduling are two applications that are well suited for the network environment. As users become more accustomed to using the computer and the network as business tools, these applications will move them closer to the paperless office.

During the 1980's, WPCorp's WordPerfect became the premier word processor for high-end/business use. One of the factors in reaching this position was the multiple platform development philosophy of WPCorp. Organizations needing a word processing solution are no longer constrained in their choice of a computing platform—they are able to use WordPerfect on whichever platform they use. Not only has WordPerfect been developed for several different computer systems, but the file format is the same throughout each product of the same version. This enables users of the various operating systems to easily exchange documents with users of the DOS version of WordPerfect.

WordPerfect Office, WPCorp's office automation software which contains E-mail, calendar/scheduler, and more, was released in 1987 for Data General computer systems. It was soon developed for DOS, VMS, and UNIX operating systems as well. The early WP Office products allowed communications only within their specific operating system environment. However, WPCorp saw the need to extend the e-mail and scheduling services of Office between platforms. The current releases of the DOS, Windows, Macintosh, UNIX, and VMS products now provide cross-platform mail and scheduling. Now, with the e-mail transport in place, users can not only exchange documents free of conversion hassles, but can also transport those documents easily through their familiar messaging environment.

OVERVIEW OF WP OFFICE FUNCTIONALITY

Currently, WP Office is available for DOS, Windows (Mail portion), Macintosh, VMS, and UNIX operating systems. It has the capability to extend both e-mail and scheduling services between these environments. This overview concentrates mainly on the DOS LAN implementation of WP Office, but applies generally to the other supported platforms as well.

The WordPerfect Office product family is comprised of four principal components: Office for DOS, Office LAN, Connection Server and WordPerfect Office Gateways.

- Office for DOS — Office for DOS replaces WordPerfect Library and includes the following desktop programs: Calendar, File Manager, Notebook, Calculator, Editor, Repeat Performance, Shell and a TSR Manager. Electronic Mail and Scheduler (which require a network) are not included in the Office for DOS product.

- Office LAN — The Office LAN package includes all the desktop programs found in Office for DOS as well as Electronic Mail and Scheduler.

- Connection Server — When two or more Office LAN hosts exist, the Connections Server is required to distribute messages (E-Mail and Scheduler) between the Office LAN hosts. The Connection Server software is bundled with Office LAN. It requires a workstation that is attached to the network and that can be dedicated to the task of running the Connection Server routing software.

- WordPerfect Office Gateways — Gateways to other electronic mail[1] systems are available to extend the services of the Office LAN system. The Connection Server acts as the "store and forward" agent to the gateway processes that are responsible for the translation, communications and transfer of electronic mail messages to the destination E-mail system.

---

[1] The WP Office Gateway to PROFS and OfficeVision/VM also supports the transparent exchange of WordPerfect Office scheduler requests and PROFS and OfficeVision calendar requests.

WP Office uses standard network/communication protocols to bridge dissimilar operating systems. Once the link has been established between these platforms, users of each platform can take advantage of any gateway services provided by the other platforms. For instance, if a DOS user needs to communicate with a user on Bitnet, and if WP Office for UNIX is available, the DOS WP Office user can simply send the message through the UNIX-based SMTP gateway. Likewise, users of platforms other than DOS can access the DOS-based PROFS gateway for mail and scheduler communication with PROFS users.

CALENDAR & SCHEDULER

The current implementation of WP Office calendar and scheduler functions is handled by two distinct programs (Calendar & Scheduler)[2] which are closely integrated. The Calendar program is a file-based, personal program for organizing appointments, to-do items, and reminder notices. The Calendar program includes a full featured auto-date programming function for entering recurring events, as well as an alarm function to notify the user at the time of the appointment.

The Scheduler program maintains a correlated record of the appointments entered into the Calendar program. Each of the defined Mail users on the network also has access to the Scheduler program. In addition, resources (conference rooms, projectors, etc.) can be defined within the Scheduler system. The resource owner is responsible for accepting or rejecting those events for which the resource is scheduled. The Scheduler program automates the process of scheduling an event. It checks for available meeting times, lists available resources, notifies participants (both users and resource owners) of the upcoming event, allows users to accept or reject schedule requests, allows the organizer of an event to easily track acceptance/rejection status of the request, and performs many other related functions.

DIRECTION & SUMMARY

WPCorp feels strongly that calendaring and scheduling functions are as fundamentally important to the business community as electronic mail is. Electronic scheduling and electronic mail share much in common—they can and should co-exist. By utilizing the same message transport as Mail, the Scheduler program can easily extend into all of the same environments as Mail. WPCorp's mail, calendaring, and scheduling functionality are being enhanced simultaneously in order to provide a truly integrated office automation system.

The major technological obstacles to the successful implementation of a computer-based time and resource management system are being removed with the introduction of notebook and palmtop computers, more functional network operating systems, and better application software. The non-technological obstacles of culture, habit, indifference, etc., will soon be all that remains to be overcome.

---

[2] The Macintosh version of WP Office features both the calendar and scheduler functionality in a single program.

Calendaring and Group Scheduling

Donald S. Campbell
President
Campbell Services Inc., Publishers of *OnTime*

Setting the Stage...

A strong case can be made that **group scheduling** is the first and most obvious of all Groupware.

By definition, Groupware means software that serves the group and makes the group as a whole more productive and efficient in whatever task in which that group is engaged. And while each individual group's mission in life may vary and even be substantially different, and therfore have different needs, there is one common denominator, one common need , that every group in the world has: **they need to meet with each other.** All groups have the need to schedule group meetings! The challenge is to accomplish this task in the shortest time and the most efficient way possible. A network, Groupware, solution is the natural and obvious solution.

A simple illustration points out the frustration and complexity of scheduling a meeting with three or more people. I want to schedule a meeting with person "A" and person "B" for one (1) hour. I call "A" and we find common time availability for tomorrow at 10 a.m. - I then call "B'" and he is tied up at 10 a.m. but is available at 1 p.m. I call back "A" and he is out to lunch. Later in the day, "A" calls back but can't make 1 p.m. time and so it goes. Trying to coordinate the calendars of three or more people is a test of Job's patience. As the number of persons attending the meeting increases, the frustration and complexity grows geometrically. May the fates smile favorably if I (or rather my secretary) have to schedule a meeting for 10 or 15 people!

The Problems...

There are basically two problems associated with group scheduling. The first problem can be summed up in a simple but profound question: *How do I determine common time availability?* In order for a group scheduling tool to work, it must represent, in a readily understood graphical interface, the consolidated blocks of time when the people with whom I plan to meet are available. I must be able to overlay my calendar on theirs and quickly and easily determine a time when all of us (or most of us) are free to meet. (I'll settle for **most** people being at my meeting, rather than not having a meeting at all).

The second problem is this: *If everyone is not willing to use the calendar/group scheduler, we're all in trouble!* Unless everyone on the system is willing to use the system, it will not support a group scheduling function. **People on the system have to use it.** And there are many reasons why people won't use a system...it's cumbersome, it's not DOS, it's not Windows, I don't understand it, I don't like meetings, it's not (some other product)....ultimately objections must be overcome, either by executive dictate, or preferably by choice, but **usage** is the goal.

A Successful System...

A group scheduling system is successful if it promotes the widest (ideally, everyone) possible usage. In building **OnTime**, Campbell Services Inc. (**CSI**) began with the conviction that *"Even an Executive"* should be able to use it. The reality is that the "executive" attitude toward software applications is typical of most end-users: don't waste my time; don't give me a complex program; don't force me to read the manual; give me some immediate gratification the first time I try it.

CSI created **OnTime** in the single-user format before developing the network version. Our philosophy of design was centered around the belief that if an executive is comfortable with it, we would achieve the highest level of usage. The single most important criteria applied to our product was **ease of use.** Following a close second in the learning stage: **instant gratification.**

These same standards have been incorporated into the formulation of our network versions; in fact, the group scheduling function within the network version of **OnTime** is the only visual distinction between that and the single-user version. We have held to the view that for a group scheduling software application to be effective, it must be universally used. For everyone to use a group scheduler, it must be (1)easy, and (2) gratifying within moments of installation.

The *OnTime* Solution...

Calendaring is built on two major scheduling components: appointments and to-do lists. A good calendar must satisfy these two requirements. **CSI** chose to concentrate on these two elements, and these two only, and do them extremely well. Others have elected to add contact managers, phone books and notepads, creating what the industry calls Personal Information Managers (PIMS). *OnTime* is not a PIM. It is a calendar/group scheduler.

In the network versions of *OnTime,* to-do lists are subordinate to the appointment function, which is taken to a higher level with the group scheduling capability: the natural extension of managing one's own appointments is the creation of a group appointment or meeting. How, then, is the first problem, determining common time availability, addressed.?

Common time availability in the group scheduling function of *OnTime* is presented in a consolidated graphic view of both the appointments and free time blocks of all those invited to the meeting. By tagging the names of individuals from the network users list, I'm able to call up a screen which combines their individual calendars into one weekly or monthly view. I then select an open day or hour, add my note and transmit the meeting announcement to their personal calendars. An on-screen window advises each of them that I've scheduled a meeting date and time. An RSVP feature enables me to confirm later whether (a)they've received my message, (b)received but not yet replied, and (c) received and replied "attend" or "not attend".

The second problem, how to get everyone to use the system, is addressed through its demonstrated utility. **CSI** has concentrated on making *OnTime* as simple and uncomplicated as possible, with almost instant success in a first-time user's efforts to schedule a group meeting. Without this effortless experience in "making it work the first time", a groupware application becomes a hard sell. Most end-users will quietly ignore or resist management's instructions to use what they believe is a cumbersome piece of network software. And if senior executives refuse to adapt to a product they believe is unfriendly, the rank and file have another reason to avoid using it.

Ease of use also translates into a platform of preference. In most group environments, it's unlikely that 100% of end-users are DOS oriented or that 100% are Windows oriented. For the next few years, it's going to continue to be a mix. Which is why *OnTime* ships its network versions together...both DOS and Windows can be loaded on the network and they communicate with each other. An end-user may have either and be able to schedule group meetings with anyone else on the network, irrespective of which platform any other end-user chooses.

Successful implementation of group scheduling software must, at least for now and the foreseeable future, allow users **at will** to select their platform of choice. Similarly, the viable products will also support OS/2, MAC and Unix operating systems...development directions being charted by **CSI**. This is clearly another spoke in the wheel of utility, because it acknowledges the essential need of the end-user to make the personal choice of how they want to manage that most personal of all information tools...their calendar.

The Expanded Solution...

Beyond the elements already acknowledged as fundamental to effective group scheduling, there are a number of ancillary issues.

Security

A successful group scheduling application must offer users the ability to **privatize** their calendars. With *OnTime,* security or privacy rights are protected by designating which network users, if any, are privileged to read the details of your calendar; otherwise, they see only that you have "an appointment".

Reconciliation

Reconciliation becomes an issue when an user has more than one installation of the program. A laptop or palm top that's been travelling with you for several days will have new and/or modified appointments. If my secretary is modifying my desk top while I'm on the road, there's a potentially greater need for reconciliation between my network information and my stand-alone information. *OnTime* provides this function. Reconciliation will align both calendars with the same information.

Enterprise Computing

The emergence of Wide Area Networking (**WAN's**) applications is evidence that traditional corporate structures (i.e., isolated departments) are yielding to more innovative, interconnected, interdepartmental work groups. File Servers must be able to talk to File Servers. Meetings must be scheduled between departments as well as within departments. **Enterprise Computing** challenges groupware to support larger corporate environments. Consequently, **CSI** has made the commitment to develop an Enterprise version of *OnTime,* in the belief that a successful group scheduling application will not only work independently in such an environment, it will also provide linkage to whatever notebook, roladex, contact manager or phone book is loaded on the server.

Paper

Embracing a new technolgy of "calendaring" often is not easy for those who for years have relied on **paper** to keep them "on time". Recognizing that old habits are not always bad habits, but they can be limiting habits, **CSI** incorporated a print option into *OnTime* that enables the user to produce an attractive two-sided paper copy of their appointments and to-do list. This makes it possible to carry a current, daily record of your calendar in place of a laptop or palm top. Regretably, for those wedded to paper calendars, they deny themselves the versatility and efficiency of the *OnTime* program that sounds an alarm, schedules recurring events with one key stroke, gives them instantaneous access to every calendar from now until the year 2079 and a hard disk archive of all past appointments. If we believe that saving time equates with saving money, the efficiencies of a PC-based system are "cash in hand".

The Future...

I believe that my calendar is the window through which I begin to see my day. What I have to do and whom I have to see today awakens my mind in the morning. Tomorrow's calendar is on my mind as I fall asleep at night. Everyone has a calendar...in their mind, on paper, in their PC. It is a common human denominator that links us together.

As technology, programming and consumer expectations combine to forge new applications, I believe there will one day be a global calendaring and group scheduling capability. Four architects, five engineers and six lawyers will come together from as many different cities or countries to one place, carrying their palm top computers. On each computer will be a calendar (I expect it will be *OnTime*), that has scheduled their meeting, and that's miraculously linked to every other calendar on every other palm top, desk top and lap top computer in the world. Summit meetings and family reunions will be scheduled easily and reliably.

Group Scheduling, whether expressed as a vision of the future or a reality of the present, has emerged in a relatively short time as a priority need of the American, indeed, the international business community. The Fortune 1000 have identified the productivity losses and costs associated with trying to schedule group meetings as a growing problem requiring an immediate solution. **CSI,** its allies and competitors, believe the time has come to designate a separate category of software publishing to **Group Scheduling**, thereby assigning it the significance it has earned and giving it the prominence it deserves.

Scheduling and Group Decision Support Systems

Arnold B. Urken
SmartChoice Technologies
614 River Street
Hoboken, NJ 07030

Norman Hughes
Nordra Technologies, Inc.
13 Kilroy Road
Newton, NJ 07860

ABSTRACT

If group scheduling is to evolve into a groupware product, the next step in its development must be integration of decision support techniques for workgroup users on their desktops. Giving individuals the ability to contribute to workgroup decision making will provide incentives to make group scheduling part of everyday work. Some opportunities for linking scheduling and group decision making support are considered.

1 INTRODUCTION

Scheduling software has evolved from a product designed to allow individuals to keep separate calendars to a tool for coordinating group activity. Group schedulers now make it possible to obtain a global view of the allocation of personnel and other resources within an organization. This perspective makes it possible for everyone to plan and execute their work more intelligently.

But group scheduling is a social process that involves two types of conflicts that must be addressed if software is to be developed that meets user needs. The first type of conflict is between the individual and the group; the second form of conflict involves disagreements between and among subgroups within an organization.

If decision support is interpreted as the timely and easy provision of information to help users make decisions, then group decision support systems may be an obstacle to collaborative work. In fact, more information may overload users so much that even those who are inclined to share information will not rely on group scheduling to plan their work! But if decision support in scheduling software provides help with the process of reaching and maintaining a consensus, incentives will be created that attract users to constantly use the tool.

2 INCENTIVE COMPATIBILITY AND SCHEDULING

A fundamental problem of what social scientists call "mechanism design" involves designing social processes in which individuals share a common set of values that allows the process to work as expected. Some processes require a learning period in which individuals adjust their expectations and behavior. For example, in games that involve a choice between cooperation and non-cooperation, so-called "prisoner's dilemma games," repeated plays of the game can lead to an equilibrium, a collective pattern of behavior in which everyone would be worse off if they deviated from the status quo. Of course, if learning does not progress and distrust takes over, such games can deteriorate into outcomes in which everyone is worse off than they would have been if they had not acted selfishly and had compromised.[1]

How are these abstractions related to scheduling? First, individuals may not employ group schedulers even if their organizations provide them. In fact, this non-cooperative practice is not uncommon. Of course, in hierarchical working environments, superiors can ask users to employ a scheduler and adapt their behavior according to meeting arrangements dictated from above. Depending on the organization, this strategy may work, though implementation may entail costs such as increased turnover and decreased efficiency. Moreover, even if users comply by employing the scheduler, they may devise strategies that allow them to circumvent the controls.[2] For instance, depending on the job, a user might schedule meetings or commitments that supervisors cannot verify without incurring unacceptable costs.

Viewed as a prisoner's dilemma situation, inducing employees to use group scheduling is easier if everyone is treated as if they were a peer even if they aren't--and they know it. As a team building, quality management practice, taking account of the preferences of members of an organization doesn't cost much. Moreover, taking preferences into consideration does not necessarily imply that the consensus of a group should be binding on the initiator of a meeting. But if employees are normally treated as if they were peers for purposes of scheduling the time and place of a meeting, group scheduling should make this possible. This collaborative process should be looked at as a positive way of resolving conflicts by pooling information that can help the group function more effectively and efficiently. Clearly, without such information, the initiator of a meeting may choose a place or time that are simply not appropriate or feasible. In game-theoretic terms, everyone would be worse off than they would have been if all parties had compromised by planning meetings collectively.

The methodology used to provide support for the collective decision making process must be implemented so that users do not have to become experts in decision theory or wade through screens of data.[3] Decision making methods do make a difference, but the differences musts be communicated in the context of decision tasks that motivate users to access the software.

If this non-traditional type of decision support is provided, group schedulers can play a constructive role in resolving con-

---

1. If the lack of trust becomes extreme and compromise is avoided, this form of behavior can devolve into a game known as "chicken," in which options for trust and collaborative behavior no longer exist.

2. For a description of how workers can adapt to electronic media to avoid management controls, see Dumais et al, 1988.

3. See Urken, 1988.

flicts to facilitate cooperative work.

3 PREMEETING PLANNING

Conflict resolution is a part of organizational learning and learning about work schedules is perhaps the key aspect of work activity. Normally, scheduling is conceived as something that stops once individuals have committed themselves to a meeting. But the realities of premeeting planning entail possibilities for taking account of employee ideas to improve meetings.

Once a meeting is established, for instance, unanticipated conflicts may need to be resolved. An existing meeting may have to be postponed or cancelled because a key person or a group of attendees must change their priorities. Scheduling software should make these changes possible.

Even without such contingencies, the meeting itself might be improved by doing asynchronous work online. The agenda and the ordering of the agenda might be clarified so that attendees are prepared to make efficient and effective use of meeting time. If meetings involve repetitive decision tasks, templates can be developed to allow attendees to reach consensus about some issues to be addressed face-to-face. In fact, consensus might be reached about all or substantial number of issues to make the meeting unnecessary!

If group schedulers develop in this way, the challenge for designers will be to create templates tailored for decision tasks that organizations face every day. In such products, support for the process of making group decisions will be the norm, not the exception.

References

Dumai, S. et al. 1988. Computers' impact on productivity and work life. **Proceedings of the IEEE/ACM Conference on Office Information Systems**, pp. 88-95.

Urken, A.B. 1988. Social choice theory and distributed decision making." **Proceedings of the IEEE/ACM Conference on Office Information Systems**, Palo Alto: IEEE, pp. 158-68.

Messaging and Mail Enabled Applications for the Workgroup

Mark B. Smith

Manager, Messaging Technology

Intel Corporation

Recent announcements have shifted focus from simple desktop mail products to more powerful applications that can interface directly with a workgroup's mail network.

The companies and consortia on this panel represent the most influential players in the mail enabled applications marketplace. Together we are shaping the next generation of enterprise wide capabilities that will profoundly affect the way we all do business in the 90's.

This panel will take a look at the complex world of mail enabled applications, and offer perspective on the elements and advantages these applications will provide.

Introduction

Today most of us depend upon a mail capability to do our everyday work. At our desktop, we use a "mail client" application such as cc:Mail or Microsoft mail that allows us to create, read, and respond to our mail. These applications communicate to a mail server or "Post Office" that stores and exchanges the mail with other users.

Several new applications that use the mail network are under development. These applications are not meant to replace the basic mail capability, but rather to extend the mail capability outside of the simple exchange of text.

These products are known as "Mail Enabled Applications", because they use the mail network to communicate and exchange information with other mail network users.

This panel will take a look at the mail enabled applications, as well as the elements needed to support them in the workgroup and on the company mail network.

Mail Enabled Applications

Mail enabled applications use the mail network as a "transport", or conveyance mechanism, to another user's mailbox. Many of these applications are currently under development, and can be categorized into two types of applications: existing applications that are being "mail enabled", which allows them to send information directly to another user via the mail network, and "accessory" or "boutique" applications that provide additional mail capabilities.

Mail Enabling Non-Mail Applications

Today, when using a word processor or spreadsheet we use a printer connected to the file server for output. If we need to send this information to someone else we either put the output in an interoffice mail envelope, or "Fax" it if it's more urgent. Wouldn't it be nice to just "mail it" from within Microsoft Word or Borland's Quattro Pro?

As these vendors mail enable their applications, that's exactly what you'll be able to do. One of your menu choices will be to simply mail the output to another user. These interfaces will look very similar to the way you save or print your work today. And when someone mails their output to you, you'll be able to receive it without leaving the application you're in!

Accessory Mail Applications

It sure would help if I could schedule a meeting with my boss without having my secretary call his secretary, play phone tag, and then reach an agreement on when and where.

Or how about receiving a purchase order from a customer 1 minute after he enters it? Your company can make customer service a competitive advantage if you receive orders several days before your competitors do, and if your customers really need quick service you can have the product on their doorsteps before your competitor gets the P.O. in the mail.

If I'm going to be out of town on a business trip I would like to have my notebook computer call a *local* phone number and collect my mail, faxes, and voice mail messages while I'm out for dinner.

These examples of accessory mail applications are all currently under development. These applications perform a specific job and use the mail network to communicate information.

Scheduling products allow quick confirmation of a date, time, and place for a meeting. Electronic Data Interchange (EDI) provides for electronic communication of forms. Mail forwarding agents send your mail to another mailbox.

Many activities are all converging to mail enable these special applications:

Operating systems interfaces and tool kits supporting mail enabled applications are being developed, groupware products such as Lotus Notes are gaining widespread use, and the various mail networks in your company are being connected together and linked to public mail networks such as AT&T EasyLink and Compuserve.

Operating System Services

Obviously an application can't communicate with another system by itself. Normally, it communicates with other software that provides the connectivity needed to get the messages through. Up until now, there have been many different interfaces that weren't consistent on systems that weren't interconnected. Application developers had a tough time supporting several different networks, choosing which networks to support, and trying to ensure that their products work the same in all environments.

This problem is being dealt with by providing standard *Application Programmatic Interfaces* (APIs) that operate at different levels of abstraction. Some APIs provide high level, send and receive functions, while others provide a much lower level (and correspondingly more complex) interface to mail transport and routing layers. Names like VIM, MAPI, and XAPI current adorn these APIs. At this time, the permanent relationship between these 3 API definitions is not yet clear. It is expected that most groupware enabled networks will actually have software using all 3 APIs present and cooperating to support mail enabled applications.

Operating System Service Layers

Operating systems such as Microsoft Windows, IBM OS/2, DOS, and UNIX will offer "service layers" that support the needs of mail enabled applications. These service layers will provide a consistent interface that hides the complexity and differences of the various networks. The application will only need to call a standard interface that is always the same. This is kind of like always opening a file using the same call even though the disks are made by different manufacturers.

This service layer is critical to allow an explosion of the many personal productivity tools that will be built as mail enabled applications. Today, much of the development time for each application is debugging the different network environments. These service layers will relieve the applications developers so they can build their applications faster and easier.

Each operating system is very different. Because of this applications developers all customize their software for the particular operating system their application must run on. The mail enabled applications will tailor their communications in such a way that the local operating system can understand it and handle it properly. Although this must be done differently on different systems, such as UNIX versus Microsoft Windows, the *basic* functions such as sending and receiving messages will be the same.

Connecting to the Network

The operating system provides a mapping of the requests from the mail enabled applications to the mail network. To do this drivers supporting the various types of mail networks must be provided. The desktop operating system must keep track of configuration information and send and receive the mail messages as they arrive.

The paths used for network mail may not always be obvious. Perhaps the system is remote, and will use a wired or wireless modem. Or maybe the desktop system's link to the world is a FAX board. A sound board may provide a direct connection from a desktop PC to a voice mailbox.

The system interfaces will provide transparency for these various communications links. The mail enabled applications will be indifferent to the communications links, and the communications links will be able to carry a variety of data in addition to plain text mail. The local operating system will provide a critical service layer that joins these two elements in a "plug and play" fashion. Two mail enabled applications will be able to communicate, even if the two end systems are running different operating systems.

Middleware and the Backbone Network

Once the mail information, or *messages*, are sent from the local system, several networks may be crossed on the way to the destination mailbox on another system. In the typical office environment where groupware will provide the critical support for distributed computing, three particular types of networks will be involved most of the time.

The Frontbone Network

Generally, the user's mailbox is not actually on the desktop. One reason for this is that the desktop system may be turned off when mail needs to be delivered. A more historical reason has to do with the fact that many systems, even today, are single tasking in nature and cannot asynchronously receive information.

To counter these problems applications were distributed between the desktop, or "client" system and "server" systems containing shared resources. Software allows the distribution of computing tasks between the client and server systems. Sometimes this software is called "middleware", because it is between the "front-end" applications on the client system and the "back-end" software on the server system.

This front-end to back-end (FE-BE) software initially allowed transparent sharing of disks and printers. Applications weren't aware that certain resources were remote or shared. The second wave, or "generation" of this software is the groupware that draws us all to this conference. In addition to simple sharing of resources, today's groupware provides support for more robust collaborative functions like mail, scheduling, document, and interactive database applications.

The client and server machines are usually in close proximity to each other for performance reasons. Most often they share a common local area network. This network is typically a local, building, or floor backbone network. I prefer the term "frontbone" to contrast this local area network backbone from the wide area network backbone.

The Backbone Network

Not all of the users and systems we need to collaborate with are in our building attached to our frontbone network. To reach the users that are located at other geographical locations we need a different kind of connectivity. Early methods used point to point connections. Today most corporate networks use a backbone network to provide connectivity between the various sites.

The backbone network provides an independent network environment where a system on one local area network, or frontbone, can transparently communicate with systems on other frontbones.

When a server on one network needs to exchange information with a server on another network, the backbone is used. The software that implements this connection is often called "back-end to back-end" software (BE-BE). Today, most of the back-end to back-end implementations use proprietary software. In the case of mail enabled applications, open systems software implementing a standard known as X.400 is increasingly providing a common "lingua franca" used between heterogeneous servers.

The Public Data Network

Sometimes mail enabling applications are located in different companies. In this case a public, or "value added network" (VAN) is used. Examples of these public networks include AT&T's EasyLink, MCIMail, SprintMail, and Compuserve.

Because these networks must often relay information between an "on-net" user and a "off-net" user, priority has been placed on VAN interoperability. Today any of these networks can be used to send mail to any other network. Sometimes these networks serve as a relay between two private corporate networks. Increasingly, VANs are providing the most cost-effective and reliable method of exchanging text and binary mail between two private companies.

In the USA, the largest public network is not a VAN at all. The *Internet* is an informal, cooperative network made up of government, educational, and commercial groups. Although Internet usage dwarfs VAN traffic combined, delivery is not guaranteed and only text mail is supported. In the next few years, VAN traffic is expected to increase much faster than Internet traffic, but this increased traffic will generally be new business traffic mandating guaranteed delivery. Existing Internet traffic is not expected to shift to the VANs.

Industry Cooperation

It should be clear by this point that there are several elements, provided by many different vendors, that must all play together for mail enabled applications to work in today's enterprises. Industry cooperation is necessary because no one vendor can hope to provide all the needed elements.

The issues surrounding mail enabled applications are very complex and the concept of plug and play mail enabled applications, desktop and server platforms, middleware, and backbone connections, while very attractive, requires an immense amount of investment to become a reality.

The Electronic Mail Association (EMA) provides a critical forum bringing vendors, systems integrators, the press, analysts, and users together. The EMA provides a neutral environment for education, cooperation, and sometimes, healthy debate and controversy. Other standards groups, such as NIST and the XAPI Association are also dedicated to ensuring interoperability across computing platforms.

Summary

Mail enabled applications won't replace our basic mail capability. Rather they are an exciting family of new capabilities that will enhance the way we conduct business. These applications will be built on top of the existing mail capability we already depend on to conduct business.

These applications will be the first true "enterprise wide" applications, made possible by interconnection of existing heterogeneous mail networks coupled with the availability of the mail enabled applications themselves.

The majority of these applications will be deployed at the workgroup level, running locally. Over time, these workgroups will be transparently interconnected using open systems protocols. We will all be able to take advantage of the best of both worlds - the proprietary richness of client applications, coupled with the "plug and play" benefits of open systems based connectivity.

400

Messaging—An OS View
Rick Segal

Operating System Objectives

☞ **Robust**
☞ **Leverage**
☞ **Migration**
☞ **Growth**
☞ **App to App**
☞ **Peer to Peer**
☞ **System to System**

Messaging - An OS View

Microsoft

OS Examples

- VMS
- SUN
- APPLE
- Microsoft

_____

_____

_____

_____

_____

_____

_____

_____

_____

_____

_____

_____

_____

_____

_____

_____

Microsoft

How come in the OS?

- **Native functionality**
- **Leverage the OS code**
- **Developer Requests**

Microsoft

The Wrong Way

- **Closed**
- **Weird Code**
- **Locked into One Vendor for everything**
- **Lowest Common Denominator**

_____
_____
_____
_____
_____
_____
_____
_____
_____
_____
_____
_____
_____
_____
_____
_____
_____

Microsoft

The Right Way

- **Standards based**
- **Open**
- **Extendible**
- **Optional**

Messaging - An OS View

Microsoft

The Relationship Between E-Mail and Workgroup Computing

Ken Einstein, Borland International, Inc.

The goal of workgroup computing is to make it as easy as possible for teams of users to share information and data with other people. Today, the sharing of data created in desktop applications is primarily limited to sharing files on a network or the infamous "sneaker net" method of walking a disk down the hall.

Traditionally, e-mail and productivity applications have been treated as separate functions given the heterogeneous nature of today's computing environment. Organizations are riddled with a multitude of mail systems, computing platforms, network operating systems and operating environments.

There are several new approaches to integrating electronic mail and messaging within the workgroup environment to improve productivity and to facilitate sharing of information. The success of these approaches requires a high level of interoperability. Achieving this requires vendors to work with one another to enable their products to interoperate so that users may work together seamlessly.

Mail-enabled Applications

Traditionally, an e-mail user shares information by attaching a file created in an application such as a word processor or spreadsheet to a mail message. The recipient detaches the file from the message and imports it into the appropriate application. This approach reduces user productivity since it requires the user to repeatedly exit and reenter the application where they actually do their work.

One solution is to mail-enable an application so that a user may share data or information without leaving the application. The user highlights the information to be shared and then uses a mail command from the application's menu to send the information. The primary benefit is that the sender doesn't need to exit the application and can resume working.

Some applications are presently mail-enabled, but they are only compatible with a specific mail system and cannot interact with the multitude of mail and message systems used in the real world. This is a problem since the workgroup of the 90s includes people within an organization, as well as outside contributors, increasing the variety of mail and message systems used.

Although mail-enabled applications make it easier to share data, they do little to advance workgroup productivity or facilitate collaboration sessions. The lack of interoperability severely limits a user's ability to share information with people using other systems. Currently, vendors are working to establish messaging standards that would make it easy for developers to create mail-enabled applications using a variety of mail and messaging transports.

Bulletin Board Systems

There are several public and private bulletin board systems that facilitate discussions among users. The primary benefit is that a cross-section of people can exchange ideas on a subject regardless of their specific function within an organization. However, these systems are not tightly integrated with popular productivity applications such as databases, spreadsheets and word processors and therefore are not useful for sharing significant amounts of structured data. In addition, these systems primarily use proprietary mail transports, thereby restricting who can participate in theses discussions.

Workgroup Architectures

Although, e-mail is well on its way to becoming a ubiquitous communication tool, man does not live by mail alone. For example, rather than receiving an e-mail message and then cutting and pasting the information into their application, some people prefer to have new data entered directly into their database or spreadsheet.

In addition, communication preferences change frequently. For example, if a colleague is traveling he might prefer to receive a fax updating him on the latest market research. Some workgroup products provide a fax capability, however, the person sending the information must know that the recipient is on the road and prefers a fax.

The most effective workgroup solutions will provide an architecture that enables users to transparently send information and data to other people and applications using a variety of communications tools such as multiple e-mail transports, fax, DDE, pagers etc...

In addition, a user should not need to know where each of his recipients are at a given moment, he should simply be able to send the information to a designated list of people. Therefore, a critical component in a workgroup architecture is an "information broker" who keeps an up-to-date directory of the different communications tools available to the users and who knows the preferred method of communication at a particular time. An information broker enables users to send information transparently and eliminates the need for a user to manually send the same information in a variety of ways.

Summary

The future of e-mail and the success of workgroup computing are closely intertwined. An effective workgroup computing solution depends upon how easy it is for a user to share information and data with a wide range of people and applications. This requires a cross-section of vendors to work together to provide a high degree of interoperability across multiple mail and messaging systems, operating platforms, network operating systems and applications.

COMMERCIAL MULTIMEDIA GROUPWARE

Earl Craighill

Network Information Systems Center

SRI International

Many commercial workstations and high-end personal computers are providing acquisition, storage and presentation capabilities for multimedia information. Furthermore, a number of products allow simultaneous interaction of multiple users sharing and manipulating multimedia information at remote locations. These initial commercial products represent a diversity of philosophical approaches to sharing presentations (commonly referred to as "shared screens") and controlling and synchronizing interactions among the participants.

This panel will include some of the leading commercial vendors and technology developers offering multimedia groupware products to discuss philosophies of shared screen and shared information presentation, coordination and synchronization; the role and expected arrival of multimedia exchange standards, and short-term strategies for multi-vendor information exchange in lieu of acceptable standards; and use of existing software applications in group environments versus special "collaboration aware" applications.

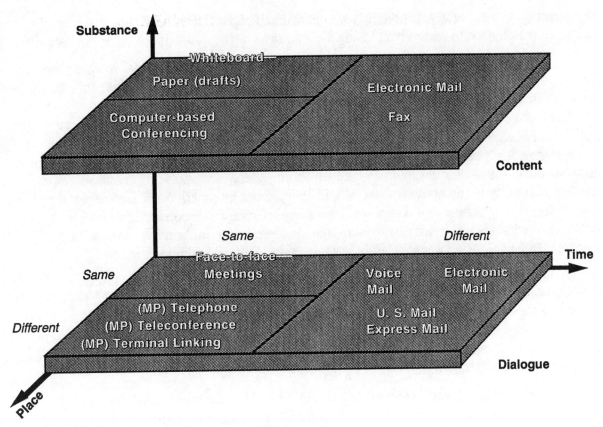

FIGURE 1. TYPES OF COLLABORATION

In order to sharpen the focus, we will discuss collaboration with respect to the framework shown in Figure 1. The usual classification of time/place (local-distant) is expanded to classify the *substance* of the collaboration to differentiate *content* (subject matter) and *dialogue*.

For instance, synchronous collaborative authoring of multimedia documents by geographically separated authors would have a multimedia document as the content and the participant's voice, graphical and pointing gestures as the multimedia *dialogue*. The content for simultaneous, multiuser VLSI chip development as a part of concurrent engineering practices would be the VLSI design. This panel will focus on such synchronous, computer-supported collaborative applications. However, we will also discuss linkages to multimedia composition systems.

1. WHAT IS THE NEED?

Personal computers have penetrated all segments of our society at work and at home. Although the end goal of computers is to assist individuals in working and interacting with each other, most of the work on human-computer interaction has focused on the often static interface between an individual and a computer. There is limited understanding today of how to use computers to enhance the activities of humans interacting in group settings. For example, the same computers that amplify the ability of individuals to write or calculate cannot usually be brought to a meeting. Consequently, people revert to pencil and paper for individual note taking, the results of which need to be fed back manually into the on-line transcript of the group activities.

The lack of computer support is the source of considerable additional work, delays, and even information loss in group-oriented information processing activities. This problem is more acute when groups are geographically dispersed, because of the inherent delays and other road-blocks incurred in sharing information remotely. Over the past few years, computer-supported collaborative work (CSCW) has emerged as a new area of interdisciplinary research. The research questions being asked relate to how groups can collaborate using computer technology: How should people work in groups to take advantage of the new medium? What software is needed to amplify group activities? How will group work be redefined to account for the interaction among people and computer technology? Clearly, our notions of group work should not be limited to such activities as face-to-face meetings while millions of people interact remotely (albeit somewhat inefficiently) by telephone, Fax, and computer mail.

On the technology side, the trend is toward more instantaneous communications like Fax, voice mail, electronic mail systems, electronic bulletin boards, and experimental computer-based conferencing systems. However, the majority of these systems have been designed to use the same mechanisms developed for individual-computer interaction. Existing systems that do address group interactions are often closed, proprietary systems that do not interoperate with the wealth of existing information processing tools and applications.

Although collaboration technology (often termed "groupware") is not yet mature and many research issues remain unresolved, increasing market interest indicates that a carefully-selected, finely-tuned product in selected markets can be successful. Furthermore, introduction of collaboration technology into user communities will both enhance our understanding of the requirements of distance groupware and increase market demand by providing a real instance of a useable first step. A successful strategy should build on an entry-level capability, adding new features as demand builds and technological issues are resolved.

2. SHARED SCREENS AND SHARED INFORMATION

Another important concept of the collaboration model is defining the *shared workspace* and its relationship to a user's private workspace. The three types of shared workspace support are: (1) message passing such as electronic mail and object-to-object messages, (2) shared storage such as shared memory, network files systems, and distributed databases, and (3) shared processing such as shared applications. The shared workspace is distinguished from private workspaces by *agreements and coordination* as follows.

Message Passing

All participants agree to a management policy. Local processes on each workstation are responsible for explicitly coordinating the behavior among all participants.

Shared Storage

All participants must agree to use common data structures. Local processes on each workstation delegate coordination of access to the common store and maintain a consistent state to a (logically) central process.

Shared Processing

All participants agree on the set of tools that will be used during the collaboration and the format of the tool inputs and outputs. Local processes on each workstation delegate to a (logically) central process the coordination of access to the tools and synchronization of the state of all tools (if replicated).

With respect to these three methods of workspace sharing, how should the presentations (views) to the participants be shared---share everything (WYSIWIS) or filtered presentations, mixture of private and shared workspaces, Does the presenter control all details of the presentation (necessitating presentation synchronization), or just offer " shared information" with individual receiver control of the presentation? How can the presentation be coordinated and synchronized using these three methods?

3. INFORMATION SHARING AND STANDARDS

People interact with one another by sharing information, an activity that may assume various forms. People collaborating with one another may establish a dialogue in real time in which visual or aural information is shared. When all the participants of a dialogue are in the same room, both the information being shared (e.g., the gestures and voices of the conferees, drawings, and written notes) and the mechanisms used to convey and record such information (e.g., pens, boards, documents, notebooks, and recorders) play a role in the nature and progress of the meeting. Hence, the sharing of information in a real-time dialogue can involve the sharing of both information and information-handling mechanisms.

People may exchange messages over computer networks synchronously or asynchronously for the purpose of transmitting copies of the information required for their collaboration, but typically, there is no consistency among such copies. Ideally, information sharing should be accomplished by sharing a common store of information (e.g., a bulletin board), whose contents can be accessed, but, again, it is difficult to maintain such a common store over large distances with multiple vendor hardware and software.

Figure 2 shows the relationship between three different factors that contribute to collaboration.

- *Internetworking Infrastructure*--The interconnection of computers to allow exchange of data.

- *Heterogeneous Information Exchange*--the standardized exchange of information between different hardware and software applications

- *Semantic Dialogues*-- The two-way interactive exchange of semantic knowledge between people supported by computer/communication systems and also between people and computer processes (such as databases).

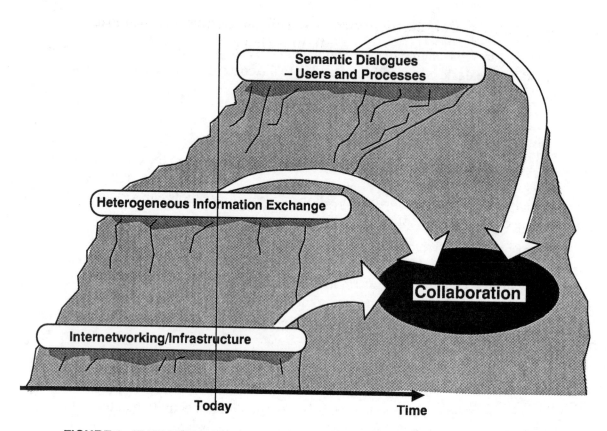

FIGURE 2. EVOLUTIONARY PLATEAUS IN WIDE-AREA INFORMATION SHARING

Each of the factors is shown as a plateau evolving in time. The progression along each plateau is closely linked to the development of standards. We are currently well along the internetworking plateau because of the strong standardization efforts. Progress in heterogeneous information exchange is hampered (and leads to the quantum step between plateaus) by the standardization process. Semantic dialogue exchange between heterogeneous programs is a research topic and beyond the scope of this discussion.

The panel will address specific questions with regard to this model.

Internetworking--Is the current (inter)networking structure adequate for commercial collaboration applications? Can you reach sufficient numbers of people with current and (near term) projected networks? Will Narrowband ISDN be satisfactory, or must we wait for BISDN? Since video is a key bandwidth driving factor, have we learned enough to say we don't need another (computerized) videophone?

Heterogeneous Information Exchange--How much compatibility is enough to sustain a commercial collaboration segment? What is the balance between innovative, collaboration-aware (but likely unique) applications and those that conform to (slowly emerging) standards? Perhaps, all we need is a collaborative wrapper around existing stand-alone applications...

Multimedia Communications: An Infrastructure for Remote Collaborations

Sudhir R. Ahuja
AT&T Bell Laboratories
Holmdel, NJ 07733

ABSTRACT

Collaborations at a distance have become more viable recently with the deployment of integrated networks such as ISDN, the availability of affordable video codec chips and wider internetworking of LAN's.

There are many different directions being pursued by researchers and companies based on their previous strengths, such as extensions to Electronic Mail, Videoconferencing, Remote Screens, Fax, etc. We believe that effective remote collaborations requires *Integrated Multimedia Communication*, not extensions in just one media. Further, that both asynchronous and synchronous interactions have to be supported in an integrated fashion.

INTRODUCTION

Collaborations, in general, involve multiple interactions over a period of time. In any real inter-personal interaction multiple media is used
in a very dynamic ways. For example, in a face to face conversation we look away many times, stop listening, think for a while, even leave and rejoin conversations, get interrupted, etc. If one examines the underlying connections in various media supporting such a conversation, they are many and get established and broken often.

Further, in most conversations we easily transition between different media, voice, gestures,etc. as well as easily transition between synchronous interaction and asynchronous interaction (like passing notes and working individually). We claim this flexibility and richness of communication is necessary to facilitate effective collaborations.

USER MODEL

In real collaborations we do not even conciously think of communications as an issue. Other issues, such as coordination, goal definition, workflow , etc. dominate our concerns. This is because we take communications for granted and we all have a common user model for communication amongst people (we address each other by names, we meet in places, we use voice as primary control media for initiating and maintaining a conversation, we have an agreed to language for exchange of information, etc.). We have chosen to support this user model as closely as possible in distance collaborations. So collaborations are amongst people (not phone numbers, or filenames or pathnames). They happen in places, called the virtual meeting rooms, and these rooms support interaction in multiple media with dynamic connections.

Further, to accommodate interactions over long periods of time that include interruptions, people leaving and joining, there must be some underlying support for maintaining consistency and providing persistence to the collaboration. In real collaborations this is provided by physical resources such as rooms, documents, white boards etc. In a distance collaboration model this translates to long lived connections and binding of connections to a virtual meeting room.

SHARING MODEL

We believe collaborations to be close interactions between people and objects (physical as well as information). In practice, most objects, e.g. a piece of paper or book, do not change their form because two persons try to use it. The sharing of objects is generally governed by physical characteristics of the object. A chalkboard can be used by one person or many because it is physically convenient to do so, whereas it is quite hard for two persons to write on a small piece of paper simultaneously. We categorize shared objects (these can be programs, databases, etc.) to be multi-user or single-user instead of collaboration-aware or not. Objects are shared in virtual meeting rooms by sharing of their Input/Output information. This is normally called collaboration-unaware model of sharing. This model assumes single instance of objects. We separate the issue of *replication* of objects as being distinct from sharing. In this model of sharing communication support for single-user or multi-user applications are similar and easliy handled through the virtual meeting room concept.

CONCLUSION

Communications is one of the key issues in enabling remote collaborations. We believe that *Integrated Multimedia Communications* is essential for supporting effective collaborations at a distance.

GROUPWARE AND MULTIMEDIA

Position Statement

David Gedye
Sun Microsystems Laboratories Inc,
and SunSoft Inc.
2550 Garcia Ave.
Mountain View, CA. 94043
gedye@sun.com

INTRODUCTION

Advanced development at Sun in the areas of groupware and multimedia has focused strongly on the real-time capabilities of these technologies. We have built desktop video conferencing systems that are completely integrated into our workstations and networks, and have developed multiuser collaborative applications to compliment the live media. The positions I outline below are based on experiences with these on-line systems.

MEDIA CONSIDERED AS GROUPWARE

There are three obvious ways in which computer technology can help a group get its job done. It can:

> Improve the efficiency of information sharing;
> Improve the processes by which groups operate;
> Improve the opportunities for, and richness of, communication.

The first of these areas is so well established that it is often not considered 'groupware' at all. Fax, shared file systems, and electronic mail are a standard part of the information infrastructure of modern companies.

A great deal of the effort of groupware developers has gone into the second of these areas, with very mixed results. While certain successes have been reported with group decision support systems for well defined tasks in structured environments, this represents only a fraction of the group work that goes on in most enterprises. Experiences with tools that attempt to capture the semantics of casual group interactions have been almost uniformly negative.

The third area is where live multimedia has a significant role to play -- and not just by adding pictures to a telephone connection. Fully integrated multimedia has the capability of creating and maintaining a shared experience for geographically separated team members.

GROUPWARE CONSIDERED AS MEDIA

The main challenge to software designers attempting to fully integrate digital audio and video is how to teach their systems about time. While it is true that 'real-time' operating systems have existed for more than a decade, these have focused primarily on providing guarantees that certain operations will be performed within a certain period of time. The realistic support of media requires that operating systems should embody notions of throughput, synchronization, and in the case of live media, latency.

It is our belief that system support for live groupware shares these requirements, and in this way we consider the inter-process communication required to support groupware as just another form of media.

The similarities in the support of live media flowing between one computer and another and multi-user application updates include:

Performance requirements are dictated by human factors. If the user cannot detect that two pieces of data (say the audio and video for a conference, or the pointer movement and the highlighting of the object under the pointer) are not perfectly synchronized, then nothing has been lost. On the other hand...

End to end performance measures are the most important.
Data captured by a camera, a microphone, a mouse, a keyboard, or any other input device must be processed, transmitted across the network, and displayed for other users as rapidly and as accurately as possible. This requires that device drivers, libraries, schedulers, network protocols and routers, and the applications themselves all recognize 'time-critical' data, and process it appropriately.

Both require flexible tradeoffs between latency and synchronization.
Latency and synchronization can often be traded against each other, and for the transmission of both media and groupware updates different situations demand different tradeoffs. For example, even though accurate synchronization between a speaker's lips and voice is desirable, we have found that if there is a large unavoidable delay in the transmission of video, many users of our conferencing system prefer to have the audio transmitted as fast as possible even though this results in noticeable failures of lip-synch. Similarly, groupware applications that support very high amounts of interactivity may wish to favor low latency over accurate synchronization. Moreover, synchronization between a media event and a groupware update is something that may or may not need to be enforced. *'See this word I'm circling'* obviously requires synchronization, whereas *'So, what about them Giants?'* probably does not.

There are however a couple of differences between the system implication of live multimedia and live groupware that need to be considered:

Media data is usually generated at predictable timed intervals, whereas collaborative application updates are often caused by user activity, and hence are not predictable.

Late media data can often be discarded, but a late application update usually must be applied to maintain consistency.

THE CHALLENGE FOR AN OPEN MULTIMEDIA ARCHTIECTURE

Existing multimedia environments such as QuickTime from Apple are open both above (to application developers) and below (to media hardware providers). They allow individuals to author and play back rich combinations of images and sounds.

The next generation of systems must be open in another direction. It must support the live exchange of media between people in a group for the purposes of communication, and it must support the integration of collaborative applications into this framework.

MANAGING MULTIMEDIA COLLABORATIONS

P. Venkat Rangan

Multimedia Laboratory, CSE Dept.

University of California, San Diego

La Jolla, CA 92093-0114

1. INTRODUCTION

Technological advances are making electronic devices with video and audio digitizing capabilities pervasive. Coupled with advances in broadcast technologies and the emergence of high-bandwidth telecommunication networks, these technological advances are revolutionizing computers to support digital multimedia. In the short term future, the power of computers unleashed on digital video and audio will trigger a wide spectrum of multimedia collaborative applications that can have a long standing effect on day to day activities. Development of such multimedia collaborative applications involves (1) modeling the behavioral semantics of several different types of collaborations, (2) mechanisms for instantiating collaborations, and (3) techniques for enhancing the effectiveness of computer supported collaborations.

2. MODELING COLLABORATIONS

Technological advances in digital audio and video processing, coupled with the availability of high speed networks, are expected to transform computer supported multimedia collaboration into an effective medium for concurrent engineering tasks. There are a wide spectrum of such tasks that involve structured collaboration among individuals, ranging from simple meetings and conferences to classrooms and examinations, and from corporate negotiations, work flow tasks, and team design endeavors to courtroom hearings, each with its own unique set of requirements for media communication.

The simplest of collaborations involve exchange of media information among all their participants, with media exchange being either synchronous (as in a telephone conversation), or asynchronous (as in electronic mail). Whereas synchronous collaborations involve contemporaneous exchange of media information, asynchronous collaborations are characterized by recipients' discretionary delays after transmission by senders. During such intervening delays, the media information in transit may have to be managed by servers (such as storage and mail servers). Traditionally, collaborations have been classified into these two categories, and different paradigms have been used by the system to manage them, thereby necessitating separate programming as well as user interfaces for their management. Unification of both synchronous and asynchronous collaborations into a single paradigm permits co-existence of both types of collaborations within a single multimedia application, and even the same collaboration may sometimes be synchronous and at other times asynchronous, shuttling from one to another depending on users' participation schedules.

Structured collaborations, whether synchronous or asynchronous, usually involve diverse modes of participation by their various participants. For instance, a session at a convention usually involves a sequence of presentations by its speakers and questions posed by its attendees, each of which must be permitted by its chairperson. A classroom is similar to a conference session except that it has only one speaker, who also serves as the chairperson. An examination, on the other hand, involves a proctor and examinees, with communication restricted to that between the proctor and examinees, but absolutely no communication among examinees themselves. Negotiations among corporate groups may involve both intra-group and inter-group communication, which may need to be separated for purposes of confidentiality. If such a wide range of collaborative activities are to be supported using computer systems, a common software framework with a sufficiently rich semantic expressibility is essential.

In order to illustrate the need for a collaboration model, consider a panel session at a conference (such as this one), that involves prepared presentations by a set of panelists followed by on-the-fly questions and answers between panelists and attendees. Whereas the prepared presentations by panelists' can be pre-recorded (and hence may need to be handled as asynchronous collaborations), the question-answer period requires contemporaneous participation of panelists and the attendees. During his or her presentation, a panelist alone has the right to transmit media information, whereas during the question-answer period, any participant may transmit. It is further desirable to permit panelists to join the panel at any time of their choice prior to the start of the panel. Modeling such collaborations, which involve multiple media exchanges (some of which maybe serial and some of which overlapped) and dynamic changes in access rights, is a research challenge.

3. INSTANTIATING COLLABORATIONS

Instantiating collaborations involve establishing media transmission channels as well as initiating various applications (such as, shared workspace, bulletin board, etc.) that characterize the collaboration. Increasing network bandwidths and improvements in compression technology will make it feasible to support real-time video transmission over metropolitan area networks. Developing media transmission protocols, which can guarantee synchronous transmission of multiple media streams, has been the focus of several research projects. Initiating shared workspace applications, and coordinating access to them is central to managing the progress of collaborations. Furthermore, designing new collaboration-aware applications as well as using existing applications in a collaborative environments provides quite a few challenges. Furthermore, heterogeneous hardware environments existing in different organizations necessitates extensive negotiation-based mechanisms for establishing and controlling progress of collaborations.

4. INTEGRATING VIRTUAL REALITY WITH COMPUTER SUPPORTED COLLABORATIONS:

Most computer supported collaboration management systems available today are very rudimentary and provide only a simple abstraction of a virtual meeting room in which each participant can view images of other participants. They usually use a bridging system in which centralized multimedia bridge mixes media streams received from different participants in a conference. Each participants receives and displays media streams transmitted by all other participants. Individual media streams are mixed together to form composite media streams suitable for playback at display devices. However, our experience with such conferencing systems indicates that the absence of face-to-face interactions will make it difficult for such conferencing systems to be preferred to real world meetings. In order to increase the effectiveness of information exchange between participants and to make computer mediated conferencing viable alternatives to real life meetings, it is necessary that collaboration management systems provide environments that closely emulate real world scenarios.

Integration of virtual reality, which involves the creation of panoramic, three-dimensional life-like video imagery and spatially distributed audio, with tele-conferencing systems yields tele-virtual conferencing systems that can enhance the effectiveness of computer supported collaborations. Different virtual environments are conducive to different types of real life interaction. For instance, in a computer mediated meeting between individuals, it is desirable for each participant to be presented with a view of the virtual meeting room, that emulates a physical meeting in most respects. In addition, the directional and iconic information about the positions of participants in the virtual meeting room can be used to emulate the exchange of audio between the participants in the meeting.

Creation of such virtual interaction environments requires that the system support stereoscopic video (which provides life-like imagery) and stereophonic audio. Stereoscopic video can be generated by alternately displaying left and right perspective (as seen by the left and the right eye, respectively), and using a stereo liquid crystal viewing device, synchronized with the monitor, that can channel the appropriate image to the appropriate eye. Stereo vision can be further supplemented by auditory systems that can combine audio streams emanating from each of the participants in a manner that enables the listener to perceive the location of the other participants. Development of such techniques has the promise to make tele-conferencing as a viable, effective, and possibly, more flexible alternative to real-world meetings and conferences.

5. CONCLUSIONS

In the recent past, emergence of digital multimedia technology have led tp the development of several computer supported multimedia collaborative applications. However, the science of building collaboration management systems, that can provide an effective, and possibly, more flexible alternative to real-life collaborations, is embryonic at best. The goal of research in collaboration management is to transform a workstation from a data processing unit to a versatile multimedia gateway to the rest of the world, thereby contributing towards the rapid ushering in of a new age of tele-personal interaction.

Commercial Multimedia Groupware

Terry Crowley
Bolt Beranek and Newman Inc.
10 Moulton Street
Cambridge MA 02138
crowley@bbn.com

1 Introduction

Multimedia groupware – e.g., real–time conferencing, desktop video, multimedia email – is a flashy and exciting area of growth. How are these areas developing and what is their impact going to be on your collaboration and communication environment?

Many of the barriers to collaboration that everyone experiences in their day–to–day affairs have little to do with these new technologies and the problems they solve. Often the problem is that the person you are dealing with does not have email or FAX or a connection to the Internet. Fortunately, this problem is disappearing rapidly. Other problems arise because of the difficulty of moving from one medium to another, e.g you need to print out that electronic memo and run it through the fax machine, or you have someone's email address but not their FAX number. Again, this situation is changing rapidly, and the technology exists to solve these problems today.

As has been historically true, these new technologies can be divided into asynchronous (like mail) and synchronous (like a phone call). Although technology allows some of these borders to slip back and forth (e.g. voice mail, fast delivery of FAX and email) the distinction between technologies that require the participants to be involved at the same time and technologies that allow them to work separately will continue to be great. In general, asynchronous technologies will have a much greater impact on the way people work – witness the migration of a synchronous communication channel – the telephone – to asynchronous use with the widespread use of voice mail. I will now look at a couple of these technologies, real–time conferencing and multimedia email, and discuss how they are developing and their potential impacts.

2 Real–Time Conferencing

For real–time conferencing (shared–screens) in the broad marketplace, the ability to use familiar applications is much more critical than the added bells and whistles provided by an application that was specifically designed for conferencing. The principal reason for conference–awareness, allowing multiple loci of control, is not something that the main body of users require (because interactions where the participants are not focused on the same area are usually asynchronous anyway). General–purpose mechanisms for providing feedback about what the other users are doing in a real–time conference (e.g., in the MCC Grove editor) are not particularly useful, because the interesting information is not WHAT the other participant is doing, but WHY he is doing it, and that information can not be provided automatically. This is true for asynchronous applications as well – it is less interesting to know that someone modified some document or program then to know why they modified it (and asynchronous groupware products need to provide mechanisms for passing along this information).

Specific audiences and application areas already use special–purpose systems for synchronous and asynchronous computer–supported collaborative work. That will continue to be the case in the real–time conferencing area. Special purpose real–time applications can address specific requirements (e.g. allowing different users different views or providing a structured interface to information about the activities of the other users).

3 Multimedia E–Mail

Multimedia Email provides the ability to mail documents that contain text, graphics, images, spreadsheets and voice. I usually reserve the term for systems that can display incoming messages in an integrated and quick way, rather than systems that simply provide the ability to add attachments to a mail message that can be passed off to some application for display (although that is a powerful and important utility).

The principal problem in wide–spread use of multimedia email is the lack of well–accepted document standards. Although there has been lots of effort put into defining standards for compound document interchange, these have not been well accepted in the industry. ODA continues to languish. SGML has made significant headway in some areas (particularly the military) but has not really penetrated the commercial marketplace for general document interchange. On the Internet, there has been recent work in defining a mail format for the interchange of compound documents (Multipurpose Internet Mail Extensions or MIME). This standard is useful for describing the data that you are moving around, but its native document structuring mechanisms are too poorly developed to be the solution to general interchange of compound documents (this is the same problem that X.400's document structuring standards – as opposed to message address and delivery – had in achieving wide–spread acceptance).

The current state of the commercial art is to provide translators from one format to another. This solution suffers from the problem that some translation may not be available or that the document models being translated between may be different enough (even if one is not necessarily inferior to the other) that the translation is not lossless.

This problem is especially annoying because the areas where current document models are lacking or diverge is exactly where some of the most interesting and important developments should come. This is in the area of providing facilities for reviewing and commenting on documents. In this area, the document model and editor need to support things like:

- quick access to where any changes are and an overview of all changes,
- the ability to switch back and forth between the original version and a change or comment,
- the ability to quickly integrate or discard a change or comment.

As with other technologies, multimedia email will also shift the border between synchronous and asynchronous communication. Compound documents will become compound multimedia presentations, with audio, video, text and graphics all synchronized to give the message with greater impact. Systems like BBN/Slate can already turn a multimedia message into a multimedia presentation with synchronized voice, video and graphics.

TRACK 5:
User Experiences

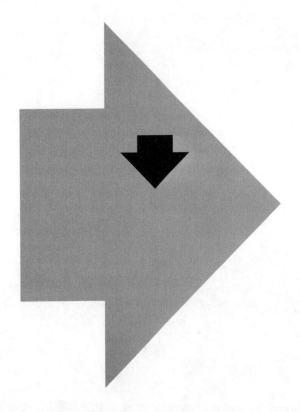

GROUPWARE IN A LAW OFFICE: A USER'S EXPERIENCES

Steve Wacker
PC Operations Analyst
Lane Powell Spears Lubersky
1420 Fifth Avenue, Suite 4100
Seattle, WA 98101-2338
206-223-7000

DETERMINING THE NEED

Choosing a groupware program for our law firm started out as a quest for "desktop organization" programs like appointment calendars, calculators and electronic rolodexes. I don't even know if the term "groupware" existed at the time, and I'm almost embarrassed to admit that E-MAIL wasn't a primary consideration for us either. We thought that E-MAIL wouldn't do much for us until we had distributed a significant number of workstations. Fortunately, because we purchased a groupware program that included E-MAIL, we realized its benefits very quickly.

One of our primary concerns was with our users' general level of computer expertise. Although the firm has a training facility and we require users to take classes before giving them access to applications, we wanted to find a program that was relatively easy to use. While this may sound rather obvious, I think end users are often overlooked when application programs are being considered and selected. While not as overused a term as "user friendly," I think "intuitive interface" probably runs a close second. Truly intuitive interfaces are few and far between.

We also determined that "ease of use" meant being able to access the program easily, and "pop-up" availability would be the most desirable. This seemed to point to programs which use TSR technology, if we could find one that was stable and didn't require massive amounts of memory. Our primary workstation configuration at the time was a 286-based PC with one MB of RAM.

Since we originally started looking for schedulers, calculators and rolodexes, we wanted to try and accomplish as much as possible with one program. At one time we considered purchasing one program for these "desktop" tools and a totally different program for E-MAIL. We're glad that we found one program which addressed most of our needs, because that meant we could minimize the effort spent on integrating and teaching separate programs.

One of the most significant factors we had to consider, however, didn't have to do with interface and features but with network configuration. At the time we had two file servers running NetWare 286. Since users on the two different servers would need to interact (send E-MAIL, make group appointments, etc.), we wanted a program that could work across multiple servers. Dedicating a server to run the application wouldn't get us very far, since NetWare 286 only allows one hundred connections per server. Even NetWare 386's ability to handle two hundred and fifty connections would, once the number of users grew large enough, limit how many people could access the program at one time.

This "available connections" problem in a multiple file server environment was solved by the program we selected in a simple but elegant manner. The program uses a special NetWare account to establish a connection for the duration of the E-MAIL exchange or group scheduling session, and then it closes the connection. I don't believe any other groupware manufacturer had this capability at the time.

Another concern was security. Although my perspective is from within the legal industry, my feeling is that implementing groupware in a law office offers some unique challenges in balancing security concerns against the need for access to information. We wanted a program that was secure enough to offer privacy but flexible enough to allow the groupware concept to work. We accomplished what we wanted through a combination of the configuration capabilities of the program and NetWare's access rights.

Once we realized that we wanted E-MAIL, we also wanted to remain flexible in terms of being able to connect and exchange messages with different systems. We determined that our primary need was for MHS compatibility. Most of the popular E-MAIL and groupware programs offer MHS compatibility or MHS gateways, so this wasn't really a problem.

TWO YEARS LATER

Not surprisingly, we have found that the most popular feature of the program we purchased is E-MAIL. Our current configuration offers instantaneous E-MAIL exchange amongst more than two hundred and seventy-five users logged in to three different file servers in two different buildings in Seattle. For remote E-MAIL capability we have installed an MHS gateway and an MCIMail gateway. The MCIMail gateway not only offers us connectivity to the outside world via MCIMail, but also offers connectivity to other systems such as the INTERNET for exchanging messages. E-MAIL has significantly enhanced communications, not only within the firm but also between the firm and the outside world.

After E-MAIL, the "electronic rolodex" feature is probably the most popular. One of the reasons this feature is so popular is the program's ability to have global data, personal data that can be accessed by others and personal data that can be password-protected. Since the program gives users the ability to cut-and-paste data between programs, everyone uses the "rolodex" feature not only to keep names and addresses (for insertion into letters created in WordPerfect) but also to store other information that previously needed to be retyped.

The personal appointment scheduler is used a great deal, for maintaining both personal and global scheduling information. We provide all users with access to each other's schedulers, so this feature is not "private," but I believe this is one of the reasons for its success. Attorneys, paralegals and secretaries all have the ability to access each other's schedules, which is very useful.

Curiously, the group scheduling feature is not used anywhere near as much. I believe this is due to a combination of not enough emphasis being placed on it during training and a lack of available time to explore its capabilities. One rather obvious thing that's easy to lose sight of is that everyone needs to keep their appointment scheduler current in order for a group scheduler to work. People generally don't like to change their work habits. It's not always easy to motivate people to use an electronic scheduler when they've used an appointment book for years.

In order to maximize the investment in technology, I believe management should play an active role in encouraging people to use available technology. I also believe that management should encourage and motivate users of groupware to try and find innovative ways to use it.

THE FUTURE

Who knows? Trying to predict the evolution of software is quite a challenge.

I believe that mail-enabled applications will become fairly common in the next few years. I also believe that E-MAIL standards will continue to evolve, but I doubt if one clear standard will emerge. I think MHS is probably as much of a standard as the industry will see.

I think the biggest challenge is to keep our minds open to the possibilities of groupware. Recent studies have indicated that all the money businesses have spent on technology in the last ten years hasn't really increased productivity. Groupware can go a long way towards solving this dilemma, because it can facilitate productivity by helping people to work together.

Electronic Group Calendaring: Experiences and Expectations

Beth Marcia Lange
Center for Strategic Technology Research
Andersen Consulting
100 S. Wacker Drive, Suite 900
Chicago, IL 60606
lange@andersen.com

ABSTRACT

Our organization began using an electronic group calendaring system in April, 1991. We found that there are two highly-related elements to the use of groupware: the set of features and capabilities these products provide, and the integration of these products into the corporate environment. The right set of features can make the use of groupware possible, while the basic ingredients for corporate adoption can maximize the benefit of groupware for an organization. Our experience provides an example of the steps to follow to successfully introduce groupware technology into an organization.

1 INTRODUCTION

It is not an easy task for organizations to adopt new technologies. There are many cited examples [Grudin, Ehrlich, Kiesler, Sproull] of the challenges presented to organizations including technical, social, and organizational issues. Our experience shows that introducing an electronic calendaring system into a corporate environment can be successful by providing these elements:

- Expected Uses: providing a baseline set of expected uses of the calendaring product

- Guidelines: establishing examples and guidelines for the social protocols of using the product

- Key Users: finding champions who lead by example and encourage adoption of the product

- Modifying Procedures: creating a process for modifying communication patterns and processes as styles of work change through use of the product

- Styles of Use: supporting the various styles of usage that will emerge.

This paper describes our experiences and findings, and identifies some requirements for group calendaring products.

2 EXPECTED USES

In April 1991 we began a pilot program to introduce the use of a Macintosh-based group calendaring product at our site. Our initial goal was to address the problem of coordinating the use of shared meeting room facilities. In addition, several people wanted to improve coordination and communication across the organization. We began our program with a core group of eighteen people and now support approximately seventy users.

One executive assistant had held the responsibility for scheduling the conference rooms. She maintained a paper calendar and coordinated the reservations. This system was ineffective as she was not always available and did not always have the necessary information for resolving conflicts.

Our goal was to replace the paper procedure with a more efficient and decentralized process, which we defined as the ability to carry out the process in a more timely manner and provide more information about the meetings scheduled. Through the use of electronic scheduling we hoped to eliminate the need for assigning a person to be responsible for this task.

3 PRODUCT FUNCTIONALITY

We selected On Technology's Meeting Maker™ product.** It is a network-based Macintosh desk accessory that allows individuals to maintain their personal calendars, propose meetings with other people, and access the calendars of shared resources, such as conference rooms.

** No endorsement of the product is implied by the author or the author's organization.

A block of time on a calendar can be scheduled in two ways, as meetings or as activities. A meeting has several attributes: a specific date (or series of dates if it is a recurring meeting), time, and duration, a meeting proposer (often the meeting sponsor), a list of proposed attendees, a location, a title which is displayed on the calendar, and an agenda. An activity is private to an individual's calendar and like a meeting is created for a specific date and time.

A user controls which meetings and activities are added to his/her calendar. While colleagues can invite a user to attend, the user chooses to accept or decline the invitation. The software does not prevent a user from scheduling overlapping events. Resources (such as conference rooms, computers, and audiovisual equipment) accept proposals automatically, on a first-come, first-served basis, and scheduling conflicts are not allowed.

A user may grant other users proxy privileges, giving them access to the grantor's calendar. The privileges may be read only, or read and write. A user can also control the degree to which a proxy can view activity details. A proxy user with write privileges can act on behalf of the grantor by proposing meetings and responding to proposals.

The product is based on a client/server architecture. A central server maintains the database, and distributes messages representing events and state changes, such as responses to proposals. Upon login, a user receives the current week's calendar from the server. Proposing a meeting requires server interaction, as well. For example, a proposer can suggest a meeting time and the server will indicate any attendee conflicts, although specific details are not provided. In "auto-pick," the server searches for a time when all of the proposed attendees are available.

4 GUIDELINES

While the product is versatile, we wanted to establish a common framework among all the users. We introduced the product by choosing a task that would motivate people to use it. We expected users to discover the multitude of product features on their own, as they used the product for reserving rooms.

We developed a four page document outlining the guidelines for using Meeting Maker. We wanted to encourage a consistent format for reserving rooms, which would provide sufficient information to anyone looking at the calendars. The document outlined the steps for viewing a resource's calendar and proposing a meeting to reserve it. Users were reminded that resources would not accept proposals for conflicting meetings and they were asked to negotiate conflicts through other means (telephone, electronic mail, voice mail etc).

The document included a glossary of terms used in the product (such as "activities," "auto-pick," "proxy," "resources," and "frequency"). It also included hints for interpreting icons and navigating around the calendar, a description of known bugs and product limitations, and the names of people to contact for help.

In addition to publishing the document we suggested that each user attend an informal demonstration of the product, at which time we reviewed the procedures, provided helpful hints, and entertained questions.

5 KEY USERS

We chose eighteen people to pilot the use of Meeting Maker. We selected people who most frequently reserved the meeting rooms, and we included the entire management team. These eighteen users represented a cross-section of the seventy people in two departments (Research and Technology Transfer). Included were one partner, four directors, four executive assistants, one part-time librarian, two network administrators, one business manager, four researchers, and one program development/marketer. All of these users had Macintosh computers in their offices; typical uses include word processing, building spreadsheets, preparing presentations, and using electronic mail. Everyone else in these two departments was informed of the new procedures and was asked to reserve meeting rooms through their executive assistants.

The current user base includes sixty-three people and seven resources (3 meeting rooms, 2 computers, 1 VCR, and 1 videocamera). Thirty-six users have Macintosh computers in their offices, the remaining 27 have other types of computers (Unix workstations or PCs).

6 USER FEEDBACK

The product does not provide tools for collecting data on usage patterns, such as frequency of use, number of meetings and activities scheduled, or communication patterns. So, instead, we relied on data collected from the users. After using the product for four months the original eighteen users completed an informal questionnaire about their uses of electronic calendaring. They answered up to twenty-three questions about their use of the product, frequency of use, significance of our procedures, meetings they propose, and use of activities. We collected data on styles of use, perceived benefits, suggestions for new features (as a way of exploring new ways in which people would use electronic calendaring systems), problems, and other comments. The remaining forty-five users were asked to submit comments on these topics in an informal manner.

7 MODIFYING PROCEDURES

We eliminated the meeting room paper calendars shortly after we started using Meeting Maker. Users' apprehensions about converting to the electronic system focused on product reliability and availability, not on the value of using electronic systems or the appropriateness of the procedures we established.

Traditionally, conference rooms were always booked on a first-come, first-served basis subject to change based on the priority of competing needs. This policy did not change when Meeting Maker was installed. Some users were initially concerned that meeting room reservations would not be based on the "right" priorities or that the process of conflict negotiation would not work as well under our new process. These concerns appear to be unfounded; users have not complained or experienced unsolvable problems. Users can view a room's calendar, and have access to all the relevant information about a scheduled meeting. [Ehrlich] describes a paper calendar maintainer's function as the "role of problem solver." In fact, we were able to eliminate the need for a single person to maintain the calendar. The electronic calendar provides distributed access to the information, removing the centralized control, which had provided no tangible functionality.

According to the users, the process for scheduling meetings and reserving conference rooms is more efficient because we are using electronic calendaring - the timeliness of the process is improved, and there is better access to information about a meeting (at a minimum who proposed it or who is the sponsor). The benefits they cited include:

- "eliminates telephone tag (or email tag)"
- "ease of scheduling meetings with standardized protocol"
- "asynchronous communications about meetings and schedules"
- "save time and energy arranging a meeting - it does the work for you"
- "it's a better way than email to communicate meeting agendas and location"
- "easy to change meetings"
- "can schedule the room simultaneously"

We asked the users how the guidelines influenced their decision to use the electronic group calendar. Most said they followed the guidelines the first time they tried using the product. This was the main motivation for people who reserve the rooms frequently. Several said they immediately experimented with the product. One user said "I knew there were guidelines but I didn't find out what they were since Meeting Maker worked fine for me and no one told me I was violating rules."

8 STYLES OF USE

Responses to our questionnaire (and informal communications with the entire user community) revealed four distinct styles of usage of the group calendaring system. We classified the users according to their answers to questions about frequency of use, reactions to the product and new process, use of activities for tracking tasks, and customized, individual utilization of the product features. All of the users honored the new process we put in place. They differed, however, in the extent to which they personally use the system.

The four styles are:
- as-needed: they use the product for discrete tasks, not on a routine basis.
- proxy: this group uses the product on behalf of others including those with user accounts and those without.
- indirect: they have accounts but do not personally use the product. They abide by the established procedures, but rely on their assistants to handle all of their proposals and responses.
- advocates: users who embraced the product and use it on a daily basis. These users, in general, stopped using paper calendars (as much as possible given that most users' computers are not portable). These users experimented with the product and identified important issues regarding product acceptance.

The 18 users who answered the survey were classified as: 9 advocates, 3 as-needed, 4 proxy, 2 indirect. Over half of the current users are as-needed or indirect users (mostly because many of these people do not have Macintosh computers). The existence of these styles is consistent with the findings in studies of strategies and styles of use of various systems, including electronic mail and Information Lens, which reveal personalized approaches to adopting to the use of these systems [Mackay].

As-Needed Users: Most of their usage is for the purpose of reserving a conference room, as outlined in the guidelines. These users login infrequently and logout after short bursts of use. They generally schedule few meetings a week, and said their schedules are generally unstructured (few formally scheduled meetings).

Proxy Users: The executive assistants all use the product primarily as proxy users for other users or to reserve the conference rooms on behalf of the people in the organization who do not have user accounts. These users do not, as a rule, use the product to maintain their own personal calendars. Like the "as-needed" users, their personal schedules include few meetings or other regularly scheduled activities. Typical use is to login for short periods of time to handle specific tasks such as proposing meetings, checking someone's calendar using proxy privileges, or checking on the availability of resources.

Indirect: These people do not personally use the calendaring system, but abide by the procedures. Either they do not have Macintosh computers in their offices, or they expect their assistants to maintain their calendars.

Advocates: This group of users gave many reasons why they use group calendaring on a routine basis. For example, eight out of nine (of the original eighteen users) mentioned increased productivity. Four of them set up recurring meetings, and six said it is more effective than scheduling by telephone. Five people said they like using an electronic calendar more than a paper calendar.

Specific examples of benefits include: "Before using [the electronic calendar] I would often not keep track (not write down) scheduled meetings or activities and just keep them in my head. It helps me be a bit more organized," "especially setting up meetings. It is light years faster than me doing it by phone and much less intrusive on my time compared to having my EA [executive assistant] do it," "reduces time spent finding when people and rooms are available," "allows my staff to save time they would otherwise spend finding out when I am available," "saves time I used to spend sending my schedule to my assistant," and "don't have to notify and catalog separately".

The advocates were motivated to create personalized uses of the product, beyond the ones outlined in the guidelines. There is diversity in the use for group calendaring (meetings) versus activities, as seen in Table 1. The percentages in the columns "group entries %" and "personal entries %" indicate how they use the calendar, not how they spend their time. The third column "work week % time scheduled" is the percentage of their time, for the week of the questionnaire, scheduled with activities and meetings. The users who indicated the highest percentage of group entries were the same people who said they had structured schedules.

person	group entries %	personal entries %	work week % time scheduled
A	35	65	>75
B	40	60	50-75
C	50	50	<50
D	60	40	<50
E	20	80	50-75
F	10	90	<50
G	70	30	>75
H	30	70	50-75
I	50	50	50-75

Table 1

These users created activities to track a wide variety of items including reminders and personal appointments, and to block out time for various tasks. In addition to typical entries such as vacation, dates out of the office, training classes, and planned lunches, users created activities for reminders on upcoming deadlines (such as submitting papers to conferences), morning reading, biweekly timesheet reminder notices, evening tasks at home, administration, and research. The advocates, in general, believe they are more organized because they are using the calendaring tool, as summarized by one user who said "It is particularly useful to me as a personal time manager. I deal with lots of due dates and deadlines and I can input an activity on the due date so I can keep track of them."

Over time some users adapted their styles of use, in part due to pressure from colleagues. For example, one person who travels frequently wanted to avoid maintaining multiple calendars. He used the application one day to check on the availability of a meeting room and "had about a dozen meeting messages. I now keep MM [Meeting Maker] active on my screen just in case one of the `group´ meetings changes." One advocate said "You work for me and I want you to use it"; next to the comment he noted "only half kidding." He actively encouraged others to use the electronic system. Another user commented that the questions we asked about use of activities prompted him to consider developing some personalized uses of his calendar.

Users were asked how they adapted to the [non-]use of the calendar by others. Responses include communicating with "indirect" users' executive assistants, or relying on other communication means, such as electronic mail. The infrequent or indirect users were asked if they missed meetings because they didn't used the product.- some of them said "yes" or "probably," but did not reflect on the consequences.

9 ADDITIONAL USES FOR GROUP CALENDARING

Through our continued use of the product we have collected suggestions for features and functionalities to include in a group calendaring product. While the product's use in our organization can be characterized as successful, missing features prevent users from always effectively communicating, sharing information, and meeting their goals. Arranging meetings, maintaining calendars, coordinating activities, and time-management are dynamic processes in the corporate world. Groupware products that support these tasks will enable organizations to work more effectively. In addition to the need for portability (by allowing a user to detach from the server and work with a snap-shot view of the database, for example) and performance improvement, suggestions include improved access to data, tools for negotiating conflicts, features for enhanced communication, and features for tracking time and using reminder notifications. Data collection tools would enable organizations to study their patterns of usage, monitor software performance, and provide valuable data to demonstrate the need for new product features.

Difficulties arise from the lack of information about the state of a proposal. Users requested improved access to:
- View users' calendars: the ability to see free times for a week or month, improving access to information such as when people are out of the office for extended periods of time.
- Status of meeting proposal: publish proposal responses for all attendees to view. Invitees' are interested in who has confirmed attendance. Proposers want the ability to set response deadlines, and view the status of responses as the deadline approaches. They want an easy way to poll users about changing the date of a meeting - the cost of rescheduling a meeting is usually assessed before making the change.
- Improve notifications: users must intentionally look for notification of conflicts and comments from invitees. Improved notifications would enable users to easily observe the status of a proposal.

Users requested these features:
- Wait list: establish a waiting-list for resources. Users often want to reserve rooms, should they become free.
- Proposal enclosures: send notes to individual attendees, include documents, circulate minutes after a meeting, enclose a note in a meeting cancellation notice.
- Forwarding: users want to forward proposals, just as they can forward electronic mail.
- Interface to electronic mail: electronic mail is used to communicate meeting proposals to potential attendees who are not using the calendaring system.
- In/Out board: a feature to quickly view team members' schedules at a high-level. For example, the In/Out board might indicate who is in town, who is on vacation, how to locate people out of town etc.
- Time management: features to track deadlines with reminders, and use the calendar for time reporting.
- Printing: users want to generate reports, calendar summaries, time-reports from the data in their calendars.

10 CONCLUSIONS

By including each of the key elements described above we have successfully introduced the use of group calendaring into our business environment. These five important elements are: defining expected uses for the product, establishing guidelines for usage, finding key users, encouraging the organization to modify procedures as a result of using the product, and supporting multiple styles of use. Our experience suggests that other organizations can have similar results if they introduce groupware by planning for each of the elements we have cited. In this new area of personal and group productivity tools we can expect individuals and groups to invent new ways of using technology to improve work coordination and communication.

ACKNOWLEDGMENTS

I greatly appreciate the comments I received on drafts of this paper from Gail Rein, Anatole Gershman, and Bill Martin.

REFERENCES

Ehrlich, S. F. 1987. Strategies for encouraging successful adoption of office communication systems. *ACM Transactions on Office Information Systems* 23, 2:340-357.

Ehrlich, S. F. 1987. Social and psychological factors influencing the design of office communication systems. *Proceedings of CHI+GI 1987 Human Factors in Computing Systems and Graphics Interface*. New York: ACM, pp. 323 - 329.

Grudin, J. 1988. Why CSCW applications fail: problems in the design and evaluation of organizational interfaces. *Proceedings of the Conference on Computer-Supported Cooperative Work*. New York: ACM, pp. 85 - 93.

Kiesler, S., Siegel, J., and McGuire, T.W. 1988. Social psychological aspects of computer-mediated communication. *Computer-Supported Cooperative Work: A Book of Readings*, I. Greif (ed). San Mateo: Morgan Kaufmann Publishers, Inc., pp. 657 - 682.

Mackay. W.E. 1988. More than just a communication system: diversity in the use of electronic mail. *Proceedings of the Conference on Computer-Supported Cooperative Work*. New York: ACM, pp. 344 - 353.

Sproull, L., and Kiesler, S. 1988. Reducing social context cues: electronic mail in organizational communication. *Computer-Supported Cooperative Work: A Book of Readings*. I Greif (ed). San Mateo: Morgan Kaufmann Publishers, pp. 683 - 712.

Conference Access Control in DCS

R. E. Newman-Wolfe and M. Montes

Computer and Information Sciences

CSE-301

University of Florida

Gainesville, FL 32611

nemo@cis.ufl.edu

Abstract

A fundamental problem in loosely coordinated distributed collaborative systems is initiating and maintaining dynamic access to the system. A common way of regulating access is to have specific stations configured for a particular conference; access to these stations during the conference implies access to the conference and its objects. However, if this level of structure is not desired, then some means for finding and joining a conference, and accessing its objects is necessary. DCS has a central conference server and conference managers to provide this capability.

1. Introduction

The Distributed Conferencing System[1] (DCS) at the University of Florida is a distributed package providing real-time support for cooperative work [11]. In this system, a set of mechanisms for conference management supports a wide range of floor control paradigms. Currently, DCS has applications that support concurrent development of text and graphic documents; remote demonstration, testing and debugging of programs; an audio channel; and automatic creation of transcripts of meetings including motions made and voting results.

Much research and development in groupware has focused on a particular application, or on sharing an existing application without modifying the application code. The philosophy of DCS is that the arena is much larger than this. We consider conferences to be a time-varying 4-tuple consisting of users, objects, operations and permissions. Conferences often endure over a long period of time, typically the lifetime of a particular project or an administrative structure. During this time, users may the conference, participate, and then terminate their membership. While the conference is in existence, many objects may be produced or modified jointly. This paper will focus on the ways in which DCS deals with finding conferences of interest; managing membership and access permissions; and controlling jointly produced objects.

2. Related Work in Groupware

Earlier systems for distributed conferencing date back to the 1960's and Engelbart's work with NLS [5] and have continued through MCC's Project Nick [2] CES [7, 13], Share [6], MMConf [4], and Mermaid [14]. Shared

---

[1] This work is partially supported by the University of Florida - Purdue University Software Engineering Research Center.

applications are bundled in DCS reflecting the cohesive nature of the conference, and indeed, conferences are grouped as a type of resource to be browsed and used. There is insufficient space here the do justice to these and other conferencing systems. An excellent introduction to work in this area may be found in [8]. Additional sources include the proceedings of the conferences on Computer Support for Cooperative Work (CSCW 86, 88 and 90) as well as the Conference on Organizational Computing Systems (nee Conference on Office Information Systems).

3. Architecture of DCS

DCS is written using Unix[2] 4.3bsd sockets [1, 10] and XWindows [9] with the X Athena Widgets package. It runs concurrently with other tools; thus other programs and sources of information are available to conference participants. Versions of DCS have been running at the University of Florida since August of 1990.

DCS is implemented as a group of cooperating processes. We term these the Central Conference Server (CCS), the Conference Manager (CM), the User Manager (UM). Of these, only the CCS need always exist and only the CCS needs to have an easily found port. Each active conference has a CM, and each user active in a conference has a UM. In addition, each application has its own logical Application Manager (AM) and architecture internal to itself. Currently, the applications we have developed all have an AM process with an application user process for each user working with that application, but this architecture is not required. These processes cooperate to provide a rich environment for collaborative work in DCS.

4. DCS Conference Control Mechanisms

Conference control is hierarchically democratic. Important control concepts in DCS are conference typing, user roles, voting, and independence [12].

User roles describe what a conference member may do. Within a conference, members may have the role of a voter, a non-voter or an observer. These are listed in strictly decreasing capability within the conference. Voters may participate in group decisions about conference actions, such as whether to allow a new user to join the conference, or what the disposition of a conference object should be. Both voters and non-voters have read and write access to all files within their conference. Observers are denied write access to most files, but may view conference files and other objects. The exception to this is that observers may append comments to the discussion log.

All conference control activities are resolved using a general voting mechanism. These actions include changing the role of a user; merging two conferences; splitting a conference; changing permissions of and disposing of conference objects. In addition to motions that have semantic content for DCS, it provides for user-defined motions. These are not interpreted by the system but are only recorded and handled through the voting mechanism.

Off-line voting is the general control paradigm, so that the conference need not be suspended while a vote is under way. When a motion is made, a small dialog box with the motion and a checklist appears on the screen of each active user. The user may then vote for or against, abstain, or defer on the motion. Unresolved motions are placed on a referendum list and members may vote on any motion for which they have not yet voted (deferral is not a vote). The referendum list may be examined by any member at any time. Once enough votes for a motion have accumulated, action may be taken. Conversely, if enough negative votes accumulate against the motion, then it will be removed from the referendum list and no action will be taken. Voting may be rollcall or anonymous, short

---

[2] Unix is a trademark of AT&T.

circuit or exhaustive. The results of voting are appended to the conference control log. By adjusting the roles of users, conference control ranges from dictatorship (one voter) to total democracy (all members are voters) to anarchy (no voters).

If a file is to be made accessible to a non-member, the group has the option of either making this user a conference member, or of changing the Unix permissions to the file. The former method has some advantages in that the user need not be able to log on to the system housing the file in question. All that is necessary is that the user have a client process that is able to communicate using DCS's message passing protocols with the servers that permit it to access conference objects. The next sections describe how users find out about a conference, create or join a conference and how their roles may change.

5. External Access to Conferences

DCS provides some operations to users who are not active participants in a conference. Once the user has started the User Manager (UM) client process, the UM connects to the local Central Conference Server (CCS), which listens at a well-known port. The user is given a status window (SW) through which she may ask for a list of conferences, initiate a conference, or request to join a conference. All operations other than direct conference file access through usual Unix mechanisms require the user to invoke DCS.

The UM and CCS together act as a limited browsing system, allowing users to examine the names of conferences to find out about what conferences exist, and to delve further into interesting conferences by requesting more information about them. Some of the information provided includes a short description of the purpose of the conference (provided by the members of that conference, usually its creator) and a list of members. If user wishes to join a conference, then the join action is selected and a message is sent to the conference manager (CM) of the desired conference requesting that the user be allowed to join. Depending on how the conference parameters have been set, the user may be allowed to join immediately, or may have to wait for the voting members of that conference to decide whether to allow membership. This process will be describe in greater detail below. Of course, if the user is already a member of the conference, then the CM allows the user to join right away.

When a user joins a conference, the UM breaks its connection to the CCS and makes one with the CM. It cannot effectively do this until the CCS tells it where to look, since the socket of the CM is randomly selected by the CCS at the time it invokes the CM and is kept hidden from any UM until the CM specifically permits the CCS to release that information. After this transition is made, the queries that could be made of the CCS may still be made of the CCS using the CM as an intermediary.

Create requests cause DCS to prompt the user for descriptive information (for external listing) and conference type. The CCS then creates a new CM and a new directory, and connects the user's UM to the new CM. The user is listed as the only member and owner, and has voter privileges. Once in the conference, the member may then set up conference parameters as desired and send invitations to other users to join.

6. Intra-Conference Access Control

Within a conference, a member may make queries, make motions, and vote. The voting mechanism has been described above, as have the queries answerable by the CCS. In addition to these, a member may ask more detailed information about the current status of a conference when they are active in the conference. For example, an active member may request a list of other members, including their roles and their status (active or inactive). Active members may also request to see motions that have not been resolved yet (the referendum list). This list is displayed along with the member's position relative to the motion (i.e., have they voted yae, nay, abstained or deferred their vote). If they have not yet voted on a motion, they may chose to do so at this time.

Control activities within a conference consist of changing user roles (joining, resigning, upgrading to voter, etc.); sending invitations to join; splitting and merging conferences; changing conference parameters; and determining the disposition of conference objects.

Of these, the only ones relevant to access control are changing a user's role and determining disposition of an object. User roles may be changed using the voting mechanism. A motion is made to make the change, and depending on the nature of the change and who made it, it is put up to a vote. An exception is made if a user makes a motion to demote herself. In this case, the motion carries automatically. If another user moves to demote a member, or if a member is moved for promotion to a higher level, then the conference voting parameters determine how many votes are needed to pass the motion. When a motion of this type is passed, the CM announces it through the status window, records it in the status log, and changes the user's role in the CM's internal structures. This approach is used to resign from a conference as well as changing levels of membership within a conference.

When an application is launched within a conference, the CM communicates the user's role to the Application Manager (AM). It is left to the AM to limit the user's access appropriately if the user does not have edit permissions within the conference. The AM is also responsible for killing application windows of a user when that user becomes inactive by leaving a conference. When a user quits out of a conference, the CM informs all the active AMs with which it believes the user to have been in contact that the user has exited the conference. The AM should then consult its list of active application windows and kill any that are associated with that user. This is done so that all access to the conference objects is done strictly from within the conference, unless explicitly allowed: application windows to conference objects should not persist after a user has quit a conference. Trusting the AM to perform these duties was a conscious design choice, trading greater security for increased flexibility and a small, clean interface between the CM and the AM.

7. Conclusions

DCS is a distributed real-time conferencing system running at the University of Florida. It provides flexible conference control and has the concept of multiple conferences. Within DCS, fine-grained concurrent text and graphics editors are available, as well as a discussion window and a general-purpose execute window for sharing a limited class of serial applications.

Conferences are treated as a collection of users, objects, operations and permissions, and may be persistent or transient. External access to conferences is mediated by a daemon listing at a well-known port, and a client process executed by the user. Through these, a user may browse summary information on existing conferences, join a conference or create a new one.

Within a conference, decisions concerning conference activities are made by a motion/voting mechanism. Users have roles, and only voting members are allowed to participate in the decision making process. Types of decisions that may be made include whether to admit a new member, change file permissions, change a member's role, or resign from the conference. A tradeoff was made in favor of keeping the interface to groupware applications within a conference small, at the expense of having to trust the application to use the information provided by the conference manager in an appropriate fashion. This tradeoff raises issues in system support for groupware applications.

Pressing research questions in this area include the following. What primitives should be available to groupware applications and conferencing systems? What protocols should be used for communication and process management within conferences and between applications? What means should exist for finding conferences and disseminating conference results, particularly over wide area networks? How does this relate to the CCITT's X.500 standard [3]? What operating system and network primitives must exist to support this type of application well, from the standpoints of performance, communication, and security?

8. References

[1] Bach, M. The Design of the UNIX Operating System Prentice-Hall, Englewood Cliffs, NJ, 1986.

[2] Begeman, M., Cook, P., Ellis, C., Graf, M., Rein, G. and Smith, T., "Project Nick: Meeting Augmentation and Analysis," Proc. of Conf. on Computer Supported Cooperative Work, Austin, December 1986, pp. 1-6.

[3] International Telegraph and Telephone Consultative Committee, "The Directory - Overview of Concepts, Models, and Service, Recommendation X.500, December 1988.

[4] Crowley, T., Milazzo, P., Baker, E., Forsdick, H., and Tomlinson, R., "MMConf: An Infrastructure for Building Shared Multimedia Applications, Proceedings of the Conference on Computer Supported Cooperative Work, Los Angeles, Oct. 1990, pp. 329-342.

[5] Engelbart, D. and W. English, "A Research Center for Augmenting Human Intellect, Proc. of FJCC 33(1):395-410, AFLPS Press, 1968.

[6] Greenberg, S., "Sharing Views and Interactions with Single-user Applications, Proceedings of ACM COIS 90, pp. 227-237.

[7] Greif, I., and Sarin, S., "Data Sharing in Group Work," Proc. of Conf. on Computer Supported Cooperative Work, Austin, December 1986, pp. 175-183.

[8] Greif, I. (ed.), Computer-Supported Cooperative Work , Morgan-Kaufmann Publishers, San Mateo, CA, 1988.

[9] Johnson, Eric F., Reichard, Kevin, "X Windows Applications Programming," MIS Press, Portland, Oregon, 1989.

[10] Leffler, S. J., McKusick, M. K., Karels, M. J., Quarterman, J. S., The Design and Implementation of the 4.3 BSD UNIX Operating System , Addison-Wesley Publishing Company, Inc. 1989.

[11] Newman-Wolfe, R. E., C. Ramirez, H. Pelimuhandiram, M. Montes, M. Webb and D. L. Wilson, ''A Brief Overview of the DCS Distributed Conferencing System,'' *Proceedings of the Summer Usenix Conference*, pp. 437-452, Nashville, TN, June 1991.

[12] Ramirez, Carmen L., "Networking Component of a Distributed Conferencing System, University of Florida CIS Dep't. Master's Thesis, 1991.

[13] Sarin, S. and Greif, I., "Computer-Based Real-Time Conferencing Systems, Computer, October 1985, pp. 33-45.

[14] Watabe, K., Sakata, S., Maeno, K., Fukuoka, H, and Ohmori, T., "Distributed Multiparty Desktop Conferencing System: MERMAID, Proceedings of the Conference on Computer Supported Cooperative Work, Los Angeles, Oct. 1990, pp. 27-38.

Experiences with Groupware:
Benefits and Limitations in a Real–world Context

James D. Gantt

U.S. Army Institute for Research in Management Information,
Communications, and Computer Sciences (AIRMICS)
115 O'Keefe Building
Georgia Institute of Technology
Atlanta, GA 30332–0800

ABSTRACT

AIRMICS (U.S. Army Institute for Research in Management Information, Communications, and Computer Sciences) serves as both a research and development (R&D) and technology transfer unit of the Army, and has been supporting over the past seven years a variety of projects in the area of groupware (among its other activities related to information technology). AIRMICS' groupware projects include development of an enhanced electronic mail system for distributed group support within the Department of Defense (DoD), video teleconferencing among historically black colleges and universities (HBCUs), development of a MAC–based distributed group support system (GSS) used for behavioral lab experiments, and a variety of work in conjunction with the University of Arizona's (Ventana's) GroupSystems product. AIRMICS currently supports groupware research at the Center for Information Management Research (CIMR), which is a joint effort between the University of Arizona and the Georgia Institute of Technology. Another current project is implementation of a portable wireless LAN with groupware included, which will be transported to a variety of Army groups to support meetings. This paper describes some of these projects, places them in the context of several groupware frameworks, and discusses benefits and limitations of groupware based on these experiences.

1. GSS PROJECTS AT AIRMICS

Johansen (1991) and others have described a framework for understanding groupware technology which is a two–dimensional grid divided into four quadrants (see Figure 1). GSS applications are often referenced with respect to whether the participants are interacting in the same or different physical locations, and at the same or different times (synchronous vs. asynchronous). AIRMICS' projects thus far have fallen into three of the four quadrants: different time, different place; same time, different place; and same time, same place.

AIRMICS' short–term approach has been to experiment and gain experience and knowledge in both group processes and technology in these three quadrants. AIRMICS' long–term goal is to provide a flexible environment for group meetings which will adapt to the needs of the particular situation and group, but will use the same technology. Johansen (1991) refers to this as an evolution toward "Any Time, Any Place" (ATAP) meeting support. Only recently has the necessary technology evolved enough to begin to make this feasible (graphics and GUIs, laptops, network speed and capacity).

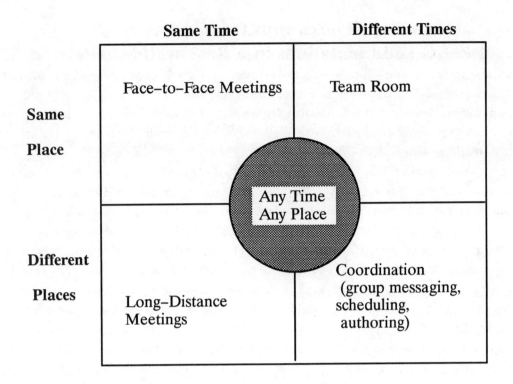

	Same Time	**Different Times**
Same Place	Face-to-Face Meetings	Team Room
Different Places	Long-Distance Meetings	Coordination (group messaging, scheduling, authoring)

Any Time Any Place

Figure 1

1.1 Different Time, Different Place

An AIRMICS–sponsored Small Business Innovative Research (SBIR) project currently in progress is the development of an electronic–mail–based system for distributed decision support, by Analytical Software, Inc.. The system currently facilitates group communication in several ways. Users can create and transmit files, database, spreadsheets, graphics, etc., as attachments to an electronic mail message. Items can be sent as fax messages from a PC, without using a fax board. The current implementation is via MCI Mail, and the software runs Lotus Express in the background to speed processing. The system allows collection, aggregation, and subsequent mass distribution of questionnaires soliciting votes and comments. In progress are enhancements for group authoring, group scheduling, and communication compatibility with the Defense Date Network (DDN), X.400, and potential EDI applications. The advantages of such a system are its widespread availability over an existing infrastructure, minimal platform requirements, and its extension of familiar individual office support tools such as spreadsheets, graphics, word processing, and communications. The disadvantages of the system are its somewhat limited set of GSS features.

1.2 Same Time, Different Place

AIRMICS has supported the development of a network of video teleconferencing (VTC) facilities among HBCUs and other locations, for the purpose of increasing and improve information–sharing and communications among the HBCUs and to strengthen their link with funding agencies such as the Army (CARTS Project, 1989). Lessons learned from this project were the importance of a critical mass of sites and users, and the unexpected creativity shown by users in thinking of new applications for the technology, once they had some familiarity with it.

A second project sponsored by AIRMICS that falls into this quadrant was conducted by researchers at Georgia Institute of Technology (Parsons & Nagao, 1989), which focused on distributed, interacting, computer–supported team work and the factors that might impact the effective performance of such groups. Using commercial software (SuperCard and Timbuktu) and Apple MacIntoshes, a distributed environment was developed to allow three or more people to be connected by both data and voice communications (via phones and computers). Lab experiments conducted for the purpose of studying both technical and social issues allowed participants to use screen sharing and discussions in order to carry out a simulated budget reduction exercise. This project included support specifically for decision–making, which places it into Level 2 of DeSanctis and Gallupe's (1987) categorization. Some interesting results of this experience were the need for private screens, secure against observation by fellow team members, in addition to shared public screens, and the need for a second communication channel for distributed GSS. ISDN (Integrated Services Digital Network), with which AIRMICS is also significantly involved, will simplify solutions to the latter problem.

1.3 Same Time, Same Place

The University of Arizona GSS tools and investigative work done using these tools have been widely published (cf., Applegate et al., 1986; Dennis et al., 1988) and are well–known in the groupware community. What is less well–known is AIRMICS' role in supporting the work in general and in collaborating on some specific projects, including the use of the GroupSystems GSS tool to define requirements for several Army information systems. AIRMICS' role was to identify the task needs within the Army and link them to appropriate support tools, i.e., the Arizona GSS tools, and also to coordinate and participate in the actual sessions, which drew Army personnel from all over the world and brought them together to rapidly define requirements for a number of different information systems (Daniels et al., 1991).

In one of these sessions, for example, twenty people participated in producing a requirements document in three and a half days that participants who were experienced in similar non–supported sessions estimated would have taken four to six weeks without the tools. A project manager who was one of the participants estimated cost savings to be between $75,000 and $125,000. Another of these sessions took four and a half days to develop a functional description for a management information system. Future sessions recommended by management were estimated to produce savings of over $1,250,000, including personnel salaries.

AIRMICS is currently supporting through CIMR two additional projects specifically involving information systems development. One is attempting to model group communications and apply the model to building extended entity relationship models (Morrison et al., 1991). The second project applies GroupSystems GSS tools to the Joint Application Development (JAD) method, an approach which brings users and developers together as a collaborative team to define requirements within a short period of time (Carmel &

George, 1991). Another CIMR groupware project involves the development of a multi–media interface for simultaeous use of applications by multiple users (Smith & Mynatt, 1991).

2. CURRENT PLANS AND FUTURE PROJECTS

AIRMICS plans to combine the use of modeling methods such as IDEF (Integrated Definition Language) and team methods such as JAD (Joint Application Design) with tools such AT&T's Application Connectivity Engineering (ACE) tool, with groupware sessions. One benefit of GSS is that a permanent record of each session is retained. The goal of a GSS–based JAD session will be to produce a formal requirements document as the primary outcome of the meeting(s). Another benefit will be the increased participation of managers and users in defining their own needs. GSS's have been shown to increase the participation of all group members in accomplishment of the task.

AIRMICS has acquired the GroupSystems software to run on a set of laptop computers connected in a wireless LAN. The purpose is to be able to transport a portable decision room to any Army group that needs it, reducing travel costs and increasing flexibility and ultimately productivity. Tasks to which AIR-MICS plans to apply the use of groupware include information systems requirements definition and business process redesign; linking systems definition with the use of rapid prototyping, re–engineering, and CASE tools; TQM; strategic planning; promotion candidate evaluation, review of grants and contracts, and source selection boards. A second purpose is to accelerate technology transfer of groupware.

Issues which have been raised by AIRMICS' experiences include the need for a group facilitator skilled in both group dynamics and the GSS tools, the importance of extensive pre–meeting planning, the identification of appropriate participants and desired outcomes, and the need for security/privacy and system reliability. In response to these research needs, AIRMICS plans to collect data while using the portable wireless LAN across a variety of applications. An additional AIRMICS' research project is gathering information about group meeting facilitation. Finally, AIRMICS is also conducting a technology assessment of the currently available commercial offerings in groupware (Beise & Evans, 1992).

3. ASSESSMENT OF GROUPWARE

There are several current obstacles to true, integrated, comprehensive groupware. Two related obstacles are the lack of standard networking technologies and the lack of cross–platform software, which prevents easy interaction between users on different networks and different hardware. Another is lack of understanding of how people work together in groups most effectively, in the office or elsewhere, knowledge which is necessary in order to design truly adequate systems to support this work. Future systems will likely incorporate advances in these areas as quickly as possible. An additional obstacle is the tendency of potential groupware buyers to focus on the features of the technology without analyzing the specific work processes that the technology is intended to support.

In the near future, organizations are likely to adopt low–end groupware tools as they have other PC LAN tools, piecemeal as needed for specific applications. It will probably be perceived as risky, except for the largest organizations, to adopt a high–end, comprehensive groupware solution. The best approach may be to base groupware tool selection on a thorough short–term and long–term needs analysis, which in turn is linked to a comprehensive, integrated, organizational–level requirements analysis, i.e., an information architecture solidly based on organizational strategic planning.

References

Beise, C.M. & Evans, M.J. 1992. *Technology Assessment of Group Support Systems.* AIRMICS Technical Report ASQB–GM–92–009.

Carmel, E. & George, J.F. 1991. Joint Application Design (JAD) and electronic meeting systems (EMS): Opportunities for the future" University of Arizona Working Paper WPS–91–06.

CARTS Project. 1989. *Army and HBCU Reference Manual.* Atlanta, GA: Clark Atlanta University.

Daniels, R.M., Dennis, A.R., Hayes, G., Nunamaker, J.F., Valacich, J. 1991. Enterprise Analyzer: Electronic support for group requirements elicitation. *Proceedings of the 24th Hawaii International Conference on Systems Sciences*, Jan 1991, Vol.3, 43–50.

Dennis, A.R., George, J.F., Jessup, L.M., Nunamaker, J.F., Vogel, D.R. 1988. Information technology to support electronic meetings. *MIS Quarterly, 12*:4, 591–624.

DeSanctis, G. & Gallupe, R.B. 1987. A foundation for the study of group decision support systems. *Management Science, 33*:5, 589–609.

Johansen, R. 1991. Teams for tomorrow. Plenary Speech. *Proceedings of the 24th Hawaii International Conference on Systems Sciences*, Jan 1991, Vol.3, p. 521–534.

Morrison, J., Morrison, M., & Vogel, D. 1991. Software to support the project and organizational requirements of business teams. University of Arizona working paper WPS–91–30.

Parsons, C.K. & Nagao, D.H. 1989. Distributed computer–supported team work: a research paradigm. *AIRMICS Technical Report ASQB–GA–90–016.*

Smith, I. & Mynatt, E. 1991. What you see is what I want: Experiences with the Virtual X Shared Window System. *Georgia Institute of Technology Technical Report GT–GVU–91–33.*

Groupware '92

User Experience Track:
Empowering Manufacturing with Notes

A presentation about how a Consumer Products Manufacturing Company is building an enterprise-wide document management system with Lotus Notes. Topics include:

- Statement of need for enterprise-wide document management
- Rationale for Lotus Notes selection
- Development approach and consideration

Presenters

Basil J. Fedynyshyn
4 Embarcadero Center, 7th Floor
San Francisco, CA   94111
Phone: (415) 362-0500
Fax: (415) 362-5528
Mr. Fedynyshyn is the Marathon project leader for this development effort and a senior manager with Marathon Systems, a leading West Coast Systems Integrator for Lotus Notes. He has over 10 years experience in a management role planning, designing, and implementing information technology. His areas of technical expertise include client/server computing, open systems, RDBMS, Imaging/Document Management, and GUIs.

Patricia F. Martin
The Clorox Company
Technical Center
7200 Johnson Drive
Pleasanton, CA   94588
Fax: 510-847-2494
Ms. Martin is the company's project leader for this development effort and the Quality Services and Standards Manager at a Consumer Products Manufacturing Company. She has 13 years of experience in manufacturing.

EMPOWERING MANUFACTURING WITH NOTES

Company Background

- A diversified international company whose principle business is developing, manufacturing, and marketing premium quality consumer products. The company's strategy for long-term growth includes:
    - ❏ The successful introduction of new products.
    - ❏ Meaningful improvements to its established products.
    - ❏ Acquisitions of new products.

- Products are sold in 70 countries and are manufactured in more than 40 plants at locations in the United States, Puerto Rico, and abroad.

Data Processing Environment

- IBM systems for business applications developed with CICS COBOL and DB2 databases.

- DEC systems for technical database applications developed with Ask's Ingres and other software tools.

- Current goals and objectives are:
    - ❏ Install Local Area Networks at all plant sites. Corporate headquarters and all plant sites will use IBM Token-Ring running IBM OS/2 LAN Servers. The technical research facility uses Novel Netware/VMS on an Ethernet LAN.
    - ❏ Install cc:Mail from Lotus as a corporate-wide electronic mail system.
    - ❏ Utilize Lotus' application suite on the desktop.

RECAP OF NEEDS

Document Management Needs

■ Today, a variety of tools and manual procedures are used to perform documentation management functions. In addition, Verity's TOPIC is installed at the Technical Center and is being used to support research and retrieval of about 9,000 scientific documents.

■ Constant change and growth are necessitating the acquisition and implementation of a corporate-wide electronic document management system.

Key Requirements

■ Automated methods to author, capture, store, retrieve, and distribute/share information (e.g., correspondence, discussions, reports, manuals, specifications, standards) which:
  ❑ Provides an intuitive method for use.
  ❑ Assures concurrency and consistency.
  ❑ Promotes sharing of collective corporate knowledge.
  ❑ Supports distribution and retrieval across a broad spectrum of users and locations.

■ Audit and security controls for access and distribution of proprietary/sensitive information.

■ Integration with existing technical infrastructure, such as applications, technology, and support resources.

■ High system availability - uptime and distributed access for an international organization.

■ Modular system design to support phased implementation and growth requirements.

■ Minimized administrative maintenance burden on end-users to keep the system operational and useful.

OUR SOLUTION

■ Use Lotus Notes to build document management applications tailored to the organization's unique needs. The following diagram describes how Lotus Notes meets these functional needs.

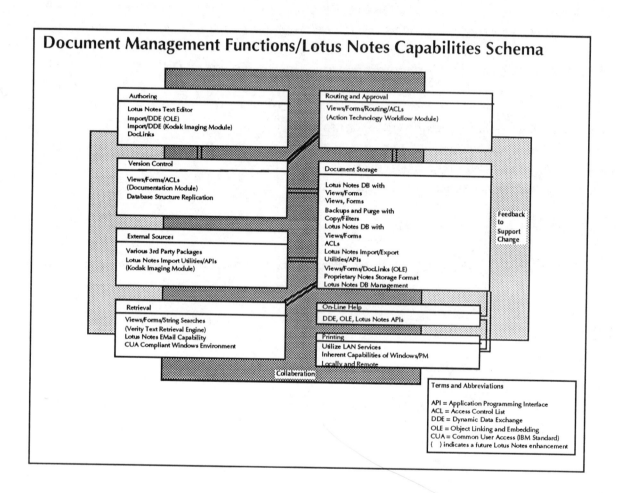

Document Management Functions/Lotus Notes Capabilities Schema

Authoring
- Lotus Notes Text Editor
- Import/DDE (OLE)
- Import/DDE (Kodak Imaging Module)
- DocLinks

Version Control
- Views/Forms/ACLs
- (Documentation Module)
- Database Structure Replication

External Sources
- Various 3rd Party Packages
- Lotus Notes Import Utilities/APIs
- (Kodak Imaging Module)

Retrieval
- Views/Forms/String Searches
- (Verity Text Retrieval Engine)
- Lotus Notes EMail Capability
- CUA Compliant Windows Environment

Routing and Approval
- Views/Forms/Routing/ACLs
- (Action Technology Workflow Module)

Document Storage
- Lotus Notes DB with
- Views/Forms
- Views, Forms
- Backups and Purge with
- Copy/Filters
- Lotus Notes DB with
- Views/Forms
- ACLs
- Lotus Notes Import/Export
- Utilities/APIs
- Views/Forms/DocLinks (OLE)
- Proprietary Notes Storage Format
- Lotus Notes DB Management

On-Line Help
- DDE, OLE, Lotus Notes APIs

Printing
- Utilize LAN Services
- Inherent Capabilities of Windows/PM
- Locally and Remote

Collaberation

Feedback to Support Change

Terms and Abbreviations
- API = Application Programming Interface
- ACL = Access Control List
- DDE = Dynamic Data Exchange
- OLE = Object Linking and Embedding
- CUA = Common User Access (IBM Standard)
- (   ) indicates a future Lotus Notes enhancement

Our Solution

- Implement the Lotus Notes-based applications within the current I.S. technical environment.
    - ❑ Utilize existing PC workstations, LANs, WAN, E-Mail, and office productivity tools.
    - ❑ Enhance PC workstations with MS-Windows or IBM Presentation Manager.
    - ❑ Install Lotus Notes on PC workstations.
    - ❑ Install OS/2 Lotus Notes servers at corporate offices, technical center, and plants.
    - ❑ Install cc:Mail - Lotus Notes gateway.

- Pilot Lotus Notes applications to validate functional and technical capabilities. In addition, gain experience developing, implementing, and supporting applications. The pilot environment is defined as a limited and controlled set of application functions/features, customers, locations, and development staff.

- Build pilot applications that could be easily upgraded for:
    - ❑ Use as a production system.
    - ❑ Roll-out to a larger customer population.
    - ❑ Enhancements and/or additions to functionality .

PILOT PROJECT APPROACH

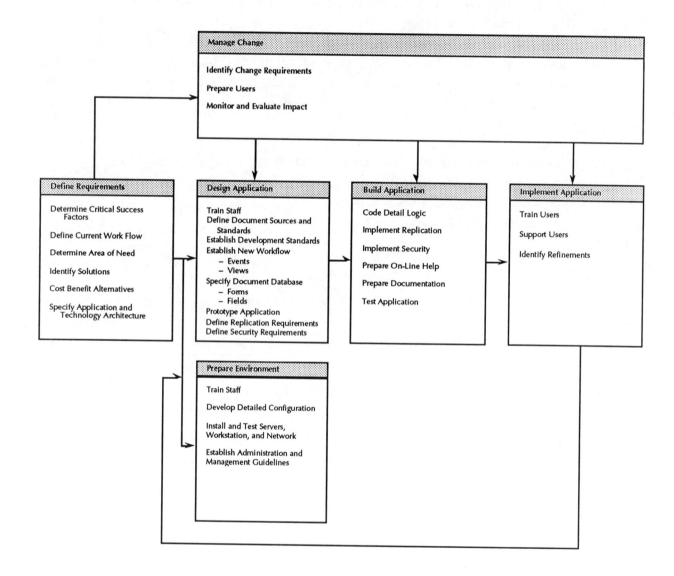

CONSIDERATIONS

- Training staff

- Establishing guidelines for:
  - ❏ Application development
  - ❏ Technology Administration/Management

- Piloting application with iterative refinements

- Leveraging tools for interactive design through prototypes

- Preparing and managing organizational changes
  - ❏ Process re-engineering
  - ❏ Document restructuring
  - ❏ New technology awareness

Meeting the Software Support Challenge
with Groupware Technologies

Louise Kirkbride
Founder and V.P. of Corporate Development
Answer Computer, Inc.
1263 Oakmead Parkway
Sunnyvale, CA 94086
(408) 739-6130 • Fax: (408) 739-2455
E-mail: lk@answer.com

Abstract

I. Introduction

The software support business is on the verge of a revolution. As companies provide increasingly sophisticated, network-intensive software, keeping these systems up and running has become a challenge for the support group. At the same time, providing excellent support has become a competitive necessity. The challenge comes primarily from the nature of the questions and answers. While we have learned how to provide increasingly reliable software products, we haven't learned how to keep our users from getting "broken." The tools and methodology that were developed in a traditional hardware support environment no longer ensure success in the rapidly changing software support arena. New tools are required – ones that are targeted specifically to software support.

With software support, the rules of the game have changed – simple facts and actions no longer meet customer expectations. The new support model must focus on managing complex information, improving quality and productivity, and, perhaps most importantly, **enhancing communication.** Keeping the customer or end user in the communication loop is <u>vital</u> when a few hours of "downtime" can mean thousands or millions of dollars in lost revenue. This communication must also extend to other areas of the software company: engineering, quality assurance, marketing, and sales.

Fortunately, a new technology is emerging to bridge the gap. Groupware is the key to increasing productivity, improving service, and enhancing communication without "upsizing" your support organization.

II. Groupware in Action A Case Study of Answer Computer

A. Objectives and Expectations

One of the advantages of groupware is that it allows you to address the concerns of your support organization **at every level.** We found that to ensure success, a system needs buy-in from management, support representatives, and end users (see figure 1).

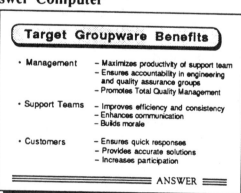

Figure 1 – Target Groupware Benefits

At Answer Computer, we wanted to implement a groupware support system that would meet all these needs. Our goals at the outset focused on:

1) Company-Wide Communication
2) Team Productivity
3) Information Management
4) Measurement ➔ Pro-Active Support

1) Communication Goals: Sharing information and expertise was one of our key objectives. We knew from experience that without automation, information exchange is often haphazard at best, accomplished by exchanging post-it notes, shouting over cubicle tops, etc. We wanted to communicate critical information to the right people **automatically.** We wanted to maintain a flow of information between the support team and other groups, such as quality assurance, engineering, and product marketing. This would allow us to track bugs and enhancement requests and facilitate product planning.

Another vital part of the process is creating **closed-loop communication** with the customer. We define closed-loop communication as involving customers in the support process, ensuring that they receive timely updates on the status of their problems, and soliciting feedback on solutions and workarounds to ensure their success with our products. We felt that increasing customer participation would improve customer satisfaction and help us capture valuable feedback about our products for use in strategic planning and development.

2) Productivity Goals: Productivity goes hand in hand with good communication. We wanted to implement a product that would maximize our productivity by eliminating duplicate research, reducing training time, streamlining our workflow and enabling the front line handle previously-solved problems. We required a groupware solution that would automate repetitive administrative tasks and let our experts concentrate on what they do best -- solving new problems.

3) Information Management Goals: We needed a solution that would manage information through every step of the support process. The ideal solution would centralize and consolidate information and expertise to **ensure accuracy** and never let good ideas fall through the cracks. When customers called, we wanted them to receive the most accurate, up-to-date information available, no matter which support representative they spoke with. We also needed a mechanism for handling solutions-in-progress and allowing people to work together on a problem while maintaining individual accountability. We wanted to make sure that every customer contact is regarded as an opportunity to gather information about product quality, company procedures, and future product directions.

4) Measurement Goals: Other key requirements were reporting capabilities that would allow us to measure performance, track information quality, and manage workload. We needed a system that would help us identify achievements and potential problems, letting us take a **pro-active** approach to support and product management.

B. Implementation

We implemented a groupware system to support our customer base of over 100 companies and 2,000 end users. Even as our product line has expanded, we have been able to contain the growth of our support team, which comprises only two frontline representatives and a group of ten experts. It interesting to note that the same groupware system we implemented is being used with even greater success by large, multinational corporations that support as many as 100,000 end users.

1) Preparation and Integration: Because the products we support are dynamic and are used in complex, rapidly changing computing environments, we chose a software-based groupware product rather than an expert system. Our chosen application adjusts automatically to support new releases or unintended uses of our products. We needed a fast ROI and had neither the time nor the manpower to reprogram the system every time our support information changed.

By selecting an application, we also avoided having to pre-load extensive documentation before using the system. We simply plugged it in and let the phone ring, loading information and solutions in response to **actual customer questions**. We found that responding to actual customer problems was a more efficient approach than spending time predicting what questions customers might ask and burdening the system with information that might not be useful. Within one month, we were able to solve over 80% of incoming problems on the first call, using the solutions that had been entered into the system in the course of handling live customer calls.

The product allows us to preserve our investment in desktop hardware by displaying on virtually any personal computer, terminal, or workstation. We use Microsoft Windows, X Window System (Motif and OPEN LOOK tool kits), and SunView graphical user interfaces in house. Our field offices dial in to the system via modems and use a character-based interface to display on dumb terminals.

2) Workflow and Automatic Communication: Our groupware system streamlines workflow and communication among individuals and groups so that we can use it for both support and product management. Here is how our workflow is organized:

Support: When the call comes in from a customer or end user, frontline support checks the groupware information base to see whether or not the problem has already been solved. If not, the problem is described, given a severity rating ("critical," "stop work," etc.), and escalated to the appropriate expert. Each expert has a prioritized "in basket" of pending problems and is responsible for documenting their solutions.. Anyone who edits one of these documents leaves his/her "fingerprints" on it, so that a complete audit trail is always available. We can specify the time limits within which all problems must be solved. Any problem not solved within these limits is escalated to management, who can then take corrective action, redistribute workload, etc.

The final solution or workaround is published in the information base, where it is read and critiqued by other experts. This keeps everyone up to date on the latest solutions and ensures that information quality remains high. The customer is automatically notified of the solution or workaround by e-mail, postal mail, or fax, and will continue to be notified whenever it changes. If any other customers call with the same problem, the frontline now has instant access to the information that will solve the problem. Our experts are freed from redundant research and also gain workload visibility, recognition for problems solved, and feedback from colleagues and customers.

We have the option of letting customers and end users dial in our information base to provide feedback, check the status of an unsolved problem, or look up the answer to their question without going through a support representative.

Product Management: We also use our groupware system for beta testing, bug tracking, and scheduling enhancement requests. During beta testing, software bugs are reported into the groupware system, queued to the appropriate expert, then sent to QA for testing. This documents the beta experience and puts it on line so that our support team is poised to answer questions from the first day of a new product release. Management can track the progress made during beta testing and run reports on the number of bugs remaining and their severity levels.

Enhancement requests are also documented and tracked so that customers can dial in and check when their suggested enhancement is scheduled to be included in the product. If a suggested enhancement does not make the current release, it escalates to the enhancement list for the next release automatically.

C.   Sample Reports

Our groupware system offers extensive reporting capabilities. This allows us to measure information quality, support team performance, call volume, reported problems for each product line, etc. A few sample reports are included on the following pages.

III. Questions You Should Ask When Evaluating Groupware Products

Based on our experience at Answer Computer, we've put together a set of guidelines to help you evaluate the various groupware systems on the market and determine which product best meets your needs. To make an informed decision, you should ask the vendor about each of these issues:

1) Evaluating the technology base
2) Fitting your computing environment
3) Fitting your support environment
4) Implementing the product
5) Managing your information
6) Enhancing communication
7) Achieving your goals

A list of questions is included below.

Achieving Your Goals

- What productivity increases have been achieved?
- How long did it take?
- What management reporting tools are available?

ANSWER

Evaluating the Technology Base

- Does it use state-of-the-art technology?
  - Graphical user interface (GUI)
  - Client-server architecture
  - Windows
  - Open
  - Relational
- Is it a "tool" or a solution?

ANSWER

Fitting into Your Computing Environment

- How does it share data with other applications?
- Does it achieve mission-critical performance?
  - Speed
  - Data integrity
  - Data Security
- How does it integrate with the existing network?
- How will it preserve the investment in desktop hardware?

ANSWER

Fitting into Your Support Environment

- How much training is required?
- How is it tailored to your workflow?
- What motivates experts to record solution?
- What kind of audit trail is created?
- How is workload management accomplished?
- Can customers use it to solve their own problems?

ANSWER

Implementing the Groupware Product

- How much maintenance is required to add knowledge to the system?
- How much programming is required up front?
- How is new information loaded into the system?
- Can this be done by the existing support staff?

ANSWER

Managing Your Information

- What happens if a solution is unknown, changes, or is incorrect?
- How does it prevent problems from falling through the cracks?
- How are accuracy and relevancy ensured?
- How is accountability ensured?
- How does it prevent duplication of data?

ANSWER

Enhancing Communication

- How are interested groups informed of new solutions and workarounds?
- How are customers notified when solutions change?
- How are unsolved problems escalated?
- Does the product "close the loop" with the customer?
- How is customer input captured?

ANSWER

Figure 2:

Incident Activity by Hour of the Day
Jan 01 1991 00:00 - May 15 1992 10:22
Report generated May 15 1992 10:35

	Incidents Created	Incidents Closed	Incidents Reopened	Solved by Document
8:00 AM	23	21	2	19
9:00 AM	38	37	3	32
10:00 AM	103	100	1	96
11:00 AM	99	80	5	66
12:00 PM	26	26	6	21
1:00 PM	78	60	11	49
2:00 PM	202	195	20	190
3:00 PM	199	176	13	169
4:00 PM	151	138	9	122
Total:	919	833	70	764

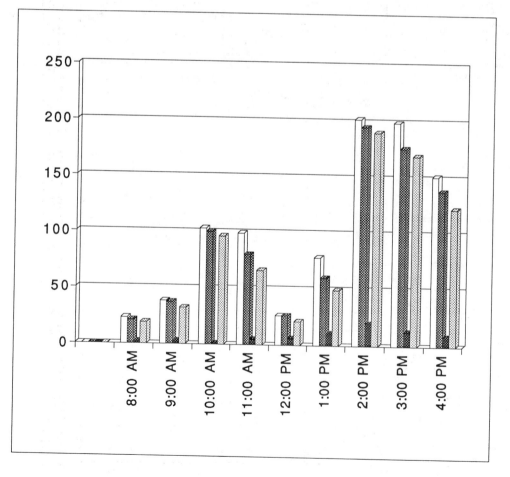

Figure 3: Bug-Tracking Report

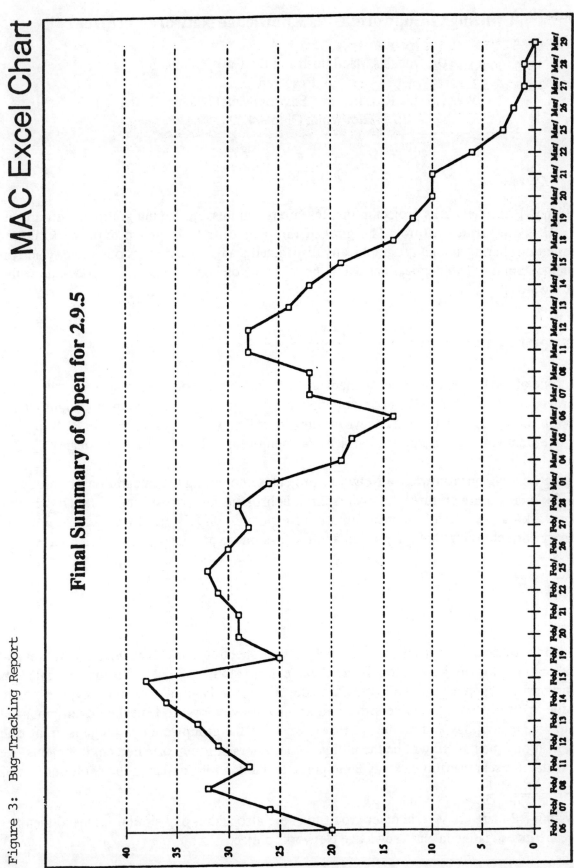

MAC Excel Chart

Final Summary of Open for 2.9.5

Utilizing Groupware: BP's Knowledge Networks Project

Dr. Douglas Mac Intosh and Dr. Ümit Yalcinalp
BP Research
Warrensville Research and Environmental Science Center
Cleveland, Ohio 44128

ABSTRACT

The Knowledge Networks project at BP Research is addressing the integration of groupware into BP's corporate culture. The goal of the project is to improve teamworking and information sharing among geographically distributed teams. We discuss our strategy and the implementation of two applications using the Virtual Notebook System. We conclude with a look towards the future.

1 INTRODUCTION

BP is one of the largest companies in the world with offices and operations spanning the globe. Improved mechanisms for sharing information and pulling people together would significantly increase BP's productivity. We believe groupware will play an important role in BP's quest to improve teamworking and information sharing among geographically distributed teams.

At BP Research, our Knowledge Networks project is addressing the integration of groupware into BP's corporate culture[1]. This research is broken into two subthemes: "Distributed Teamworking" and "Intelligent Information Retrieval". In this article we will outline our strategy for achieving this integration and discuss our experiences, obstacles, and lessons learned.

2 A LAYERED APPROACH

Our plan for integrating groupware into BP's corporate culture involves the cooperation and collaboration of many groups both internal and external to BP. Since BP's business interests are primarily centered around oil, and not in developing collaborative technology, we look to outside institutions (e.g., Universities and groupware vendors) to lead the development of groupware technology and products. However, since the groupware challenge is great, and organizations such as BP will be the ultimate consumers of group oriented environments, we feel that our research effort can play an important enabling role, assisting the evolution of this

---

1. Within BP there are several other groups that are also addressing similar issues to the ones we are investigating in our Knowledge Networks project.

technology. We can provide insights to the developers about our needs. We can identify internal obstacles and barriers that will inhibit the use of the technology in production environments. We can provide real application domains to test the technology. Consequently, BP research is working closely with the ForeFront Group and Digital Equipment Corporation to pilot test innovative groupware environments, designed to address specific business needs.

Our approach for integrating groupware into BP's corporate culture, and for developing business applications that exploit groupware technology has three layers. These layers are shown in Figure 1. In this model, University research and groupware vendor products provide the foundation, or framework, for groupware applications. These products and tools should be generalized and flexible so that they can be easily customized and tailored for each new application. Problems such as non-homogeneous computing environments (both hardware and software) should be addressed by these tools so that the tools can be easily integrated into existing environments with minimal impact (e.g., they should run on PCs, Macintoshes, Unix and VMS workstations, etc.).

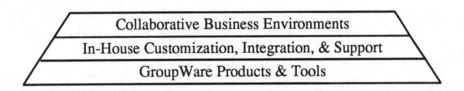

Figure 1: Layered Approach For Groupware Application Development

The middle level in the layered architecture represents our corporate R&D program. The goal of the Knowledge Networks project is to extend, customize, and adapt groupware frameworks into real collaborative business environments. The business environments we seek to build must facilitate information sharing and team collaboration, but must also support the ability for finding and retrieving information from the collective whole. Therefore, two distinct subthemes have emerged: "Distributed Teamworking" and "Intelligent Information Retrieval". Our goal is to integrate these subtheme technologies and to use them as building blocks for building customized collaborative business environments.

Our strategy for achieving this goal is:

1) Identify a group of people, or team, in the corporation that are already interacting, or recognize the need to. The goal is not to change or force new ways of working together on the team. Instead, we want to enhance and/or facilitate the process that is already in place, or which is beginning to surface.

2) Based on the needs of the team, build a customized collaborative business environment to facilitate team interaction and information sharing. This is accomplished by:

- tailoring the existing groupware functionality to meet the needs of collaborative teams.

- integrating existing information sources and programs into the evolving collaborative environment.

- adding functionality to improve information management and retrieval.

3) Deliver, maintain, and support the Collaborative Business Environment.

3 A GENERALIZED GROUPWARE FRAMEWORK

A generalized groupware framework that we have been investigating is the Virtual Notebook System (VNS) of the ForeFront Group, Houston, TX (Baylor College of Medicine) [Burger91]. The VNS provides a generalized concurrent blackboard structure based on a notebook paradigm for wide area network (WAN) use. See references for more information on the Virtual Notebook System.

There are several reasons why we have chosen the VNS as a foundation for groupware application development. First of all, it has a "open system, client/server architecture" [Gorry91] which supports access from a multitude of platforms. This is very important since BP is a world wide organization with a heterogeneous computing environment. (It cannot be expected that all team members will have identical hardware/software platforms.) Secondly, the VNS supports a robust Application Programmer's Interface (API). This is crucial for both customizing the application environment, and for integrating it with other applications. Finally, the VNS has an advantage over other groupware products in that it is based on a notebook paradigm, something that potential users are already familiar and comfortable with. These properties make the VNS a flexible, generalized groupware tool.

4 EXAMPLES OF BP GROUPWARE APPLICATIONS

We have developed numerous prototypes and applications using the VNS. For the purpose of this paper we will give two examples. The first example is a "pure" VNS application which pulls together geographically distributed Petrophysical Scientists located in the US and UK. This system takes advantage of two VNS servers, one in each country. To optimize performance, each team member primarily interacts with the local VNS server. Because the VNS supports access to information across multiple servers in a transparent fashion, team members have no difficulty in accessing and sharing all the information distributed across both servers.

The significance of this application is that this geographically distributed team now has the ability to share complex color images in a *concurrent* fashion. Multi-colored "pointers" are used by the Scientists to draw attention to regions of interest in real time. This is something that could not be achieved previously using conventional methods (e.g., fax, email, telephone, etc.) for many reasons. For instance, faxing this information is not feasible because resolution and color is lost. Even if each team member had a high quality hardcopy in front of him/her, the complexity of the images does not permit them to collaborate over the telephone. In this scenario, too much effort is required to communicate to other team members where to look in the image.

In contrast to the pure VNS application above, the second example demonstrates the importance of being able to extend and customize existing groupware frameworks to meet the needs of the application domain. This application was developed for a team of chemists who perform Mossbauer Effect Spectroscopy analyses on various physical samples. Because this team is already using traditional lab notebooks in the analysis process, it was easy for them to accept the electronic notebook paradigm of the VNS. This is consistent with our strategy as outlined in the first item of Section 2.

Although the ability to share and record information electronically through the VNS is in itself very useful, it was not enough to meet the group's needs. There were several domain dependent requirements (obstacles) that had to be addressed before full-time use of the collaborative environment could be expected. Therefore, the following extensions were added to improve the functionality of the environment: automatic table of contents generation, enhanced information retrieval, page locking, and automatic form and template generation.

Most of these extensions are based on what we learned from our studies of the current work processes of the group and were implemented using the robust API of the VNS. For example, we found that researchers frequently reference information based on experiment date, sample name, and resulting data files. For this reason, an automatic table of contents generation based on this knowledge was implemented. Likewise, it was important to provide the researchers with the ability to retrieve information using keyword search[2] .

Because signed, witnessed, and dated physical lab notebooks are important when applying for patents, the electronic counterpart must have the ability to be used in the same manner. Since electronic notebooks have not yet been tested as legal documents, we added page locking. Once a page is locked (published) by a researcher, it can never be altered again. At the same time, a hardcopy is generated to meet legal requirements.

The last feature, automatic form and template generation, was added to support repetitive requirements that were already in place. For example, a written sample request form was

---

2. For this application, keyword search is sufficient. However, for future applications the ability to retrieve conceptual information will be necessary.

required for every new sample submitted for analysis. With automatic form and template generation, the sample request form can now be entered electronically with minimal effort.

5 FUTURE

Currently, our Knowledge Networks project is generating a lot of interest within the organization. There are several groups within BP who already using the Virtual Notebook System (with and without enhancements), and many other teams which expect to do so in the near future. The initial success, acceptance, and use of the VNS technology by these teams leads us to believe that groupware will play an important role in pulling people and information together within BP.

We plan to continue using the strategy outlined in this paper as we move to further integrate groupware technology into the corporation. We have found that hands-on-experience is the best way for people to become familiar with groupware technology and to gain an appreciation for the potential use of groupware in their work environment. Likewise, an appreciation for a team's work process is an important ingredient when tailoring and customizing groupware technology to fit team member needs. We strongly believe that the success and acceptance of groupware technology is directly dependent upon how well it can be used to enhance and facilitate the current work process as opposed to dramatically changing it.

ACKNOWLEDGEMENTS

We thank Geoffrey Bock (Collaborative Systems Group (OSAG), Digital Equipment Corporation) for his constructive editorial comments. We would also like to thank several of our BP colleagues who have contributed to this project: David Stepien, Arun Jain, Mike Hallam, John Connors, John Haberfield, Rande Burton, Steve Kimminau, Robert Swofford, and Mark Antonio.

REFERENCES

Burger, A.M., Meyer, B.D., Jung, C.P., and Long, K.B. 1991. The Virtual Notebook System. *Third ACM Conference on Hypertext Proceedings*. San Antonio, TX: ACM Press, pp. 395-401.

Gorry, G.A., Long, K.B., Burger, A.M., Jung, C.P., and Meyer, B.D. 1991. The Virtual Notebook System: An Architecture for Collaborative Work. *Journal of Organizational Computing* 1(3):233-250.

GroupWare In Investment Banking: Improving Revenue and Deal Flow

Jeffrey J. Held, Partner
Network Computing Practice
Ernst & Young

Investment banking is a very information intensive business, where possessing the latest or most accurate information can be the difference between winning and losing. As a result, many investment banking organizations have invested heavily in information technology, but most of this investment has been focused on "back room" operations. Until recently, front office operations, the activities of investment bankers and analysts, have not benefited from automation, primarily because traditional mainframe based systems did not have the necessary flexibility. This paper describes a recent project in which an international investment banking concern used the latest groupware technology to substantial improve its front office operations, with great success.

Background

The International Capital Markets Division (ICMD) of Barclays Bank plc is one of the most successful such organizations in the world. With principal offices in London, New York, and Tokyo, ICMD is a leader in global private placements, syndications, and asset securitization, and other complex financial transactions. ICMD had achieved this position without benefits of any automation beyond the use of personal computers for analysis, but its very success began to affect the efficiency of its operation. ICMD found that it was becoming increasingly difficult to gather, analyze, and manage the information needed to analyze a potential deal; to coordinate the activities of originators, analysts, and salesmen all over the world; and to assemble the large and complex offer memoranda needed in the short time intervals required. ICMD subsequently engaged Ernst & Young to develop an implement a technology solution in a pilot group of ICMD professionals.

Key Business Drivers for Groupware

As we began to learn more about ICMD, we found that three major types of activities consumed most of the staff time and were the best candidates for automation:

- Deal Coordination - Since many potential deals were being analyzed or negotiated at any given time, and since most deals involved parties on at least two continents, coordination was both vital and extremely difficult. The current environment provided no method for sharing information other than telephone and facsimile, and the security of this information was also very important.

- Deal Tracking - Knowing was going happening in the worldwide marketplace was the single most important requirement for success in this business. ICMD felt is was vital that it have access to information concerning all deals that were in process or completed, both by ICMD and other investment banking firms, on a worldwide basis.

- Research - Every analysis of a prospective deal required an enormous amount of research to obtain financial data, market data, competitive information, and industry background information. This consumed large amounts of analysts time, was very expensive, and was especially difficult for international companies whose operations were global.

Our solution focused on these three areas, but also provided other benefits as well, as will be discussed in the following sections.

Technology Solution

Our solution was based on Lotus Notes, with several add-on products that included Hoover, by SandPoint Corp., and NewsEdge, by Desktop Data. The application architecture for the solution is shown below:

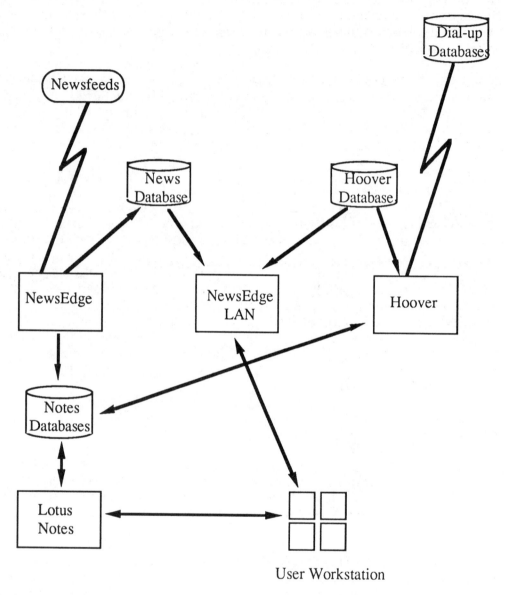

User Workstation

This solution supported each of the three primary needs using a combination of technologies and products:

- Deal Coordination: This function was addressed using a variety of Notes databases, including a deal tracking database, and numerous discussion databases. The users at ICMD very quickly understood the power of the discussion database, and many substantial, if somewhat undisciplined, discussion databases appeared.

- Deal Tracking: The deal tracking database contained summary information about all ICMD deals, as well as any other deals that were known in the marketplace. In addition, the Deal

Tracking database included phone logs, contact reports, correspondence tracking, and action item tracking, all of which has proven to be very useful.

- Research: The functions of NewsEdge and Hoover provided access to two types of information. Current news about potential deal candidates was provided through NewsEdge, which was used to access newswires from the U.S., Europe, and Japan. Retrospective information was provided by Hoover, which would automatically search a variety of databases available from Dow Jones or Dialog to obtain general information about a candidate.

The technology used in this pilot project was "garden variety" personal computers and LANs, as shown below:

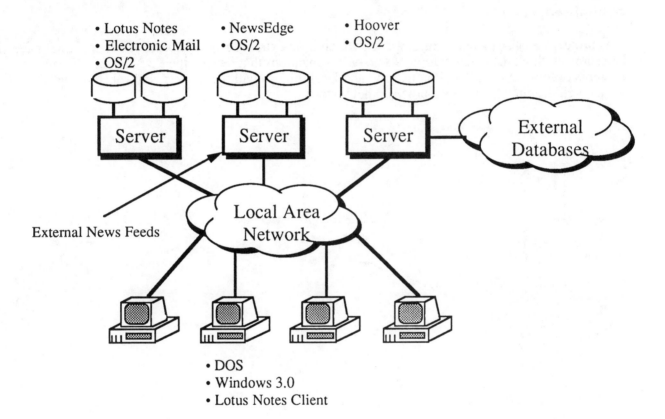

Initially 486 based PCs with 650 Meg hard drives running OS/2 1.3 were used for the servers, with mostly 386 PCs used as user workstations. A 10BaseT LAN using LAN Manager 2.0 connected the workstations and servers. We found that this configuration provided adequate performance for the initial pilot project group of 20 users.

Results to Date

The system, known as MarketTalk, has been enthusiastically received by the users. A measure of their enthusiasm has been the continuing need to upgrade server performance and disk capacities. Within a few weeks of pilot initiation, the 650 Meg hard drives were operating at 95% of capacity, as were most of the OS/2 servers. A combination of careful tuning, purging, and adding servers kept performance from degrading, but it was a continuing challenge. We are now in the process of installing 486 50 Mhz servers using EISA bus technology, and high speed disk arrays to improve performance and reliability. Both these measures have resulted in marked performance improvements. We have also examined several superserver options, including the Compaq SystemPro and the NetFrame product, however, the current limitations imposed by OS/2 make those options less attractive.

In addition, the system has already expanded to around 100 users, and has been declared to be an operational system in ICMD. ICMD has developed plans to expand MarketTalk worldwide, with an eventual users community of over 700 users in 10 cities on three continents. It is also important to note that ICMD senior management are active users of MarketTalk, and this is especially impressive considering that prior to this project, most of these individuals did not even have computers. Other units of Barclays are also expressing interest in Notes, and are beginning to experiment with it as well, and we expect substantial growth in the user of Notes through the bank.

Acknolwedgements

This project was completed in eight weeks, which is an extraordinarily short time. It could not have been done without the collaboration of several organzations that formed the E&Y team: Distributed Systems Solutions, Inc., SandPoint Corp., and Desktop Data all performed vital roles in a very difficult environment, and we appreciate their efforts.

ELECTRONIC COLLABORATIONS IN A MULTI-CAMPUS NETWORK

John P. Witherspoon
San Diego State University
San Diego, California 92182-0117

ABSTRACT

We are developing virtual institutions: non-geographic communities of interest made possible by applications of information technology. BESTNET (Binational English-Spanish Telecommunications Network) is a consortium of nine university and college campuses in the southwestern United States and northern Mexico, with a growing number of users elsewhere as well. Based on off-the-shelf VAX technology for electronic mail, conferencing, and videotext, and riding the Internet, BESTNET has provided experience in developing and managing virtual institutions; collaborative research and course development; peer-to-peer work in "electronic classrooms;" and cross-cultural collaborations (involving multiple national and organizational cultures) in teaching and research.

1. INTRODUCTION

As we learn more about the possibilities of everyday information technology, we find ourselves living in new kinds of organizations. BESTNET is one example. BESTNET -- created as the Binational English-Spanish Telecommunications Network -- began as an experiment in cross-border communication between campuses in southern California and northern Mexico. Now there are nine formal members: two Mexican institutions, four campuses of the California State University system, one campus of the University of California, the University of New Mexico, and Texas A&I. More telling than a membership roster, however, is that with virtually no promotion the idea has attracted so much attention that the MicroVAX at the San Diego node is now host to nearly four thousand accounts from throughout the United States and several other countries.

Why are all these people attracted to BESTNET? The answer does not lie in some new technical magic. The technology is straightforward and familiar to many: with the sponsorship of the Digital Equipment Corporation, we're based on VAX computers, using VAX Notes for conferencing, VAX Mail, and VTX videotext. Transmission is via the Internet. The technology, then, is not the most glamorous in anybody's product line. Its great virtues are that it does what it was designed to do, it can be used with a minimum of training, and when used appropriately its power can be leveraged to great effect.

The key to the emergence of BESTNET lies in using this technology in the service of an old-fashioned idea: communities of interest; people collaborating to serve their common purposes. In short, it's groupware, usefully applied.

This conclusion is more than a hunch expressed by one who is caught up in the idea. BESTNET is based in universities accustomed to conducting research, and its members have been studying the process of creating and managing this virtual institution. We've also been deliberately examining the effects of what we do in courses and other applications of the system.

2. STUDENTS, BESTNET, AND THE UNIVERSITY

Following is one illustrative example of BESTNET applied to teaching and learning in today's university. It is based on a non-technical course on telecommunication trends and policy, taught by the author at San Diego State University. Last fall the course did not have conventional class meetings, instead using a combination of BESTNET electronic mail and computer conferences, specially prepared videos in lieu of lectures, a hefty package of print material, plus individual meetings, phone conferences, etc. The format was chosen to meet some real-world issues:

- <u>A desire to meet the difficult schedules faced by students.</u> The stereotypical 18-22 year old undergraduate is now a minority population. The typical undergraduate in the California State University system is now 25 and working at least half-time. The fastest-growing population in U.S. higher education is women over 35. These students may be on campus many hours each week, but they often find it difficult to coordinate their working lives and fixed course schedules.

- <u>A desire to improve the quality of instruction.</u> It is well established that no one medium or method of instruction is best under all circumstances. Collaborative learning is known to be effective but is seldom tried.

- <u>A desire to accommodate the individual characteristics of students.</u>
Students appear in the classroom with varying degrees of prior understanding about the subject matter.   International students, often new to
English, find themselves studying unfamiliar material in a strange language.   In the course reported here, one benefit turned out to be that students relatively new to English could rewind and replay portions of the
videos, or take as long as necessary to enter material into the BESTNET
system, in order to be sure they understood the material.   Furthermore, in
their online collaborative work these students could take the time to be
sure that they were communicating the ideas they intended.

The student, then, could take the course on his/her own schedule,
staying in step with the class week by week but participating in the computer conferences, viewing the videos, and doing the reading literally at
any time of the week, day or night.   The practical result of this approach to
course design was that the focus shifted from a lecture-oriented classroom,
in which students come to listen and take notes, to a situation in which the
emphasis is on the work of the students and their online association and
collaboration with peers and professor.

A suite of a half-dozen conferences involved collaboration of several
kinds:
- discussions of current issues in the field based on questions posed
by the professor;
- the development of online "term papers" by groups of students;
- online discussions with guest experts, the most active of whom was
outside the United States during the whole of the course;
- the preparation of an ongoing "abstracts service" in which students
reported on developments in the field by preparing abstracts of leading
articles from current trade publications, sharing their findings via a conference designed for the purpose;
- an informal "TelePub," in which students could take some virtual
refreshment and discuss the subject matter of the course and other matters of interest which, as it turned out, included some truly awful jokes
and plans for a party held at the home of a class member who knew most
of her colleagues by name (or username) but not face-to-face until they
arrived at her door.

During the course a group of graduate students conducted a set of
surveys and focus groups, with a basic groundrule that respondents would
not be identified to the professor.   At the end of the semester the author
conducted a final focus group with a self-selected (but, as it happened,
representative) group of students.   Among the findings:

- 64% of respondents believed that this class format "enhanced learning, compared to conventionally taught classes."

- 66% agreed with a statement that the course format "made it more comfortable for me to express my thoughts and opinions."

- By nearly 2 to 1, students agreed that "the format of the class allowed me to learn more from other students' input than is usually the case in traditional classes."

- By nearly 3 to 1, students agreed that the professor was more accessible than is normally the case, and 60% characterized the professor's attention as more personalized than would have been the case in a traditional class environment.

Aspects of collaboration -- the ability to read others' ideas and share work with them -- turned out to be a leading benefit of the course, according to those participating in the final focus group.

The value students place on collaborative work is almost certainly behind an important (if subjective) observation by the professor: the quality of student writing was clearly better than in earlier, more traditional versions of the course. The only explanation to have surfaced to date is that the students wrote better because they were writing for each other, and not merely to satisfy a course requirement.

While this course was focused on one campus, BESTNET provides access to conferences from anywhere on the network, and a multicampus (perhaps multinational), collaboratively developed version is under study.

3. CULTURES AND COLLABORATION

From the discussion above one should not conclude that the academic work of BESTNET is restricted to communication or information technology. Among the earliest purposes of BESTNET was transborder study of peoples and cultures, via courses and related research in sociology and anthropology. At Texas A&I, for example, BESTNET was used during the past academic year to support collaborative work for courses in Social Psychology and Chicano Studies. The University of California at Irvine (often in collaboration with California State University, Los Angeles) uses multisite, U.S.-Mexican conferences in courses and research programs including Ethnographies of the U.S.-Mexican Border, Intercultural Communication, and Theory and Practice of Longterm Social and Economic Development.

4. BESTNET AS A COLLABORATIVE VIRTUAL INSTITUTION

At first glance BESTNET might seem to be a conventional consortium of university representatives. From time to time, members of the Board of Directors meet face to face to discuss matters of organizational interest. Typically, however, while issues are raised in face-to-face meetings or by electronic mail, they are examined collaboratively over time in VAX Notes conferences and are resolved via the resulting consensus. BESTNET is a distributed network which is home to a genuinely distributed organization.

5. CONCLUSION

Like many useful ideas, BESTNET began as a straightforward response to a real-world requirement. It was never a solution in search of a problem or a technology seeking an application. With the support of the Digital Equipment Corporation, which has been very important, and with the active participation of users who seem to multiply day by day, BESTNET has become an environment in which collaboration, specifically for education and research, takes place easily and naturally. And that, of course, is what groupware should be about.

GroupWare '92
San Jose Convention Center
San Jose, CA
August 3rd - 5th, 1992

Groupware—One Experience

Til Dallavalle, Red Bank, NJ   Alicia Esposito, Livingston, NJ
Steve Lang, Piscataway, NJ
Bellcore

What Is It

What is this thing called Groupware? Perhaps an understanding of what it is not will hasten an understanding of what it is. It is not a new technology nor is it a new management or process technique. Groupware is a set of tools which uses Computers and Communications to increase productivity and effectiveness of team and group related work or processes. Many names and titles have been applied to this *thing* called Groupware. It has been generically referred to as; Computer Assisted Communications, Interpersonal Computing, Group Decision Support Systems, and Work group Computing to mention a few.

Some of the most common communications tools such as: electronic mail, voice mail, overhead projectors, electronic blackboards, meeting rooms, audio/video teleconferencing and of course the "ubiquitous" telephone are also fundamental tools for groupware applications. The magic is in the synergy of these tools when they are integrated for groupware applications.

Within Bellcore the term Teamware has evolved as a descriptor for our implementation of groupware. As stated earlier, groupware is not new a technology; however, it is a more effective and efficient use of existing computer and communications technologies to support team and work group collaborative efforts. During the mid to late 1980s, Bellcore installed thousands of personal computers some of which were connected to Local Area Networks. The productivity improvements as a result of this embedded technology were primarily related to individual gains rather than the synergistic increases which derive from collaborative efforts.

The notion of integrating traditional stand-alone applications using Computers and Communications is not new to Bellcore. Robert Kraut, working in Bellcore's Applied Research Lab, and his team developed a computer-based tool, "*Quilt*", for collaborative writing several years ago to promote rapid production of documents which required the input and review of many individuals. In 1989 Bellcore's Corporate Telecommunications Department began an investigation of groupware's potential by becoming a member of the Groupware User's Exchange Project which provided research funding to the IFTF (Institute For The Future). The Institute is a non-profit future oriented research group in Menlo Park, CA. that researches and documents current groupware applications and the potential for future ones.

As a spin-off from what was learned from the IFTF research, the Corporate Telecommunications Department teamed with Bellcore's Quality Advisors to test the potential benefits of groupware in support of Quality Team meetings. Groupware appeared to offer some immediate benefits to the quality process by accelerating the idea generation activity for the development of possible solutions to reengineering and work flow problems. In addition to the involvement of Quality Advisors, members of other departments were brought into the early planning stages to assess the potential benefits of groupware when applied to planning activities and work group communications processes.

Why Use It

Exactly what was it that motivated us to explore the use of a combination of tools and technology? First, consider some of the problems associated with traditional meetings. For example, the problem of lost ideas that do not surface in a meeting. This may be due to dominating extroverts in the meeting, an individual's fear of sounding "silly", or some individuals' hesitation to challenge authority. Ideas also have a hard time surfacing when meetings focus on personalities and not on content.

Some other problems experienced in traditional meetings include time wasted on "*political*" posturing, and the serial nature of communications (e.g., one person discussing one topic at one time). In addition, documenting the meeting may be time consuming, long in coming and lose something in the translation.

So why use groupware to address problems like these? In today's global economy we all face an increasingly competitive business environment. As a result we are consistently expected to shorten our business cycles to compete. Our teams must do more than just communicate effectively. The contribution of each employee must be focused and integrated with the whole. In short, we must achieve collaboration.

Expected Benefits

By introducing groupware in Bellcore we anticipated that teams through the use of this technology would reach agreement more quickly on sensitive issues and be more productive than those teams that do not use groupware tools. The teams will use electronic groupware tools which will jump-start team activities such as: electronic brainstorming, consensus testing, voting, idea categorization, evaluation of alternatives, and team document preparation to name a few. Our expectation is that this groupware facilitated collaboration will promote team ownership and support for group decisions. Specifically, the tools will facilitate team functions by:

1. Supporting group decision making and consensus building
2. Improving communications
3. Promoting greater innovation and creativity
4. Enhancing the ability to focus on the task
5. Increasing the number of ideas generated
6. Improving team productivity, team building and ownership

While improved communications among participants may occur, the bigger payoff will come from the expected increase in ideas and input which supports innovation and creativity as the result of greater participation by individual team members.

What Is Required

Groupware as stated previously is not a new technology nor is it a replacement for team/group dynamics. More importantly it is not the "end all solution". Rather it is an approach to using technology, communications and computers, as an effective and efficient tool to support true collaboration. Five essential ingredients were needed to successfully employ the groupware meeting support tools within Bellcore:

1. A meeting room
2. A meeting facilitator/team guide
3. A set of computer workstations (PCs) on a Local Area Network
4. A set of groupware software tools
5. A disciplined process

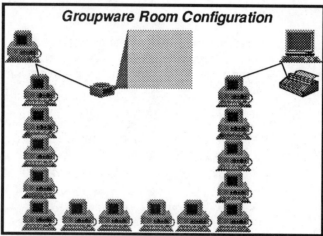

Figure 1.0   *Groupware Room*

The process includes three major steps. To begin the process, there is a preplanning session where the facilitator reviews the objectives of the meeting and designs an agenda to achieve the objectives.   The second step is conducting the actual meeting with the facilitator using the groupware tools.   And finally, there is follow-up by the facilitator to evaluate the meeting's effectiveness and plan the next steps when appropriate. This three step process will support several different types of meeting activities including:

- strategic planning sessions
- idea generation/brain-storming
- resolution of sensitive ideas
- problem solving
- requirements gathering
- negotiations
- systems analysis and design
- team building
- policy development

Some specific characteristics that make groupware meetings productive are:

1. Anonymity - the use of the electronic tools prevents the specific identification of the participants
2. Ability to focus on content, not personality
3. Equality of participation - ideas are not inhibited by dominant personalities, all participants have equal access to the tools
4. Parallel and simultaneous communications - accomplished through a Local Area Network
5. Provides a complete written record of the meeting - each participant can leave the meeting with a record of the   meeting accomplishments in the form of a paper copy, a computer floppy diskette, or both
6. Efficiency - participants have fewer meetings

7. Enjoyability - participants appreciate the creative and innovative environment it promotes

Armed with the introductory experience, Bellcore's Corporate Telecommunications Department implemented a groupware lab to gain more experience with specific applications and understand how they might support Bellcore's business processes.

Bellcore's Experience

Our experience with groupware tools developed in today's marketplace began with an exploratory visit to a vendor's location to use their groupware facility. Members of a Quality Improvement organization in Bellcore were so impressed with the potential of these tools that quality improvement teams were invited to explore this approach. Between February and March 1991, four quality improvement teams used this facility. These teams were working on ways to improve their products, services, and basic business planning processes within the company as well as improving teamwork across diverse work groups.

In follow-up surveys participants indicated how they felt about the sessions as compared to traditional meetings (*figures 2.0 & 3.0*):

- 40% felt that the groupware supported meetings were more than three times as productive.
- 40% felt that the groupware supported meetings were three times as productive.
- 20% felt that the groupware supported meetings were twice as productive.

Additionally:

- 40% felt that their task was accomplished in less than 1/3 the amount of time
- 60% felt that their task was accomplished in 1/3 the amount of time

Productivity & Time Comparisons

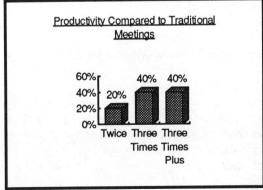

Figure 2.0

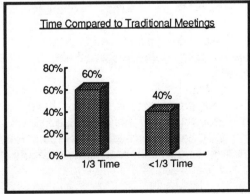

Figure 3.0

Some of the participant verbatim comments were:

> "I would recommend this tool to all levels of management."
> "...it's a time saver, it saves ideas, and analysis is rapid."
> "This helps to get everyone's input, regardless of level or personality."
> "Without a doubt, groupware could be used to augment the quality process..."

One of the Quality Teams that participated had come to the session expecting to complete their assignment (i.e., making recommendations on how to improve team effectiveness in their organization) sometime in July, 1991; however, as a result of the productivity from using the groupware tools for one day, they revised their expected completion date to April, 1991 and met the revised date.

Coming On Board

Bellcore's experience with the groupware trial provided support for the development of a "lab" site to continue to test the feasibility of using this new tool in our business environment. Our objective was to begin to trial the use of groupware with selected teams in January 1992.

In order to meet that objective, the "lab" site was developed and constructed during November and December 1991. Facilitators were given six days of formal training by the vendor. A one-day application training session was also conducted by a consultant experienced in the use of groupware with actual teams.

We learned that the formal training needed to be supplemented with "hands on" experience in using the tools. Prior to using the groupware tools for the first time with teams, our facilitators received about ten days of informal practice using the equipment. The facilitators also developed a peer group support network. In addition to jointly designing meetings, the members of this network informally certified each other in the use of the tools. This collaborative teaming maximized the group's knowledge and ideas about the application of the groupware tools and helped to reduce what otherwise might have been steep learning curves during the start-up process.

Initial Applications: "Same Time, Same Place"

"Same time, same place meetings occur when the participants are face to face in the same room at the same time. It is the most frequent format for meetings in Bellcore.

With the "lab" site implemented and facilitators trained, we were able to begin using groupware with teams. During January and February 1992, we used groupware with 12 teams or roughly 120 people.

Thus far, our groupware applications have focused primarily on business-planning and quality-improvement activities. We have used groupware to: design organizational vision and mission statements, develop business objectives, explore customer product and service needs, analyze the strengths and weaknesses of our products and services, and to improve team effectiveness.

Managing The Meeting Process Using Groupware

Through these applications, our facilitators have developed insights into the use of groupware as a tool to enhance the process of holding meetings. These insights fall into the following categories:

1. pre-meeting preparation
2. meeting facilitation
3. post-meeting follow-up

Pre-meeting Preparation

Facilitators learned that they need to follow the same pre-meeting process steps, with or without groupware. These steps include such activities as consulting with the person who is originating the meeting to define the purpose and objectives of the meeting. A meeting must then be designed, including the use of tools and techniques, to meet the desired objectives. Our facilitators have found that it usually takes about the same amount of time for pre-meeting activities, with or without groupware.

Additionally, the facilitators found that it is very helpful during pre-meeting consultation with the meeting originator to manage the meeting originator's and participants' perceptions and expectations regarding groupware. Sometimes, facilitators discovered that the meeting originator and participants had totally unrealistic expectations about groupware; facilitators had to provide information to participants prior to the meeting to help them develop a more realistic picture of how groupware would be used.

In the initial applications, facilitators found that meeting objectives could usually be met by using a basic set of groupware tools for generating, organizing, evaluating, and selecting ideas, as well as building implementation plans. This meant that the facilitators really only had to master a manageable set of tools in order to meet the objectives of the meetings. This was extremely helpful during the learning curve.

Meeting Facilitation

The facilitators found that they needed the same basic facilitation skills, with or without, groupware. These skills focus on managing group dynamics, the needs of the individuals, and the task itself. Overall, however, the facilitators discovered that the use of groupware tools requires increased sensitivity to group dynamics. This sensitivity focuses on the following areas:

- Communication and sharing
- Anonymity
- The management of data
- The environment

During the 1991 trial, feedback from the participants indicated the need for ensuring the careful balance of "live talk time" with "electronic talk time". In our initial applications, therefore, the facilitators designed discussion periods into the meeting. This also addressed the tendency for groups to become mesmerized or lured into simply using tools because they were there, at the expense of the meeting purpose or objective. Simply put, the facilitators tried to use groupware as a tool to facilitate a given task, rather than designing a groupware session to use as many tools as possible.

Another communication challenge for groupware facilitators is the need to deal with group members who are used to being in control of meetings. With groupware, some participants may have to share perceived power and control with other members of the group. This loss of control may manifest itself through a lack of interest and participation in the meeting. Facilitators have developed ground rules that they share with meeting participants at the beginning of the meeting to sensitize participants to the need for equal sharing and participation in the meeting.

Another ground rule developed by facilitators and discussed with meeting participants involves creating a sensitivity to anonymity in the groupware environment. The facilitators found that the anonymity feature of groupware requires a heightened awareness by the facilitators and the meeting participants about the impact of anonymity on the group. For example, because the groupware tools may allow group members to remain anonymous as they input ideas and comments, the group may become insensitive to individual perspectives on an issue. Further, if a conflict emerges as a result, and if the group does not get the opportunity to "socially enact" and resolve the conflict, participants may become frustrated, and team dynamics may suffer.

The facilitators also discovered that because some of the groupware tools enhance a group's ability to generate a large volume of ideas, the group may be unable to process such a large number of ideas. In the pre-meeting design, the facilitator must plan for managing the potential volume. Some techniques facilitators have found helpful include cutting down on the time associated with the idea-generation tools, having the group work in pairs or small groups to generate and prioritize ideas, and limiting the time spent during a meeting to edit the group's ideas.

Finally, facilitators found that because groupware enables a group to work more intensely and quickly, the group sometimes tires more easily. Thus, facilitators offer more frequent breaks and are extremely cognizant of environmental factors such as proper heating, lighting, and air flow during the meeting.

Post Meeting Follow-Up

Facilitators found that quantitative data-collection tools such as questionnaires, along with qualitative feedback from the meeting originator and participants, are important to improving the effectiveness of using groupware. Further, the facilitators now hold debriefing sessions with other facilitators after each application to share information and to constantly improve the process of applying groupware to meet our customers' needs. The data collected during these initial applications will also be used in a business case to support the implementation of groupware in Bellcore.

Implementation: July - December 1992

Implementation activities for the July through December 1992 time frame include building a business case for the potential implementation of groupware in the Bellcore environment. As previously mentioned, part of the business case will be built on customer feedback collected during the initial applications.

Another key implementation activity for this time frame will be the expansion of the initial applications to include senior-management applications, cross-organizational teaming applications, and the integration of the tools in the normal day- to-day business environment; e.g., to improve staff meetings. Other activities will include work with distributed-access applications initially focused on *"same time, different place"* meetings where participants are collaborating using groupware at the same time but from different locations.

"Any Time, Any Place"

Although most of our efforts from late 1990 through early 1992 have focused on identifying applications and preparing plans for implementing groupware in the *"same time, same place"* environment. The ultimate objective is to achieve *"any time, any place"* meetings where participant collaborations occur at any time, day or night, and from any location. It has become very clear that to achieve the maximum benefits of groupware technology the *"any time, any place"* mode must become part of the future implementation.   The ubiquitous availability of communication networks has prompted groupware meeting participants to request that groupware applications in addition to being in a meeting room should be accessible from their office or home computer/workstations to expand opportunities for collaboration.

Physical and logical connectivity to groupware applications in the *"any time, any place"* collaborative environment will be through personal computers/workstations using public telecommunication networks including Integrated Services Digital Network (ISDN) and other architectures such as Local and Wide Area Networks.

Future Applications: 1993 ----

As groupware applications become widely deployed in Bellcore, we anticipate these applications will supplement the face-to-face meetings between project teams and their customers. This is especially true in those cases where geographical separation precludes frequent face-to-face meetings for project reviews. Other applications will facilitate meetings between Bellcore and industry representatives in the generic requirements development process. These are only a few of the many possible ways where groupware can be used in addition to its present uses in Bellcore.

Literally, with each passing day, we are discovering additional applications where groupware enhances the processes by increasing productivity and customer focus in teams and work groups. Groupware is helping us become a **"best managed"** company which translates to reduced operating costs and increased value to our customers.

In our trial we have only brushed the tip of this productivity improvement iceberg.

Look Ma, No Prototype!

Brad Post
TeamFocus Group
Boeing Computer Services
Professional Services Organization PSO

and

Doug Vogel, Associate Professor
Management Information Systems Department
University of Arizona
Tucson, Arizona 85721

Doing business today means accomplishing group work. The modern organization depends on the participation and consensus of its employees and interested others--all of whom are potential stakeholders in the many business processes and decisions that create success.

Groups and teams now form the bedrock of most business operations and as such, have merged as the crucial resource in our continuing effort to increase the quality of our products and services. Business group behavior alone cannot produce the results that are necessary to sustain the competitiveness, growth and rich rewards we seek for ourselves and our customers. We can only produce significant business improvements through enhanced group activity that we closely fit to the strategies, processes and technologies of our work.

There has been a growing interest in computer-based technologies that promise to make groups work more effectively and efficiently. This field of interest is now popularly called Group Decision Support (GDS). Over the last few years a trend had developed toward the use of shared information technology such as electronic mail, distributed databases, teleconferencing and group decision support systems.

Group support technologies include a wide range of tools that support group work and increase productivity. These "groupware" tools assist activities such as electronic brainstorming, issue analysis, alternative evaluation and voting.

Evaluation Mission and Objectives

The GroupSystems/TeamFocus product was evaluated. It was developed by the University of Arizona and its spin-off company Ventana Corporation and marketed by IBM. TeamFocus is the IBM private label for GroupSystems.
The mission of the evaluation was to appraise the value of the TeamFocus product so as to:

- Develop insight into group decision support. Determine whether the TeamFocus technology would enhance or detract from current business team practices and expand our knowledge in matters important in the decision support system area.

- Determine customer impact.   Answer such questions as: "What are the measurable benefits of the technology?" "How does the technology improve group work quality?" "What is the return on investment?"

- Assess integration issues with existing PSO services. Explore the impacts and efforts required of systems integration, management consulting and group facilitation services inside the company to the application of Group Decision support technologies.

The objectives of the evaluation were to:

- Help customers make significantly faster decisions (flowtime).
- Support quality assurance in customer decision processes with quantification, traceability and increased participation (quality).
- Significantly improve the leverage of PSO resources (cost-benefit).
- Add value by enhancing customers' impact on their businesses (effectiveness).

Project History

Planning for this business technology evaluation began in the fall of 1990 with a technical feasibility review of leading GDS products that support team collaboration functions.   This involved the formation of a small group of specialists who reviewed current research and product literature. They also consulted with Company researchers who kept abreast of GDS issues and technologies and participated in product demonstrations. They then prepared a statement of work focused on reviewing a leading group support technology product. The technical feasibility review included an analysis of the product literature, technical description and user documentation. The technical assessment also included an evaluation tour of IBM TeamFocus facilities in Washington D.C. area. In October 1990, the technical feasibility report recommended that the Professional Services Organization proceed with the formation of an evaluation team and identification of a project manager.

TeamFocus software acquisition began in December 1990. In parallel with the acquisition efforts, the evaluation team proceeded with TeamFocus facility development, evaluation metrics design, customer identification, evaluation procedures and process definition. A key project activity was the identification and training of the initial TeamFocus facilitators. By February 1991, the team was ready to begin the first internal learning and training TeamFocus sessions. Before the formal evaluation could begin, the necessary evaluation vehicles (questionnaires, surveys and database) had to be designed and put in place. The formal evaluation of the TeamFocus technology began in March, 1991.

The evaluation TeamFocus facility was created using surplus XT workstations, and AT class facilitator workstation and a 386 file server. This was considered a "shoestring" configuration to keep the evaluation costs low. Additional equipment included a portable color projection system for a public screen and a state-of-the-art screen grabber that would allow screen capture and VGA display of computer screen data. Despite "teething problems" with the hardware and software, the facility was operational for the evaluation of the TeamFocus product by March, 1991.

Along with these infrastructure developments went the definition of an evaluation methodology, data architecture and business case metrics. Outside experts assisted to help ensure both sound measurement procedures and sound criteria. The metrics were tested on internal team members during mock TeamFocus sessions, then refined to meet production requirements of customer sessions.

The TeamFocus evaluation methodology and process were fleshed out and defined in the Customer Lifecycle Procedures created by the evaluation team. The Customer Lifecycle Procedures standardized the approach for the "cradle-to-grave" process of conducting a TeamFocus session. Standardization was crucial to an objective evaluation and to ensuring a quality service that adds value to the customer. It also helped establish a firm basis for the rapid deployment of the product as a business service offering. The Customer Lifecycle Procedures cover five distinct phases of activity:

Phase 1: Customer Acquisition
Phase 2: Session Planning
Phase 3: Session Activities
Phase 4: Evaluation Administration
Phase 5: Post-Session Follow-up

By examining the standard tasks within each phase it was possible to estimate time and resource requirements of the various evaluation team members (facilitators, marketing and session schedulers, evaluators, data entry, etc.). But most importantly the lifecycle procedures provided a standard and model for the delivery of a quality session and evaluation for each customer.

The formal TeamFocus evaluation ran from March, 1991, through the end of August, 1991. This evaluation included 64 sessions covering a wide spectrum of customers and business applications throughout the Company.

The business case for the development of the recommended TeamFocus prototype and service offering (practice) is based solely on the cost benefit analysis. This analysis was developed from evaluating 64 customer sessions using TeamFocus at The Boeing Company. As discussed elsewhere in this report, these customer sessions measured costs and benefits according to those customers involved in this examination. In every case, the data used for this analysis was either collected directly by the evaluation team or was provided by customer management based on their direct experience in the measurement of these activities. These financial data make it clear that combined Phase 1 and 2 productivity gains exceed investment and further that each "Production" facility has a life cycle savings (NPV) potential of $1M on an initial investment of less than $300,000. The data indicate that the Phase 2 TeamFocus activities concerning the development of a prototype facility and customer service offering will generate savings for the Company in excess of $2,208,000 over a five year period. Phase 2 costs will average $557,000 per year.

Perhaps more dramatically, quantified data collected during the Phase 1 evaluation period showed an average flowtime savings of 91%, when compared to other group work methods currently used without TeamFocus. The bottom-line value of flowtime savings of this magnitude, represents highly significant additional potential savings to the Company. Taken together, the business case for TeamFocus is striking. As a result of this evaluation, an objective case has been demonstrated that the use of TeamFocus is clearly a major source for productivity in terms of labor hours saved and monumental flowtime reduction.

TeamFocus Case Study: Tooling Shop Floor Control

Background:

BCAG needed to define a user requirement set to support the development of the Tooling Shop Floor Control (TSFC) computing system. Although some design work had already been started by the TSFC group, this requirement set was crucial to producing a system that could efficiently support the people on the floor. However, gathering the requirement data meant risking a schedule slip. The TSFC group found the solution to gathering requirement data in the flowtime reduction promised by TeamFocus.

Objectives:

The objectives of these sessions were twofold:

1. Specify the current business functions.
2. Identify user requirements specific to TSFC.

The TSFC group believes that these objectives were met and exceeded with many additional benefits.

TSFC Benefits

By using TeamFocus, the TSFC group was able to deploy its resources more effectively and compress activities avoiding the expected schedule slide. The AS-IS models of each division's functions will yield further savings as the computing system is integrated into the shop floor.

The customer has realized additional benefits:

- Requirement and process data gathered exceeded all expectations.
- Users felt they had ownership in the system since they contributed to its design.
- The TSFC group was able to redeploy its resources to other critical areas.
- No data input required. All data already on magnetic media for analysis with computers.

TRACK 6:
Special Sessions

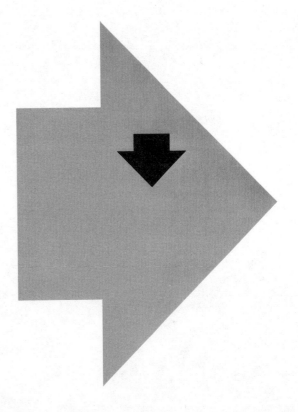

GroupWare '92

End-User Multimedia and Integrated Messaging Trends:
Shifting Priorities

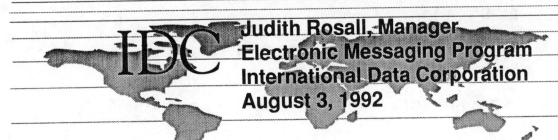

Judith Rosall, Manager
Electronic Messaging Program
International Data Corporation
August 3, 1992

Agenda

Siginificant shifts in end-user priorities reveal that electronic mail in the corporate environment is moving beyond its traditional role as an interpersonal communications vehicle to become a universal platform for a wide variety of integrated messaging technologies and services.

■ **Understanding today's environment**

■ **What kind of messaging products and services are end users looking for?**

■ **What areas of the market are growing?**

■ **What are some key messaging trends?**

■ **Predictions**

■ **Conclusions**

Understanding Today's Environment

- What are some of the most popular e-mail applications worldwide?

- What is the penetration rate of electronic mail, fax and voicemail in the corporate environment?

- Are users standardizing on specific electronic mail platforms?

- What is the corporate use of messaging technologies?

- What are some key emerging technologies?

IDC

Understanding Today's Environment

What are some of the most popular e-mail applications worldwide?

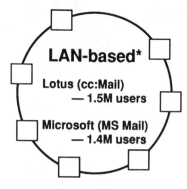

LAN-based*

Lotus (cc:Mail)
— 1.5M users

Microsoft (MS Mail)
— 1.4M users

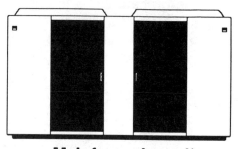

Mainframe-based*

IBM (Office Vision/Profs) — 1.5M users
Verimation — 1.2M users

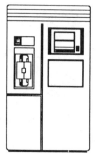

Midrange-based*

DEC (All-In-1) — 3.5M users

*Worldwide count for year ending 1991

IDC

Understanding Today's Environment

What is the penetration rate of electronic mail, fax and voicemail in the corporate environment?

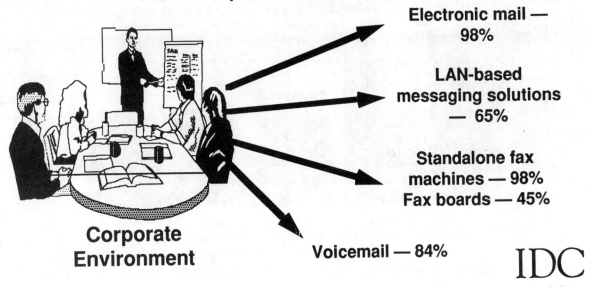

Electronic mail — 98%

LAN-based messaging solutions — 65%

Standalone fax machines — 98%
Fax boards — 45%

Corporate Environment

Voicemail — 84%

IDC

Understanding Today's Environment

Are users standardizing on specific electronic mail platforms?

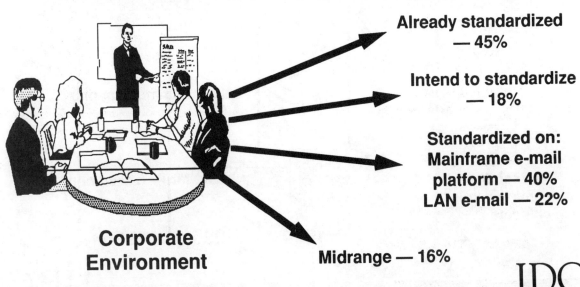

Already standardized — 45%

Intend to standardize — 18%

Standardized on:
Mainframe e-mail platform — 40%
LAN e-mail — 22%

Corporate Environment

Midrange — 16%

IDC

Corporate Use of Messaging Technologies Increases

Survey respondents say a high priority is to integrate e-mail, fax, EDI and online information systems.

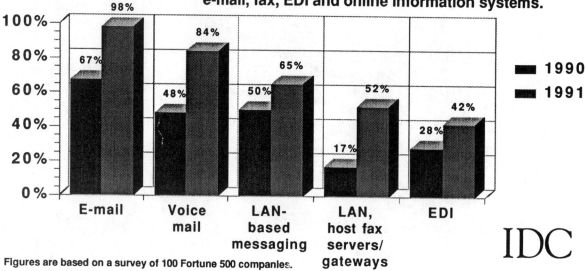

Figures are based on a survey of 100 Fortune 500 companies.

IDC

Understanding Today's Environment

What are some key emerging technologies?

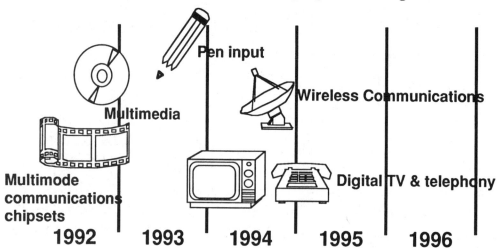

IDC

Trends: What Kind of Messaging Products and Services Are U.S. (Multinational) End Users Looking for?

End user preferences for:
- **Integrated messaging services**
- **Public messaging services**
- **Messaging application integration services**

IDC

Trends: End-User Preferences for Integrated Messaging Services
(Importance Rating: High to Very High)

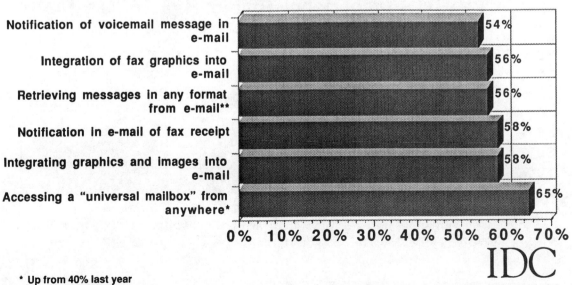

IDC

* Up from 40% last year
** Up from 35% last year

Trends: End-User Preferences for Public Messaging Services

(Major end-user external messaging purchasing trends over next 20 months)

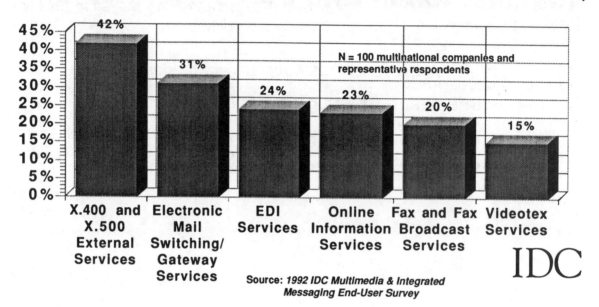

Source: *1992 IDC Multimedia & Integrated Messaging End-User Survey*

Trends: End-User Preferences for Messaging Application Integration Services (Importance Rating: High to Very High)

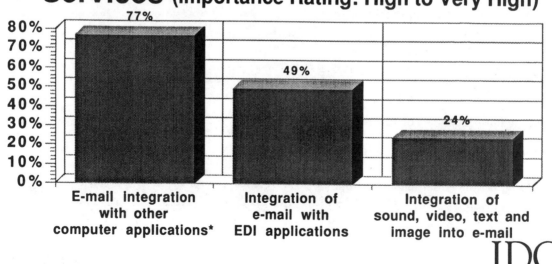

*Up from 45% last year

Trends: What Areas of the Market Are Growing?

Global (public) electronic messaging services	The worldwide public e-mail users base is expected to grow from 4.9 million in 1991 to 38 million by 1996
LAN-based electronic mail systems	LANs will become the dominant e-mail platform for the 1990s. By 1995, LANs will support 36 million users worldwide, or 63% of the total market. This compares to 20% of the total market in 1990.
Electronic mail gateways LAN X.400 vs. host X.400	LAN X.400 gateway revenues will increase at a CAGR of 104%, compared to 27% for host X.400 gateways over the next four years.

IDC

What Are Some Key End-User Messaging Trends?

- End users shift to LAN solutions
- Integration of public and private electronic mail systems
- Increased commitment to X.400-based products and services
- Increased demand for customized integrated messaging applications and services

IDC

End Users Shift to LAN Solutions

Transition to LAN-Centric Networking

- LAN dominance
- Building corporate internetworks
- Network coexistence

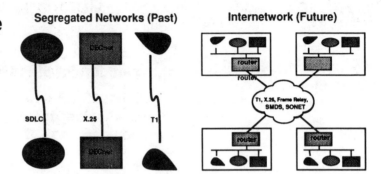

IDC

End Users Shift to LAN Solutions

Transition to LAN-Centric Application Solutions

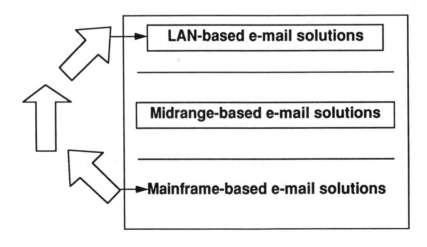

LAN-based e-mail solutions

Midrange-based e-mail solutions

Mainframe-based e-mail solutions

Trend	Vendor Response
Integration of public and private electronic mail systems*	**Sprint MailExchange** **Compuserve's Novell MHS Interconnection Service** **Infonet's Email Switching Outsourcing service (via SSW central)**

*Source: IDC Multimedia/Integrated Messaging
End-User Survey, 1992

Trend	Vendor Response
Increased commitment to X.400-based products and services*	**AT&T:** **Sprint International:** Commitment to ADMD interconnections Commitment to X.400 services **ISOCOR — X.400 Lite** **SoftSwitch — EMX (Enterprise Mail Exchange)**

*Source: IDC Multimedia/Integrated Messaging
End-User Survey, 1992

IDC

Trend	Vendor Response
Increased demand for customized integrated messaging applications and services	**IBM Information Network** — "Electronic Markets" in the insurance, retail apparel and health care industries **GEIS** — CargoLink; UPC*Express COEP **AT&T** — ABA Net **Lotus** — Lotus Notes — numerous vertical turnkey applications

IDC

Predictions

Four predictions about short-term directions of this industry

IDC

Prediction #1

Electronic mail will reach critical mass and become an indispensable utility by 1994

Prediction #2

Electronic mail will become the corporate backbone providing an infrastructure for all key business applications

Prediction #3

Expect more consolidations and partnerships taking place among key electronic mail suppliers

Prediction #4

OSI is in the mail!

IDC

Conclusions

■ **End users are beginning to reshape the corporate infrastructure**

■ **Messaging providers will react with products and services more closely aligned with end-user strategies**

■ **Messaging provider specialization critical**

■ **OSI is a messaging provider imperative**

gw1-01.n08 5/19/92:

Workgroup Applications from the Network Point of View

Banyan Systems Inc.
Ed Harnish

seh2-03.n08 4/14/92:

*In the future, modern man will have the
'Know How' to construct lightning fast
computing devices, what he will lack is the
'Know What' needed to fully exploit such devices...*

"The Human Use of Human Beings"
Norbert Weinhart, 1955

seh2-04.n08 3/24/92:

Myths about Technology

- Every technology advancement must be utilized
- Connectivity of systems guarantees success

- **Greatest Return:**
  - Increased efficiency
  - Administrative assistance
  - Performance of mundane tasks

seh2-05.n08 3/24/92:

Truths about Technology

- Advancements provide choice
- Complexity of user environment prevents single technology solutions
- Standards are broad-based rules for heterogenous interoperability
- **Greatest Return:**
  - Increased effectiveness/productivity
  - Geographically dispersed offices are united
  - Human intellect is augmented

seh2-06.n08 3/11/92:

Challenges of the '90s

- Empower users to work smarter rather than faster
  - Global competition will be based on quality, service, knowledge

- Maintain competitive advantage
  - Increase user effectiveness and form new partnerships

- Tap two largest corporate assets:
  - Employees - Ultimate beneficiary of technology decisions
  - Information resources - Augment decision making process

seh2-15a.n08 3/24/92:

Modern Business Environment

Shifting Corporate Assets:

- Industrial Age

  - Real estate holdings
  - Manufacturing equipment
  - Material inventory

- Information Age

  - Information resources
  - Employee education

seh2-16.n08 4/14/92:

Cost of Isolation

Office Tower - NYC

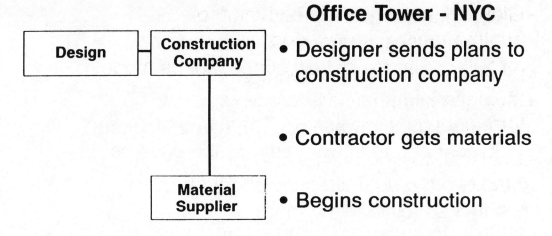

- Designer sends plans to construction company

- Contractor gets materials

- Begins construction

"Enterprise Networking: Working Together, Apart."

seh2-22.n08 3/13/92:

The Office of the Future

Advances in multimedia, telecommunication, and interoperability create single, graphically-dispersed organizations

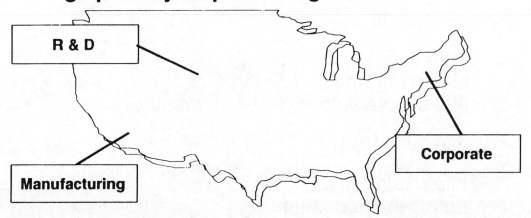

seh3-04.n08 3/13/92:

Global Directory Examples

- Telephone System
  - One number always rings same phone
  - Caller unaware of how connection is made

- Postal System
  - One address always goes to same location
  - Sender can mail from any location (zip code)

- A network global directory should provide
  same capabilities and more

seh3-05.n08 4/14/02:

Directory Requirements

- Intuitive

- Adaptable to corporate changes

- Single addressing format for all resources

- Available in LAN and WAN environments

- Implemented as a Distributed Directory Service

- Single information community

seh3-06.n08 4/14/92:

Banyan's Global Directory

StreetTalk

- Like a telephone number, it has 3 parts:
  ITEM @ GROUP @ ORGANIZATION
  (508) - 898 - 1000

Examples:

Resource	Item	@	Group	@	Organization
User	John Doe	@	Sales	@	CDC Computers
File Service	Private	@	Acct	@	CDC Computers
Print Service	LaserJet	@	Eng	@	CDC Computers
Other	3090	@	MIS	@	CDC Computers

seh3-07.n08 4/14/92:

StreetTalk

Transparent Access to All Resources

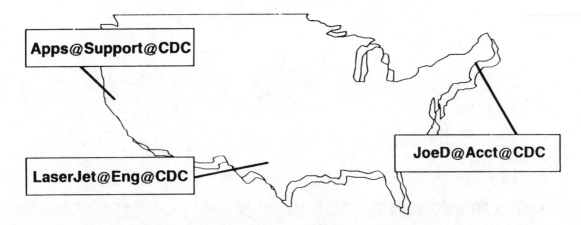

soh3–43.n08 3/13/92;

Summary

- Design based on industry standards
- VINES is a logical network
- Distributed services ease administration and use
- Modular architecture allows adoption of new technologies
- Transparent access and management boosts productivity
- Flexibility addresses unique customer requirements
- Most mature and integrated directory service on market

BRINGING THE MEETING TO THE GROUP:
GROUPWARE ON A PORTABLE WIRELESS LAN

Catherine M. Beise*
AIRMICS
115 O'Keefe Building
Georgia Institute of Technology
Atlanta, GA 30332–0800
(*on leave 1991/92 from
West Georgia College, Carrollton, GA 30118)

Michael J. Evans
AIRMICS
115 O'Keefe Building
Georgia Institute of Technology
Atlanta, GA 30332–0800

ABSTRACT

The U.S. Army, like many organizations faced with cost reductions and downsizing, is expected to increase its use of team–related activities such as strategic planning, systems requirements definition, and quality improvement programs. Group support systems offer potential for greater efficiency and effectiveness in group work. The U.S. Army Institute for Research in Management Information, Communications, and Computer Sciences (AIRMICS) has configured a portable wireless LAN with groupware installed to assist constituent groups in adopting and using this emerging technology to support their group–related activities.

1. INTRODUCTION

In the current era of downsizing, re–organization, and cost–cutting, the U.S. Army and other entities in the Department of Defense (DoD) are having to resolve conflicting requirements. More meetings, ad–hoc teams, and collaborative efforts are needed to plan and implement organizational transformation and streamlining of operations. The well–known high cost of meetings resulting from travel from disparate locations and staff–hours lost, however, conflicts with directives for cost–containment. Group support systems (GSS) appear to provide a partial solution, by speeding up the decision–making process for a variety of tasks. However, to reduce travel expenses and the significant start–up cost of installing of a permanent electronic decision room, AIRMICS (the U.S. Army Institute for Research in Management Information, Communications, and Computer Sciences) has undertaken a project to implement group support system software on a portable, wireless LAN.

AIRMICS is drawing on seven years of involvement and experience in the area of GSS, also referred to as GDSS (Group Decision Support Systems) (DeSanctis & Gallupe,

1987), EMS (Electronic Meeting Systems) (Dennis et al., 1988; Grohowski et al., 1990), CSCW (Computer-supported Collaborative Work) (Stefik et al., 1988), and groupware (Johansen, 1988).

Results of AIRMICS' and their clients' experiences with these systems have included: 1) estimation of hundreds of thousands of dollars in productivity gains when used for information requirements definition (Daniels et al., 1990), 2) critical success factors (CSF's) of system reliability, meeting planning, and good facilitation, and 3) partial success with distributed GSS used for decision making (Parsons & Nagao, 1989). (For a more detailed description of those experiences, see AIRMICS Report ASQB-GM-92-009, Beise & Evans, 1992.) These results have motivated continuing exploration of: 1) technical advances in GSS, 2) how and for what types of tasks the systems can be most effectively utilized, and 3) what factors are most important in successful implementation of GSS.

1.1 Goals

AIRMICS' short-term goal is to successfully implement a GSS on a portable environment and use it for appropriate tasks by constituent groups. In the longer term, AIRMICS' vision is to provide an "Any Time, Any Place" (Johansen, 1991) distributed environment for group work and group decision-making throughout their constituent organizations. Finally, in both the short term and long term, AIRMICS expects to use the practical and research-related experiences with GSS to develop management guidelines for implementation and use.

1.2 Assumptions and Constraints

Based on prior experiences with GSS and research evidence, AIRMICS is assuming that GSS can be used to increase meeting and work group productivity, when properly implemented. Thus, the primary thrust of the GSS implementation effort is to discover *how* to best use GSS, rather than *whether* to use it. Potential outcomes desired from successful implementation of GSS are listed in Appendix B. Measurements of some of these variables are being taken when feasible, as part of a longitudinal field research project on the use of GSS.

In keeping with its role as a technology transfer unit of the Army and the DoD, AIRMICS has developed and has begun implementation of a plan for introducing GSS in these constituent organizations. The remainder of this paper discusses AIRMICS' GSS implementation and technology transfer plan, a key component of which is to use GSS on a portable wireless LAN platform.

2. GSS IMPLEMENTATION

AIRMICS is supporting technology transfer of GSS in several ways. The first is to monitor and encourage existing and planned GSS installations elsewhere in the military and in government, and to provide these as potential resources for interested end–users. A second approach is to compile information about commercial GSS and groupware products, on the basis of their applications. A partial summary of such a product survey can be found in AIRMICS' Report ASQB–GM–92–009 (Beise & Evans, 1992). Third, AIRMICS continues to support the research and development of GSS at the University of Arizona, whose early Plexsys system is now available commercially as GroupSystems from Ventana Corporation and as TeamFocus from IBM. Finally, AIRMICS has acquired a portable wireless LAN as a platform for GroupSystems and potentially for other groupware products. The configuration for the portable system is shown in Appendix A.

AIRMICS is initially gaining experience with the system by using it for group tasks internally. The second overlapping step is to transport the complete system (including LAN, software, and support), to interested constituent groups wherever they want to see a demonstration or hold a live meeting. The portability of the system is expected to increase the rate of exposure to the technology, to enhance awareness of the potential benefits of using GSS, and to educate potential users about system limitations.

Applications for which the system is being used or planned include information systems requirements definition, strategic planning, TQM–related activities, curriculum development, source selection boards, and promotion candidate evaluation.

3. PORTABLE GSS ISSUES

A number of interesting issues have arisen in configuring and implementing a portable wireless technology. One of these was selection of an appropriate wireless technology. At the time of this writing, wireless technologies from which to choose included infrared, radio spectrum, microwave, and laser (Francett, 1991). Infrared and radio were candidates for AIRMICS application. Among the tradeoffs are speed, flexibility, and legal issues (Kerr, 1992). Although infrared is faster, line of sight is needed, and radio seemed more suited to a portable system. The licensing requirements for the use of FCC–regulated radio frequencies were handled by the vendor and did not present a major obstacle.

For portability, computer weight was a factor, but this had to be balanced against the necessary network peripherals. In the current configuration, Ethernet cards are internally installed, simplifying the process of quickly getting the system up and running when taken to a new location. (Currently, it takes two people only about ten minutes to plug the system together and have the groupware up and running, after having arrived at the meeting location) Screen size was important for participants who might be using the system for several hours at a time. The quality of the public display required in the GroupSystems product was also a consideration, leading to the acquisition of a high–quality projection system for use with the GSS.

Since a key element of the project is to transport the system to a variety of locations, practical transportation alternatives are an issue. Custom carrying cases are eventually expected to be used either for separately shipping the system or for carrying it as airline excess baggage.

Ventana's GroupSystems product was selected as the initial GSS, due to its current market prominence, prior successful Army experience with GroupSystems, and AIRMICS' past support of its development by the University of Arizona. However, AIRMICS also intends to use the portable GSS to test and evaluate other commercial and research–oriented groupware products.

Since effective facilitation is one of the key success factors in using products like GroupSystems used for face–to–face meetings, AIRMICS is conducting a research project which is intended to identify facilitation skills and sources, and is also in the process of developing a facilitator training program. The program includes formal training as well as observation and apprenticeship approaches. Finally, training and resources for on–site technical support for the LAN and the GSS is also an important consideration.

4. GSS RESEARCH PLANS

Prior AIRMICS–supported groupware projects have suggested a number of factors important to the success of GSS implementation. These include the need for a skilled facilitator, the need for adequate training and education of participants, the importance of pre–meeting planning, the identification of appropriate participants and desired outcomes (Daniels, 1991), and the need for security/privacy and system reliability (CARTS, 1989; Parsons & Nagao, 1989). Another topic which offers significant research potential is the use of GSS in a distributed environment (one in which participants are not in the same physical location as they meet, and/or their interactions are asynchronous).

4.1 Research Questions

The following questions are thus guiding AIRMICS' research program in GSS:

1) What are the Critical Success Factors (CSF's) for implementation and use of GSS?

2) What are appropriate and inappropriate tasks for GSS?

3) How does GSS technology support, hinder, or change group processes?

4) What are positive and negative impacts of GSS?

5) What is the role of the group facilitator?

6) What are the social and technical constraints (barriers) to use of a GSS?

7) Do the answers to any of the above questions vary for distributed GSS?

4.2 Research Framework and Methods

Pinsonneault and Kraemer (1989) suggest a framework for analysis of computer-augmented group sessions into which these issues can be placed and which will provide the initial basis for structuring the field study data collection planned by AIRMICS. They categorize variables into contextual, group process, and task- and group-related outcomes (Pinsonneault & Kraemer, 1989). Appropriate variables suggested in this model will be collected when feasible, using existing, previously-validated instruments where possible. Some of these variables are listed in Appendix B.

4.3 Technology Transfer of GSS

A long-term perspective that AIRMICS is also tracking are the factors that have positive or negative impacts on the assimilation of the technology throughout their client organizations (Army and DoD). Past research on this topic has suggested that early visible successes, organizational champions, and user communication (awareness and education) about the technology may be critical success factors for acceptance of a new information technology (cf., Leonard-Barton & Deschamps, 1988). However, success factors for information technology implementation may change from early stages of the process to later ones (Cooper & Zmud, 1990).

How will the process of implementation of GSS technology be similar to or different from that of more traditional information technologies? Applegate (1991) provides a framework for GSS assimilation in organizations that suggests it will be successful when there is alignment between technology, task, and group characteristics of structure, process, and goal or outcome. Attempts will be made to track these variables as the technology spreads through the constituent organizations.

5. CONCLUSION

AIRMICS' history of R&D in the areas of MIS/DSS/GSS, systems development, and data communications provides a foundation for synthesis and innovation around the issue of computer support for the team communications and tasks. AIRMICS' past, current, and planned experiences with GSS provide a solid basis for continued study of group technologies and their interactions with group processes. AIRMICS' activities will continue to support improvements in individual, group, and organizational efficiency and effectiveness through innovative information technology such as GSS. Finally, GSS and groupware provide a vehicle for supporting and facilitating organizational tranformation and business process redesign through the potential that GSS holds for helping to change how people work together.

References

Applegate, L.M. 1991. Technology support for cooperative work: A framework for studying introduction and assimilation in organizations. *Journal of Organizational Computing, 1*:1, 11–39.

Beise, C. M. & Evans, M. J. 1992. Technology assessment of Group Support Systems. *AIRMICS Technical Report ASBQ-GM-92-009.*

Francett, B. 1991. Wireless LAN makes moving a snap. *Data Communications*, September 21, 91–93.

CARTS Project 1989. *Army and HBCU Reference Manual.* Atlanta, GA: Clark Atlanta University.

Cooper, R.B. & Zmud, R.W. 1990. Information technology implementation research: A technological diffusion approach. *Management Science, 36*:2, 123–139.

Daniels, R.M., Dennis, A.R., Hayes, G., Nunamaker, J.F., Valacich, J. 1991. Enterprise Analyzer: Electronic support for group requirements elicitation. *Proceedings of the 24th Hawaii International Conference on Systems Sciences*, Jan 1991, Vol.3, 43–50.

Dennis, A.R., George, J.F., Jessup, L.M., Nunamaker, J.F., Vogel, D.R. 1988. Information technology to support electronic meetings. *MIS Quarterly, 12*:4, 591–624.

DeSanctis, G. & Gallupe, R.B. 1987. A foundation for the study of group decision support systems" *Management Science, 33*:5, 589–609.

Grohowski, R., McGoff, C., Vogel, D., Martz, B., & Nunamaker, J. 1990. Implementing electronic meeting systems at IBM: lessons learned and success factors. *MIS Quarterly*, Dec., 369–383.

Johansen, R. 1988. *Groupware: Computer support for business teams*. New York, NY: Free Press.

Johansen, R. 1991. Teams for tomorrow. Plenary Speech, *Proceedings of the 24th Hawaii International Conference on Systems Sciences*, Jan 1991, 3:521–534.

Kerr, S. 1992. Wireless works, within limits. *Datamation*, February 1, 38–40.

Leonard–Barton, D. & Deschamps, I. (1988) "Managerial influence in the implementation of new technology" *Management Science, 34*:10, 1252–1265.

Parsons, C.K. & Nagao, D.H. (1989 Dec) "Distributed computer–supported team work: a research paradigm" *AIRMICS Technical Report ASQB–GA–90–016.*

Pinsonneault, A. & Kraemer, K.L. (1989) "The impact of technological support on groups: An assessment of the empirical research" *Decision Support Systems, 5*, 197–216.

Stefik, M., Foster, G., Bobrow, D.G., Kahn, K., Lanning, S., & Suchman, L. (1987) "Beyond the chalkboard: Computer support for collaboration and problem solving in meetings" *Communications of the ACM*, 30:1, 32–47.

Appendix A:
Portable GSS System Specifications

10 Toshiba 3200 386SX laptops, 2 MB RAM, 120MB disk, VGA

    (1 used as file server)

1 Toshiba 5200 386SX laptop, 2 MB RAM, 200MB disk, color display

    (used as facilitator station)

Novell Netware LAN, Ethernet cards inside laptops

Motorola Altair wireless modules (up to 6 laptops per module),

Ventana GroupSystems GSS

Public Display (NView ViewFrame Spectra)

Overhead Projector (3000 lumens)

Printer (Canon Bubblejet BJ–10ex)

Liteshow (InFocus – computer–generated slide storage and display)

Carrying Cases

Appendix B:
Desired Outcomes of Implementation and Research

A. Desired Outcomes:

1. Decrease meeting time
  - a. # hours
  - b. # meetings per task

2. Increase group process quality
  - a. increase creativity & idea generation: depth of analysis
  - b. increase participation
  - c. first decrease then increase consensus
  - d. increase task focus

3. Increase outcome quality
  - a. decision quality
  - b. requirements specification:
    - accuracy
    - completeness
    - consensus

4. Increase satisfaction
  - a. individual
  - b. group
  - c. process
  - d. outcome

5. Minimize technology barriers & resistance
  - a. education
    - technology
    - group process
  - b. training
    - # hours
    - by whom
    - for whom
    - evolution toward standard method

B. Outcome measurement
  1. Time
  2. Cost
  3. Quality of decision-making
  4. Quality of system when used for system definition
  5. Satisfaction/attitudes of users
  6. Level of communication, awareness, education

COMPAQ COMPUTER CORPORATION'S
WORLD-WIDE USE OF LOTUS NOTES

Mark C. Wozny, Ph.D.
Compaq Computer Corporation
20555 SH 249
Houston, Texas 77070

1. HISTORY OF NOTES AT COMPAQ

Compaq Computer Corporation has a long history of involvement with Lotus Notes, which has helped in our deployment of that product world-wide. A strategic relationship has existed between the two companies for almost a decade. Thus, in 1990 when Lotus was looking for a partner to stress test their new product, Notes, which was then in beta test, Compaq was the logical choice. Compaq at that time was in the process of using many client-server applications to benchmark and stress test our systems and subsystems in order to optimize and improve our system's performance. This marriage of interest offered benefits to both parties.

It was during this benchmarking process that Compaq realized the potential and strategic advantages of the Lotus Notes product offering and the emerging groupware market.

The Systems Integration group within Systems Engineering, which was performing the benchmarking test, had been searching for a platform for distributing technical publications, problem solving and performance optimization information, and software utilities to our Accredited Systems Engineers (ASEs) within the Specialized Dealer Channel. The group evaluated over twenty products. Lotus Notes was selected because of its good match with the technical information system requirements, as well as its suitability as a rapid development and deployment platform. The system, TechPAQ, was developed and began shipping to ASEs in May of 1991, which included copies of the Notes workstation software and access to our TechPAQ Notes server.

As Notes gained more exposure within Compaq, the demand for Notes and the number of Notes applications increased significantly and rapidly. As a result, Compaq negotiated with Lotus the purchase of a large number of licenses with the right to world-wide distribution and support of Notes whereby Compaq can send the desired volumes of software in the appropriate language anywhere we need. Because Compaq has subsidiaries around the world, this agreement has been a key factor to the success in implementing and deploying Notes on a world-wide basis.

2. WORLD-WIDE USE OF NOTES

2.1 International Notes Applications

Following the domestic roll out of TechPAQ, Compaq International selected Lotus Notes as a platform for offering not only the on-line, current technical information in TechPAQ, but also as a preferred medium for all communications between Compaq and its business partners. This led to the development in Europe of the Compaq Link program, which incorporates the TechPAQ databases with sales and marketing data, and a reseller to Compaq mail application.

The sales and marketing databases use the Notes API to transfer corporate data from our HP minicomputers into Notes databases in subsidiaries where it can then be accessed by resellers. The Compaq Link application relies upon our international Banyan VINES corporate network to transfer data from our domestic and international business offices to subsidiaries. Unlike other implementations of Notes that have heterogeneous local area networks or rely on replication via modem, the Compaq network offers real-time access to Notes servers virtually anywhere in our corporate world. The only reason we have to replicate databases is load balancing on our network. (Compaq offers dial-in access to resellers and other business partners as well as Compaq field personnel in remote areas who do not have network access.)

In addition to our Compaq Link applications, Compaq uses Notes globally to handle International Service Case Tracking and Escalation. These cases are escalated from Notes servers in each subsidiary to our international centers, then on to Houston, Texas. In addition, we have Enterprise Network Workgroups connecting our major business centers: Singapore; Houston, Texas; Erskine, Scotland; and Munich, Germany.

2.2 Notes Platform Infrastructure at Compaq

Use of Lotus Notes world-wide by Compaq has the following characteristics:

Banyan VINES network for internal, corporate world-wide access: This offers connectivity between servers and workstations anytime, anywhere in our corporate world.

Internal use of VINES, LAN Manager: Where appropriate, we have used LAN Manager in addition to VINES for server to server replication (usually for TCP/IP connectivity under NetBIOS). This enables us to isolate specific servers from the corporate network (such as those used for dial-in access by external groups and individuals), and manage servers directly across campus using standard LAN Manager services by coexisting the Notes Server as LAN Manager file server.

Notes to VINES mail gateway for Non-Notes mail interface: Not all Compaq personnel have Lotus Notes on their desktops. Therefore, we have implemented a Notes mail gateway to offer mail integration between VINES and Notes.

External access via dial-in: a key to the success of TechPAQ domestically and Compaq Link internationally, has been the ability to use multi-port boards like Digiboard to provide extensive dial-in access. This has provided Compaq with insight into a number of issues related to dial-in access (e.g. speed of access, traffic patterns, peak hour usage, number of ports required/server, setting up multi-port boards, analyzing usage statistics, and so on).

2.3 Administering Notes

Developing Notes Administrations Guidelines has been critical to our successful use of Notes domestically and internationally. We anticipated that the flexibility of Notes was a two edged sword: on the one hand, it is a platform that can accomplish many tasks easily in many different ways. On the other hand, Notes offers an opportunity for a corporate Tower of Babel, which we wanted to avoid.

Through a gradual, evolutionary, and international process, Compaq developed Notes Administration Standards for Domestic and International Notes use. These standards include topics such as:

   o   Security guidelines

   o   Training offerings: internal courses, standard and customized versions

o   Standard roles and responsibilities
            Notes server and systems administration
            Network administration
            Database development and administration

o   Naming standards: users, groups, servers, networks, domains

o   Server roles: Hub, production or application, development, gateway

o   Database development and deployment guidelines

o   Server administration standards

o   Operational procedures
            Issuing licenses
            Server backup/recovery
            Virus scanning software and procedures

2.4 Criteria for selecting hardware

Because Compaq offers a range of system platforms, we are sensitive to matching appropriate hardware to the problem at hand. Notes offers two major dimensions to consider: the volume of data and number of users. In Notes current implementation running under OS/2, Notes servers do not reflect performance improvement from multi-processor support. Therefore, we developed the following recommendations for server and workstation configurations based upon the current Notes implementation. These are internally distributed guidelines and the categories are nominal at best.

Recommended Notes Hardware

Servers:

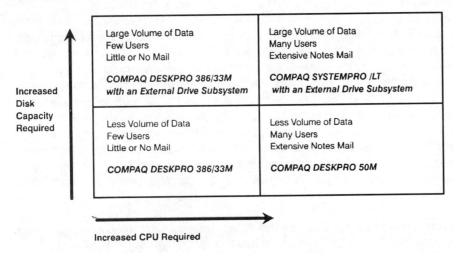

Increased
Disk
Capacity
Required

Increased CPU Required

Distinguishing between COMPAQ DESKPRO /M family and COMPAQ SYSTEMPRO /LT is based on the number of slots needed: COMPAQ DESKPRO /M family if you need fewer slots, COMPAQ SYSTEMPRO /LT of you need more (e.g. multi-port boards or multiple NICs can take up extra slots for ease of installation and accessibility).

As a Notes (or any kind of network) Administrator, utilization of the COMPAQ Server Manager/R Board for Server Administration is an invaluable added benefit. This board offers remote Notes console server administration regardless of the network operating system, as well as remote notification of server problems to the administrator.

Workstations:

Remote access: The COMPAQ SLT 386s/20, COMPAQ LTE 386 or COMPAQ LTE Lite 386/20 or faster laptops with COMPAQ Enhanced 9600 Baud Modems or COMPAQ Enhanced 2400 Baud Modems (2400 baud non-compressed modem speed usually is unacceptable to users).

Network access: COMPAQ DESKPRO 386/20e or faster with at least 6 MB RAM, 110MB Fixed Disk Drive and VGA graphics.

3. CURRENT COMPAQ DIRECTIONS WITH NOTES

More and more, Compaq is using Notes for doing our business in many areas: Sales, Marketing, Product Development, and Customer Service, to name a few. The Compaq MIS department views Notes as an important platform for rapid application development and dissemination. It fits in with our philosophy of moving toward distributed, client-server technology. The future functionality of Notes Version 3 should offer a closer marriage between Notes and our other platforms of choice. This should lead to increased productivity and decreased application development and maintenance costs.

Active evaluation of Lotus Notes, future Notes versions or enhancements and Notes add-on products has been instrumental to our successful deployment of Notes at Compaq. This has provided us a great advantage by allowing us to foresee how our applications may grow in parallel with the functionality in Notes and the groupware market.   Feedback from our own field employees offers valuable insights for fine tuning our own use of Notes, as well as allowing us to mold our offerings to business partners.   Additionally, we provide Lotus with input on desired product features and enhancements.

Not only does Compaq view Lotus Notes from a customer perspective, we also see it as a strategic application platform to proactively test and integrate with our products and our network operating system partners (Novell, SCO, Microsoft and Banyan). As the result of our integration efforts, Compaq has developed ToolKits that help our customers integrate their applications on NOVELL NetWare, SCO UNIX, MICROSOFT LAN Manager and BANYAN VINES. These toolkits are available not only in paper form, but also electronically through Lotus Notes. A critical area that we feel needs attention is server and application management. We are working with our partners and important application vendors like Lotus to extend management capabilities to the application level for both in band and out of band alerting and trouble shooting. In addition, we feel it is important to participate in other forums such as the Notes World Wide User Group, and events such as Lotus Week to stay in touch with Notes developments at Lotus and among users.

Compaq is committed to not only investigate and understand emerging technologies and application integration markets, such as groupware, we are also committed to disseminating the information and knowledge gained. We feel we are helping to push the envelope on groupware systems and technology.

Designing Group-enabled Applications: A Spreadsheet Example

Irene Greif
Lotus Development Corporation
1 Rogers Street
Cambridge, MA
email: igreif@lotus.com

1. Introduction

To date, the most successful groupware products have been products that facilitate general group communication. Email systems and Lotus Notes are examples. But there are many situations in which a workgroup's business is already conducted using products that support the individual -- spreadsheets, word processing, graphic design. Communication and sharing happen outside those products and often off-line entirely. We believe that the next wave of innovation in workgroup computing will come from integrating such desktop tools with the communications and data sharing capabilities of groupware systems. The result will be products that encourage collaboration in the application domain.

In order to leverage existing successful software, both the communications infrastructure of the general purpose groupware tools and the application-specific software need to change. Groupware products must be "opened up" to provide communications and data storage infrastructure to applications. Trends towards this kind of architecture are evident in the race among system vendors to offer new system services for object stores and standard messaging interfaces. Application software then needs to be modified to interface with groupware infrastructure, and to make it possible to share the objects created in the application. As we group-enable today's products, the design challenge is to introduce these changes in ways that naturally extend the product metaphor while substantially changing the ways the product can be used.

At Lotus, we've learned that there is an unmet need for what could be termed a "workgroup spreadsheet." This paper is a case study of the design of the series of products that will respond to that need. The paper describes the original target application -- budget planning -- and explains how spreadsheet characteristics and user input influenced the design. The next three sections cover the three main threads of the design: application analysis; software design;

and user input. The result is a product very different from our initial prototypes: instead of a new "workgroup spreadsheet" product, we have group-enabled 1-2-3 and are incrementally adding group support by using Lotus Notes technology.

A significant outcome has been that customers find the group-enabling features very attractive for individual use. Not only will our group spreadsheet be based on the standard 1-2-3, but the new features that we add will have a very good chance of becoming part of the standard repertoire for individuals who use spreadsheets. We expect that this will play an important role in increasing customer acceptance of workgroup spreadsheet technology, since people will not need to learn the features solely to participate in the group process. There is also some basis for expecting this kind of incidental pay-off for the individual to emerge in other personal productivity products as they are group-enabled. An individual working over time often needs assistance remembering what they were up to -- this can be provided by the same features that help the user understand a new contribution from a co-worker.

2. Group Spreadsheet Applications

2.1. Consolidation and Budget Planning

Budget planning is the quintessential group financial application. At most large corporations, people across the organization are involved in discussions, negotiations, planning and approval cycles for corporate budgets for months out of every year. During the rest of the year, changes to plan result in *ad hoc* adjustments to budget -- rarely is a complete revision of the corporate budget done more than annually.

For spreadsheet users, budget planning is equated with a batch process called "roll-up" and is supported through data entry templates. A financial officer builds a model for the whole organization. Sections to be filled in by departments are extracted and sent to each department. These sections are spreadsheets in their own right usually with some data filled in. For example, the formulas for computing results would be typed in ahead, as would some basic assumptions about target headcount, expenses, etc. Spreadsheet protection features are often used to ensure that data can be entered only in certain areas, leaving formulas and assumptions protected and unchangeable. In some organizations, macros are written that guide data entry into the sheet.

As the templates are completed, they are collected and consolidated. Typically, data collection is done completely off-line through exchange of files on floppy disks. Occasionally exchange happens through email, by attaching spreadsheet files, or by placing files in shared directories on file servers. When files are all collected in one place, a "roll-up" macro is invoked. It brings in each section, places it in the spreadsheet, and triggers calculations as each is read in. For a large organization, this can be a lengthy process. Mainframe spreadsheet programs have been developed in part to help these massive roll-ups run more efficiently.

2.2. Limits of this process: Departmental Consolidation

While roll-up is a very successful application of spreadsheets, it supports only a small segment of the work involved in developing a budget for an organization. Much more work happens as each department in the organization prepares its own contribution to the budget. This preparation involves complex interactions among groups of people before they are ready to "fill in" the corporate template.

A large department will need to divide up its own "template" budget, request numbers from subgroups, roll them up, consider the results and iterate the process. Few departments will institute a formal roll-up -- the overhead is too high and not all of the contributors use spreadsheets. What is more, the process requires people to work in many different settings -- alone at their desks, on the road, in meetings, by phone. Since the spreadsheet program is not used in some settings -- for example, while in a meeting room -- even experienced spreadsheet users revert to the "lowest common denominator" of paper. Confusion results when each participant at a meeting leaves with private notes on paper which may reflect differing ideas of what's been agreed to. There's delay after the meeting while a transcriber tries to reconstruct what happened into a new spreadsheet version. Finally, the new spreadsheet printed on paper is different from the old, but there are no easy ways to make a comparison and find out what has changed.

There's a missed opportunity here, not just for the department, but for the organization as a whole. An on-line budget can become a strategic tool in an organization. It can be reviewed and revised to reflect changing circumstances throughout the year. The main obstacle is that no one has time to keep up with it. The departments that spend several months of each year in the "budgeting exercise" can't spend more time on it. If the process could be made more efficient through more extensive use of technology, the budget could be a more dynamic and reliable part of business operation.

Quality of decisions could also be affected by introduction of spreadsheet sharing technology. Today, people work privately on their own sections of the budget. Department resources like headcount must be allocated by central authority who can put target figures into each template. Shared spreadsheet technology would *allow*, *not require*, more flexible resource allocation. Using this technology, target figures for the whole department could be put in a shared spreadsheet and groups could negotiate allocation, as long as total for department met the overall target number. Even if the manager continued to set group targets, a shared spreadsheet would allow individuals to see more contextual information as input to their planning. Sharing the full budget would of course depend on good access control that could protect sensitive information such as current salaries. With the right tools, not only would today's process run more efficiently, but also innovative uses of spreadsheets would be facilitated making new work processes practical.

2.3. Integration of Information Management Tools and Spreadsheet

This broad picture of the full budget planning process emerged as we interviewed planners from several companies about their budget processes.* A full workgroup spreadsheet system would support people as they:

- ask for numbers for parts of the sheet (distribute templates);

- share parts of the sheet, or the entire sheet, with ways of focusing attention to specific sections;

- set access control on sections of shared sheets;

- collate sheets after they are filled in;

- compare alternative versions;

- look at partial roll-ups with assistance from the system in understanding what's "good" data, "partial" data and "inconsistent" data;

- monitor progress: assign responsibility; review list of outstanding requests; send reminders;

- discuss and comment on parts of the sheets.

The requirements amount to identifying a set of "communication gaps" in today's process that inhibit spreadsheet use in a group setting. Integration of spreadsheets with communications and data sharing technologies fills these gaps:

- email: easy exchange of spreadsheets;

- database: spreadsheet sharing and concurrency;

- access control: hiding sensitive information;

- annotations: document reasoning;

- versioning: track changes and alterative suggestions (supports meetings, both in conference rooms and at-a-distance);

- workflow: tracking requests for information; iteration.

Most of the communication gaps described above can be filled using email, shared database and workflow technology. However, there are application-specific aspects to access control and versioning that require some support directly in the application product.   For spreadsheets, the internal structure of the sheet must be enriched so that components can have their own version histories and so that users can work in separate parts of the sheet at the same time. Today, the spreadsheet is a relatively unstructured object: that's its strength for the

---

*The budget planning analysis was done in collaboration with Kate Ehrlich of Sun Microsystems.

individual, but may be a weakness in the group setting. Our design challenge was to add some structure to the sheet without impinging on spreadsheet usability.

3. Designing the Group Spreadsheet

3.1. Objects in Spreadsheet: Named Ranges

Group spreadsheet applications strongly motivate versioning, so we were particularly interested in how versioning of objects would work out. Since cells are the "objects" of which the spreadsheet is composed, we considered an automatic versioning mechanism that tracked changes to cells throughout the sheet. However we found such cell tracking would have little value to users who were trying to go back to known states that cut across these versions. We needed a "transaction mechanism" -- a way for the user to indicate that a group of values made sense together and were worth saving as a version. This led to the idea of working with *named ranges* within the spreadsheet.

In the spreadsheet, structure is implicit in the layout of a model -- in the labels on rows and columns. But that structure is in the minds of the designers and reader of the sheet, not in the internal data structure of the spreadsheet. A range is a rectangular block of cells in a sheet defined by two cells -- the top left and bottom right cells. By selecting and naming ranges, the user makes explicit the structure of the spreadsheet.

We also let the user indicate when a range contains a set of values worth saving as a new version. At the time the user saves these versions, they can be given a name and an annotation about the reason they are of interest. The system automatically adds a user id, date, and time stamp.

3.2. Named Versions, Range Alternatives and Scenario Management

Source control systems for software and CAD have sophisticated version control and configuration management features. This was a lot of new functionality to consider adding to the spreadsheet, particularly as it is apparently unrelated to current use of spreadsheets for model building and analysis. The features are needed only at certain points in the process and would also be of greatest benefit to the manager of the budget planning process, rather than to the individual contributor. We needed to simplify configuration management and looked for ways to make it natural for the end-user to manage the versions themselves.

Our solution came out of considering how an individual would work with the range versions. If each version has a meaningful name, they become "alternative versions" that represent different cases. (See Figure 1.) They are no longer just being saved for historical reasons and back-up, but rather to represent several different meaningful situations that should be evaluated, analyzed and perhaps even shared. Sharing is enhanced by adding annotations,

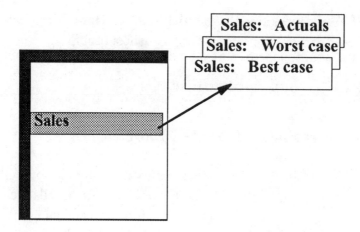

Figure 1: Ranges have Alternatives

timestamps and user names (See Figure 2). (Alternatives also appear in configuration management system as distinct from automatically generated revisions.)

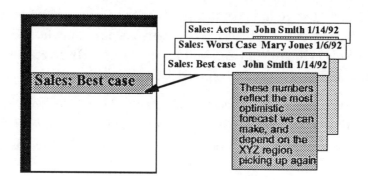

Figure 2:   Alternatives have Name, Date & Annotation

The individual will use these "alternatives" in "what-if" experiments and will want to mix and match alternatives from different parts of the sheet to form "scenarios" for the model. For example, a user might define alternatives for ranges SALES and EXPENSES. They might include "best case" for SALES, "moderate expectations" for SALES, "Joe's forecast" for EXPENSES and "Sally's thoughts" for EXPENSES.   A planning and analysis phase might involve mixing and matching these to build new scenarios, such as "best case" for SALES combined with "Sally's thoughts" for EXPENSES. Today, scenarios are built by making changes directly in the spreadsheet and saving to files with cryptic names. If two scenarios -- say one with all high numbers, and another with all low numbers -- contain numbers that ought to be looked at in another combination -- say HIGH SALES and LOW EXPENSES -- the new scenario has to be created manually by cutting and pasting, then saved to yet another file. With range alternatives and scenario management, users can keep all the scenarios in one file and can mix and match easily.

3.3. Email versus Database Integration

With the additional structure added through range alternatives, spreadsheet information can be made available for sharing. We mentioned integration with email and shared databases. Email is the natural communication medium for automating today's central process. Group members will send sections of spreadsheet in emails, collect them over email, use email filters and email-based workflow tools to track progress.

We would expect a shared spreadsheet to be used by a group that wants to collaborate on building a model. Concurrency and access control would be set relative to component ranges. Sections of the model common to all group members would be shared this way with confidence that updates would be seen by all group members. The shared spreadsheet would be implemented by using database technology rather then email.

As we designed out first prototype, we stayed closer to current practices in which spreadsheets are exchanged rather than shared. Thus we integrated with email first.

4. Testing the Ideas with Customers

4.1. Customer Reaction

The analysis of budget consolidation took a broad view of financial applications. Instead of focusing on spreadsheet usage alone, we examined a full process that had impact on both spreadsheet users and non-users. This kind of analysis is different from the traditional feature-driven customer input. For example, Lotus has worked with customers for some time to understand how to make our products more useful on their networks. Customer requests have led us to introduce features that make our products easier to load over networks, and to modify our licensing scheme to accommodate sharing of licenses. In addition, all of our products share a common "file reservation" scheme for managing conflicting updates to files.

The budget planning analysis gave us a new perspective on product requirements. We shared that perspective with customers at focus groups where we showed a "Chronicle" prototype. The prototype consisted of a separate Chronicle product that worked with 1-2-3. Chronicle saved alternatives and scenarios, and managed some email-based support for requesting information from group members.

It was interesting that even among the more "network aware" of the focus groups, customers were initially cautious about the idea of the broad value of a workgroup spreadsheet. This came across in distrust of their networks and file servers and a nervousness about what other people would do to their work. However, their comments after seeing the first prototype were more open and positive.

Customers understood and liked the "what-if" and scenario management application. We received very strong feedback that this was a feature that could be used right away, to solve a common problem for the individual doing "what-if" analysis and scenario management. They wanted that feature to be more closely integrated into 1-2-3, and they did in fact appreciate that it would help them manage the input of multiple users to the spreadsheet.

Once they saw this feature, they started to explore its uses and slowly returned to the workgroup theme. By the end of the sessions several customers were telling us that they could see how these features might serve as a gentle first step towards sharing. One group talked about the opportunity for "consensus building" if a model could be on a network for all to see. As the groups started to see the potential for sharing, they also became more creative in generating additional requirements, particularly in the area of security and information hiding. They could see the value of sharing if they could be assured of the ability to hide sensitive information.

4.2. Impact on Design

Overall, the focus groups had a strong influence on our product strategy. It was their strong positive reaction to "scenario management" for the individual that resulted in making this a standard feature of 1-2-3, rather than a part of a separate workgroup spreadsheet product. The fact that they became more open to spreadsheet sharing after seeing Chronicle led us to accelerate the use of database technology to facilitate sharing (see section on Chronicle with Notes).

Design partners have contributed ideas for further applications such as sales forecasting, acquisition analysis and resource monitoring. Like budget planning, these are workgroup activities that use today's spreadsheets and currently get no explicit support for sharing.

The response from our design partners indicates that we are designing a smooth migration path for current spreadsheet users to workgroup spreadsheets. The scenario management features will be incorporated as a valuable addition to the standard spreadsheet repertoire. Because the features include name and time stamping and annotations, they make spreadsheets more shareable, even when exchanged through file transfer or floppy exchange. Follow-on versions or companion products will offer additional workgroup features and will be targeted at the users who will benefit the most -- the consolidators and the decision makers who have responsibility for managing the workflow and sharing aspects of financial applications. Their satisfaction with the product will be enhanced by the ease of getting group members to participate: other group members will already have the basic tools in hand for participating in group projects.

5. Chronicle Products

5.1. Implementation Approach

The design project we have described is code-named Chronicle. It has resulted in a multi-stage plan for workgroup-enabling spreadsheets and integrating the spreadsheet with communications software. Thus, several "Chronicle Products" will be developed. In the first phase, we are building an alternative scenario manager that will be part of the standard spreadsheet package. The second phase is to use database technology to upgrade from file sharing to sharing with concurrency and access control. By leveraging existing database technology, spreadsheets can be stored on secure network servers and shared across wide area networks. Users can update spreadsheets concurrently, set access constraints, and query spreadsheet information. In later stages, additional workflow support can be added in complementary products and alternative user interfaces provided for individual roles in the group process. We describe the first two stages in the following sections.

5.2. Chronicle in 1-2-3 for Windows

The first implementation of Chronicle is a scenario management capability in Lotus 1-2-3 for Windows 2.0. It allows spreadsheet analysts to save alternative values for sections of the sheet -- named ranges -- and to combine them into alternatives "scenarios" for the overall spreadsheet model. Values may be data or formulas. Alternatives are created by typing directly in the spreadsheet. Scenarios are created by selecting an alternative for each of several ranges and naming the combination.

Alternatives and scenarios are marked with name and time stamp at creation and whenever modified. The name used for the user identification is taken from the best available source on the machine -- either Notes ID, ccMail name or network name. Each alternative also carries with it an annotation provided by the user to document reasoning about the values in the alternative.

Alternatives and scenarios can be viewed by placing the numbers in the sheet causing recalculation of other formulas. The user can also browse through an index of these alternatives viewing them by range name, by user name, by time, or organized as scenarios. In all views, the user can also read the annotations, and select alternatives to place in the spreadsheet. For example, it might be useful to collect a set of alternatives all by the same person into one scenario.

The scenario management features are integrated in to Lotus 1-2-3. Users can flip between alternatives directly on the sheet. Spreadsheet sharing is at the file level -- users will take turns updating files on servers. The workgroup that chooses to share files on file servers will find the name and time stamps and the documentation of reasoning in annotations helpful for auditing changes and understanding each other's contributions. Design partners frequently discussed the value of auditing or tracking "who did what to the sheet, when they did it and why."

Chronicle will provide a number of report formats. Information from alternatives will be put back into a spreadsheet file and formatted for printing. One report format might highlight differences between alternatives for each range. Another might be organized to collate all annotations together for each range. Report formats specifically designed for auditing will be available.

5.3. Chronicle with Notes

Using database technology for storing ranges and alternatives, we can add new functionality that lets users:

- see new and unread alternatives contributed since they last viewed the spreadsheet;

- work concurrently on the same spreadsheet;

- be notified of changes (when more than one user is working on the spreadsheet, a user can be notified as new alternatives are added);

- control access.

We are working first with the Lotus Notes database technology, because there is an especially good match between the versioning support Chronicle adds to spreadsheets and the Notes replication mechanism. Lotus Notes technology provides a document store with a unique replication scheme that supports sharing information over wide-area networks. Applications that work best with Notes technology are ones in which communication is accomplished primarily through additions of new information. Because Chronicle will encourage people to make changes through additions of alternatives rather than by directly overwriting data in the sheet, spreadsheets stored in Notes databases can be replicated over wide area networks. Users at any site can add changes concurrently. The effect will be to meet a long-standing customer request for finer grained concurrency, but without introducing yet another kind of lock that must be explicitly set and unset in order to manage updates. What is more, the version history implicit in a set of alternatives supports communication about the changes, allowing people to see what used to be in the sheet as a way to understand the new numbers.

One important benefit of using the Lotus Notes technology is that we now have a common data representation between two applications: the spreadsheet and Lotus Notes. Lotus Notes is a flexible application development environment for workgroups. New "forms" and "views" can be added to the database through the Notes user interface without affecting the 1-2-3 view. These new views can include review of requests, automatic notification of overdue information and other management support. The forms can also be used for data entry, as an alternative to typing into the spreadsheet. Data entered this way is made available immediately to anyone looking at the database through 1-2-3.

6. Conclusion

A significant lesson of Chronicle is the importance of looking beyond current use to view products in the workgroup setting. Even though customers can quickly appreciate the value of the Chronicle features for sharing, their current work practices had not led them to ask for these features as enhancements to 1-2-3. What is especially interesting about their reaction, is the enthusiasm with which the basic group-enabling feature -- range alternatives -- has been received by individual users. The value of this feature to individual users should significantly ease overall group acceptance: it means that the consolidator who decides to use the product will find group members already comfortable with the basic features because they use them in everyday work for their own scenario management and "what-if" analysis.

Once the broad requirements were established, group-enabling was a two-step process: first the application-specific changes were introduced; then the application began leveraging workgroup technologies -- email and shared databases -- to support groups. The first step added value for the individual, even before the connection was made to the communication infrastructure. Customers say that a file that contains alternative scenarios, documentation of assumptions, and history of cases analyzed, is much easier to understand and is, therefore, more shareable. The second step is actually a sequence of planned enhancements as the product is used with different kinds of groupware software from email, to databases, to workflow engines.

We expect that much of what we did for spreadsheets will generalize to other applications. Other applications will also have new requirements for structure, versions and user identity as part of the initial step of group-enabling. These enhancements to the application extend its functionality for the individual even if it's only a matter of making it easier to manage one's own revisions and reworking of data. Just as 1-2-3 users will create scenarios and do "what-if" experiments with named alternatives, a word processor user could write alternative paragraphs to be used in different "editions" of their document for different audiences. In a product like Lotus' Freelance Graphics for Windows, alternatives for slides and scenarios can be used to assemble presentations on the same topic for different audiences. We anticipate the wide appearance of such features in the future as group-enabled products appear on desktops of individuals.

"Intelligent Agents in Groupware"

By Jon Ramer, ELF Technologies, Inc.

I. Introduction

The conference advisory board recently asked me to write this paper for the GroupWare '92 conference. The subject the advisory board asked me to write about is, "Intelligent Agents in Groupware." When I first heard the title I thought to myself, "Wow, two of the latest high-technobabble[1] phrases strung together to form one paper... and I am being asked to write it!"

Actually, I am grateful for the challenge. We have been using computers to help groups work more effectively for the past nine years.   And since 1989, when we developed and introduced "Bubba" -- what we called then an electronic organizational actor -- the focus of our work remains the employment of electronic helpers who assist groups of people in carrying out their everyday work.

Experience to date has convinced us that the role of intelligent agents has great merit. However, at this time there appears to be more *hype* than *understanding.* As we all know, it takes time for an industry to agree on the meaning of specific terminology. It takes trial and error to understand the impact, potential harm and value of any new technology.

In our judgment, we have **not** reached these mature levels of time and trial and error with "intelligent agents in groupware." The subject is still very young.   Therefore, it is our intent for this paper to report on and interpret some of the current language being used to talk about "intelligent agents in groupware."   It is our hope to offer a useful framework that will help bring greater clarity to our communications with each other.

II. Research Method

Given how quickly terminology changes in our industry, we decided to review what others have recently said about Intelligent Agents in Groupware. We did a search for recent articles that mentioned the words "intelligent agent."   Upon completion of the search, we had a file that contained thirty-three documents found in a search of thousands of articles published over the past six months.

To gain another perspective on Intelligent Agents in Groupware, we checked various dictionaries.

In-tel-li-gent
Able to perform computer functions. When applied to agents, intelligent usually means programmable. A person defines logical rules for an intelligent agent to apply in a given situation.

A-gents
A means or instrument by which a guiding intelligence achieves a result. In general, Agent usually means something capable of producing an effect.

Group-ware
Webster was no help. Groupware is not in Webster's Ninth Collegiate Edition. Our industry has only recently accepted Groupware as a common substitute for: Workgroup Computing, Cooperative Processing, Computer Supported Cooperative Work, Collaborative Work, etc.

III. Our Interpretation and Approach

In this section, we begin to outline our interpretation and framework for discussing Intelligent Agents. On the basis of our work and research, we have defined three common characteristics:

- An Intelligent Agent is *programmable*.

- An Intelligent Agent is *automatic* and acts as a buffer between people and other systems.

- An Intelligent Agent has an *identity*.

Programmable
In our judgment, calling anything around computers "intelligent" begs for a return to the debate over artificial intelligence. Fortunately, I did not see many claims about Intelligent Agents possessing human intelligence. In our opinion, an agent is Intelligent if it does what we tell it to do. It is programmable.

Automatic
Today, the term "Agent" has a number of different uses in the computer industry. There are references to User Agents, Message Transfer Agents, Network Management Agents and others. In general, the term Agent usually means something capable of automatically acting. An Agent works automatically.

Identity

Sometimes, we talk about Agents in anthropomorphic terms, i.e., describing them as taking on human characteristics, e.g., names such as Bubba, Liza or Casper. This approach can lead to surprising secondary benefits that help make the technology more usable and understandable. We intend to dedicate an entire paper to this subject at a later time.

So What? And Who Cares?

Even if we did all agree on what an intelligent agent is, why ought we care? What is an intelligent agent in groupware good for, if anything?   To address this, we distinguish two parties with different interests and concern: Groupware Developers and Employers of Intelligent Agents.

Groupware Developers Building Intelligent Agents

When developing groupware applications that include intelligent agents, the interests of Groupware Developers include adding value to existing tools. Their tools and others' tools. As mentioned earlier, Intelligent Agents can extend the boundaries of today's groupware. "Mail-enabling" applications are one step in this direction.

Note the evolution of the answering machine. In its primitive state you waited for the beep and recorded a message. Now the answering machine has become an "automated attendant" offering a menu of options to choose from. By pressing a few buttons you can re-direct your call, leave a message, send or even receive a fax.

For Groupware Developers, Intelligent Agents can act as an interface between their application, other applications, and people.

Employers of Intelligent Agents

When re-designing work practices and employing intelligent agents for administrative purposes, the interests of business managers are to extend and enhance their peoples abilities to know and produce.   Intelligent Agents can help with the production, distribution and management of routine tasks.

For employers of intelligent agents, there are social and economic outcomes to consider.

The social impact will effect what people stop and start doing. The tasks or jobs well suited for an intelligent agent are those requiring stored memory, logical rules and computer processing power[2]. An Intelligent Agent can remember what to look for (stored memory), apply rules (logic), and autonomously act (process or communicate).

What we seem to value most about ourselves are those ways in which we add common-sense, intelligence and creativity to the work process. We suspect that organizations will increasingly support on-going education, training and re-design of work practices. In general, specific *in-human work* can and ought to be delegated to an electronic labor force.

As organizations handle more administrative activities through intelligent agents, the economic impact may lead to a re-allocation of human resources. The labor savings can free up capital to support expansion, research and development, and customer service. Historically, the modern multi-unit business rapidly grew through greater productivity, lower costs and higher profits as a result of improved administrative coordination.[3]

At the same time, these economic benefits, which in the past lead to large-scale enterprises, might generate more profit for a few. We shall see.

IV. Two Classes Of Intelligent Agents in Groupware

Whether you are a Groupware Developer or an Employer of Intelligent Agents, we are all new at working with Intelligent Agents. On the basis of our work on the structure and functions of intelligent agents (we call an Intelligent Agent an ELF), we suggest that the order of growth will evolve with more use and understanding. We organized all references to Intelligent Agents into one of two classes; **information** agents and **coordination** agents.

A. Information Agents

Information Agents inform. They locate, retrieve and deliver information when pre-defined conditions or events occur. A good Information Agent will process data into user-specific knowledge.

Job instructions to Information Agents provide access to data elements, information views, exception conditions, alarms, etc. To date, most offerings of Intelligent Agents are Information Agents. Examples of Information Agents include:

•   Network and System Management Agents

There are a number of system management tools that monitor servers and workstations and alert network administrators when pre designated thresholds are reached. Examples of Information Agents include the SNMP Agents, Tivoli Systems WizDOM and HP's PerfView, described in writing as an "Intelligent Collection Agent."

•   According to John Sculley, Apple's Portable Digital Assistants will contain "intelligent agent" technology. Sculley recently demonstrated Reporter and Casper. Reporter is able to search through databases and prepare for you a customized report.

•   Edify corporation offers the "Information Agent" that can retrieve and deliver information and send it via e-mail, fax or phone.

B. Coordination Agents

The role of Information Agents can evolve to become what we call Coordination Agents. They do more than inform. They integrate, track and act within the flow of work. They support organizational functions taking place across applications, for a client, or a group.

Distinct from Information Agents, job instructions direct Coordination Agents to issue and carry out directives if and when a trigger event occurs[4]. For example, at a law firm, every time a New Case Assignment gets composed, the Intelligent Agent (or ELF as we call them) OWHolmes creates a Conflict Search request. OWHolmes then tracks the state of the Conflict Search, following up if no one acts after a specified period of time.

Experience has shown that preparing for successful coordination is more complex than keeping people informed. Coordination requires consistency between groups of people and applications.

Examples of Coordination Agents include:

. Beyond Mail offers' rule based agent technology that filters and acts upon incoming e-mail according to pre-defined procedures.

. SmartStream routes data and integrates in-house and public databases.

. Communicating Agents in the Cyc Knowledge Base help navigate through worldwide directly services.

When more and more people understand and use Information Agents, we anticipate a greater appreciation and interest in the kinds of jobs that Coordination Agents perform.

V.   Closing

From our biased perspective, no single technology we know of holds greater potential for economic and social change than Intelligent Agents in Groupware. We will have to think seriously about what we are trying to do in organizations and how we deploy labor to get it done.

Integrating Intelligent Agents into everyday life will lead to new requirements for human knowledge and skill. We anticipate an increasingly high value being placed on creativity, common-sense and human intelligence. We also expect there will be less interest and value placed on the administrative handling of routine and repetitive tasks.

Clearly we must do more work, before we can complete an effective assessment of the overall impact and value of Intelligent Agents in Groupware. However, we have seen repeated success and remain encouraged by the prospects.

---

[1]From "Technobabble" the title of John A. Barry's book about new computer lexicon.
[2]For more on dividing work, review The Economist 1992 Survey of Artificial Intelligence
[3]For a thorough understanding of this phenomena, we recommend "The Visible Hand" by Alfred Chandler.
[4]For a more thorough understanding of the importance of directives and commissives, we recommend you read Understanding Computers and Cognition by Winograd and Flores.

Alternates

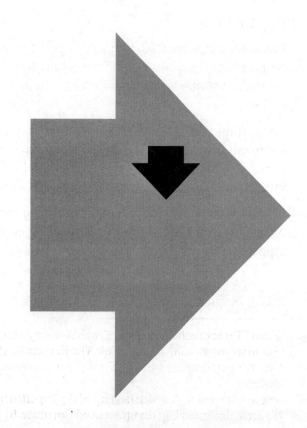

Practical Aspects of Implementing Computer Supported Collaboration (CSC)
Vertical Solution: *Residential Real Estate Transactions*

Karin Kundargi and Ramesh Subramaniam, Intel Corporation.

Introduction : The Changing Role Of Personal Computing

Personal computers powered by more powerful microprocessors, improved operating environments and new applications are poised to change the way we do business. Now, almost every desktop has a personal computer and they are increasingly being interconnected with other PCs and Servers in a reliable local area network (LAN) or wide area network (WAN). The latest introduction of Notebook and Pentop computers (mobile PC's) provide the traveling individuals access to their business environment. Thus, in addition to personal productivity gains, personal computers are being harnessed to improve information management, inter and inter-group communications and business collaborations. This paper describes the experience to-date of designing and implementing an Intel X86 based environment to improve business collaborations in a specific case of residential real estate transactions.

Goal and Scope of the Project

Project Goal

The primary goal of this project is to implement a proof-of-concept "Computer Supported Collaboration" (CSC) solution for a business which needs a substantial amount of collaboration. The residential real estate market is a good example of a business situation where CSC can play an effective role. The project goal is to:

- Understand the collaborative nature of the business,
- Understand the activities which could benefit by a CSC solution
- Identify the mechanisms to implement the solution
- Primarily use off the shelf hardware and software components to implement a solution as a proof-of-concept.

An additional inherent goal in this project is to gain a better understanding of CSC in general and the issues in implementing it using today's technology.

Definition of Computer Supported Collaboration

Individuals with different backgrounds may have different definitions of what CSC really means. Additionally, one can enter into strong discussions on how collaboration relates to other business activities such as negotiations. As a result, we restrict our definition of collaboration in this project to mean "ongoing, possibly recursive, transfer of dynamically changing information among individuals using a network of business workstations, including desktop and mobile. The information may contain not only text but also other rich-data types (e.g., images)."

To implement a Computer Supported Collaboration, we encapsulate the information in three different classes: *WHAT*, *HOW* and *WHEN*.

- *The "WHAT" refers to the information about which the collaboration is occurring*. In a residential real estate transaction, it would be the information on properties (description of the properties such as square footage, age, price and so on) which are available for sale.

- *The "HOW" refers to the means with which the participants share information among each other.* In a real estate transaction, this refers to the purchase contract forms, property appraisal forms etc., in addition to the simple mail-messages that may be used by individuals for ad-hoc communications.

• *"WHEN" information is maintained to track the status of collaborations in progress.* For example, once an agreement takes place between a seller and a buyer regarding a property, a number of activities occur in parallel and need to be completed within specific time frames. The status of these activities is an important factor in the overall transaction.

Overview of Residential Real Estate Transactions

The principal collaborators in a residential real estate transaction are the seller and the buyer. However, because of the size of the investment on the part of the buyer and to satisfy the legal requirements of the local and state authorities, a number of people are typically involved in a complete transaction. These people need to communicate with others and also need to know the overall status on an ongoing basis.

A typical residential real estate transaction goes through the following (simplified) scenario.

1. A property owner (Seller) and a Real Estate agent (Seller's agent) enter into a contractual agreement whereby the real estate agent will market and sell the property within a stated duration of time for a specific commission.

2. The agent advertises the property through a centralized computer database, newspapers, office discussions and so on.

3. A potential buyer talks to a real estate agent (Buyer's agent) and searches for a property that fits his/her criteria. The search continues until the buyer finds an appropriate property.

4. The two agents discuss the offer with the seller. *Assume* the seller accepts the offer (although it is quite common for certain amount of negotiation to happen at this stage).

5. Buyer then applies for (and hopefully qualifies for) a loan via a loan agent. An escrow is opened to collect all the "closing material" in one place.

6. Meanwhile, the property is appraised by an appraiser. Pest inspection and other inspections take place. All the information is collected by the real estate agents as well as the escrow agent. A title search takes place to verify that no previous liens on the property exist.

7. When everything is in place, the seller and buyer sign the papers. The property deed is recorded with the county. The agents get their commissions. The transaction is complete (as far as the seller and buyer are concerned) when the papers are signed and the deed is recorded with the county.

Although details of an actual transaction are omitted in the description above, the key points here are:

•   It is a collaborative activity requiring substantial communication.
•   A number of activities occur in parallel (particularly after an agreement is in place between the buyer and the seller). Therefore up-to-date information on the status of each individual activity is required. Additionally, time-critical events must be monitored according to the contract agreements; any deviations need to be raised as warnings to the appropriate individuals.

Design and Implementation of the CSC solution

As discussed above, the computer supported collaboration in this project involves three information repositories - The WHAT, HOW and WHEN information bases.

- The WHAT information is a database containing *active* properties - that is, the properties available for sale. Example data on active properties are price, age and so on. The database could also contain other rich data (such as digitized motion video, sound) but that is not included at this stage in the project.

- The HOW information base consists of predefined real estate transaction forms. These forms, in general, are expected to reflect the contents of the actual forms used in the industry.

- The WHEN information contains information regarding each collaboration event and some comments. The status of any activity can be checked at any time.

Figure 1 shows the project environment.

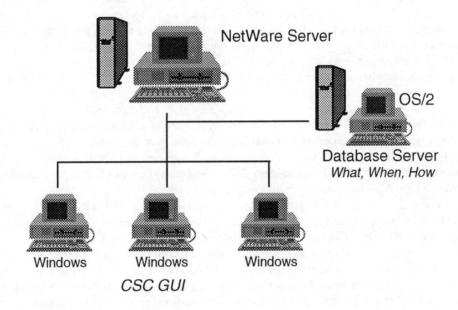

Figure 1. Project Environment

These three databases are implemented using Microsoft's SQLServer running on an OS/2 (1.3) server. The project does not really need a full SQL-compliant database server at this time; however, it was selected based upon possible future enhancements.

The access to all the databases is via graphical user interfaces (GUIs). In the proposed implementation, the GUI's are implemented entirely on the WINDOWs operating system; however, there is no restriction on implementing these on other platforms such as Motif and/or OpenLook.

The underlying Network Operating System is Novell's NetWare (3.11). All the databases are currently implemented on a single database server and therefore the project does not need much message passing between various hosts. However, since a real solution would probably employ multiple database servers for practical reasons, an underlying message handling service needs to exist. Novell's Message Handling Services (MHS) will be used for this purpose.

The hardware platforms used in this project are all Intel X86-based. At this stage, the project includes only the desktops. Notebooks and/or Pentops are planned to be included in the project in the future.

The GUI's are built using the WINDOWs SDK, rather than using GUI Builders. Although more complex, we feel this approach would be better in view of later integration of rich data types (multimedia) as well as Pentops in to the project scope. The user interface flow of the collaboration is as shown in the following figure:

Analysis

There are commercial turnkey products available today - such as Lotus Notes, NCR's Cooperation - which could be used to implement solutions similar to the one being implemented in this project. However, in a business environment where some of the components already exist (for example, a database server), implementations such as the one being implemented in this project may be a good alternative instead of using new turnkey solutions. Additionally, as the commercially available operating systems begin to support true pre-emptive multitasking, a peer-to-peer paradigm may become more beneficial in some situations, as compared to the client-server architecture. Because of these reasons, we believe that although turnkey solutions such as Lotus Notes are available today, other alternatives should exist and may indeed be more appropriate in some situations.

What have we learned from this project so far? We believe that there is definitely a need for a single-source, single-vendor software development tool kit for client-server application developments. In this project, multiple SDK's needed to be used. For example, the SQLServer libraries work only with Microsoft C libraries. Novell's NLM's cannot be built using Microsoft C. Thus it appears that one has to get familiar with multiple SDK's to implement client-server applications today.

Open database accesses is another problem. For example, as part of the WHAT information, we intended to include geographic information which could be presented using GIS (Geographic Information Systems) mapping tools. However, the internal database of the GIS tools is either not accessible directly by application programs and/or the tools have limited capability for accessing external databases such as SQLServer. This can be solved if the databases provide open access to applications. It appears that the industry is indeed moving towards such Open Database access technology (for example, ODAPI from Borland). We feel this is an important step for the proliferation of client-server applications in general.

Summary

The powerful networked computing platforms are increasingly harnessed for improved information management and inter and intra-group collaborations. In this project, we have attempted to implement a specific collaboration solution for a specific business situation. The project is under implementation. Additional features such as Multimedia and new platforms such as Notebooks, Pentops are planned to be added as the project progresses further.

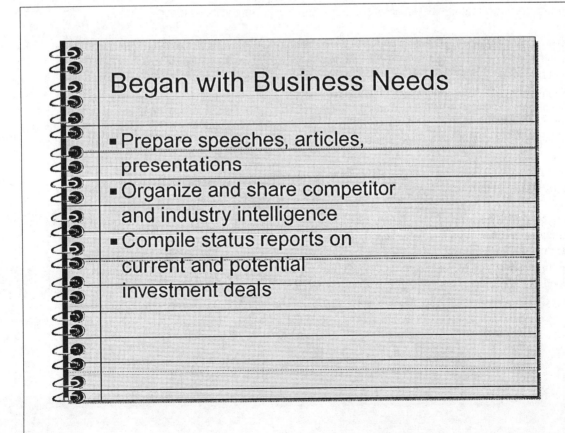

Lotus Notes as a Knowledge Workshop: Experiences at MetLife

David Daniels
Executive Information
Investments

Began with Business Needs

- Prepare speeches, articles, presentations
- Organize and share competitor and industry intelligence
- Compile status reports on current and potential investment deals

Overview of Lotus Notes Implementation To-Date

- Decision to purchase, 12/90
- 325 licenses, 175 used
- 10 servers
- 150 applications
  - handful are strategic
  - most are *ad hoc*
- 5 support staff
- Inter-organizational replication
  - Lotus
  - Seybold

How are We Doing?

- No formal metrics or requirements for communication/collaboration systems
- Mainframe orientation
  - desktops/LANs not ready
  - relatively inexperienced with complex end-user information systems
  - unsure how to integrate with existing systems

How are We Doing? (cont'd.)

- Have only begun to come to terms with decentralized organization
  - extremely hierarchical
  - information is protected
  - tendency towards control
- And yet...
  - operations are becoming increasingly distributed
  - greater need for both flexibility and coordination

How to *Think* About All This?

- Coordinated Information Services for a Discipline- or Mission-Oriented Community by Doug Engelbart
  - Collaborative Dialogue
  - Document Development, Production, and Control
  - Research Intelligence
  - Community Handbook Development

How to *Think* About All This? (cont'd.)

- Computer-Based Instruction
- Meetings and Conferences
- Community Management and Organization
- Special Knowledge Work by Individuals and Teams

What Notes Allows Us To Do as Work Groups and Teams

- Collect electronic documents
- Organize electronic documents
- Link electronic documents
- Inter-organization collaboration
- Step in the right direction for ubiquitous computing
- Alleviates immediate need to resolve LAN issues:
  - communication/replication
  - security
- Learn and mature

But... "You Pays Your Money and You Takes Your Chances!"

- Proprietary document database?
- General purpose with limited extensibility?
- A substitute for a mature, sophisticated network infrastructure?
- Capable of evolving into one?
- Desirable to evolve into one?

And, What About People?

- MIS professionals in our organization have not come close to mastering our complex computer systems, much less our social/cultural systems?
- Are they prepared?
- Are they interested?
- Are they incented?

Author Index